AF577192

Illusion and Reality in Franco-American Diplomacy 1914–1945

Illusion and Reality in Franco-American Diplomacy 1914–1945

Henry Blumenthal

Louisiana State University Press
Baton Rouge and London

Manufactured in the United States of America

Designer: Christopher Wilcox
Typeface: Palatino
Typesetter: Moran Colorgraphic
Printer: Thomson Shore, Inc.
Binder: John Dekker & Sons, Inc.

Library of Congress Cataloging in Publication Data

Blumenthal, Henry.
Illusion and reality in Franco-American diplomacy, 1914–1945.

Bibliography: p.
Includes index.
1. United States—Foreign relations—France.
2. France—Foreign relations—United States. 3. World War, 1914–1918—Diplomatic history. 4. World War, 1939–1945—Diplomatic history. I. Title.
E183.8.F8B545 1986 327.44073 85-24183
ISBN 0-8071-1278-X

The author gratefully acknowledges that the following libraries and publishers have granted him permission to quote from the works cited:

ARCHON BOOKS: Karl E. Birnbaum, *Peace Moves and U-Boat Warfare: A Study of Imperial Germany's Policy Towards the United States, April 8, 1916–January 9, 1917*. Hamden, Conn., 1970. PRINCETON UNIVERSITY LIBRARY: Two letters, dated February 17 and 19, 1919, in the Robert Lansing Papers. FRANKLIN D. ROOSEVELT LIBRARY: A. A. Berle, Jr., Papers. SIMON & SCHUSTER, INC.: Paul Reynaud, *In the Thick of the Fight, 1930–1945*. Translated by James D. Lambert. New York, 1955. HARRY S. TRUMAN LIBRARY: Dean Acheson Papers, "Princeton Seminars." YALE UNIVERSITY LIBRARY: Manuscript material from the Gordon Auchincloss Papers, Box 2, Folder 26, pp. 21–23; the Vance C. McCormick Papers, Diary, March 5, May 15, 1919; and the Henry L. Stimson Papers, Diary, June 23–25, July 24, September 13, 1931, January 13, 1941, and "Conversations and Memos, 1929–32."

Contents

Tables

Acknowledgments

I am grateful for the courteous professional assistance of archivists and librarians throughout the United States and in France. Fortunately, the archives of the French Foreign Ministry permit consultation of Franco-American documents up to 1940. General de Gaulle's papers, embracing his London and Algiers activities, go up to 1945. American source materials and major collections of British and German records have been readily available.

I am also indebted to the specialists whom the LSU Press consulted. Their comments and suggestions improved the final version of the manuscript. Furthermore, the editors of the LSU Press have earned my gratitude for their care and cooperation in the final stages of the publishing process. John Easterly's remarkable editing skill deserves special recognition. I also wish to thank Margaret Dalrymple for preparing the index.

Finally, I wish to thank Mrs. Susanne Lang for typing this manuscript. Her professional excellence has been much appreciated.

Abbreviations

AHR	*American Historical Review*
AMAE	Archives du Ministère des Affaires Étrangères (Paris)
BIS	Bank for International Settlements (Basel)
CPEU	Correspondance Politique, Etats-Unis, AMAE
DDF	France, Ministère des Affaires Étrangères, *Documents Diplomatiques Français, 1932–1939*
FCNL	French Committee of National Liberation
FDRL	Franklin Delano Roosevelt Library, Hyde Park, New York
FRUS	U.S. Department of State, *The Foreign Relations of the United States* series
FSP	Fondation des Sciences Politiques (Paris)
JAH	*Journal of American History*
NA	National Archives, Washington, D.C.
OSS	U.S. Office of Strategic Services
POF	President's Official File, FDRL
PPF	President's Personal File, FDRL
PSF	President's Secretary File, FDRL
RG	Record Group

Illusion and Reality in Franco-American Diplomacy 1914–1945

Introduction

One cannot discuss Franco-American diplomatic relations realistically without paying attention to the international web of which they were a part. This immensely involved interdependence was not always understood by the statesmen charged to cope with it, and students of history would not be on track if they concentrated merely on French or American policies. History is a constant process of action, reaction, inaction, and interaction impacting on a multitude of global interests and conditions.

This study, based on extensive research in France and the United States, also incorporates the valuable contributions of German and English scholars. Instead of tracing well-known details, it emphasizes functional and procedural aspects of often decisive significance. Interpretations emerging from the broad panorama overlooking the period from the First to the end of the Second World War assume a persuasiveness often obscured in studies of limited episodes seen in a narrow time frame.

The friendly, though frequently strained, diplomatic relations between France and the United States that had marked the nineteenth century did not undergo significant changes up to 1939, despite the fact that the two powers operated in a profoundly changed world after World War I. This war accelerated the pace of America's industrial development and transformed it from a debtor to a creditor nation. It elevated the United States to the status of a major world power. France, on the contrary, emerged from the war in a generally weakened condition. But the United States was not fully conscious of its new global responsibilities, and France entertained power-political ambitions beyond its actual capacity. Franco-American frictions caused by each nation's failure to estimate realistically its degree of power clouded the international horizon.

Other factors also darkened it. Germany's assertion that its military had not lost World War I was as untenable as France's assertion that Germany alone was responsible for its outbreak and was capable of paying ruinous reparations. It was equally erroneous for France to claim that the Americans and the French had been fighting for "a common cause." These illusions could not but lead to political distortions.

In the field of foreign policy, political judgments of the American administrations were often badly flawed. In their desire to share with Great Britain a position of parity in the world markets, they overrated Britain's postwar economic and financial strength. And by assuming that Europe's financial dilemmas were primarily Europe's business to solve, they underrated their own stake in the interdependent world of business. By the same token, America's policy of neutrality in the 1930s failed to recognize the generating thrust of international tension. Like France and Great Britain, furthermore, it focused narrowly on the Ethiopian and Spanish conflicts, not anticipating the far-reaching consequences of their potential by-products.

France worried about the high degree of Anglo-Saxon cooperation, which did not actually materialize during this period. Up to 1930, moreover, it tended to exaggerate the potential danger it faced from resurgent Germany. The French did not seem to understand that their policies actually enlarged this danger. While these Western powers anxiously watched the shadow of Soviet communism, their commercial competition and financial transactions, greatly complicated by unbusinesslike approaches to the settlement of debts and reparations, helped create conditions conducive to social explosion and political instability. Steadily growing armaments and budget deficits were hardly designed to promote peace and prosperity. The world thus moved along a road marked by unrealities, the illusory nature of which its leaders obscured with verbose rationalizations and appealing principles and slogans. Whatever the virtues of democracy, the prejudices of uninformed or brainwashed masses on the whole supported this process of self-deception.

When this process also governed relations with Hitler's Germany, it led to an unnecessary tragedy. The unsteady course of French policy toward Germany, characterized by severity followed by moderation and weakness, failed to deal sensibly with Weimar Germany, permitted Hitler to overtake France militarily, and finally challenged his perilous designs only when it no longer possessed superior power. Like Great Britain, France realized much too late that one cannot do business with a leader who does not feel bound by traditional standards of international morality and law. Concessions for the sake of peace remain moral, noble, and worthwhile only as long as they are reciprocated in the same spirit they are made. It has been equally axiomatic in diplomacy that incoherent policies tend to fail stress tests. France's fate in 1940 merely confirmed the accuracy of this observation.

It was remarkable, though, that with the help of Great Britain, the Soviet Union, the United States, and Hitler's miscalculations, France managed to emerge from the war as a democratic entity. As trying as the French situation was during the war years for all parties concerned, including the United States, it is noteworthy that, even before Hitler invaded Russia, Vichy's collaboration with Nazi Germany stopped short of making France an enemy of the United Nations. Nevertheless, convinced of Germany's ultimate victory, Darlan went further than any other leader, including Laval, in his effort to preserve France as an important continental power by cooperating with Hitler. Reflecting the shifts of military tides, later Darlan also helped General Eisenhower more than any other highly placed Frenchman.

De Gaulle was dependent on Great Britain and the United States, but as soon as he was satisfied that Hitler would be defeated, he began to concentrate on restoring France to its former status in the family of nations. In this respect the general and President Roosevelt held irreconcilable views. Their political differences created problems that at times interfered with military operations and foreshadowed serious frictions in the postwar era.

In the end, though unplanned and uncoordinated, the mosaic of free and captive Frenchmen's diplomacy produced a result that did France credit. Annoying as it was that its various spokesmen always placed France ahead of the United Nations, its disappointments and humiliation had obviously been so great as to explain, though not really justify, this tendency.

It is not the function of the historian to promote good relations, but to analyze the past without prejudice. History has much to teach if we really want to avoid the mistakes of the past. The passage of time and access to essential records enable us to see what happened more comprehensively and dispassionately than contemporaries could. The truism that it is easier to judge policies from hindsight makes altogether insufficient allowances for foresight. How else can foresight be acquired if not by analyzing the consequences of past alternatives?

I

World War I Diplomacy

FRANCO-AMERICAN DIPLOMATIC RELATIONS TO 1917

French interest in the United States had its roots in the eighteenth-century Anglo-French competition for control of the North American continent. When at the end of the Seven Years' War France lost Canada, its great explorer Samuel de Champlain's vision of developing and dominating the vast region from the Atlantic to the Mississippi vanished for the foreseeable future. As the Anglo-French struggle for empire continued, the English colonies in America and, subsequently, the independent United States benefited from it. The decisive participation of France in the American War of Independence was primarily prompted by its determination to weaken its imperial rival. Early in the nineteenth century, Napoleon preferred to sell Louisiana to the United States, destined to become an important commercial sea power and competitor of Great Britain, rather than to treat it in a way likely to bring about an Anglo-American reconciliation. Future French leaders translated Napoleon's extraordinary farsightedness by counting during most of the nineteenth century on the pooling of Franco-American naval power as a counterweight to Britain's control of the seas.

Although Americans appreciated these French moves, they treasured their independence too much to allow their national interests to become permanently entangled with those of France or any other European power. While France counted in its basically pragmatic decisions on America's eternal gratitude, it also disregarded fundamental principles in international relations. Moreover, its subsequent attempts to block America's penetration of the North American continent, the unreliable attitude of Napoleon III during the critical period of the American Civil War, and French fears by the turn of the twentieth century that the dynamic Yankees might endanger Europe's future tended to justify growing mutual reservations. Also, France never developed its potentially prosperous economic relationship with America.

In the midnineteenth century François Guizot denounced the spread of republicanism, one of the manifest objectives of the United States. The influential French statesman rationalized his opposition by expounding the principle "What is not good for the universal monarchy is not good for the universal republic." The monolithic growth of any one power or political system, he feared, would not bode well for the safety of other countries and their institutions.

Once the United States set out to become an empire, Jules Cambon, the distinguished French ambassador to the United States, warned in 1898 that America's attempt to monopolize world sugar production was "the beginning of the economic war the United States will soon undertake against the Old World." As a response to this potential destruction of the complicated European structure, about which Americans were in his opinion incredibly ignorant, Cambon recommended much closer ties among the continental powers. Typically, he warned that without such European cooperation the Anglo-Saxons would eventually dominate the world.

The fact that the United States did not interfere with French imperialism in Asia and Africa and that it now carried on significant trade relations with France did not diminish French anxieties concerning America. As many Frenchmen saw it, America had disappointed them when it did not send an expeditionary force to rescue them in the Franco-Prussian War of 1870–1871. But such a thought was sheer fantasy at a time when America had not yet recovered from its civil war and when Napoleon III's irritating courting of the Confederacy and his ill-fated maneuvers in Mexico had not been forgotten. Contemporary Americans saw no reason to abandon their traditional policy of staying out of Europe's perennial wars.[1]

Despite major political strains, in their public statements American and French diplomats perpetuated the myth of the uninterrupted historic friendship between their two countries. Except for the undeclared naval war during President John Adams' administration, they had indeed always avoided war. The Franco-American alliance of 1778 and French participation in the War of Independence were traditionally cited to substantiate this friendship, as if

1. See Henry Blumenthal, *A Reappraisal of Franco-American Relations, 1830–1871* (Chapel Hill, 1959), and *France and the United States: Their Diplomatic Relations, 1789–1914* (Chapel Hill, 1970).

nothing had disturbed it with the passage of time. The marquis de Lafayette became and remained an emotional symbol for Franco-American solidarity. Whatever political differences divided their respective governments, allusion to this symbol psychologically conditioned Americans to remember, with fondness, only the crucial assistance France had rendered at the time of the birth of the American republic. The French gladly played up this friendly notion.

Cultural factors also contributed to the distortion of political realities. It was fashionable in the nineteenth century for steadily increasing numbers of affluent Americans to visit France and admire its remarkable contributions to modern civilization. In literature, the arts, and science, French genius assumed a position of leadership. Also, their *savoir vivre*, courteous manners, stimulating salons, and gastronomical distinction appealed to the finer instincts of people in all parts of the world. Those Americans who tried to hold on to traditional mores and values naturally objected to too much looseness in French morals and the restlessness of their culture. But on the whole, Americans, particularly southerners, looked upon France as a cultural trailblazer. The same people who resisted political involvement in Europe welcomed its cultural and intellectual stimulation. The British, French, and Germans assumed the leading role in this cross-fertilization. But culture was one thing and politics another. Friendly cultural contacts at best facilitated the process of dealing with conflicting interests.

By the same token, many Europeans from all walks of life pointed to the free institutions in the American republic as a model and hope for a better life. Unlike citizens of other countries, however, few Frenchmen visited the United States and even fewer immigrated to it. They preferred to stay in La Belle France. Their general ignorance about life in the United States, particularly its cultural developments, led them by and large to assume a condescending attitude. By the late nineteenth century, educated Americans deplored the fact that Frenchmen tended to underrate American culture and overrate their own.

America was a continent inhabited by a steadily increasing, industrious population and blessed with political stability and immense resources. Although the momentum of its enormous growth caused concern, in the late nineteenth century America's challenge to European leadership merely loomed on the horizon. It was by no means a foregone conclusion that the United States would ever want to engage Europe in a struggle for supremacy. On the contrary, its traditional decent respect for the opinions and welfare of other peoples and its preoccupation with domestic developments suggested nothing more than a desire for reasonably open trade and cultural opportunities abroad. Even a very powerful United States constituted only an imagined threat reflecting a mentality grown out of European experiences. Thus, instead of reaping profits from sizable investments in, and solidifying their ties with, the United States, in the nineteenth century France made politically determined investments only in its colonies and in Czarist Russia. Historical experience taught the French too late to question this policy.

As France knew only too well, it was Germany that posed a real threat to its territorial integrity and aspirations. Germany, too, looked upon France as a threat to its territorial integrity and aspirations. It had not forgotten that in past centuries, during which England, France, and Holland had built up their kingdoms and empires, they had deliberately kept Germany weak and decentralized. The policies of Bismarck and the kaiser were designed to catch up with the powers that had denied Germany full participation in shaping modern Europe. Repeated French attempts to detach the Rhineland from Germany and to prevent the incorporation of Austria into the Reich were as much resented by Germans as they seemed essential to French security.

During the period from the creation of the German Reich to the First World War, France watched with alarm the modernization, industrialization, and militarization of its neighbor. It did not keep pace with these important developments or with the comparative size of the German population. Naturally, projecting this trend into the future, France feared for its future safety. What was equally disturbing, Germany's rise threatened to block the realization of French dominance on the European continent. Without such hegemony, French ambitions for a major role as a world power would, of course, also be put in jeopardy. Lacking sufficient strength on its own to implement such objectives, France tried to enlist the help of other powers to reduce Germany's competitive potential.

Germany felt itself in a similar situation. For Germany to rise to a prominent position on the Continent, the potential power of France had to be contained. By the beginning of the twentieth century, the kaiser aimed not only at continental hegemony but also at making his nation a major world power. Significantly, at this stage of history such a goal involved taking on Great Britain rather than France, since the conquest of world markets and the attainment of an empire—the objectives of Germany's *Weltpolitik*—necessitated a confrontation with the leading empire. Interestingly, the kaiser and his chancellor, Theobald von Bethmann-Hollweg, were occasionally disposed to consider a cooperative, though subordinate, role for France in their German-controlled continental system.

Obviously, France would have been too proud to dignify such a scheme with a response had it ever been officially suggested. France took the German danger seriously and tried to protect itself, in addition to maintaining its own military strength, by a series of alliances with England, Russia, and several smaller Eastern European countries. Such reliance on a policy of encircling Germany brought with it liabilities as well as reassurance. Beginning in 1910, the noted statesman and historian Gabriel Hanotaux deemed it also prudent to promote close personal contacts with leading Americans, "to assure American support of France in the eventuality of a European conflict."[2]

For more than a year prior to the outbreak of war in Europe, President Wilson was concerned about its approach, fearing that it would interfere with the further development of his domestic programs. He admitted to himself that American foreign policy contained a duality of habitually enunciating "handsome principles of equity in international dealings" even while having "shown ourselves kin to all the world when it came to pushing an advantage." Although he recognized the existence of "material interests" in world affairs, he rather vaguely wished to see them developed in an enlightened liberal fashion. This thrust toward international liberalism called for the active participation of the United States in international politics. America's phenomenal material growth and active rivalry in world trade could no longer perpetuate the questionable contention of its traditional disinterest in European affairs. The underlying causes of the gathering war clouds in Europe involved, after all, economic rivalries on a global scale. The nation that came out on top economically was also expected to emerge as the politically dominant force.

President Wilson was much too detached from this kind of rough rivalry to feel comfortable in dealing with it. Therefore he found it

2. Gabriel Hanotaux, *Le Comité "France-Amérique": Son Activité de 1909 à 1920* (Paris, 1920).

useful to be assisted by such advisers as Colonel Edward M. House and Walter Hines Page, the American ambassador to Great Britain. They evolved concrete, though still general, notions about how to improve the existing world order and thereby reduce the danger of war. They suggested that, instead of spending huge amounts on competitive military establishments, the great powers, including the United States, should take the more constructive approach of cooperating in the development of the backward regions of the world. The significant new element in this suggestion was the emphasis on truly enlightened international liberalism. In his letter to House dated August 28, 1913, Page defined it in these ethical terms: "Everything must be done for the good of the tropical peoples and nobody may annex a foot of land." He expected that such a nonimperialistic, cooperative effort would enormously benefit the native populations and greatly reduce the burden of armament and the likelihood of war. This would be a great improvement over the existing situation. Under it, the exploitation of colonial populations and resources provided Europeans a higher standard of living, and selfishly, each empire was prepared to fight its rivals to maintain this superior life-style.[3]

A strong advocate of Anglo-American entente, Page suggested, on July 20, 1913, that Wilson make an unprecedented presidential journey to England. "I have a feeling," he wrote the president, "that such a visit . . . might possibly prevent an Anglo-German war, which seems almost certain at some time, and an American-Japanese war, which is at least conceivable a decade or so hence. I think the world would take notice to whom it belongs and—be quiet." But Wilson refused to leave the country and would not consider embracing such an objectionable version of the balance of power concept.[4]

A few days before the crisis in August, 1914, reached its climax, the American ambassador to France, Myron T. Herrick, sent a confidential note to Secretary of State William Jennings Bryan in which he recommended that President Wilson make "a strong plea for delay and moderation" before Germany mobilized.[5] Coming from the president of the United States, he believed, it would carry weight

3. Ray Stannard Baker, *Woodrow Wilson: Life and Letters* (6 vols.; Garden City, N.Y., 1927–37), V, 26–28.

4. *Ibid.*, 30–31.

5. T. Bentley Mott, *Myron T. Herrick, Friend of France* (New York, 1929), 18–19.

and be "met with the respect and approval of Europe." But instead of bringing this communication to the prompt attention of the president, Bryan asked Page in London whether an offer of America's good offices "would be acceptable or serve any high purpose in the present crisis." Only when it was too late to produce any immediate results, on August 4, 1914, did President Wilson notify the representatives of the belligerent states that he would "welcome an opportunity to act in the interest of European peace, either now or at any other time." In the meantime he officially proclaimed the neutrality of the United States, "in fact, as well as in thought." However obscure the causes and objectives of this war appeared to American citizens, most of them of European descent, they could not really be neutral in thought. Like their president, the majority sympathized with the Allies. German-Americans, though loyal to the United States, tended to pray for the success of the Fatherland. Even neutrality "in fact" turned out to be an extremely complex and controversial matter, for American merchants could legally trade and bankers could grant loans as long as, technically, they engaged in such transactions at their own risk. The implementation of this laissez-faire principle led to many vexing situations.[6]

As early as August 10, 1914, Secretary Bryan presented the president with a question that had far-reaching ramifications. The banking house of J. P. Morgan and Company had just inquired whether there would be any objection to its making a loan to the French government. The secretary's legal counselor, Robert Lansing, an international law expert, saw no impediment to such a loan. But in the mind of Bryan, "Money is the worst of all contrabands because it commands everything else. . . . I know of nothing that would do more to prevent war than an international agreement that neutral nations would not loan to belligerents." He also feared that the precedent of approving a loan to France would entitle all other belligerents to the same consideration and ultimately confront the country with divisive lending camps. The powerful financial interests making the loans would develop a high stake in the victory of their respective clients and thus violate the spirit of strict neutrality. When the president judged these arguments sound, the house of

6. Albert Pingaud, *Histoire diplomatique de la France pendant la guerre* (2 vols.; Paris, 1938), II, 232–33.

Morgan was promptly advised that American loans to nations at war could not be reconciled with our neutral position.[7]

It remained to be seen whether this principled decision could withstand the mounting pressures to which it was exposed at home and abroad. The banking community wished to support the policies of the government, but it had certain financial responsibilities that affected the economic stability of the country. On October 23, 1914, the vice-president of the National City Bank of New York explained to the acting secretary of state that, as a debtor nation, the United States had to send sizable sums to Europe before the year's end to honor short-term drafts. Since war conditions interfered with the shipments of cotton normally available during autumn "for the settlement of this balance against us," the bank executive observed, "it can only be wiped out by the shipment of the goods, in lieu of cotton, that are now needed and desired by the various European countries." The magnitude of this developing trade threatened to exhaust the existing cash credits of the European governments. Both American manufacturers and foreign governments called on the banks to provide temporary credits. Some of the National City Bank's American clients, who were offered short-term treasury warrants of the French government in payment for goods, asked the bank to "discount them or purchase warrants direct from the French government for the purpose of replenishing their cash balances." If American banks could not find adequate solutions, very profitable trade opportunities would be lost, to the benefit of other neutrals.

Provided the Wilson administration did not object, the National City Bank was willing to advance short-term credits to belligerent and neutral European governments. When Wilson fell back on the distinction between legitimate credits to pay commercial debts and loans to finance the war, three New York banks granted the French government in the spring of 1915 short-term credits "to meet their obligations for American products and continue their purchases in this country."[8]

As the war continued and the urgency for large American credits became self-evident, the expedient distinction between "credit loans" and "general loans" proved to be an inadequate solution. The secretary of the treasury, William Gibbs McAdoo, approached this

7. U.S. Department of State, *Papers Relating to the Foreign Relations of the United States: The Lansing Papers, 1914–1920* (2 vols.; Washington, D.C., 1940), I, 131–35.

8. *Ibid.*, 136–41.

financial question as broadly as possible. Despite their sale of American securities and gold shipments, the British and French needed huge credits to finance the war. McAdoo, supported by Secretary of State Lansing, impressed upon the president that large gold shipments "would disastrously affect the credit of the European nations, and the consequence would be a general state of bankruptcy." In their opinion, if for lack of finances Europeans would have to halt their purchases in the United States, the country would be faced with a disastrous industrial depression. In Europe, the military masters of Germany would be the beneficiaries.[9]

It did not escape McAdoo that the war had transformed the United States from a debtor into a creditor. By the end of 1915, he estimated its trade balance against Europe to be about $2.5 billion. He knew that the advancement of huge credits to the Allies involved risks. Although the United States could afford them, he reminded the president that the credits would necessarily lead to increased American identification with the cause of the Allies. He also pointed out that at the end of the war the accelerated pace of the country's industrial expansion to accommodate the Allies' war requirements would elevate the United States to the status of a major world power. Under these circumstances, the troubled president reluctantly retreated from his original position of "sound" neutrality. The developing pressures had thus compelled desirable theoretical principles to yield to complex realities that gradually pushed the United States into unneutrality.

Wilson's determination to steer a neutral course and to keep the United States out of the war was also shaken by the belligerents' violation of neutral rights and by their political objectives. From the beginning, the Allies and the Central Powers ignored the fact that their war created serious dislocations for American trade, and they showed little respect for America's desire to remain neutral. They all tried to use the United States to their advantage whenever possible. The French request in mid-September, 1914, to add cotton to the contraband list disregarded the vital significance of this commodity for the South. Rather presumptuously, the French and the British took it for granted that, whatever inconveniences they caused, Americans would stand by them, help finance the war, and supply them with arms, munitions, oil, horses, food, and other nec-

9. Baker, *Wilson: Life and Letters*, V, 380–82.

essary supplies. The longer the war lasted, the greater grew the Allies' dependence on America's industry, agriculture, and finance. Naturally the Germans resented what they saw as an indirect attempt by the United States to help their enemies defeat them. Since the scope of American shipments to the Allies assumed enormous proportions and those to Germany were minimal, the Central Powers decided on drastic actions to stop the dangerous trans-Atlantic flow of war supplies. Considering diplomatic protests practically useless, they decided early in 1915 to sabotage American factories producing war materials. The exposure by British and American intelligence of the chief instigators of this sabotage compelled the recall of several German and Austro-Hungarian diplomats who were declared personae non gratae. A much more effective, though in the end counterproductive, approach was tried with the sinking of ships suspected of carrying cargo across the ocean.

Although not the first ship sent to the bottom of the Atlantic by German submarines, the *Lusitania*, flying the flag of Great Britain and with many American passengers on board, suffered this tragic fate on May 1, 1915. The loss of American lives brought the war closer to home and outraged the American people. The torpedoing of this liner without prior removal of the passengers violated international law and led to several stern protest notes by President Wilson. If the Germans had an interest in avoiding America's entry into the war, they could not defiantly ignore the president's warning that the United States would hold the imperial German government to "strict accountability." But Berlin must have been puzzled by the president's note of June 9, in which he expounded this noble thought: "The government of the United States is contending for something much greater than mere rights of property or privileges of commerce. It is contending for nothing less high and sacred than the rights of humanity."

A compromise resolved the *Lusitania* crisis temporarily. In contrast to the German navy's high command, which opposed any concessions in the belief that the United States would not actively enter the war, Germany's political leaders did not exclude the possibility of America's eventual military intervention. On July 8, 1915, they therefore guaranteed the safety of American citizens in the proclaimed war zone provided they traveled under neutral flags. This offer amounted to a face-saving concession, but it did not satisfy America's insistence on the observation of more humane rules in submarine warfare.[10]

Had the United States been determined to maintain a strict neutrality and avoid serious complications growing out of Germany's U-boat attacks, it could not afford to supply and finance the Entente powers. Evidently it permitted its political sympathies and profitable trade to shape its immediate policies without being overly concerned about their long-range consequences. In April and June, 1915, the diplomatic spokesmen of the Central Powers requested the United States to do what other neutrals had done, namely embargo the export of war supplies to the belligerents. Quite uncomfortable with Lansing's view that such a decision would be "an unjustifiable departure from the principle of strict neutrality," Wilson nevertheless went along with the State Department's pragmatic explanation in its communication to Vienna on August 12, 1915: "It has never been the policy of this country to maintain in time of peace a large military establishment. . . . The United States has always depended upon the right and power to purchase arms and ammunition from neutral nations in case of foreign attack. This right, which it claims for itself, it cannot deny to others."[11]

While the Central Powers tried to force the United States not to aid their enemies, the Entente powers also treated American principles and policies in a most irritating way. The British blockade interfered with American commerce as well as with German interests. It severely restricted American trade with European neutrals near Germany. The capture of American ships, subsequently brought to British ports, reopened ancient controversies. The British and the French aroused President Wilson's anger when they committed the blunder of seizing American mails. But a strongly worded protest note to Britain accomplished hardly more than conveying the appearance of evenhandedness. Wilson's advisers House and Page had actually seen to it that Sir Edward Grey would not be too upset by it.

Rightly or wrongly, the British and French were convinced that as defenders of Western civilization they fought as much for America as for themselves. By mid-1915 they began to deplore the fact that

10. Karl E. Birnbaum, *Peace Moves and U-Boat Warfare: A Study of Imperial Germany's Policy Toward the United States, April 18, 1916–January 9, 1917* (Hamden, Conn., 1970).

11. Quoted in Z. A. B. Zeman, *A Diplomatic History of the First World War* (London, 1971), 176–77.

America was reaping huge profits while they were fighting the war. Disappointed Frenchmen began to hint at dire consequences. On June 1, 1916, Colonel House relayed to Wilson the opinion of Ambassador Jean Jules Jusserand that Russia, Japan, and Germany would form an alliance after the war and attack the United States. Revealingly, the French ambassador "hinted we would have no sympathizers in our [hour] of trouble unless we more actively took the part of the Allies," House noted. As Jusserand explained to Aristide Briand, he wanted to discourage House from pursuing his visionary peace schemes. To leave no doubt in the American diplomat's mind, Jusserand reiterated the determined French position: "Germany has started the war; we intend to write the peace." President Raymond Poincaré was more optimistic. He confidently expressed the view that after an opportunistic interval, during which Americans were cashing in on the war, they would eventually intervene militarily on the side of the Allies. Jusserand, once a member of Theodore Roosevelt's "Tennis Cabinet," found Wilson less congenial to work with. As a result of his loss of the inside track, his effectiveness had declined sharply. To the regret of the Quai d'Orsay, even French war propaganda in the United States left much to be desired.[12]

The assumption that France was fighting this war as much for America as for European civilization and therefore had a right to call on America to share the burden of sacrifice merits further scrutiny. Was it historically sound? It is appropriate to remember that President George Washington's experience with French diplomacy and British high-handedness prompted him to emphasize in his Farewell Address that the United States and Europe had separate interests. The Monroe Doctrine underscored this point with its distinction between the New World and the Old World. And to these policy differences between France and the United States during the nineteenth century must be added those regarding culture. Although rooted in Europe, the nation of immigrants had developed its own distinct civilization. As much as many educated Americans appreciated France's cultural contributions, they did not accept French culture as a model.

The United States played no direct role in causing the war being fought in Europe and had not been consulted about it. America did

12. Baker, *Wilson: Life and Letters*, VI, 227.

not participate in the parleys and political maneuvers of the various belligerents prior to its outbreak and knew nothing of their secret treaties. In fact, the European powers tried to keep the United States politically at a distance and feared the prospect of its economic penetration of their continent. In view of this background, the French contention of an identity of Franco-American interests appears extraordinary. And as far as war aims were concerned, Wilson and the French, in fact the president and all the European belligerents, were far apart, as we shall see.

There remained one weighty consideration that those responsible for the security and defense of the free institutions of the United States could not reject out of hand. The French used it as a trump card. They contended that a victorious Imperial Germany would in time challenge America, which would then have to face Germany's ruthless military masters alone. To prevent such a calamity, the argument ran, the vital interest of the United States demanded that it join with the Entente. As legitimate as this hypothesis sounded, it did not entirely pass the test of analysis. Significantly, it did imply the possibility of a French defeat. It was, in the first instance, an attempt to enlist the aid of the United States to rescue France from such a debacle. Undoubtedly the sympathies and self-interest of the United States favored the prevention of such a disaster, as long as it could be accomplished without undue risk to its own future. The developing trend in recent Franco-American relations, however, had suggested that there was merely a difference in degree between France and Germany with respect to their limited acceptance of the United States as a world power. And it was at least possible that America and a victorious Germany could peacefully coexist. The insulation of the United States by the Atlantic Ocean and its phenomenal industrial momentum afforded it advantages Imperial Germany could not recklessly ignore in peace or war. Should Germany nevertheless challenge the United States directly, then would be the time to throw America's might against the aggressor. Prominent Americans could be found on either side of the question. No wonder President Wilson wavered until the last moment before, even then, he hesitatingly made his momentous decision.[13]

He would have preferred to avoid it altogether. But his patient efforts to mediate an early diplomatic conclusion to the war produced

13. *Ibid.*, V, 64–71.

only endless frustrations. Each of the three key European countries—Germany, Great Britain, and France—reacted so differently to Wilson's soundings that, for the sake of clarity, it seems advisable to discuss their responses separately.

Wilson, of course, had his own ideas about peace. He was greatly aided and influenced by his roving ambassador-at-large, Texas-born Colonel House, an amateur diplomat. Initially the president condemned all the belligerents for having thrown the world into turmoil. Critical as he was of German militarism and British navalism, he was also suspicious of despotic and imperialistic Russia. Nearly all of the possible alternative outcomes of the war depressed him. As Colonel House told him on August 22, 1914, an Allied victory would mean the domination of Europe by Russia, not France. A German victory would enthrone militarism for an unforeseeable time. Unrestrained British dominance would also pose vexatious problems. Wilson firmly believed that only as a neutral could he hope to help bring about more promising solutions. As much as he respected President Charles W. Eliot of Harvard, he thus rejected Eliot's proposal, early in August, 1914, to organize a grand alliance to punish the Central European bullies, with the American navy taking part.

What strengthened Woodrow Wilson when he undertook the thankless task of peacemaker was the support of his people. Despite their sympathies for one or the other side in this war, the American people were militarily and psychologically totally unprepared for war. When Wilson ran for a second term under the slogan "He kept us out of war," they voted for him because their aloofness from European affairs was even more firmly rooted than the president's. The inhumanity and lawlessness of this war disturbed them deeply, and its economic repercussions made them restless. The European leaders, preoccupied with their heavy war responsibilities, simply did not appreciate how extraordinary it was for the president of the United States to assume an active world role. The scope of Wilson's peace efforts made them a significant departure from America's historical aloofness. Frenchmen who were disappointed because he did not act more vigorously on behalf of French security from the war's outset did not evidence any realistic conception of the American political scene.

Wilson and his right-hand man, Colonel House, realized the delicacy of their undertaking. They could not be sure whether the belligerents would be willing to accept a neutral outsider as an honest broker. The timing of any approach required careful consideration, because the responses of foreign governments depended on such factors as the military situation at any given time, the morale of their respective peoples, and internal political complications. The pacifists and annexationists in each of the countries at war usually deprived policy makers of complete freedom of decision. Civilian and military leaders, moreover, did not always see eye to eye in regard to tactics and strategy. Wilson and House realized the importance of the procedural question of whether to make specific peace proposals or merely try to bring the opposing sides together to explore the possibility of ending the slaughter and suffering. In addition to these complexities, they also had to convince the Europeans that they would not favor one side or the other and had no overriding selfish American policy objectives in mind.

None of the belligerents made it easy for the president: each was guided by its own interests. When the Germans realized that their original Blitzkrieg strategy, embodied in the Schlieffen plan, had not succeeded, they sought alternative ways to accomplish an early victory. By November, 1914, their civilian and military leaders were banking on an effort to drive a political wedge between their enemies by separating, for an attractive price, one of the members of the Entente from its allies. This strategy held out little hope in view of the Pact of London, signed by Great Britain, France, and Russia on September 5, 1914, and pledging the signatories not to make a separate peace. Despite the Allies' promise to make war and peace as a unit, the Germans pursued their strategy with perseverance. Their military and political leaders, however, were not in agreement on whether France or Russia would be the desirable target of such endeavors. The chief of staff, General Erich von Falkenhayn, believed that by bringing Russia to terms, "we could then deal France and England so crushing a blow that we could dictate peace terms."[14] To Undersecretary of State Arthur Zimmermann, the kaiser's favorite foreign policy adviser, France, not Russia, appeared to be the weakest link in the enemy camp. No bargaining was conceived possible with tenacious England except perhaps at the final peace conference. Germany did not exclude the possibility, however, of maneuvering the United States into a conflict with Great Britain over

14. Quoted in Zeman, *Diplomatic History of the First World War*, 83–85.

the issues of neutral rights and freedom of the seas. The Germans were prepared to make slight concessions to the United States in U-boat crises so as to appear more conciliatory than Britain, which refused to back down on its blockade.[15]

On the whole, the German government desired to keep the lines of communication with the United States open, just in case the military situation should warrant its diplomatic assistance. But its responses to American peace feelers were deliberately vague. It evaded all invitations to be specific about its terms of peace. It shied away from all exploratory peace conferences in which it would have been in a minority and, therefore, at a disadvantage. But as Chancellor Bethmann-Hollweg explained in a note to Ambassador Johann-Heinrich von Bernstorff on August 18, 1916: "We gladly accept a mediation by the President which endeavors to promote the beginning of peace negotiations among the belligerents. Strongly encourage the President to proceed. Of course, acceptance of such mediation does not oblige us to any concrete peace conditions."[16] As long as it appeared possible to achieve, the kaiser and his supreme military commanders did not abandon their goal to dictate a peace that would establish Germany's hegemony in Europe. When Zimmermann told the American ambassador in Berlin that "Germany desires, above all else, to conclude the war with a lasting peace," he meant, of course, a total German victory.[17]

In this respect, the leaders of the opposing camps were of one mind. When in the summer of 1914 it appeared that the Germans were about to conquer Paris and the kaiser would thereafter make a peace gesture, Britain and France were apprehensive about Wilson's reaction to such a diplomatic trap. In September, 1914, Ambassador Page sounded the alarm that "the Allies can't and won't accept any peace except on the condition that German militarism is uprooted."[18]

A month later, Colonel House explained to Page that President Wilson approached the consequences of this war with dispassionate vision. Guided by ancient hatreds, he believed, Europeans often

15. Birnbaum, *Peace Moves and U-Boat Warfare*, 74–75.

16. *Ibid.*, 124–26.

17. Quoted in Ernest R. May, *The World War and American Isolation, 1914–1917* (Cambridge, Mass., 1963), 107.

18. Burton J. Hendrick, *The Life and Letters of Walter H. Page* (4 vols.; New York, 1924), I, Pt. 2, 401–14.

did not know what was best for them. If Germany were crushed, the president feared, Russian militarism would become dominant in Europe, merely replacing German militarism. Such a prospect made the future look grim indeed. For Russia's "government is so constituted that friendly conversations could not be had with her as they might be had even with such a power as Germany, and the world would look forward to another cataclysm." Without wishing to offend the sensibilities of any of the belligerents, but earnestly objecting to the complete annihilation of any of them, the president simply would not be dissuaded from taking the initiative for the construction of a truly peaceful world. According to Ambassador Page, the British had no desire for vengeance. But inasmuch as "Germany set out to rule the world and to conquer Britain," they wanted to make sure that German militarism would be in no position to threaten them again in a generation or two. While the English people and their military and naval personnel no longer cared about the feelings and thoughts of neutral America, the cabinet and many thoughtful British subjects knew better. Precisely because Sir Edward Grey considered good relations with the United States a paramount necessity, he listened patiently to whatever was on the president's mind.

Fortunately, Colonel House, Wilson's second self, succeeded in gaining Grey's full confidence, which assured him of many contacts at the highest level, enabling him to carry on genuinely frank exchanges. In the course of his mission to Europe early in 1915, as well as on many subsequent missions, House discussed with various leaders the president's ideas about the reconstruction of the troubled world. In essence, it called for the abolition of German militarism, British navalism, and competitive nationalism—the underlying causes of war. Wilson believed that cooperative investments in underdeveloped regions would benefit the peoples of these regions, as well as the participating industrial nations, and contribute to peace. In his view, only such a nonexploitative and nonimperialistic approach would do honor to "white" civilization.[19]

Such idealistic notions sounded so utopian that the prophetic advocate of this new world appeared a greater enigma to the leaders of the Old World than ever before. Preoccupied first and foremost

19. N. Gordon Levin, Jr., *Woodrow Wilson and World Politics: America's Response to War and Revolution* (New York, 1969), 24–25.

with winning the war, Grey sought to convince the president that only through America's participation in the ongoing conflict could it effectively shape the future world. And if the American people wanted to see the war come to an early end, he suggested, it could hasten it by fighting on the side of the Allies.[20]

France was not even sure of that. Its policies and the tone of its communications annoyed the president. As early as September, 1914, Ambassador Herrick alerted the State Department that "a proposal for mediation would be refused by the Entente Powers." The first mediation soundings, indirectly engineered by Bernstorff at a private dinner party at which America's former ambassador to Turkey, Oscar Straus, was present, looked suspicious to the Allies. The French and the Russians actually resented any attempt by the Germans to escape, temporarily or permanently, from the consequences of their ruthless invasion. Like Great Britain, France and Russia left no doubt that they intended to crush their aggressive neighbor and impose a victor's peace on him.[21]

On March 15, 1915, at his first meeting with Théophile Delcassé, the energetic French minister of foreign affairs, Colonel House was primarily interested in letting him know that President Wilson was thoroughly familiar with the situation in Europe. Initially uncertain that he would be accorded a cordial reception, House considered it an important step forward that Delcassé indicated his readiness to talk with him again after his return from Berlin. Perhaps reading too much into the foreign minister's polite appreciation of Wilson's "keen interest and noble desire to bring about peace," House felt that "France has at least tentatively accepted [Wilson] as moderator." His superficial impression, however, led him to the conclusion that the ruling class in France did not desire peace at that time. House respected France as a great power without whose participation no negotiated peace would be possible. But the French showed a cold shoulder to his diplomatic soundings, despite the ambiguous pleasantries. He regretted that he could not talk as openly and directly with French leaders as he could with the British. The colonel had to use third parties, friends of Delcassé, to prepare the ground for fu-

20. E. M. House, *Intimate Papers*, ed. Charles Seymour (2 vols.; Boston, 1926–28), II, 54–55.

21. Ambassador Jean Jules Jusserand discouraged House's visionary peace schemes. Jean Jules Jusserand to Aristide Briand, June 1, 1916, in Guerre 1914–18: États-Unis, Dossier 501, AMAE.

ture interviews. He desired the foreign minister to know how much the Allies had to gain from the president's good will and that he, Wilson's confidant, had immediate access to him. Above all, he wanted the message to sink in that the president strove for a permanent settlement, not just territorial changes, which would be likely to produce new troubles.

President Wilson was preoccupied with the massive destruction caused by this conflict, the disruption of normal economic channels, and the prospect of highly undesirable power constellations emerging from it, House emphasized. If the belligerents continued to decline his mediation overtures, Wilson did not rule out American intervention in order to shorten the war. He would not make such a decision lightly; but too much was at stake for the future of civilization to permit the ruinous conflict to drag out.

With all this in mind, House arrived in London on January 5, 1916. It did not take him long to realize that since his last visit the situation had generally become worse and that the United States would have to step up its search for diplomatic solutions. Grey, in the past a moderating influence, had been politically weakened, and the British attitude toward the blockade had been stiffened. House's exploratory trips to Berlin and Paris also left him with the impression of a generally worsening trend. Under enormous pressures from Germany's military leaders, Bethmann-Hollweg's relatively flexible position had been weakened, and early resort to unrestricted submarine warfare seemed likely.[22]

In Paris, House reviewed the whole situation at an important conference with Briand, the French premier, and Cambon, chief of the foreign ministry. After reassuring them of the president's friendly disposition toward France, House made another pitch for French support of Wilson's peace bid. But should the time come for America's military intervention, he did not want to leave them in doubt about Wilson's insistence on a peace of justice, not vengeance. House promised that "in the event the Allies are successful during the next few months . . . the President would not intervene. In the event they were losing ground, the President would intervene." For good measure, anticipating the major battle of Verdun, he reiterated that "the lower the fortunes of the Allies ebbed, the closer the United States would stand by them." When Colonel House

22. May, *World War and American Isolation*, 352–55, 374.

read the memorandum in which Cambon summarized these conversations, he took strenuous exception to its version of the latter statement, according to which he was reported to have said, "No matter how low the ebb of the fortunes of France got, when they said the word, we would intervene." This inaccuracy eliminated the independence of America's ultimate decision. House also advised Grey that it would make no sense for the United States to come into the war when it was about to be lost. These Franco-American discussions deepened the mutual skepticism in Paris and Washington. America's apparent disposition to accept a negotiated peace based upon the status quo ante bellum caused considerable concern in France.[23]

In any case, at this time France showed no interest in sitting down with anybody to discuss peace. On the contrary, on January 21, 1916, Ambassador William Graves Sharp forwarded to Secretary of State Lansing a copy of Poincaré's message to the French troops, which left no doubt in this respect. In it the French leader declared: "Any peace that would come to us in a suspicious figure or in equivocal terms . . . would only bring us, under deceiving appearances, disgrace, ruin, and slavery. . . . The free and pure genius of our race . . . the soul of our land . . . all that makes us ourselves, would be a prey to German brutality. We will not grow tired."

To House it seemed more urgent than ever for the president to call for a conference in which the belligerents should explore the basis for peace. Sir Edward Grey was willing to attend it. For House had indicated that if, as expected, Germany refused to participate, then the United States "will throw in all our weight to bring her to terms." Between February 12 and 22, 1916, Colonel House and British leaders conferred and dined frequently, informally drafting a very far-reaching formula concerning America's future role in the war. Although they rather casually explored the future political map of the world, the British statesmen did not reveal the secret territorial treaties the Allies had previously negotiated.[24] Whether or not the president knew of the secret treaties, it is certain that under no circumstances would he have taken his country into war just to distribute such spoils. On February 23, Grey handed House his memorandum containing the understanding arrived at in their bilateral

23. "Conversation du Col. House avec Jules Cambon," February 2, 7, and 12, 1916, in Guerre 1914–18: États Unis, Dossiers 498 and 499, AMAE.

24. Zeman, *Diplomatic History of the First World War*, 182–85.

discussions. According to it, the president, once given the signal by France and England, would propose a conference to bring the war to a diplomatic end. The extraordinary commitment of the United States was couched in these terms: "Should the Allies accept this proposal, and should Germany refuse it, the United States would enter the war against Germany . . . and, if it [the conference] failed to secure peace, the United States would leave the conference as a belligerent on the side of the Allies, if Germany was unreasonable." It now depended on the British cabinet and the French to follow through.[25]

Two developments frustrated the implementation of this understanding. President Wilson, who was much less inclined to intervene militarily than either Colonel House or Secretary Lansing, cautiously added the word *probably* to the text so that it read, "The United States would probably leave the conference on the side of the Allies." This one word made, of course, a great difference because it added an element of uncertainty that the British foreign secretary did not like at all. He therefore merely informed the French government of this understanding without urging Paris to accept it. He did not want the French to think that Britain's willingness to take American peace overtures seriously amounted in any sense whatsoever to its willingness to abandon the Anglo-French Entente. Grey was so sensitive about this that he thought the president should approach France directly.

The proposed conference could not come off anyway, because the French pushed the Grey-House understanding aside. Briand reacted to it with eloquent silence, and Cambon, one of the leading French experts on the United States, "laughed it to scorn." On May 22, 1916, the French ambassador to the United States advised the State Department that "France could not consider peace until it could be assured that it was a real peace and not a breathing spell for Germany." Although courteous and even complimentary, Jusserand could also be emotional and irritating. His parting observation that "anyone suggesting peace now would be considered by his people a friend of Germany" honestly reflected the prevailing view of his government.[26] The French clearly wanted to fight this war to the finish and annihilate their rival, with the help of Great Britain, Russia,

25. House, *Intimate Papers*, II, 201–202.

26. Frank L. Polk, memorandum, May 22, 1916, in Box 17, Folder 18, Frank L. Polk Papers, Yale University Library.

Italy, and Belgium, a coalition not to be duplicated soon. Alone, the French could not hold Germany down, much less dominate Europe. They were determined, with the help of their allies, to deal with Germany on their terms, not on Wilson's terms. The United States could best contribute to victory by continuing to send and finance massive supplies. Like the Germans, they totally underestimated America's military potential. Its military unpreparedness was so incredible that the war was likely to be over, they assumed, before Americans could throw armies into battle.[27]

Confident that their gamble for military victory would pay off, the French were essentially fighting this war for strictly French objectives. The United States and democracy stood to benefit only indirectly. As the leading power in Europe, France was unlikely to be more hospitable than Germany to opening its markets to Americans. And while Wilson occasionally spoke disapprovingly of the balance of power system, he was too intelligent not to expect serious complications to arise from hegemony by any power in Europe. His peace bids had made this very plain.

In the final week of March, 1916, the British prime minister and his foreign secretary went to Paris to confer with their French allies. Remarkably, they did not impress upon the French the extraordinary significance of the Grey-House understanding, which left the door open for America's intervention, an event likely to shorten the war. Perhaps they were afraid of the political concessions such an entry would exact.

Instead of agreeing to such concessions, the British tried to exhaust another possibility. They encroached more severely on the rights of neutrals, hoping that food shortages and signs of sinking morale would provoke Germany into a direct confrontation with the United States, the Allies' arsenal. Appreciating America's usefulness, Sir Edward Grey continued to hold out a degree of hope for cooperative peace efforts when, in fact, Britain had moved much closer to the French view of dealing with Germany. Indeed, by the end of 1916, Britain's intensified blockade and imperial ambitions led Colonel House to the conclusion that Britain threatened America's long-term interests far more than Germany. He did not dis-

27. Yves-Henri Nouaihat, *La France et les États-Unis, août 1914–avril 1917* (Paris, 1979), 421.

count the possibility of a future Anglo-American showdown. It loomed on the horizon.[28]

As a power, the Allies did not rate the United States on a par with them. Thinking in terms overtaken by history, they jealously kept America away from their councils. In their analysis, they, particularly the French, failed to perceive that their concentration on immediate objectives in this war might help them win battles but, in a large perspective, still lose the war. The longer the war lasted, the more Europe's exhaustion foreshadowed economic difficulties for its reconstruction. In the meantime the massive acceleration of neutral America's industrial capacities enabled it to forge ahead of Europe. As a creditor, moreover, America became a power to reckon with in its own right. The ironic consequences of this war thus indicated results contrary to all calculations.

Soon after President Wilson had been reelected and David Lloyd George had formed his war cabinet, Colonel House made plans to resume his aborted mediation efforts. This time, however, Wilson decided first to find out the specific peace terms and general war aims the belligerents had in mind. He just wanted to receive essential information. Even so, such a request confronted the belligerents with a delicate diplomatic dilemma. Despite frozen battle lines and their peoples' yearning for an early end of their suffering, both sides still anticipated victory. It seemed childish to them, therefore, to put their political cards on the table. Each side expected greatly accelerated naval warfare to starve the enemy into surrender.[29] So far, American policy had striven, not entirely successfully, to restrain British and German naval excesses. When on December 3, 1916, Ambassador Jusserand criticized the United States for not really having held Germany strictly accountable in recurring submarine controversies, Colonel House justified the president's restraint on the ground that unrestricted submarine warfare would practically isolate England and be a disaster for the Allied cause. For a moment the French envoy saw this point, but he still charged Wilson with pro-Germanism. This irritating comment annoyed House so much that he had to control his temper not to tell the Frenchman "things he would have remembered a long while."

28. V. H. Rothwell, *British War Aims and Peace Diplomacy, 1914–1918* (Oxford, 1971), 32–37.

29. Zeman, *Diplomatic History of the First World War*, 186–87.

Following a meeting with Jules Cambon on December 9, Ambassador Sharp sent a confidential report to Lansing informing him that at this time the French diplomat did not believe in the likelihood of any negotiated end to the war. Sharp found it incredible "that those well informed of the true situation can believe," as Cambon stated emphatically, "that the forces of the Central Powers can be conquered or even driven back to the Rhine" in three to six months. In Sharp's opinion, both sides had developed trench warfare to such an extent that "it has become almost impossible to make any marked advances even at the expense of enormous quantities of matériel as well as the loss of great numbers of men. Only acute domestic conditions can change the outlook for many months to come." Despite Cambon's views, Sharp noted that the French press reacted to the president's latest initiative more fairly and temperately than the British press.[30] These different reactions reflected their respective peoples' morale. Playing on this morale factor, the Central Powers attempted to draw out the Allies about the basis for diplomatic explorations. Rather contemptuously, the French government labeled this sounding "a mere ruse having an insidious purpose to discourage and demoralize the forces of the Allies."

From Berlin, Joseph C. Grew, the temporary chargé d'affaires, also apprised Lansing of the German people's steadily declining morale, their hardships, and their willingness to express and listen to liberal ideas. The notions that "Germany by virtue of the leadership in the arts of civilization and the moral superiority of her people must spread her power and methods throughout the world, are now generally relegated to obscurity," he said. But from what he could gather, Grew assumed that the Allies would make peace only on terms teaching the German people the futility of future wars of expansion.[31]

Neither side had the vision to see that they were engaged in a conflict they could not really "win" in the sense they intended to use their victory. They sneered at Wilson's statesmanlike "Peace Without Victory" speech on January 22, 1917. As Secretary Lansing explained in the draft of his war memoirs, Wilson did not say "War Without Victory." By peace without victory, he meant to look ahead,

30. Sharp to Robert Lansing, December 29, 1916, in Robert Lansing Papers, Seeley G. Mudd Library, Princeton University, Princeton.

31. Joseph C. Grew to Robert Lansing, December 21, 1916, in Lansing Papers, Princeton.

not backward, to lay a solid foundation for a stable, cooperative world. The economic and imperialistic rivalries of the past had, as Wilson interpreted them, brought instability and war. Now was the time to learn from history and find a compromise peace that could lead to an enlightened league of nations.[32]

When Wilson's patient perseverance did not bring results, suspicions of the ultimate peace aims of both belligerent camps made him fear for the future. In June of 1916, Secretary Lansing had already alerted him to the Allies' intention "to continue the war industrially after actual warfare ceases." The chances were that such a course would also at least peripherally affect the American economy. The rejection of all his peace efforts inspired no faith in the Allies' future good will. On the contrary, the president became increasingly convinced that regardless of what the United States did for the Allies, they, like the Germans, were fighting for strictly selfish nationalistic objectives. Therefore, as late as January 4, 1917, he declared to Colonel House: "There will be no war. This country does not intend to become involved in this war. We are the only one of the great white nations that is free from war today, and it would be a crime against civilization for us to go in." As much as his concern for the future of mankind guided him in this view, he also felt a profound sense of obligation toward the American people, who had only recently honored him by reelecting him as their peace president.[33]

What, then, happened between January and April, 1917, to make the president change his mind and, with the approval of Congress, throw America's full weight into this world conflict? Although the Allies responded to the president's inquiry of December 18 in general, studiedly friendly terms, they nevertheless reiterated their old positions. They would be ready to listen to American peace plans for the future only after they themselves had drawn the new map of Europe. They preferred to discuss these issues directly with their antagonists rather than through an intermediary, a euphemistic way of saying "once victory is ours."

In January, 1917, Field Marshal Paul von Hindenburg and Admiral Henning von Holtzendorff, chief of the admiralty staff, considered the time ripe for resumption of unrestricted submarine war-

32. See draft of Lansing's "War Memoirs," in Lansing Papers, Princeton.

33. House, *Intimate Papers*, II, 411–12.

fare, to bring starving Britain to her knees. Hindenburg assumed that Wilson's latest peace sounding had been prompted by the British, with the intent to delay Germany's all-out naval war. As far as the German high command was concerned, the United States had for all practical purposes been an unfriendly power from the beginning of the war. Germany expected little support from America at a peace conference and was confident that the American reaction to unrestricted submarine warfare would be limited to protests. But even if, unexpectedly, the United States should join the Allies, the German high command thought that America's military capabilities could be dismissed. "The sole, serious danger to U-boat war," declared Admiral Holtzendorff, "does not come from America, but from hesitating to resort to it now, after poor harvests in America and before the next harvest in England. . . . If we miss this opportunity for victory, time will be against us."[34] Chancellor Bethmann-Hollweg and Ambassador Bernstorff, concerned that unrestricted submarine warfare would lead to a break with the United States, counseled against resorting to it. But the pressures of the military leaders gradually compelled the civilians to yield. Supporting every chance to save his throne and the Hohenzollern dynasty, the kaiser accepted the recommendations of his high command. On January 31, the disappointed German ambassador delivered the declaration of unrestricted U-boat warfare to the State Department. He knew better than Germany's generals and admirals that it was foolhardy to dismiss the United States as a harmless democracy, incapable of fighting a modern war. Four days later, the United States severed diplomatic relations with the Reich.

Although approaching the point of utter exhaustion, both Germany and France treated this severance as of little consequence. Jusserand was so amazed at the break that he asked for official instructions. But, not knowing that it would soon be followed by a declaration of war, the optimistic French did not interpret it as a decisive turn in the war. If they feared anything, they feared that President Wilson, as a participant in the war, would try to assume the role of the world's ombudsman instead of accepting a *paix française*. Only Lloyd George, now faced with the greatest challenge to his country, welcomed the direction in which the president was moving. He flattered Wilson by letting him know that, above all, En-

34. Birnbaum, *Peace Moves and U-Boat Warfare*, 254–77, 316–19.

gland wanted him "to come into the war not so much for the help in the war as for help with peace. . . . If he [the president] sits in the conference that makes peace he will exert the greatest influence that any man has ever exerted in expressing the moral value of free government." Unlike the French and the Germans, British leaders understood American psychology so well that they could skillfully exploit it. Throughout the war, German propaganda in the United States had been clumsy and ineffective. French attitudes had often been annoying. As the war came closer to a climax, the Anglophile Wilson and British leaders sensed the possibility of Anglo-American solidarity extending to the postwar period. Neither the French nor the Germans could be entirely comfortable with such Anglo-Saxon solidarity.[35]

Theoretically, following the severance of relations, the president could have sat back and persevered in his peace course. He could have decided on armed neutrality to protect American shipping, nonbelligerency, or a declaration of war against Germany. Several developments in February and March, exposing him successively to extraordinary pressures, compelled him to make up his mind for war. The unrestricted U-boat war constituted a serious threat to Great Britain. It also accelerated the sinking of American ships, with consequent loss of American lives. Fearing such a fate, many American shipowners decided to stay in port. By doing so, they not only hurt the American economy but also played right into the hands of Germany's blockade. In view of these dilemmas, Secretary of the Treasury McAdoo urged the president to provide merchantmen with defensive armament. While this issue was under discussion, a diplomatic bombshell shook Washington on February 24, when the British foreign secretary, Arthur J. Balfour, transmitted to Ambassador Page a transcript of the decoded Zimmermann telegram of January 16. The telegram revealed Germany's duplicity of having talked in mid-January with Wilson about peace while at the same moment offering Mexico an alliance in case the United States should enter the war following the declaration of unrestricted submarine warfare. The stunned American public did not have long to wait for Zimmermann himself to confirm the telegram's authenticity. By promising Mexico the return of Texas, New Mexico, and Arizona as a reward for its participation in a war against the United States, Ger-

35. Zeman, *Diplomatic History of the First World War*, 202–205.

many succeeded in antagonizing the American people as never before. This provocation, rather than any serious concern about a war with Mexico, brought about a decisive change of public opinion in the United States. Coming as it did soon after the inauguration of Germany's new U-boat policy, the Zimmermann note contributed to building a momentum of crisis proportions.

However, Congress' readiness now to approve the arming of merchantmen tended to divide the country into pacifists, who were to some extent financially supported by Germany, and patriots, who clamored for energetic actions against Gemany's challenge on the high seas and its threatened violation of America's territorial integrity. The very prospect of such division disturbed Wilson because he wanted a united people behind him if and when he decided to go to war.

Finally, the outbreak of the Russian Revolution, and the danger of the breakdown of the eastern front and a separate peace between Germany and Russia, portended an ominous crisis for the Allies. The transfer of German forces from the east to the west confronted France, already at a straining point domestically, with the imminent possibility of military collapse. Coupled with Britain's inability to withstand the German blockade for any length of time, Germany seemed to be within reach of controlling the French ports on the English Channel, the European shore of the Atlantic, and eventually the waters of this ocean. This realistic scenario turned what so far had been a European war into one of vital interest to the defenses and trade of the United States and the Western hemisphere. According to Walter Lippmann's analysis, this turn of events influenced President Wilson more than any of the other provocations and considerations. "When it was seen that Britain could not hold the other shore of the Atlantic without American help, America intervened." In the words of Theodore Roosevelt, who had all along criticized Wilson's patient pacifism, "First and foremost we are to make the world safe for ourselves."[36] On April 2, 1917, President Wilson finally asked Congress to declare war against Imperial Germany, to bring it to terms for its "warfare against mankind" and its recent course, which he described "to be in fact nothing less than war against the Government and the people of the United States." By

36. See also Algernon Gordon Lennox (ed.), *The Diary of Lord Bertie of Thame, 1914–1918* (2 vols.; London, 1924), II, 316.

April 6, the United States was officially at war with Germany. America also promptly broke relations with Austria-Hungary, though it saw no reason for the time being to declare war against that nation.

THE UNITED STATES AS AN ASSOCIATE OF FRANCE, 1917–1918

It is important to note that the president deliberately entered the war as an "associate," not an ally, of the Entente powers. Similarly, the subsequent insistence on employing American forces, led by American officers, as a separate military entity, though cooperating with the Supreme Allied Command, was politically motivated. Furthermore, Wilson preferred not to appoint a representative to the Inter-Allied Blockade Council, so that American exports "should not be regarded as controlled by an agreement with the Allies." The Allies were fighting their war; the United States was fighting its war. Wilson clearly signaled to the Allies that their war aims were dis-

Table 1

French Loans in the United States, 1914–1919
(in millions of francs at the average yearly exchange rate)

Year	Amount
1914	.051
1915	1.845
1916	1.624
1917	7.532
1918	5.388
1919	9.267
Total:	25.707

Source: Henri Truchy, *The War Finance of France* (New Haven, 1927), 17.

Table 2

United States Exports to France, 1914–1919
(in thousands of dollars)

Year	Amount
1914	170.104
1915	500.792
1916	860.821
1917	940.791
1918	931.199
1919	893.369

Source: France, *Statistique Générale*, IX (1919–20), 104.

tinct from America's war aims. Although they were opposing the same enemy, they were fighting for different political objectives. Significantly, when at the end of the war France attempted to "share" the cost of the entire conflict with the United States, Colonel House went so far as to declare that American entry into the war had not been an absolute necessity. "We were never afraid of the Germans," he recorded in his diary, "and would not have been afraid of them even if France and England had gone under." In case of a future German challenge, he maintained, the United States would not have "feared that they could defeat us or dominate us."[37]

America's entry into the war was a red-letter day for the French. Premier Alexandre Ribot gratefully acknowledged that it amounted to the financial salvation of his hard-pressed nation. By this time the French were finding it extremely difficult to finance purchases of war materials and food supplies from America. To private bankers France had become a poor risk. Although the sums the Federal Treasury henceforth made available mortgaged France's future, they relieved the government of immediate pressures.[38]

In an eloquent address to the Chamber of Deputies on April 5, 1917, Ribot used the occasion of American entry as a means of bolstering the declining morale of the French people. He declared that it was an illustration of the common cause to which the Allies and the United States were committed. Now that the conscience of peoples throughout the world was protesting against the atrocious victimization of the French people, he said, "we feel more vividly that we are not fighting only for ourselves and for our Allies, but for something immortal and . . . a new order."[39] Similarly, President Raymond Poincaré lauded President Wilson for having made himself "the eloquent interpreter of the civilization threatened by Germany." As the war progressed, he stressed repeatedly the necessity of keeping the wartime "alliance" intact when peace returned. The greater the contribution of the United States to the final victory, the

37. Colonel Edward M. House, Diary, January 4, 1919, in Colonel Edward M. House Papers, Yale University Library, New Haven.

38. Pierre Renouvin, *La crise européenne et la première guerre mondiale (1914–1918)* (Paris, 1948), 443; G. Olphe-Galliard, *Histoire économique et financière de la guerre (1914–1918)* (Paris, 1923), 140–47.

39. France, *Journal Officiel de la République Française: Débats Parlementaires*, Chambre des Députés, April 5, 1917, pp. 1140–41.

more the French preferred to see the continuation of the tested league of the Allies, rather than the creation of a League of Nations.

President Wilson, "the political Pope of the future," as the conservative editor of *Le Correspondant* called him, of course opposed the substance of this play with words. He was not interested in a new order essentially perpetuating the old order of power-political leagues. He was guided by a vision more worthy of Judeo-Christian civilization, an uplifting world order. When late in 1918 the Allies began to belittle America's military and financial contributions, which had saved them, the president vowed not "to let those Europeans forget it." He deplored the fact that "England and France have not the same views with regard to peace as we have by any means." But in order to avoid public disagreements during the war, he postponed a showdown on this issue. According to Ray Stannard Baker, despite Wilson's often lofty thoughts, he was capable of acting in a very realistic, pragmatic way. Nothing demonstrates this better than his observation to House on July 21, 1917: "When the war is over we can force them to our way of thinking, because by that time they will, among other things, be financially in our hands."

It was typical of Wilson to take the United States into the war without prior consultation with the Allies. Since wars are fought for political ends, one might have expected him to seek an understanding regarding final political objectives prior to joining the military phase. If the Allies refused to yield to American goals when they needed the United States desperately, what chance would there be for them to underwrite a Wilsonian peace when victory allowed them again to be much freer agents? Wilson's comment to Colonel House holds one of the answers. He believed that the gradual ascendancy of the United States would place it in a controlling position by the end of the conflict. That reality appeared to be basically more solid than promises that could be later ignored. Aided by such a reality, he also possessed an extraordinary faith in his own ability to conduct the ultimate political phase successfully.

Following America's declaration of war, the French people felt relieved and began to see the light at the end of the tunnel. The hoisting of the American flag at the pinnacle of the Eiffel Tower symbolized their grateful sentiments toward the United States. Besides experiencing material sacrifices and fear for the future, hardly a family in France had escaped personal tragedy. With countless men dead or permanently disabled, the French could not continue to suffer such loss of life much longer. Unfortunately, their euphoric expectations anticipated immediate American miracles. As the people overestimated the instant effects of America's military intervention, their military and political leaders completely underestimated American military capacities and potential contributions. The French general staff were "not particularly interested in having American troops in France." Considering them unready for combat, they intended to limit their role to giving moral support. Marshal Joseph J. Joffre thought "it will cheer our people" to see a division show the Stars and Stripes. The French attaché in Washington had previously advised his War Department not to count on any effective military assistance in case the United States entered the war. Ambassador Jusserand even expressed the opinion that in such a contingency, equipping an American expeditionary force might interfere with the immediate needs of the French command. None of the European belligerents had the slightest inkling that the citizens of the American republic, who loved hunting and sports, were accustomed to rifles and teamwork. All they needed was a little time and the tools to forge them into effective military units. In the meantime the United States continued to send food, steel, and military supplies, mobilized its industrial capacity, and developed its war machine. America's phenomenal organizational genius produced within a year the soldiers, ships, and supplies that, to the utter amazement of the British, French, and Germans, tilted the scales of the war in favor of the Allies.

This American effort came just in the nick of time. In April of 1917 alone, German submarines had sent 874,000 tons of shipping to the bottom of the ocean. At that rate Great Britain's ability to stay in the war became doubtful. The morale of the war-weary French people had sunk alarmingly. The internal situation in France gave as much rise to doubts as the bleeding military front. Mutinies in May of 1917, recurrent strikes in munition factories, the incarceration of the minister of interior (accused of treason), the worsening food situation, and the corruption of a portion of the French press that accepted subsidies from the Germans to spread defeatism—all these factors created a discouraging atmosphere. In August, 1917, Professor Felix Frankfurter submitted to the secretary of state his officially requested findings about the situation in France. He concluded, "If

American troops in great numbers will not be in France by the end of the year, if winter should again be a hard one, if the Russian situation should become worse instead of better, the diverse elements of impatience may well give Caillaux and his friends their opportunity."[40]

Joseph Caillaux, a politician of considerable influence, rallied French support for an early peace. Although the followers of Georges Clemenceau and French royalists continued to advocate vigorous military action, by the spring of 1918 large segments of the French populace had become "impregnated with the virus of pacifism." In a trial for treason Caillaux was found innocent of "intelligence with the enemy" but guilty of "damage to the external security of the state." It is noteworthy that he was motivated by more than pacifism. He also contended that the continuation of the war was likely to favor England rather than France. Ideally, Caillaux would have preferred France's closest ties be with such Latin neighbors as Italy and Spain, not with the English. In his opinion, continuation of the war would ultimately weaken France rather than lead to any significant gains. In view of these various defeatist signs, Frankfurter recommended that the United States preach the doctrine of optimism, based upon the gigantic military campaign America would mount in the near future.

In anticipation of the arrival of American troops, Marshal Henri Philippe Pétain marked time with largely defensive moves. When they did arrive, all kinds of complications awaited them. Their combat inexperience and insufficient military hardware was deemed sufficient ground to amalgamate them in Allied, particularly French, units. Aside from betraying a lack of confidence in American combat readiness, such an arrangement would have used American troops to fight for whatever political aims the French had in mind. For this reason alone, amalgamation was not acceptable. To the chagrin of Pétain, General John J. Pershing insisted that his troops be assigned to a sector on the front as an American unit under American command, even though French leaders did not regard American officers and their staffs sufficiently competent to assume such responsibilities. Fortunately, Marshal Ferdinand Foch's experience had taught him "that the soldiers of any country only give their best when fighting under their own leaders and under their own col-

40. U.S. State Department, *Lansing Papers*, II, 38–42.

ours." General Pershing's view did not only prevail, but American officers, in their turn, criticized the French conduct of the war. They were particularly annoyed by long bureaucratic delays. Eventually they bypassed them and operated in their own way, admittedly offending French sensitivities. But their remarkable military accomplishments vindicated them.

Although Marshal Foch praised Pershing's troops for their splendid successes in the Saint-Mihiel and Meuse-Argonne sectors, Clemenceau sent a very critical letter to Foch on October 21, 1918, deploring the "marking of time" of the American army. As president of the council and minister of war, he concluded that General Pershing's invincible obstinacy caused faulty utilization of the American troops. "I would be a criminal," he wrote, "if I allowed the French Army to wear itself out indefinitely in battle" while American troops were "unused." In his judgment, it was "high time to tell President Wilson . . . the whole truth concerning the situation of the American troops." In his response to the constitutional head of the French armies, Foch confined himself to informing Clemenceau that of the thirty American divisions fit for battle, ten were distributed among the French and British armies and twenty constituted the autonomous American army under General Pershing's orders. According to Foch, "there is no denying the magnitude of the effort made by the American army." Marshal Joffre also attested to the "glorious part" American divisions played along the fighting front. What, then, was Clemenceau up to? Was his attempt to downgrade America's contribution to the final victory and to extol the sustained sacrifices of the French armies politically motivated? Subsequent diplomatic developments strongly suggest that Clemenceau's maneuver was designed more to reduce Wilson's political influence at the approaching peace conference than to undermine Pershing's position. In this context it is noteworthy that only three months prior to Clemenceau's communication to Foch, President Poincaré observed that the British and some French deputies would have liked to see American forces facilitate the reduction of Allied fighting divisions. Poincaré objected to such a cynical attitude because it would "weaken ourselves at the moment of supreme efforts."[41]

In his "History of the United States Naval Attaché in Paris,"

41. T. Bentley Mott (trans.), *The Memoirs of Marshal Foch* (New York, 1931), 346, 402, 434–38. See also Lennox (ed.), *Diary of Lord Bertie*, 268, and Raymond Poincaré, *Au service de la France: Neuf années de souvenirs* (10 vols.; Paris, 1928–33), X, 278–85.

Franklin Delano Roosevelt, the U.S. assistant secretary of the navy during the First World War, described the outstanding performance of the attaché. Virtually in charge of the entire naval activities of the United States in France, Lieutenant Commander William R. Sayles realized from the beginning the vital importance of coordination between the French and American naval forces. Toward this end he cooperated closely with Admiral Lucien Lacaze, who was the French minister of marine, and with other French officials. Preparations had to be made for the docking and discharging of cargoes and for rail transportation. High priority had to be assigned to the establishment of naval bases in France, the transportation of supplies and men essential to France, assistance in the warfare against submarines, naval intelligence, and a steady flow of information concerning ship movements. To invest himself with adequate authority, the attaché enlisted the full cooperation of his American superior, Rear Admiral William Sowden Sims, in London. On April 30, 1917, he informed Sims that Admiral Lacaze had "expressed his intense gratification at the effort . . . to bring about real co-ordination between the Naval Forces of France, England, and the United States." Coordination was necessary in every respect. The governments of France, England, and Russia, for instance, were all asking for American destroyers to be sent to them immediately, without making certain that the limited number of these destroyers really obtained their utmost usefulness. Despite the alert initiatives of the attaché, the naval bureaucracies in Washington and Paris moved too slowly, in part because they were understaffed, to develop maximum efficiency. The French chief of the general staff, Admiral Ferdinand de Bon, complained to the attaché that as of May 22, 1917, "he was all in a fog as to preparations to make in advance to receive the American Forces."[42]

The financial cost of the war caused the French government many headaches. André Tardieu, the French commissioner in America who did a superb job as a lobbyist and aid coordinator, later acknowledged the value to France of America's crucial financial aid. Early in April, 1917, Premier Ribot was pleased to receive Ambassador Sharp's assurance of America's readiness to assist France financially. This tender of help at a most precarious moment came as

42. Franklin D. Roosevelt, "History of U.S. Naval Attaché, Paris," in Assistant Secretary of the Navy File, Group 10, Container 191, Franklin D. Roosevelt Papers, FDRL.

a godsend. Referring to the precedent set by the king of France at the time of America's distress in 1782–1783, Sharp offered to recommend to his government to forgo any interest on a loan "for the duration of the war and for a limited number of years thereafter." In view of the controversies that disturbed Franco-American relations in the 1920s, Ribot's reply was significant: "This is a very generous thought, but my country would accept no favours that it would not agree to pay for. It wants no gifts."[43]

Although Secretary McAdoo authorized loans for short periods only and expected them to be spent primarily in the United States, France obtained in the period from April to December, 1917, a total of $1.13 billion. Successive loans brought the total to more than $3 billion. Altogether, the American treasury had been authorized to advance to the Allies up to $10 billion. Immense as these amounts were, the Allies "stubbornly opposed the American proposal for an inter-Allied financial board" to coordinate their loan requests. As much as they needed these loans, they were careful not to lose their "financial autonomy." In March, 1918, when McAdoo, as a prudent protection for American finances, did tighten the conditions for granting loans, the French minister of finance accused the United States of undermining the stability of the franc.[44]

The problems of war and peace could not be entirely compartmentalized. The essential priority of winning the war made it easier for Wilson and the Allies to plan jointly for the prosecution of the war than for the peace to follow it. Nevertheless, the pressure of circumstances confronted them every so often with opportunties to touch on political questions. Felix Frankfurter was struck by the silence with which French politicians and the press, with the notable exception of the French statesman Léon Bourgeois, treated the American scheme of a league to enforce peace. Frankfurter deemed it wise for the United States to take the initiative in efforts to enlighten the French public about America's vision of the postwar world. The contributions of the United States and the commanding authority of its president, he thought, provided ample leverage for such education.

By coincidence, late in July, Premier Ribot invited Wilson to elab-

43. Warrington Dawes (ed.), *The War Memoirs of William Graves Sharp, American Ambassador to France, 1914–1919* (London, 1931), 186–87.

44. Lucien Petit, *Histoire des finances extérieures de la France pendant la guerre* (Paris, 1929), 787; L. L. Klotz, *De la guerre à la paix: Souvenirs et documents* (Paris, 1924), 180.

orate on his proposal for a league. Ribot intended to appoint a commission to study this issue, but in his response the president cautioned against such a premature commission because it was likely to bring divisive differences to the fore among the nations associated against Germany. In principle, Wilson believed then that "such a society of nations would of necessity be an evolution rather than a creation by formal convention." He envisioned it as the by-product of organic growth. It would be the natural result of functional cooperation in the end producing a concert of nations. Even as late as December 9, 1918, he explained to his advisers on board the *George Washington* that he did not strive for "any hard and fast constitution of the League of Nations." The main purpose of a council of regularly meeting ministers was to alert the powers to any war danger and to step in and stop it. "War," he emphasized, "must no longer be considered an exclusive business. Any war must be considered as affecting the whole world." The powers composing the league would, if necessary, have to organize an all-inclusive boycott against any country defying the advice of the league.[45]

As advisable as the creation of the Supreme War Council appeared, Wilson insisted that it concern itself exclusively with military questions and leave political issues alone. He regarded them largely his prerogative. The Allies, who distrusted the president's political judgment and motives, set out early to fend off his political thrusts. To corral this wild idealist, they invited him time and again to "coordinate" policies with them. At first erroneously believing Austria-Hungary to be behind the pope's peace initiative in the summer of 1917, the Quai d'Orsay instructed Ambassador Jusserand to impress upon the American government the desirability of close and deliberate consultation with the Allies before drafting its response. Jules Cambon actually intimated to the American ambassador in Paris that France was disposed to turn down the pope's all-too-vague appeal. Evidently not aware of the extent of Germany's grasp for power, Pope Benedict misinterpreted the kaiser's attempt to use the Vatican for his political snares to promote a negotiated peace that would favor Germany. When President Wilson disregarded the Allies' plea, Ambassador Jusserand strongly criticized him for having sent his independent reply to the pope. But all he

45. Bullitt Diary Notes, December, 1918–January, 1919, pp. 3–4, in Select Correspondence, Box 21, House Papers.

managed to accomplish was his further alienation from the president. The chief executive told House that "he was growing tired of Jusserand's excitable impertinence." He was tempted to have him recalled if he could do it without hurting French sensibilities. In his message to the pope the president made it plain that there could be no lasting peace on the basis of prewar conditions and practices, which had produced the war in the first place. In this instance Wilson adopted Secretary Lansing's arguments that the pope's appeal amounted to little more than "an invitation to negotiate . . . on the basis of the *status quo ante bellum*." The Allies had every reason to feel greatly relieved when they studied the president's adroit reply.[46]

As a result of the Russian Revolution and America's participation in the war, governments became more inclined to explore peace possibilities. In the spring of 1917 the Austro-Hungarian government put out peace feelers to France and Great Britain. Although inadequate from the Allies' point of view and also unacceptable to Germany, these overtures strengthened the assumption that a separate peace with Austria-Hungary might be a serious possibility. Even Clemenceau was willing to "listen" to what the Austrians had to say in secret negotiations that began in the summer. In June, Baron Oskar von Lancken, a prominent German diplomat, proposed to meet Aristide Briand in Switzerland to convey his government's willingness to make certain concessions regarding Alsace-Lorraine. Unlike Ribot, who was afraid that such a rendezvous might be a diplomatic trap, Briand felt confident that such an informal meeting might prove to be productive.[47]

Loyal Frenchman that he was, Briand deplored the fact that his government did not try to circumvent the military stalemate by using its brains as well as its might. He noted that the Germans prosecuted the war with ideological as well as military weapons by telling their people that the war must go on "because if the Allies were successful the condition of the German people would become one of abject servitude." In his long conversation with Colonel House on December 3, 1917, Briand echoed the thrust of the views previously published by Lord Lansdowne in the *Daily Telegraph*, namely, that the Allies would not try to annihilate or oppress Germany in the future. Prominent individuals in England and France had finally

46. House, Diary, September 10, 1917, in House Papers.
47. House, *Intimate Papers*, III, 274–81.

come to realize the advisability of a clear statement of revised war aims. It might weaken the moral power of German defense and induce the German government at last to take peace negotiations seriously. House believed a joint statement of liberal war aims at this time held out more promise than in the past. But all he could accomplish was to prevent any declaration of an imperialistic nature. Lloyd George and Clemenceau were not prepared to abandon conservative policies. As Ambassador Paul Cambon observed, any French government that attempted to negotiate a peace on liberal terms would be thrown out of office within twenty-four hours. Asked about his war aims, Clemenceau replied simply, "*Je fais la guerre.*" Whatever his political aims, his preoccupation continued to be with winning the war. In the session of the Chamber on November 20, 1917, he responded to critics who charged that he was not sufficiently concerned with peace. He stated that as long as the war was going on he would not tolerate defeatist peace campaigns and that in any case he had no faith in the much-talked-about League of Nations as a realistic solution for the peace of the world. Even if Germany were a member of the league, he snarled, the guarantee of its signature would mean nothing. "Ask the Belgians what it is worth!"[48]

Gradually, the impact of the Russian Revolution caused growing concern in the camps of both sides. At times it threatened to overshadow America's new role in world affairs. As long as the Kerensky government remained in power, the danger of a separate peace remained merely a remote possibility. Its ability, however, to convince the war-weary Russian people to keep fighting until a general peace secured the motherland's vital interests grew ever more questionable. The escalating popular clamor for "peace at any price" encouraged the Germans in April, 1917, to permit Nikolai Lenin to return to Russia through Germany in a sealed railroad car. No matter how much Germany fundamentally opposed Lenin's revolutionary aims, it considered the breakdown of the Russian front worth the temporary expediency of facilitating the Red leader's taking command of the revolution. This cynical gamble promised to help them win the war. Its political consequences could be dealt with after Germany's victory.

48. George Bonnefous, *Historie Politique de la IIIe République* (7 vols.; Paris, 1956–67), II, 345–51.

Lenin lost little time. On May 4, 1917, he appealed to the Russian people to overthrow the provisional government. Although not successful immediately, the rapidly deteriorating domestic and military situation in Russia enabled him to seize power in November. President Wilson had looked upon the end of the Czar's autocratic regime as a welcome manifestation of democratic ideals. In the president's mind, this development appeared to be of such transcending significance that the potential military consequences of the revolution dwarfed by comparison. In his message of May 26, 1917, to the government in Petrograd, he limited himself to reassuring the Russians: "She [America] seeks no material profit or aggrandizement of any kind. She is fighting . . . for the liberation of peoples everywhere from the aggressions of autocratic force." With reference to revolutionary slogans, the president advised: "We ought not to consider remedies merely because they have a pleasing and sonorous sound. Practical questions can be settled only by practical means. Phrases will not accomplish the result." Again, in response to Jules Cambon's inquiry of July 23, Wilson stated he felt that should the provisional government propose an Allied conference on war aims, it would be wise to agree to it. With the obvious intent of apprising France as well as Russia's revolutionaries, he wished to let the whole world know that "the object of the war is not aggrandizement but the freedom of the peoples to secure independence—and free themselves against aggression whether by physical force or successful economic arrangement."[49]

Tragically, the leaders of the Allied and Associated Powers still did not see eye to eye on any purpose of the war except the defeat of Germany. Their divided councils could not but confuse and play into the hands of their actual and potential challengers. Back in February, 1916, when they had failed to accept and implement the Grey-House understanding, they had missed an opportunity to cut the war short by at least a year and, consequently, to avoid what now confronted them—their disastrous physical exhaustion, their power-political decline, and the haunting specter of a communist epidemic.

Shortly before the Bolsheviks took control of the government, they

49. George F. Kennan, *Soviet-American Relations, 1917–20* (2 vols.; Princeton, 1956–58), I, 132–47.

bitterly castigated the warmongers of Europe and denounced capitalistic America. Once in power, Lenin and Leon Trotsky moved fast. By March, 1918, they had concluded peace with the Central Powers. Harsh as the terms of the Brest-Litovsk treaty were, Bolshevik leaders were content to risk everything as long as it promised the ultimate survival and success of the revolution. Should Germany in the end be defeated, they anticipated no difficulty in tearing up this treaty. As the Germans had originally used Lenin as a military trump card, Lenin and Trotsky looked upon the Brest-Litovsk treaty as the revolution's potential savior. For all concerned onlookers, the ramifications of such unprincipled conduct were practically incalculable.

These developments produced far-reaching reactions. The Germans rejoiced in the success of their diplomatic strategy. They no longer saw any need for political concessions. At last their victory was within reach. While Stéphen Pichon, the French foreign minister, tried to play down the loss of his country's Russian ally by asserting in the Chamber of Deputies that America would take up the slack, the Germans counted on an Allied defeat before American troops would arrive in sufficient numbers. But as before, they made several miscalculations. The Brest-Litovsk conference cost them four precious months. To compel Ukrainian peasants to deliver their grain and cattle and to make sure that the Bolsheviks could not resume war activities, the Germans decided to leave about a million soldiers in the East. In their spring offensives in 1918, the absence of these soldiers on the western front proved fatal. Furthermore, contrary to their expectations the American command surprised them with massive assaults.

The prolonged fighting and the propagandistic effects of the Bolshevik Revolution also taught the conservative Allied leaders the folly of their stubborn insistence on imperialistic goals. They were overtaken by the political earthquake in Russia and shaken by the persistent challenge from the American prophet. With the publication of the secret treaties, the Bolsheviks exposed the cynical nature of Europe's old leaders. Politicians, labor leaders, and other spokesmen of the war-weary peoples, as well as their public opinion organs, no longer hesitated to call for peace negotiations. The fear of the bolshevization of Europe, in Germany as well as in the Allied countries, spread rapidly. The realization that this long war had exhausted Europe to an extent that it may have lost its preeminence was indicated by the growing popular appeal of ideas coming from Russia and America.

Their simultaneous appearance on the world scene ushered in a new era. Lenin's demand for a "peace without annexation or indemnities" sounded much like Wilson's "peace without victory." The president's faith in a nonimperialistic league of nations, though capitalistic in structure, did not ultimately differ so much from Lenin's and Trotsky's belief in the virtues of international socialism. Both envisioned a better world for the masses. Whereas the extension of Wilson's New Freedom beyond the frontiers of the United States and the Bolsheviks' "democratic rule of the international proletariat" seemed to converge the tides of history, however different their respective systems, the officials of British, French, and German societies continued to uphold the traditional order of the competitive national state system. For many liberals and leftists in Europe, including the labor unions, the choice between Lenin and Wilson presented no problem. America's democratic tradition and Wilson's proven record as an enlightened statesman clearly outdistanced the as yet limited performance of the fiery Red Pope. Wilson enhanced his position further with the enunciation of his Fourteen Points.[50]

Late in November and again on December 29, 1917, Trotsky invited the Allies to support the Soviet peace effort and to state their program for the future. The Soviet "program of consistent socialistic democracy," he proclaimed, aimed at the establishment of "entire liberty of national development" and the union of all nations "in an economic and cultural collaboration." He suspected the Allies' principle of national self-determination as much as that of Germany and Austria-Hungary. In his view, both had anchored it in imperialistic notions. Now that the Russian Revolution had opened the path to genuine universal peace, he summoned the Allies to lay their cards on the table.[51]

Colonel House and Ambassador David R. Francis in Petrograd urged the president to counter Soviet propaganda in order to aid the

50. Arno Mayer, *Politics and Diplomacy of Peacemaking: Containment and Counterrevolution at Versailles, 1918–1919* (New York, 1967), and *The Political Origins of the New Diplomacy* (New Haven, 1959).

51. FRUS, Supplement I, *Russia, 1918* (2 vols.; Washington, D.C., 1933), I, 405–408.

Allied cause psychologically and to prevent German domination of Russia. Early in 1918, Lloyd George was worried about a possible Russo-German alliance. It would hurt England's long-range interests in the Near East, India, and South Asia, in addition to its immediate military impact on the war. He was therefore prepared to do what he could to maintain diplomatic relations with the Bolshevik government. Clemenceau, on the other hand, was unwilling to recognize the Council of Soviet Commissars as a legitimate government or to appease them by accepting their terms of a peace "without annexations or indemnities." On the contrary he wished to overthrow the Bolshevik regime. Secretary Lansing could sympathize with Clemenceau's views. He cautioned the president not to take the Bolsheviks' democratic slogans at face value, indeed, to beware of these fanatic doctrinaires.

Without prior consultation with the Allied governments, Wilson decided to announce his war aims and terms of peace. He chose a joint session of Congress on January 8, 1918, to inform the world. In an effort to inspire the armies and peoples of both belligerent camps, the substance of his message denounced the military and imperialistic minority among the citizens of the Central Powers who pitilessly pursued a policy of conquest and subjugation. A peace-loving Germany, he stated reassuringly, would be free to develop its legitimate influence. This olive branch encouraged the necessarily silent minority of German industrialists, bankers, academicians, and ordinary citizens more interested in postwar economic stability than in "glorious" wars. They discovered in America's call for freedom of the seas and open markets an identity of interests, whereas the British and French empires tended to erect inhibiting barriers to trade and access to raw materials.[52]

Reaching out to the Russian people, Wilson applauded their "true spirit of modern democracy" and paid his respect to the compelling voice of the Russian people, whose "soul is not subservient" and whose "universal human sympathy" commanded universal admiration. He then proceeded to issue his warning that "the day of conquest and aggrandizement is gone." The concern of the United States in this war was to make the world "fit and safe to live in." To ac-

52. Leo Haupts, *Deutsche Friedenspolitik 1918–19: Eine Alternative zur Machtpolitik des Ersten Weltkrieges* (Düsseldorf, 1976), 151–56, 180–82.

complish this essential condition, he outlined his program, which called for open diplomacy, absolute freedom of navigation, removal of economic barriers, disarmament, fair colonial adjustments with special consideration for the well-being of local populations, various territorial settlements based on the principle of self-determination, and an international organization to guarantee political independence and territorial integrity to all states. With respect to France, the president asked for complete restoration of all French territory and the righting of the wrong done to the French in regard to Alsace-Lorraine. And finally, he reached his friendly hand out to Russia, asking for the evacuation of all Russian territory and "an unhampered and unembarrassed opportunity for the independent determination of her own political development and national play."

The peoples of the world received the Fourteen Points with a greater sigh of relief than did the leaders of the old empires. At last a statesman had risen above narrow national interests and eloquently spoken for the struggling and tired masses of the world. Although Foreign Minister Pichon seemed to react favorably to Wilson's address, his polite compliments could not really be taken literally. In his address to the Chamber he skillfully conveyed the impression that he referred to the president's league in his statement "As for the society of nations, victory alone can bring its realization," while in context his remarks actually seem to allude to the French proposal for a "society of victorious nations."

Although officialdom in France, including Clemenceau, never questioned the integrity of President Wilson, it maintained strong reservations with respect to his realistic understanding of European affairs, which were rooted deeply in centuries of history. No wonder that in a moment of exasperation Clemenceau was reported to have exclaimed: "God Almighty gave us Ten Commandments—and we broke them. Wilson gave us his Fourteen Points—we shall see." The French government did not officially accept Wilson's program. Public sentiment, however, reacted positively. French conservatives, still thinking and operating in anachronistic terms, doubted the efficacy of a League of Nations and open diplomacy. They were determined to settle longstanding political accounts with Germany and make it pay for the war. They wanted "to get from under the shadow of Germany" forever, if they could. But Wilson received strong support from the French political Left. *L'Humanité* saw in the Fourteen Points a workable basis for peace. In general, the French press appreciated the president's references to the complete reestablishment of Belgium and the return of Alsace-Lorraine, "matters of universal moral value." The noted writer Gustave Hervé thought of Wilson as the "impartial judge of the international tribunal which someday will prevent wars among the reconciled nations."[53]

In many respects, Lloyd George's views differed less from Wilson's than they did from Clemenceau's.[54] They all, however, attempted to keep Russia fighting for the Allied cause as long as possible. A couple of weeks after the signing of the Brest-Litovsk treaty, the leaders of the Entente issued a scathing attack against the merciless German rulers who compelled prostrate Russia to sign a treaty the Allies refused to acknowledge. It had become clear by now that "the battles of freedom are everywhere interdependent," the Allied leaders said. Convinced of Germany's drive for world mastery, Wilson pledged "force without stint or limit . . . [to] cast every selfish dominion down in the dust."

Following Brest-Litovsk, Germany's strong position in Russia cast many shadows. They ranged from the immediate shift of troops to the possibility of a Russo-German alliance threatening Entente interests as far as South Asia. Germany's exploitation of Russian resources endangered the effectiveness of the Allied blockade and reduced the prospect of an Allied victory. The Entente's failure to defeat Germany would, of course, improve Germany's chances for world domination. And if these prospects did not confront the Allies with enough calamities, the fear that bolshevism might spread to other countries and undermine the existing social order haunted all leaders of Western civilization. Suddenly the power-political military conflict threatened to be overtaken and consumed by this revolutionary nightmare.

As far as the Allies were concerned, they now had to cope simultaneously with both problems, the early defeat of Germany and possible Bolshevik contagion. Unlike in vigorous America, the internal conditions in most European countries presented fertile ground for the gospel preached by Lenin and Trotsky. Even the

53. Dawes (ed.), *War Memoirs of William Graves Sharp*, 233. See also William C. Bullitt's memorandum of December 21, 1918, in Select Correspondence, Box 21, House Papers.

54. See the British war cabinet's "War Aims," dated January 3, 1918, and drafted by Lord Robert Cecil, in Box 3, Folder 101, Sir William Wiseman Papers, Yale University Library, New Haven.

Germans could not lose sight of unexpected turmoil fanned by Bolshevik infiltrators.[55]

As it turned out, it amounted to wishful thinking that the Russian Revolution would not long survive. Nonrecognition of the government directing it, as Clemenceau preferred, accomplished as little as Wilson's continued hope for genuine democracy once the propagandistic flames of revolution ceased to burn. France and many of its citizens had a high financial stake to protect in Russia. Prior to the war they had invested in Russia fully 25 percent of all securities held in France. Before 1914 they seemed financially safe and politically profitable. But would the anticapitalist Bolsheviks honor their country's obligations?

The French government did not want to take a chance. Starting in early December, 1917, Clemenceau repeatedly asked the Allies to organize an intervention in Siberia to protect the Trans-Siberian Railway against German penetration of Russia and to be prepared to assist anti-Bolshevik forces in the south of Russia. Such a maneuver also promised to pay additional dividends by compelling the German command to tie up some of its forces in the East. Marshal Foch not only urged such an undertaking; he would have liked to see the United States and Japan assume the major burden in the attempt to occupy the Trans-Siberian Railway from Vladivostok to Moscow. Early in 1918, Ambassador Jusserand formally approached the State Department with this suggestion.[56] Then and for several months afterward, President Wilson firmly opposed any foreign intervention in Russia, hoping for the revolution's excesses to end and regular contacts to become possible. Also, the prospect that Japan might establish a foothold in Siberia worried him. While in November, 1917, he had reluctantly conceded to Japan "special interests" in China, the basic objective of the Lansing-Ishii agreement, after all, had been to restrain Japanese expansionism. Prodded by the British and French governments, the president eventually condoned Japan's limited intervention in Siberia, provided that the final peace conference would settle Siberian questions.

55. See New Scotland Yard's secret report "The Progress of Bolshevism in Europe," dated January 28, 1919, in Box 207, Folder 2/796, House Papers, and Marshal Foch's memorandum of January 7, 1919, in Select Correspondence, Box 44, Folder 1415, House Papers.

56. Jean Jules Jusserand to Robert Lansing, January 8, 1918, in Box 25, Folder 250, Polk Papers.

At that moment, William C. Bullitt of the State Department, Elihu Root, the respected Republican expert on Russia, and Colonal House cautioned Wilson to tread carefully. Intervention in Siberia, they warned, would destroy his "prestige as a fair and impartial statesman" and cost him "his position as moral leader of the world." Certainly, German propaganda would accuse the hypocritical Allies of "doing in Siberia, through the Japanese, what the Germans are doing in the West." Colonel House gave the president the benefit of his opinion: "I cannot understand the fatuous determination of the British and French to take such a step. Leaving out the loss of moral advantage, it is doubtful whether there will be any material gain." Impressed by the weight of these arguments, the president continued to oppose American intervention in Russia, but he left it up to the Japanese to determine their own course.[57]

Wilson agonized about the correct policy regarding Russia. He did not want to be sidetracked from the supreme objective of this war, the defeat of Germany. Ultimately, the military necessity of restoring the eastern front, to prevent German troop transfers to the West, reconciled the president to yield reluctantly. Clemenceau considered intervention so imperative, particularly when in June of 1918 the Germans were within forty miles of Paris, that he dispatched, among others, the distinguished philosopher Henri Bergson to plead for it in Washington. The realization of the vital interconnection between the eastern and western theaters of war finally tipped the scales in favor of intervention.

A convenient pretext for Allied intervention in Siberia was offered by the presence of some fifty thousand Czech troops who prior to the revolution had been attached to Russian forces fighting the Central Powers. The president went reluctantly along with the decision to "rescue" them, provided the limited operation in northern Russia should not aim at "any restoration of the ancient regime or any other interference with the political liberty of the Russian people."[58] But the British and French thought otherwise. However sincere Wilson's proviso was, the Allies soon exposed his naïveté. Their plan called for the formation of a solid front from the White Sea to the Pacific. On June 20 the French government issued instructions

57. House, *Intimate Papers*, III, 394; David F. Trask, *The United States in the Supreme War Council: American War Aims and Inter-Allied Strategy, 1917–1918* (Middletown, Conn., 1961), 108–19.

58. Kennan, *Soviet-American Relations*, I, 300–23, II, 82–100, 270–76, 394–99.

to the effect that the "Siberian and Cossack partisans of the re-establishment of order" should attach themselves to the Czech Legion. Along with the Japanese, they started the intervention in Siberia on August 5. A small Anglo-French force formed the nucleus for activities in northern Russia.

The Soviets interpreted this intervention as an interference in their civil war with the object of overthrowing their regime. They did not hesitate, therefore, to turn to the Germans, who had recently been defeated in the West and now realized the necessity of protecting their back in the East. Under these circumstances, they worked out a mutually satisfactory agreement of collaboration. Thus, in their desperation to keep the revolution alive, the Bolsheviks enlisted even the aid of the Germans, whom they did not trust. Traditionally obsessed with fears of the West, the Soviets learned from the intervention by their former capitalist Allies to rely on nobody but themselves. By yielding to Anglo-French pressures, President Wilson violated his principle of nonintervention in the internal affairs of other countries. But his basic disagreement with the Allies appeared to be founded on more realism and understanding of the Russian situation than the Allies themselves demonstrated. The Allies' apparently minor operation in southern and northern Russia resulted in lasting consequences. Actually, it was launched as the first step in a major strategic scheme, which came to light at the very end of the war.[59]

When decisive military defeats compelled the Central Powers to plead for an armistice on the basis of Wilson's Fourteen Points and subsequent explanations, they approached the president in the hope of receiving the fairest deal from him. Typically, they also endeavored to drive a wedge between him and the Allies. Allied leaders—both military and political—were extremely irritated by this procedure. It was an open secret that they intended to take control of the peace negotiations away from Wilson, whom they considered utopian. Indignantly, Wilson directed Colonel House on October 29: "If it is the purpose of the statesmen to nullify my influence, force the purpose boldly to the surface. . . . I am ready to repudiate any selfish programme openly, but assume that the Allies cannot honor-

59. Pierre Renouvin, *War and Aftermath, 1914–1929*, trans. Remy Inglis Hall (New York, 1968), 98.

ably turn the present discussions into a peace conference without me."

At an informal meeting in Pichon's study at the Quai d'Orsay, attended by the Allied leaders, House was struck by their unanimous objection to the acceptance of the Fourteen Points as a basis for peace. They did not feel bound by them, because they had not been consulted before their enunciation. Nevertheless, they accepted them when Colonel House administered shock treatment by stating that if their "conditions of peace are essentially different," the president would probably feel obliged to ask Congress "whether the United States shall continue to fight for the aims of Great Britain, France, and Italy." Looking at each other with consternation, Lloyd George and Clemenceau realized instantly that the time for protracted discussions, which might have led to a falling apart of the grand coalition, had passed. They did, however, make reservations with respect to the freedom of the seas and reparations. But by not abandoning at this time their secret treaties, they acted with duplicity.[60]

On November 4, 1918, the Supreme War Council approved the terms of the pre-Armistice agreement, thus strengthening the legal position of President Wilson at the forthcoming peace conference. But the final test of his leadership still lay ahead. Verbally, Clemenceau pledged cooperation in building the more splendid ethical era conceived by Wilson. Did Clemenceau mean it when he asserted that "the United States and France are the only nations willing to make an unselfish settlement"?

As the war against the Central Powers was reaching its successful climax, Clemenceau, premier and minister of war of the Third Republic, officially instructed General Franchet d'Esperey to make preparations for the continuation of the fight against Bolshevik Russia. According to a German study, Clemenceau's directive of October 27, 1918, soon became a matter of utmost importance to Marshal Foch. It was he who had developed the plans for an Allied army in south Russia and who saw to the reinforcement of French troops in Black Sea ports. He counted on England's cooperation. Once peace was concluded, he was prepared to offer Germany, too, a role in the

60. Gordon Auchincloss, Diary, October 29–30, 1918, in Box 2, Folder 26, Gordon Auchincloss Papers, Yale University Library, New Haven; Trask, *The U.S. in the Supreme War Council*, 166–71.

overthrow of the Bolshevik regime. In a move reminiscent of Napoleon's grand strategy, Foch was prepared to accept Germany as a subordinate partner in his country's Russian policy.[61]

General d'Esperey assured officials in Odessa that the Entente powers had no intention of invading and conquering Russia. They were prepared, however, to extend material and financial aid to Russians willing to raise an army against the Red usurpers. The security of France called for a solid Franco-Russian alliance. If, however, Russian nationalists failed to rise to the occasion, France would regrettably have to recall its troops from southern Russia. Andreas Hohlfeld's account ascribes to France much more far-reaching objectives: to destroy bolshevism and to control and exploit the rich provinces of southern Russia, thus reassuring France of its leadership in Europe. Whatever happened at the peace conference, the success of this plan was conceived as an insurance policy for the future greatness of France. Under the pretext of an ideological crusade, England and France envisioned great economic and political advantages for themselves. On balance, though, France had more to gain from the scheme than England. As much as England opposed German hegemony, it had no interest in helping France establish its predominance. This scheme also ran counter to President Wilson's policies and principles. The French leaders would of course have liked to demonstrate their ability to be a great power without having to depend on the United States. But without England and America, they did not possess the strength and the support at home to carry out their ambitious plan.

In the end Clemenceau also realized that Marshal Foch, not he, would emerge as the hero in case of its successful execution. Distrusting Foch as he did, he did not go through with these risky operations. In any case Foch had the last word in this matter. Regardless of their victory over Germany, he opined, "The Allies have lost the war if they do not find a satisfactory solution for the Bolshevik question." Thinking in essentially political rather than military terms, President Wilson, too, feared there could be no genuine world peace without Russia.[62]

61. Andreas Hohlfeld, *Versailles und die russische Frage, 1918–1919* (Hamburg, 1940), 7–11, 66–78. See also *Documents Historiques: Les alliés contre la Russie avant, pendant et après la guerre mondiale* (Paris, 1926), 285–87, and Jean Xydias, *L'intervention française en Russie, 1918–1919: Souvenirs d'un témoin* (Paris, 1927), 287–89, 365.

62. Hellmuth Rössler (comp.), *Ideologie und Machtpolitik 1919: Plan und Werk der Pariser Friedenskonferenzen 1919* (Göttingen, 1966).

America's relations with France during the war were greatly influenced by worldwide developments. Anglo-French cooperation, for instance, frequently depended on prior Anglo-American understandings and, occasionally, on conflicting interests between England and America. In the final analysis, the United States approached the traditional rivalry between France and Germany with the detachment of a sympathetic pragmatist. It respected and valued both, but dealt with each in accordance with its own national interests. Like France, the United States regarded the continental ambitions of Germany's military leaders as a serious threat to a peaceful world. It learned to distrust Germany's political spokesmen and to be on guard against its military planners. Although fully aware of the conflicts and interplays between Germany's civilian and military leadership, Wilson and his advisers at best underestimated the far-reaching differences between German generals and admirals. Essentially, the generals were land-oriented and looked eastward to insure Germany's predominance on the continent. The admirals looked westward and were determined to control the oceans to insure Germany's political and economic leadership in the world.

Originally, the prewar naval program of Admiral Alfred von Tirpitz was largely directed against England's sea power. The war aims of the chief of the admiralty staff, Admiral Henning von Holtzendorff, as presented by him late in 1916, affected all naval and industrial powers, including the United States. With the kaiser's approval, he aimed at nothing less than the German Empire's naval supremacy. As chief of staff of the army supreme command, Field Marshal Paul von Hindenburg endorsed this ambitious objective. General Erich Ludendorff's conception of a mighty Germany controlling and expanding in Eastern Europe was downgraded by the navy as being of secondary importance. Indeed, if Russia were ever to join in efforts to frustrate Anglo-American domination, the navy preferred it to be a cooperative ally rather than a weak and reluctant partner. Germany's naval hierarchy manifested little interest in continental France, a power too weak to resist Anglo-American pressures. What mattered was to break Great Britain's maritime dominance by annexing the Belgian coast, the Danish Faeroe Islands, and the central coastline of western Africa. The acquisition of naval bases at Dakar and the Azores and the control of the east African coast were primarily directed against Great Britain's lifelines. In the Far East, its naval stategists hoped to add Tahiti to their existing bases to be in a better position to interfere with American trade between the Panama Canal and the Pacific region. For good measure, Germany aimed to be on such terms with Russia, Japan, and Mexico as to blunt any future Anglo-American alliance.[63] Soon after the end of the war, General Wilhelm Groener admitted Germany's fundamental strategic mistake of striving to achieve world dominion without first having consolidated its position on the continent.

Superficially, the Allies and their American associate were fighting a military war against the Central Powers, especially Germany. Such convenient simplification, however, tends to distort the immensely complex nature of this conflict. In both camps, each participating belligerent aimed at its own primary and secondary national objectives, which were in varying degrees in competition with those of both the enemy and its "allies" as well. While military battles are fought to defend a country's territorial integrity and independence, the paramount war aims of major powers include the acquisition of power and control of trade channels and raw materials.

Even during the military phase of World War I, none of the major belligerents lost sight of these ultimate goals. As Germany challenged Britain's imperial position, the Allied and Associated Powers found Germany's grasp for power intolerable. The phenomenal rise of the United States alarmed the Allies sufficiently to check its potential competition. All these powers were in favor of competition except when it dashed their dreams. Rising to this challenge, President Wilson maneuvered to protect the interests of America and those of a more enlightened future by steering a course that would create a world in which neither Great Britain, Germany, nor France would be dominant or crushed.

Caught in this whirlpool of international politics, France had little choice but to devise flexible alternatives, siding expediently with Britain or the United States, depending on the advantage it could gain. Defense of its empire and close association with East European countries, preferably including Russia, offered additional opportunities for safeguarding its future. Wilson, too, turned to France and England, respectively, to implement his views of world affairs. France found his concern for the future viability of Germany particularly disturbing because the French firmly believed that only a

63. Holger H. Herwig, "Admirals Versus Generals: The War Aims of the Imperial German Navy, 1914–1918," *Central European History*, V (1972), 208–33.

Germany deprived of aggressive capabilities would not pose a threat to its security. In the light of these realities, France developed doubt about the reliability of the United States as a dependable friend. As history has long permitted us to observe, allies of today may become antagonists in the future, just as international rivals in a world of flux may at times find it advantageous to cooperate.

Specifically, the outbreak of hostilities on land and at sea disrupted international trade so alarmingly that both belligerent camps took protective measures of an immediate and long-range nature. Commercial interdependence on a most-favored-nation principle gave way to exclusive trading areas based on preference. The prospect of economic warfare designed to cripple antagonists did not augur well for the period of postwar reconstruction. The Central Powers, embodying such a change in their notion of *Mitteleuropa*, planned as early as 1915 to perpetuate their wartime emergency commercial policies in peacetime. Following preliminary discussions, the Entente powers met in June, 1916, to coordinate their trade policies, making plans that would reach far beyond the immediate needs of the war. At this Paris Economic Conference, France and Britain tried to introduce a new mercantilism that would not only fence in but deliberately cripple the German economy. Although not explicitly stated, it would also hurt America's future prospects for essential trade expansion. The wide range of proposals at the conference included such measures as colonial preference systems, differential shipping rates, cooperative development and purchase of raw materials, and a variety of restrictions favoring their own trade and putting that of all other countries at a disadvantage.[64]

Having at no time been consulted about the resolutions of the Paris Economic Conference, many American officials, including President Wilson, suspected the Allies of endeavoring to establish exclusive privileges for themselves at the expense of all others, including the United States. More than ever, the president disapproved of the direction of both camps, their neomercantilism, German militarism, British navalism, and the French push for hegemony. At a time when the welfare and sustained prosperity of the United States required an open door to the markets and raw materials of the world, the Entente and the Central Powers appeared inclined to close it. Whether

64. Carl P. Parrini, *Heir to Empire: United States Economic Diplomacy, 1916–1923* (Pittsburgh, 1969), 15–16; Burton J. Kaufman, *Efficiency and Expansion: Foreign Trade Organization in the Wilson Administration, 1913–1921* (Westport, Conn., 1974), 166–69.

or not the consequences of the plans adopted at the Paris Economic Conference would have been as damaging as Americans conceived them, the Allies lost Wilson's trust enough to encourage his assertive independence.

The European war accelerated the economic development of the United States at such a pace and with such momentum that it began to make the Europeans very apprehensive. Initially, the war caused abrupt shocks to American exports and severe commercial dislocations. Before long, however, the Allies' needs transformed the United States from a debtor into a creditor with extraordinary industrial capacity. Opposed to embargoes "in any form," Wilson would not have hesitated to permit goods to be shipped to Germany as well, had the Allied blockade not endangered such trade. Between 1916 and 1919 the United States moved into the vacuum created by Europe's inability to supply Latin America. It practically tripled its Latin American port trade. During 1917 alone the American merchant marine practically doubled its tonnage. The building up of its navy and of an army of 3.5 million men suddenly elevated the United States to the position of being a power to reckon with in war and peace.[65]

President Wilson gave every indication of being fully aware of international crosscurrents. He assumed the unaccustomed role of world leader with a global vision. That is why he wanted to see Germany have a healthy economy, capable of making constructive contributions to a lasting peace. He also desired to see the German navy remain a counterbalance to British sea power at the end of hostilities rather than be dealt with in a way that would augment Britain's naval might. At the same time, he helped the Allies head off a decisive German victory. Significantly, he could, and apparently did, increase or decrease American military, shipping, and financial aid to the Allies for purposes of political and diplomatic manipulation.[66]

The official members of Wilson's administration naturally supported his policies, certainly on the whole. As the election results of 1918 attested, he also encountered a great deal of opposition at home, to the delight of Allied leaders. Americans who believed in the wis-

65. Edward B. Parsons, *Wilsonian Diplomacy: Allied-American Rivalries in War and Peace* (St. Louis, 1978), 44–47, 142–58; Burton J. Kaufman, "The United States Trade and Latin America: The Wilson Years," *JAH*, LVIII (September, 1971), 342–63.

66. Jeffrey J. Safford, *Wilsonian Maritime Diplomacy, 1913–1921* (New Brunswick, N.J., 1977), 146–71.

dom of close ties with Great Britain, such as Theodore Roosevelt and Admiral Sims, took strenuous exception to a policy prolonging the war unnecessarily and possibly enabling Germany to become a threat to a later generation. The wartime correspondence between Josephus Daniels, the secretary of the navy, and Vice Admiral Sims, commander of United States destroyer forces in European waters, substantiates these major tactical and strategic differences. Asserting "hearty cooperation with the Allies" and hoping for "a successful termination of the present war," Secretary Daniels nevertheless advised Sims on July 10, 1917, that "the future position of the United States must in no way be jeopardized by any disintegration of our main fighting fleet. . . . The primary role in all offensive preparations must perforce belong to the Allied powers." Sims responded on July 16 that he assumed "our mission was to promote the maximum cooperation with the Allies in defeating a common enemy." He deemed it possible "to accomplish our mission without in any way involving the so-called disintegration of our fleet as a whole. . . . Our course of action, in order to throw our main strength against the enemy, would be to move all our forces, including the battleship fleet, into the war area. . . . The most effective defense which can be afforded to our home waters is an offensive campaign against the enemy which threatens these waters."[67] During the period of active participation in the war, the United States dispatched only one-fourth of its antisubmarine vessels to the admiral's command, and it preferred to employ its merchant marine in its expanding trade and let the British take care of most of the dangerous transportation of supplies for the Allies. Admiral William S. Benson, chief of United States naval operations, frankly admitted at Senate hearings in 1920 that he was primarily concerned with safeguarding America's interests, "regardless of any other duty." He kept the main fleet in home waters to protect the coast and to be fully prepared for all contingencies at the end of the war and thereafter.

The Allies showed their cards sufficiently to alert American observers. As early as 1915 they restricted the sale and transfer of ships to foreigners, thus reducing America's chances for accelerating the acquisition of cargo ships and oil tankers. They coordinated their purchase and transportation of foodstuffs from Latin America. And they acted quite independently in regard to German vessels in-

67. William Sowden Sims, *The Victory at Sea* (New York, 1920), 391–99.

terned in South American ports. Not only had France, Italy, and Japan cast their eyes on acquisitions in Asia, to the detriment of American trade and capital, but France, Great Britain, and Italy also planned to control the oil resources of the Mideast in a way that would have been totally unacceptable to the United States. When for bargaining purposes the British, who for the time being held most of the territories in the Ottoman Empire and Africa desired by the French, explored French reaction to a possible American mandate in the Levant, the French got up in arms. They were firmly opposed to seeing efficient American corporations jeopardize the future of family-oriented French enterprises in the region.

Finally, when in the months prior to the Armistice the French and the British successively reduced their estimates of American divisions needed on the Continent from a hundred to eighty to forty, they sent a clear political signal to the American president. The forces of the Entente had been fighting and sacrificing from the start of the war, and it was the Entente—not the United States, its significant contribution to the final victory notwithstanding—that was entitled to guide the destiny of Europe. As ugly as these realities were, the various industrial powers facing each other obscured underlying economic needs and ambitions with self-righteous references to ideology and security.

The coordinated Allied military campaigns produced such results that by early October, 1918, Germany's military leaders considered it imperative to halt further useless sacrifices. On October 3 the German high command urged Prince Max of Baden to sue for peace immediately. Two days later, the new chancellor of the Reich requested the Swiss government to advise President Wilson of his readiness to enter peace negotiations on the basis of the Fourteen Points and conclude an armistice at once. The Austro-Hungarian government expressed the same desire.

Evidently expecting the fairest treatment from President Wilson, the Central Powers addressed this request to him rather than to Marshal Foch. As welcome as these developments were, Wilson had to be extremely careful in his dealings with the enemy lest he be caught in a military-diplomatic trap. An outright rejection of Germany's offer could prolong the war and strengthen the declining morale of the German people. A prompt acceptance might afford Germany's military leaders the breathing space they required to regroup their forces, and it might also cause frictions among the Allies. The president's astute adviser Colonel House impressed upon him that, before passing on the German proposal to the Allies, it would be necessary to insist on the most stringent guarantees from Germany to implement armistice conditions. And Joseph P. Tumulty, his secretary, cautioned him "not to accept a German offer which came to us under the auspices of the Hohenzollerns." Tumulty also agreed with the commonsense observation in the Springfield *Republican* that Germany's acceptance of the Fourteen Points as a "basis" for negotiations left an escape valve wide open. To close it Germany would need to give "a clear, specific and binding pledge in regard to the essential preliminaries." These included restitution, reparation, and guarantees. In his reply to the imperial chancellor, the president intimated his willingness to follow up on the German armistice proposal, provided the chancellor spoke for the people and not for their discredited military autocrats. Wilson also insisted on the implementation of both the letter and the spirit of the Fourteen Points and on the evacuation of all invaded territories.[68]

As soon as the German government had officially asked Wilson for an armistice, the prime ministers of Great Britain, France, and Italy met in Paris. On October 7 they informed General Tasker H. Bliss, the American military representative on the Supreme War Council, of the armistice terms they had tentatively agreed upon. In the context of this study, several of their conditions deserve to be singled out: 1) there was to be total evacuation, by the enemy, of France, Belgium, Luxemburg, and Italy; 2) the Germans were to retire behind the Rhine into Germany; 3) Alsace-Lorraine was to be evacuated by German troops without occupation by the Allies.[69]

In view of the delicate diplomatic exchanges then taking place between Washington and Berlin, General Bliss had absented himself from the deliberations of the Allied military and naval representatives on October 8. Following this meeting these representatives submitted to their respective prime ministers a more elaborate ver-

68. Joseph P. Tumulty, *Woodrow Wilson as I Knew Him* (New York, 1921), 309–21. On the kaiser's abdication and secret German-American discussions prior to the Armistice, see the important work by Klaus Schwabe, *Woodrow Wilson, Revolutionary Germany, and Peacemaking, 1918–1919*, trans. Robert and Rita Kimber (Chapel Hill, 1985).

69. Tasker H. Bliss, "The Armistices," *American Journal of International Law*, XVI (1922), 509–22.

sion of the armistice conditions. In the absence of instructions from his government, Bliss declined to sign this document. But he promptly cabled its text to Washington. In compliance with the request of the council of ministers, he also drafted his views with respect to the armistice conditions. While on the whole accepting them, he took particular exception to the second one. As it stood, he argued, "the Germans could retire to a strong position behind the Rhine with their army, armament and supplies intact." He proposed, instead, virtual unconditional surrender by suggesting the "complete military disarmament and demobilization of the active land and naval forces of the enemy." In the view of General Bliss, such armistice terms would have removed the haunting fear of Germany's military revival and would have immediately facilitated a preliminary treaty of peace. General Pershing went even further. In his communication to the Allied Supreme War Council dated October 30, 1918, he recommended that the Allies "continue the offensive until we compel her [Germany's] unconditional surrender." Any armistice terms, he held, "should be so rigid that under no circumstances could Germany again take up arms."[70]

The president's provisos caused consternation at German headquarters. They had hoped for his quick and unconditional agreement to an armistice, which would enable them to save their army as a future instrument in peace or war. Although they had little choice but to accept Wilson's conditions, they asked for preliminary armistice negotiations by a mixed commission, a request the president rejected. He also made it plain that there could be no armistice interfering in any way with "the present military supremacy of the armies of the United States and of the Allies in the field" or leaving their governments in any doubt about "with whom they are dealing" in Germany. The answer to these uncompromising statements was drafted by Germany's political leaders, who disregarded the last-minute maneuvers of the generals. The civilians yielded to Wilson's demands. It was now up to the Allies to end the hostilities with an armistice based on the Fourteen Points.

The president communicated his correspondence with Berlin to the Allies and asked them, if they were "disposed to effect peace upon the terms and principles indicated," to draft appropriate ar-

70. See Auchincloss, Diary, October 30, 1918, in Box 2, Folder 26, Auchincloss Papers.

mistice terms. As has already been noted, the Allies accepted the Fourteen Points, with reservations regarding reparations and the principle of freedom of the seas. Officially authorized to represent the United States at the deliberations of the Supreme War Council, Colonel House arrived in Paris on October 26, one of the most hectic days in his life. After seeing many distinguished Americans and foreigners, he finally paid his respects to Clemenceau. Unlike British Field Marshal Douglas Haig, Clemenceau and Foch were convinced that Germany had no realistic choice but to accept any terms. In strictest confidence, Clemenceau entrusted Marshal Foch's armistice terms to Colonel House. Already reassured by Wilson's firmness during the prearmistice period, the Allied leaders appreciated the president's willingness to leave the terms of the armistice to the military commanders and in all military matters to be guided by Marshal Foch's recommendations. The French leaders liked to interpret this disposition as an indication of Wilson's ability to modify his idealistic principles in international affairs under the pressure of actualities. It enhanced their hopes of steering him away from a Wilsonian peace and of succeeding after all in drafting an essentially French-dominated treaty.

General agreement existed that the armistice terms should not be so harsh as to lead to their rejection and yet should be harsh enough to prevent Germany's resumption of hostilities during the peace negotiations. On the whole, Generals Pétain, Pershing, and Bliss wanted to lay down more severe terms than Field Marshal Haig. The British officer would have been satisfied with the evacuation of occupied France, Belgium, and Alsace-Lorraine, in addition to the return of French and Belgian rolling stock. Marshal Foch's additional conditions by and large accommodated the views of Pétain and Pershing. For he asked for the occupation of the left bank of the Rhine and the establishment of a neutral zone on its right bank, and he demanded the surrender of 150 submarines and the withdrawal of the German surface fleet to the ports of the Baltic. To make sure that the Allies accepted full responsibility for the armistice terms to be presented to the Germans, Colonel House deliberately asked Foch at a meeting of the political and military leaders: "Solely from the military point of view, do you prefer the Germans to reject or sign these armistice terms?" The marshal replied: "We fought this war to obtain certain political objectives. If the Germans now sign the armistice determined by us, we have accomplished what we set out to do. Therefore, no man has the right to cause another drop of blood to be shed."

The Allied Supreme War Council completed its work by November 4. Upon Wilson's notification to this effect, the German armistice commission departed for Paris. There they were taken to a railroad car in the forest of Compiègne to meet Marshal Foch, representing the Allied armies, and Sir Rosslyn Wemyss, representing the Allied navies. If the German delegates found this setting undignified, the subsequent conversation, as reported by Clemenceau to House, was painfully humiliating. When, upon Foch's inquiring about the purpose of the Germans' visit, Matthias Erzberger, a moderate civilian political leader, replied they had come to receive the Allies' propositions for an armistice, Foch icily advised him, "I have no proposition to make." Then, asked about the conditions of the armistice, he replied in the same manner. "I have no conditions to offer." Perplexed, Erzberger referred to President Wilson's notification informing the German government that "Marshal Foch is authorized to make known the conditions of the armistice." In this needlessly offensive cat-and-mouse game the marshal finally explained that he could reveal the conditions only if the German delegates asked for an armistice, as indeed they now did. Claiming that the conditions presented to them required "careful examination," the Germans inquired whether, to avoid unnecessary bloodshed, "Marshal Foch might agree to fix immediately and for the entire front a provisional suspension of hostilities." Foch reacted negatively to this anticipated suggestion. He simply reiterated that "hostilities cannot cease before the signing of the armistice." In order to keep their army as nearly as possible intact, the Germans probed for various modifications of the terms. They justified them primarily on the ground that they needed the means to prevent the spread of bolshevism and to keep order at home. In view of possible chaos in Germany following its military defeat, the collapse of the Hohenzollern dynasty, the proclamation of the People's Republic, and the nihilistic exhortations by Lenin and Trotsky, the Allies had reason to feel uneasy. They therefore provided some respite for the despairing German population. The news of the signing of the Armistice early on the morning of November 11 came as a great relief.

Despite the exhaustion and turmoil after the long war, the Allies proceeded so slowly with genuine peace efforts that the Armistice had to be renewed each month. Henry White, one of the American commissioners in Paris, not only deplored the failure to expedite the business of the peace conference, but he also interpreted French pleas of unreadiness as a deliberate technique to use these monthly renewals for the purpose of adding new conditions. To his mind, this was hardly a straightforward process.[71]

In the meantime, the Allies began to reduce their armies even though the fear of a German military revival, however exaggerated, lingered on. By February 11, 1919, the time for a third renewal of the Armistice, the council of the heads of the four Allied governments finally decided to take the wind out of the sails of German extremists on the right and left who were bent on overthrowing the young republic. This time, the brief renewal of the Armistice was to be followed up with the final military terms of peace. As General Bliss pointed out, such a preliminary treaty disposing of military issues would have permitted subsequent negotiations of political and territorial questions without undue apprehensions. During the president's temporary return to Washington, however, the council decided to leave all types of questions to be decided by the peace conference. This procedural delay, whether or not designed to do so, tended toward the deteriroiation of the Reich's position, both internally and externally.

The continuation of the blockade months after hostilities had ceased left Germany to the mercy of its enemies. An armistice is essentially a military matter. The French admittedly used it as a means of enforcement as well. Marshal Foch possessed the power to increase or diminish the severity of the blockade. It was his judgment that the blockade "will remain the best and most rapid means of obtaining the respect for the armistice agreement and, in a general way, for compelling Germany to bow to our wishes."[72] Clemenceau defended the maintenance of the blockade as a means of applying pressure to Germany without resorting to military force. But taking a longer view, Lloyd George feared that German memories of starvation might one day reap a bitter harvest for the Allies. "They were piling up agony, not for the Germans but for themselves," he said. President Wilson pleaded at the Supreme War Council meeting of January 13, 1919, for immediate food shipments to Germany, not just

71. Allan Nevins, *Henry White: Thirty Years of American Diplomacy* (New York, 1930), 379.

72. Suda L. Bane and Ralph H. Lutz (eds.), *The Blockade of Germany After the Armistice, 1918–1919* (Stanford, 1942), 91–93, 206–18, 472–73.

for humanitarian reasons but to prevent hunger from destroying the foundations of government. Four months later, he expressed his disgust about the callous French position, which preferred the starvation method of enforcement rather than expensive military occupation. The blockade was not lifted until Germany formally accepted the treaty of peace. Notwithstanding the likelihood of similarly callous conduct on the part of victorious German generals, these attitudes cast long shadows over the peace conference and the postwar period. As Vance McCormick, one of Wilson's advisers, summed it up, "We are living on top of volcano; if relief not immediate, bound to have trouble and will affect France."[73]

THE VERSAILLES TREATY FROM PARIS TO WASHINGTON

The history of World War I diplomacy illustrates how much the resolution of substantive issues may be influenced by procedural and functional considerations. For better or worse, the elements of time and timing and the skill with which they were made use of played a significant part throughout this period. The initial failure of Germany's blitzkrieg, the stalemate character of trench warfare, the exhausting and costly duration of the war, Germany's sudden request for an immediate end of hostilities in October, 1918, and the extension of the blockade for several months after the Armistice all affected the course of future developments. Whether the United States could have shortened the war by effectively implementing the Grey-House understanding of February, 1916, is a matter of fruitless speculation, but Marshal Foch did believe that the Allies had a real opportunity to end the war in 1917. In his judgment, because of the hesitancy displayed by Allied political leaders, full advantage was not taken of Germany's weakened condition following the battles of Verdun and the Somme. They failed to aggressively exploit the situation, and in the end they lost much more than several months' time. By carrying the war into 1917, they brought the United States into the central picture and failed to head off the collapse of the Russian front and the outbreak of the Russian Revolution. Conse-

73. Vance C. McCormick, Diary, March 5, 1919, in Vance C. McCormick Papers, Yale University Library, New Haven. See also Herbert Hoover's letter to Colonel House in Auchincloss, Diary, December 11, 1918, Box 2, Folder 28, Auchincloss Papers.

quently, instead of a peace dictated by the European powers, the "foggy notions" of the American president obscured Europe's horizon, and bolshevism poisoned the international atmosphere.[74]

After the Armistice, Clemenceau and Foch used the time element in a skillful attempt to outflank Wilson. If they could quickly gain support for the kind of security to which they felt France was entitled, they were ready to conclude the peace treaty without delay. When Wilson, however, stood in their way, they stretched out the peace proceedings long enough to expose the president's limitations and to induce him to make debilitating compromises. Concerned with more than just Europe and rejecting its old-fashioned type of power politics, Wilson had all along aimed at a new concert of powers to raise the living standards of the entire family of nations and remove the underlying causes of war. If it took time to sell his ideas, he was prepared to take it. And if he could not convince governments of the merits of his new diplomacy, he counted on the yearnings of their peoples for peace to help him in his crusade. As will soon become evident, the president lost precious time and ground fighting for his ideals.

To a political leader of Clemenceau's caliber and outlook, the distinction between governments and peoples seemed devoid of practical significance, particularly in times of war. Since Clemenceau, overwhelmingly authorized by the French parliament to speak for his people, needed little time to state precisely what France wanted, he occupied a much stronger position than the American president. Not only had the November election eroded Wilson's leadership, but his imprecise notions with respect to the League of Nations also handicapped him in his efforts to sell it as an effective catchall solution for the troubles of the world. Nebulously expounded, the most worthy ideal loses its popular appeal, and without mastery of procedural skills the effectiveness of its cause can be lost. It is, after all, axiomatic that diplomacy is bound to founder without precision and steadfastness. At the end of the six months from the Armistice to the presentation of the final peace terms, the United States no longer occupied the controlling position it had only recently imagined to be within its reach. The president himself in the meantime had lost

74. Raymond Recouly, *Foch: My Conversations with the Marshal*, trans. Joyce Davis (New York, 1929), 52–64.

his elevated place at home and abroad. Perhaps a detailed consideration of the peacemaking process can explain what happened.

The unprecedented decision on the part of the occupant of the White House to fight at the peace conference for the kind of peace he desired caused concern at home and abroad. His exposure to the pressures of making important on-the-spot decisions seemed as risky as his failure to ask a delegation of prominent senators of both parties to accompany him. Regardless of his determination not to permit lawyers to ensnarl the peace treaty in a maze of technicalities, ultimately he would need the consent of the Senate. But his belief in his personal indispensability and his powers of persuasion simply were not enough to shape the treaty he wanted or to have it ratified.

When Colonel House asked Clemenceau late in October "what place he had in mind for the peace conference," the shrewd Frenchman picked Versailles. Lloyd George and Colonel House would have preferred Geneva or another neutral location. It did not matter to Vittorio Emanuele Orlando, the Italian prime minister, where the conference was held. President Wilson thought of Lausanne as the best place because of its ample hotel and other accommodations. It did not occur to him or his close advisers that from a functional point of view Washington, D.C., would have offered him the most likely, perhaps the only, chance to promote a truly Wilsonian peace, with the advice and consent of the Senate. In every respect, the president of the United States sat at the end of the World War so solidly in the driver's seat that he was in a position to insist on holding the peace conference in Washington. However impertinent the symbolism of such an unprecedented suggestion might have appeared to Europeans, at least Wilson would have asserted his New World leadership. He would have enjoyed a multitude of procedural advantages that the strong undercurrents of political intrigues in Paris denied him. As Lord Castlereagh had observed as far back as 1814, "Paris was a bad place for business." Several of the president's aides warned him that it was in principle unwise for him to go to Europe. He did not like it when Secretary of State Lansing felt it his duty to tell him that it would be a mistake for which he would be sorry. The president "said nothing, but looked volumes" when Lansing pointed out to him that "he held at present a dominant position in the world . . . he could practically dictate the terms of peace if he held aloof;

he would be criticized severely in this country for leaving at a time when Congress particularly needed his guidance." All these arguments were to no avail.[75]

At first Wilson's intention to head the American peace delegation also shocked Poincaré, the president of the French republic, and it annoyed Georges Clemenceau. The premier did not like to see himself outranked at the conference by a non-European whose political theories ran counter to the interests of France as its leaders defined them. Clemenceau's personal vanity, moreover, could be satisfied only by presiding over the conference. When the president tactfully yielded this "honor," really a powerful functional advantage, to the French premier, the Tiger graciously welcomed Wilson's impending arrival. Before long, Poincaré, too, changed his attitude. He could essentially agree with the observation of the nationalistic *Action Française* that the president's presence in Paris was preferable to his remote direction of the proceedings from "his ivory tower in Washington." Many perceptive Frenchmen expected that Wilson's personal involvement would acquaint him with European realities and that, in the course of this educational process, he would come down to earth or be cut down to size.[76]

As much as they could, the Allies maneuvered in the weeks prior to the peace conference to reduce the president's domination of it. Portraying him as a noble but naïve man who lacked intimate familiarity with Europe's problems and destiny, they tried to disqualify him as a leading arbiter and architect of the forthcoming peace. To appear civilized and friendly, they flattered him while at the same time attempting to downgrade him. Any functional analysis of this technique, however, cannot fail to discover that the United States, not Wilson, was the real target. Belittling the president merely served as a convenient camouflage to redress the inter-Allied balance of power. The emergence of the United States as a major world power, apparently on the way to replacing Europe as the dynamic world center, confronted the Old World with a painful challenge. It was one thing to enlist the resources of the United States

75. House, Diary, October 29, 1918, in House Papers; Confidential memorandum, November 12, 1918, Book III, Box 66, and Desk Diaries, December 5, 1918, Box 65, both in Robert Lansing Papers, Library of Congress, Washington, D.C.

76. George Bernard Noble, *Policies and Opinions at Paris, 1919: Wilsonian Diplomacy, the Versailles Peace, and French Public Opinion* (New York, 1935), 68–69.

to win the war and to reestablish Europe's place as the world's director; it was another matter to accept a subordinate role in the new constellation of power. Rejecting the inevitability of such a fate, Europe was determined to regain its former position.

At least as instructive as the final provisions of the peace treaty were the procedural moves leading up to them. While the president and his company of experts and advisers, whom he later consulted and informed sparingly, crossed the Atlantic, the Allied leaders convened in London to discuss peace terms. Perseveringly, Marshal Foch pushed for a military frontier at the Rhine and for the removal of future German threats by detaching the Rhenish provinces. This exploratory conference furthermore decided to set up the Inter-Allied Commission of Reparations and Indemnities to study Germany's capacity to pay. As soon as Wilson learned what had transpired at this meeting, he cabled to Colonel House his insistence that these issues could not be acted upon until his arrival in Paris. But the very fact of this discussion gave the president a foretaste of what to expect from his "honorable friends" in the Allied camp. Airing his views before his company of experts, known as the Inquiry, on board the *USS George Washington*, Wilson saw the "poison of Bolshevism" as a protest against the social injustices of the old order. Unless it was fundamentally changed, he believed deeply, the future held little in store but more unrest and war.

President Wilson's arrival in Paris and the adulation he received from the masses in France and elsewhere in Europe gave him an immense psychological lift. He interpreted this popular reaction as a mandate to implement his new diplomacy. At a luncheon at the Elysée palace, President Poincaré's toast roughly sketched the peace terms of the old school of French diplomacy: "For the misery and sadness of yesterday, the peace must be a reparation; against the dangers of tomorrow, it must be a guarantee." The French president alluded to the desirability of continued collaboration among the victorious powers. In his reply President Wilson sought to set the stage for an international order based upon "the eternal principles of right and justice," far apart from the perpetuation of parochial power politics. Speaking on December 28 at the Guildhall in London, he elaborated on this theme by attacking the old balance of power system that set nation against nation and periodically climaxed in war. In his judgment, lasting peace could only be established by the cooperation of all nations, assembled in a league serving as "the trustee of the peace of the world."[77]

On the next day Clemenceau decided to go on the verbal counteroffensive. It was easy, he argued, for distant America to express lofty thoughts. France, the country nearest to Germany, has been bled white and devastated. It must think in the practical terms of "solid frontiers" and a "system of alliances" to safeguard its territorial integrity without having to resort to war. He did not object to the concept of a League of Nations as a "supplementary guarantee." As Secretary of State Lansing interpreted Clemenceau's defense of the balance of power system, essentially dependent upon might rather than right, it offered France the promise of status as a world empire. In view of contemporary power constellations, namely, with the United States and Great Britain likely to demobilize their armies and with Germany, Austria-Hungary, and Russia in political disorganization, France stood to emerge from the war as "the greatest military nation in the world." An effective League of Nations would threaten this superior position.[78]

Wilson promptly responded to Clemenceau in a speech he delivered in Manchester, England, by raising the possibility of America's return to prewar noninvolvement in inter-European affairs. "The United States," he warned sternly, "will join no combination of powers which is not the combination of all of us. She is not interested merely in the peace of Europe, but in the peace of the world." Despite efforts by the French press to minimize the differences between Clemenceau's and Wilson's political philosophies, a liberal journal in Lyons drew the honest conclusion: "The disparity stares one in the face." This disparity certainly demonstrated the need for a preliminary educational process, but it also practically eliminated the possibility of meaningful compromise. Compromises might be made on relatively minor details; they were out of the question in regard to the general direction of the peace.

The president's oratory occasionally carried him so far away that the French could identify with its thrust, as they interpreted it, even though French politicians, with the exception of the Socialists, were generally opposed to Wilson's political concepts. For example, in his

77. *Ibid.*, 86–90.

78. Confidential memorandum, January 3, 1919, Book IV, Box 66, in Lansing Papers, Library of Congress.

address to the French senate on January 20, 1919, he assured France, the land standing "at the frontier of freedom," that its peril, "if it continues, will be the peril of the world. It knows that not only France must organize against this peril, but that the world must organize against it." On February 3 he brought the deputies in the Chamber to their feet by proclaiming: "America . . . is helping to reunite world forces so that never again shall France be isolated; never again will France have to ask the question who will come to her assistance in her battle for right and justice."[79]

Soon after the peace conference had been solemnly opened on January 18, it elected Clemenceau its president. From then on, the French premier, a virtuoso of affability and firmness, was in the driver's seat to end "his war" in his stern and shrewd fashion. Certainly he treated the delegates representing the major powers with the respect they commanded. The delegates of the smaller countries, however, often had reason to complain that they were not accorded the courtesy of a full hearing. Clemenceau used his control of the time element to expedite or delay particular decisions. Issue papers on complicated questions, which the Quai d'Orsay had studied and prepared, were often handed to the delegates of other nations shortly before discussion of them was scheduled. American and British diplomats took exception to this improper procedure. It tended to intensify their distrust of the Quai d'Orsay.

It must also be kept in mind that Marshal Foch controlled the implementation of the Armistice. The controlling combination of Clemenceau and Foch offered France extraordinary functional opportunities. It is hard to understand why Wilson and Lloyd George did not foresee the potential danger of such concentration of power.

Unlike Lloyd George, who preferred to discuss matters with Wilson directly, Clemenceau frequently relied on his Franco-American expert, André Tardieu, and Colonel House as intermediaries. As Lloyd George put it, Clemenceau attempted to tame Wilson by cultivating his closeness with House. Despite the frank and courteous relationship between the Tiger and the Prophet, their personalities were as different as their philosophies and methods. A hardened and skeptical realist, the dynamic and eloquent French patriot was never entirely comfortable with the optimistic American idealist, whose sincerity and good faith he appreciated more than his rem-

79. Quoted in Stephen Bonsal, *Unfinished Business* (New York, 1944), 29.

edies for a world in perpetual conflict. Alarmed by Wilsonism, Clemenceau cautioned the Chamber on the eve of the conference that it would be "more difficult to make peace than it was to make war."

Franco-American tactical emphases reflected their substantive disagreements. Whereas the president assigned the highest priority to the League of Nations as the long-range adjuster of difficulties arising from the final treaty, the French were primarily concerned with tangible arrangements assuring them of immediate territorial and financial gains and contributing to their security. Secretary of State Lansing and Colonel House considered it more expedient to conclude the peace treaty first and only subsequently take up, with due deliberation, the League of Nations project. But the president, acting as his own secretary of state, disregarded such advice, although he himself had in 1916 preferred to let the league develop "organically," as the outgrowth of step-by-step practical cooperation among the various nations of the world. Ironically, Wilson's order of priority played into the hands of the French.

The private correspondence of Secretary Lansing sheds much light on these issues. In a letter from Paris dated February 19, 1919, he expressed the opinion that the French viewed with complacency the president's insistence on giving the League of Nations issue priority over anything else. "It was what they wanted since it delayed peace and left Foch in control," he said. More specifically, "They have, through Marshal Foch, control of the armistice and of the armies, and they wish to keep that control until they receive certain property, such as machinery, seed grains, cattle, sheep, etc., from Germany and have complete mastery of certain territory which they propose to keep." For the same reason, Lansing believed, the French government regarded with satisfaction the stagnation caused by the president's temporary absence starting in mid-February. These delays contributed to uncertainties and complications inside Germany. They made the Germans anxious to sign a peace treaty as soon as possible and deal with the objections to it later. The president probably never realized that if he considered his presence in Europe crucial, he could not afford to interrupt it.[80]

In his letter of February 17, 1919, to Ambassador John W. Davis, Lansing aired his irritations even more explicitly: "I do not think that

80. Robert Lansing to Edward Smith, February 19, 1919, in Lansing Papers, Princeton.

our French friends are keen about making peace very quickly. Foch controls the armistice and does what his government tells him to do. They are after more territory before peace is negotiated. They are not at all anxious to have Germany's industries reestablished. It is a strange game they are playing, a political game which one cannot admire." Proud of America's idealistic heritage, Lansing became disgusted with the dominant spirit at the peace conference, which he characterized as one of "selfish materialism tinctured with a cynical disregard of manifest rights." Lansing was aware of what was common knowledge—that the French government was afraid of being turned out of office unless it brought home the spoils of victory. Having taxed their people insufficiently to pay for the war, French politicians hoped to find alternative sources of funds by collecting huge indemnities from Germany and by negotiating sharp reductions of their debts to the United States.[81]

One of the unforeseen by-products of the slow progress made at the conference was the growing friction between American soldiers and the French population. An ugly situation developed when the doughboys, restlessly idling their time away and anxious to go home, began to resent their unfair treatment by some French storekeepers who overcharged them. The French government naturally deplored this development, particularly when it also became aware of the friendly attitude of American soldiers toward the Germans. This unfavorable comparison created politically undesirable and possibly lasting impressions. It also contributed to the early withdrawal of United States forces. By the early spring of 1919, some 300,000 men a month were being shipped home. Their premature demobilization before the peace treaty was signed and ratified demonstrated how little contemporary Americans understood that war was merely an extension of diplomacy by different means. Declining military strength automatically translated itself into reduced diplomatic maneuverability.

In the process of drafting the guiding rules for the conference, the French succeeded in making distinctions of far-reaching importance. The section entitled "Bases of Negotiations" labeled Wilson's Fourteen Points "principles of public law by which the negotiations

81. Robert Lansing to John W. Davis, February 17, 1919, in Lansing Papers, Princeton.

may be guided, but which have not the concrete character which is essential to attain the settlement of concrete provisions." The distinctions, moreover, between the "settlement of the war" and the "organization of the peace," as well as between the authority of the conference and that of the council, facilitated two-track procedures designed to accommodate major Allied war aims without appearing to reject Wilson's propositions. Under the cover of defending public law and morality, the conference's agenda provided for consideration of "the means of punishment" for "violation of the laws of nations and . . . crimes against humanity." In view of these procedural arrangements to insure a "realistic" peace that would compel Germany to acknowledge its responsibility for the war, Wilson's "Peace without Victory" ceased, strictly speaking, to be an alternative. Since the president's peace concept was thus thoroughly compromised before the conference even got under way, one wonders why he remained in Europe. His so-called concessions in the course of the deliberations could hardly be referred to as concessions at all.[82]

As minimum conditions for its security, France expected the military neutralization of the Rhineland, the annexation of the Saar, the return of Alsace-Lorraine, and "the complete repayment of all the costs of the war." French leaders and public-opinion organs made no secret of their preference for the kind of peace that would insure them against any future German aggression.

About the time the peace conference was to begin its work, Warrington Dawson, confidential adviser and special assistant to the American embassy in France, met with Marshal Joffre, commander-in-chief of the French armies from 1914 to 1916, for more than an hour. In the course of their friendly conversation, Joffre stated that he considered the occupation, not annexation, of the left bank of the Rhine for twenty or thirty years to be a necessary guarantee for the

82. The experts of the Quai d'Orsay skillfully laid the groundwork for a peace far removed from Wilson's ideals. The president's advisers were evidently too inexperienced to appreciate the crucial importance of procedures in international conferences. See Arthur Walworth, *America's Moment, 1918: American Diplomacy at the End of World War I* (New York, 1977), 94–98; David Hunter Miller, *My Diary at the Conference of Paris: With Documents* (21 vols.; New York, 1924), II, Documents 4 and 13; and Robert C. Binkley, "New Light on the Paris Peace Conference," *Political Science Quarterly*, XLVI (1931), 335–61, 509–47.

fulfillment of the final peace treaty. "Only the Rhine as a frontier can offer to France absolute security against future aggressions," he said.[83]

It may have been just coincidence that Marshal Foch warned about the dangers of unduly delaying the treaty while the president's duties required his temporary presence in the United States. In Foch's opinion the Germans, afraid of a renewal of hostilities on their soil, were ready to accept the victors' terms. All the peace conference had to do during "the next few days" was to stipulate the three principal conditions—Germany's military strength, frontiers, and indemnity payments. He anticipated arguments from the Germans, but no serious resistance. Should they unexpectedly become militant, Peace Commissioner Henry White had little doubt that it would have given Foch much satisfaction "to enter Germany at the head of an Allied army, to overturn the country completely . . . and to squeeze out every bit of money obtainable anywhere throughout the land."

Basically, though, the marshal considered the following terms proper and necessary: First, Germany's military capacity for war had to be eliminated. Second, whatever the ultimate fate of the Rhenish provinces, he insisted that Germany's western frontier must not be allowed to extend beyond the Rhine. And whatever the ultimate indemnity to be exacted from Germany, he preferred it to be stated in terms of a lump sum, perhaps twenty billion dollars. Speedy liquidation of these issues would, he urged, free the Allies to turn their attention to the Russian problem, perhaps even with the help of the Germans. For his part, Clemenceau, with respect to the Rhineland, would have liked to see the creation of a Rhenish Republic with a population of between four and five million Germans. He wanted such a neighbor to be exempt from any indemnity and forever outside the German federation.

These French demands ran into strong Anglo-American opposition. Lloyd George and Wilson were not willing, in the name of French security, to resurrect Napoleon's design for the Rhineland. Not only would it violate the principle of self-determination, it was also likely to poison Franco-German relations and in time lead to another conflict on the Continent. The Anglo-American statesmen frowned upon such a prospect as much as on the French expecta-

83. FRUS, *Paris Peace Conference, 1919* (12 vols.; Washington, D.C., 1943–47), I, 381–85.

tion of an Allied occupation force at the bridgeheads of the Rhine for an indefinite period.[84]

This troublesome frontier question threatened to prolong the deliberations or perhaps even end them abruptly. Under these circumstances, Lloyd George confided to Wilson on March 14 Britain's willingness to offer France a guarantee against German aggression. Remarkably, the president did not hesitate to agree that America would join in this unorthodox solution, even though, if consummated, such a pact would constitute a complete break with the traditional nonentangling diplomacy of the United States. Two optimistic assumptions led the president to this extraordinary decision. The very existence of such a guarantee, he believed, would bolster the chances of lasting peace. And it seemed, therefore, unthinkable to him that the Senate might turn it down. Although in basic agreement, many British observers questioned the French insistence on both the guarantee and the occupation.

Clemenceau could not but be pleased with the Anglo-American guarantee against German aggression. Nevertheless, he looked for tangible guarantees and would accept the guarantee pact only under certain conditions. They included the occupation of the Rhineland for thirty years, the demilitarization of Germany for a distance of fifty kilometers east of the Rhine, and a joint commission of inspection to make sure of German compliance. In the next few weeks the developing impasse reached crisis proportions. Aside from such operative details as the duration and implementation of the proposed guarantee and, possibly, its emasculating effect on the League of Nations, such astute advisers as Lansing, Bliss, and White disapproved of it altogether.

As André Tardieu has pointed out in his discussion of the treaties of guarantee, France, too, ran great risks making concessions to the guarantors, because the pact would go into effect only if ratified by the legislative bodies of both countries. The failure of the United States Senate to ratify, for instance, would automatically make the guarantee inoperative even if Parliament approved it. But that was a chance France was prepared to take. In late April the French agreed to the compromise formula: acceptance of the proposed pact, a demilitarized zone, and the occupation limited to fifteen years unless

84. Seth P. Tillman, *Anglo-American Relations at the Peace Conference of 1919* (Princeton, 1961), 178–82.

the guarantees proved to be inadequate. Despite many reservations, the French press, well prompted by Clemenceau and the Chamber of Deputies, supported these final arrangements. On balance, the pledge by England and the United States "to come immediately to the assistance of France in the event of any unprovoked movement of aggression against her made by Germany" seemed worth the withdrawal of unobtainable measures with respect to the Rhineland. Surely many questions remained unanswered and could be tested only by actual future developments. What did "immediately" mean? What form would the "assistance" take and how effective would it be? Who would determine whether Germany's aggression against France was "unprovoked"? And would not France stand stripped of any genuine international guarantee if the British Parliament or the American Senate refused to underwrite it?

Thinking in strictly military terms, Marshal Foch objected forcefully to this compromise. Emphasizing his desire for permanent French occupation of the Rhine, not the entire Rhineland, he protested that a temporary occupation was worthless. "If you are master of the Rhine," he explained, "you are master of the whole country. But if you are not on the Rhine, you have lost everything. . . . From the military point of view . . . the mere occupation of the Rhineland has no value without a hold on the Rhine." The French military and their wily friends in politics naturally sided with Foch. The hard-boiled marshal, who had never cultivated the habit of concealing his views, reserved contemptuous sneers for his civilian chief and a shrug for America's internationalist dreamer. He pleaded for the fullest political exploitation of the existing military situation.[85]

This attitude begain to concern American observers. They read into it an attempt to use Foch's military authority for the purpose of advancing French domination of Europe. Taking a longer view, General Bliss anticipated that French militarism would endanger the present and future peace because it would compel the rest of Europe to remain under arms and make a farce of the League of Nations. Secretary Lansing suspected Foch of desiring "to be a second Napoleon, a dictator of the destinies of Europe." And inasmuch as

85. FRUS, *Paris Peace Conference*, III, 384–88; Alexandre Ribot, *Journal et correspondances inédites, 1914–1922* (Paris, 1936), 274–76; André Tardieu, *The Truth About the Treaty* (Indianapolis, 1921), 204–13.

many French military officers had already begun to display an arrogance and insolence in dealings with officers of other nationalities that had been characteristic of many Prussians, the substitution of French militarism for German militarism did not hold out much hope for a better future.[86]

Soon after the Rhine dispute, a serious crisis arose over the Saar question. On March 28, the French claimed political annexation and ownership of the Saar coal basin. A special political status was to be established for the territory of the basin remaining under German sovereignty. The French justified this demand on the grounds of history, the inhabitants' attachment to French traditions, and rightful reparation. The possession of this valuable region offered much-coveted insurance. With the exception of the Socialists, the press defended the official policy. As strenously as Lloyd George reacted against French designs in regard to the Rhineland, he saw some justification for granting the French ownership of the mines, but not outright annexation. To Wilson, more was at stake in this instance than economic and territorial questions. To him, French annexation of the Saar was completely out of the question. It would be inconsistent with the Fourteen Points and amount to a breach of the Armistice agreement, an act, he protested, the American people would not condone. The original pledges involved the correction of the wrongs done to France in 1871, not in 1815. Tempers began to flare when Clemenceau intimated that Wilson's "pro-German" attitude put the entire treaty in jeopardy. Without satisfaction of France's claim to the Saar, he indicated, there could be no treaty. Following an acrimonious exchange, the Tiger abruptly walked out of the council session and left the troubled president wondering whether the peace conference would break up. Clemenceau acted the way one would have expected Wilson to fight for his goals. Lansing had no doubt that from this moment on, the unforgiving president "will look upon Clemenceau as an antagonist." This episode was also likely to convince the president of the French premier's ruthless spirit of revenge, which led him to make "the most extravagant demands."[87]

86. Confidential memoranda, March 24, April 10, 1919, Book IV, Box 66, in Lansing Papers, Library of Congress.

87. Confidential memorandum, March 28, 1919, Book IV, Box 66, in Lansing Papers, Library of Congress. See also Jean-Baptiste Duroselle, *From Wilson to Roosevelt: Foreign Policy of the United States, 1913–1945* (Cambridge, Mass., 1963), 99–100.

In the end Wilson yielded to a complicated compromise establishing for fifteen years a special regime under the League of Nations and a customs union between the Saar Basin and France. At the end of this period a plebiscite would determine the definite sovereignty of the Saar Valley, with the proviso that Germany would have to compensate France for the mines should the outcome of the plebiscite favor Germany. As was often the case, informal understandings smoothed the way for this compromise. Wilson struck a personal bargain with Clemenceau. He promised to modify his stand on the Saar in exchange for a French pledge to support an exemption for the Monroe Doctrine in the league's covenant. Such an international recognition of the Monroe Doctrine, Wilson hoped, might appease many opponents of the league back home.[88]

There were other territorial questions of direct concern to France. Alsace-Lorraine posed no problem, because its full restoration to French sovereignty redressed the wrong done by Germany in 1871. But the frontiers in Eastern Europe, particularly those of Poland, led to many irritating exchanges. France's interest in weakening Germany in the East by securing solid frontiers for Poland conflicted with Wilson's defense of the principle of self-determination. In the end, most of Posen and West Prussia were assigned to Poland. East Prussia was separated from the rest of Germany, and coal-rich Upper Silesia's future was made subject to a plebiscite. The decisions to create a Polish corridor through Germany and to provide Poland with access to a port in predominantly German Danzig promised to be troublesome arrangements. Similarly, Czechoslovakia, a potential ally of France in Central Europe, had to cope with a large German population, in violation of the principle of self-determination. Concerning the issue of Austria's merger with the German Reich, both Wilson and Lloyd George went along with the French veto of Anschluss.[89]

The loss of its colonies also weakened Germany, but actually hurt its pride and prestige more than its economy. The rather cynical manner in which the former German colonies were distributed also hurt President Wilson's prestige. His anticolonial principles lost credibility. Similarly, though Germany's military capacity was

88. House, Diary, April 3, 1919, in House Papers; Paul Mantoux, *Les délibérations du Conseil des Quatre: 24 mars–28 juin 1919* (2 vols.; Paris, 1955), I, 204–206.

89. Erich Eyck, *Geschichte der Weimarer Republik* (3 vols.; Zurich, 1954–57), I, 118–38, 158–59.

sharply limited and its possession of submarines altogether forbidden, this one-sided disarmament could not but embarrass Wilson's call for universal disarmament.

The Allies advanced their territorial and military demands for a variety of political and psychological reasons. It was therefore understandable that they would try to see how much they could get away with. Was it too much to expect them to take a businesslike approach to the question of reparations? Instead of weighing the ramifications on the world economy of their contemplated compensatory penalties, they displayed an incredible degree of irresponsibility with respect to the interlocking aspects of international trade and finance. The basically unselfish attitude of the United States, which asked for neither territory nor reparations, contrasted sharply with the bills presented by the Allies. The physical destruction committed by the Germans and the enormous sums needed for reconstruction led the French seriously to entertain the illusion that they could put into effect the slogan "Let the Boches pay." No burden imposed upon Germany appeared to them unjust. Besides, they wanted Germany so weakened for decades to come that it would not be able to muster the strength for a repeat performance. Were these notions a recipe for recovery, to be followed by peaceful cooperation?[90]

The first order of business of the Commission on Reparations called for the clarification of the principles of reparation. The American principles referred to Germany's pre-Armistice agreement to compensate "for all damage done to civilian population and their property." The American delegation had surveyed the damage and roughly calculated it at $15 billion. Other delegations held Germany generally "responsible for all the loss and damage, direct and indirect," that resulted from the war. This terminology led to costly semantic quibbles. When in his run for reelection Lloyd George campaigned on the platform of collecting from Germany "the costs of the war," the French saw a welcome opportunity to expand their claims for damages. But President Wilson disapproved of the inclusion of the costs of the war because they were "clearly inconsistent with what we deliberately led the enemy to expect." He was, however, persuaded to stretch the "damages" principle of the pre-Ar-

90. For a more sensible French opinion, see Warrington Dawson's confidential report "French Exaggeration About Indemnities," in Auchincloss Correspondence, March 23, 1919, Box 10, Folder 255, Auchincloss Papers.

mistice agreement to satisfy the Allies' insistence on including pensions and separation allowances, raising the total reparations to about $30 billion. In Paris, some wild estimates ran as high as $120 billion for indemnities. Americans would have preferred to fix a reasonable lump sum and relate it to Germany's capacity to pay within financially sound time limits. Without speedy German recovery, they apprehended, social radicalism would upset the entire European economy and delay the restoration of financial stability, a matter of high priority to the United States. For good measure, Wilson reminded his colleagues in the council that without adequate liquid assets and credits Germany would not be able to pay any reparations.

Clemenceau resisted these conditions, which would have accelerated the pace of European reconstruction and of improvement in the world markets. To leave the total amount of reparations open and to disregard Germany's capacity to pay reflected political motivations irreconcilable with sound statesmanship. What particularly annoyed the president and Colonel House was the French tendency to press for ever new concessions, exasperating amendments, and definitions of details. Thoroughly discouraged by the long delays in March and April, the president indicated that his patience had been exhausted. Disgusted with the narrow, and in many respects hateful, parochialism pervading the atmosphere at Versailles and anxious to return to his duties at home, Wilson inquired on April 9 how soon the *George Washington* could arrive to take him home.

An inconclusive compromise finally left it up to the Reparations Commission to determine by 1921 "the amount of damages as set forth in the specific categories."[91] Wilson pleaded with Clemenceau and Lloyd George to agree to a fixed sum at the conference. He felt let down by Lloyd George, who acknowledged the wisdom of such a decision when he talked with Wilson alone. But in the presence of Clemenceau, the president noted, the British statesman never followed through.[92]

While these discussions were going on, the rumor circulated in Paris that "an international agreement" was in the offing to pay for the expenses of the war. According to it, the United States would assume by far the largest share of them. This trial balloon was soon

91. House, *Intimate Papers*, IV, 398–406; Bernard Baruch, *The Making of the Reparation and Economic Sections of the Treaty* (New York, 1920), 18–55.

92. McCormick, Diary, June 9, 1919, in McCormick Papers.

punctured when the French foreign minister alluded to this possibility, unofficially and confidentially, in a private talk with Commissioner Henry White. White did not for a moment hesitate to tell Pichon that the American people would never agree to it. Up to 1919, the war had already cost the United States $26 billion.

On January 15, 1919, Édouard de Billy, French deputy high commissioner, suggested to Secretary of the Treasury Carter Glass that the "closely interwoven" financial relations among the Allies, particularly the question of reimbursing the Allies' debts to the United States, could "be satisfactorily settled only at a conference to be held in Paris during the peace conference." Secretary Glass promptly declined to encourage this. He showed himself accommodating as far as the question of equity of inter-Allied settlements was concerned. He also assured de Billy that he did not intend to press for immediate repayments. But he insisted that the question of debts due the United States should be discussed at a later day in Washington. Continued French attempts to take up the "reapportionment and consolidation of war debts" while the peace conference was at work terminated when Assistant Secretary of the Treasury Albert Rathbone bluntly advised de Billy, "The Treasury cannot contemplate continuance of advances to any allied government which is lending its support to any plan which would create uncertainty as to its due repayment."[93]

Repeated British and French proposals for pooling inter-Allied resources in the reconstruction of Europe were also turned down. The United States government intended to get out of the money-lending business and leave international finance to private channels. It allowed, however, that it was generally prepared to lend support to Europe's recovery, provided its various governments pursued sound fiscal policies and strove for greater economic cooperation among themselves. Perpetuation of their ancient political rivalries, Americans warned, would result in lingering economic instability.

A negative response also awaited a French proposal in April, 1919, for a postwar Allied raw-materials cartel. The Wilson administration flatly opposed such governmental interferences with free trade. Unlike private initiative and competition, state-sponsored and preferential trade arrangements, Wilsonians maintained, created un-

93. United States World War Foreign Debt Commission, *Combined Annual Reports of the World War Foreign Debt Commission* (Washington, D.C. 1927), 64–67.

wholesome economic conditions. Wilson's concept of collective security to preserve peace treated exclusive preferences in international trade as an inadmissible weapon.[94]

If the way the Allied powers behaved at this conference of peace served as a political barometer, the promise of the League of Nations held out little hope. The problems created by the war convinced President Wilson that the time was ripe for promoting a new, enlightened order to benefit the masses of the modern world. Although the idea had not originated with him, he made it his special mission to go to the peace conference and steer it personally toward a more peaceful international order. Firmly believing that "the key to peace is the guarantee of the peace, not the terms of it," he labored long and tirelessly until on February 14 he could proudly announce to the full peace conference: "A living thing is born. . . . While it is general in its terms . . . it is a definite guarantee by word against aggression." If the spirit of the league prevailed, Wilson prayerfully assumed, even the worst features of the final Versailles treaty would in time be straightened out. For this optimistic reason, it seemed to him absolutely essential to make the league covenant an integral part of the treaty. This rationale permitted him to grant concessions short of seriously violating his general principles. The president underlined his transcendent faith in the imperative nature of his priorities by disregarding for the time being voices raised in France and the United States against welding the league and the treaty and for a league of victors. But it was pathetic for the president even to entertain the notion that cunning and stalking political forces would change their behavior to honor a verbal pledge.

The French had anticipated Wilson's thrust and had in 1917 entrusted a commission to draft a framework for a league of nations. This groundwork enabled them to come to the peace conference with a detailed blueprint. They had worked out a scheme that deflected Wilson's thrust so as to serve traditional national interests of France. By appearing to be in sympathy with the president's favorite project, the French hoped to gain various tangible concessions. But they joined the international parade in the garb of the tricolor. To insure

94. André Kaspi, *Le temps des américains: Le concours américain à la France en 1917–18* (Paris, 1976), 216–17, 346–48; Paul Abrams, "American Bankers and the Economic Tactics of Peace," *JAH*, XLVI (1969), 572–83; Michael J. Hogan, "The United States and the Problem of International Economic Control: American Attitudes Toward European Reconstruction, 1918–1920," *Pacific Historical Review*, XLIV (1975), 84–103.

their security, they preferred to rely on their own strength and alliances. They assigned the highest priority to the perpetuation of the wartime alliances, and they counted heavily on the United States. If the league could offer additional guarantees, so much the better. But for the league to be effective, the French insisted its structure and means must make it so. Only a strong league could carry out its mission and serve France, as well as the rest of the world.

The differences between Wilson's concept of the league and that of the French reflected their contrasting mentalities. Since the British notion of the league did not essentially differ from Wilson's, it is noteworthy to observe that the Anglo-Saxons' view mirrored the sense of their own security as much as their intellectual tendency to allow for flexibility. The French had been much more concerned with threats to their security and with attempts to satisfy their proclivities by relying on precise details and definitions. Clemenceau was taken aback by Wilson's mystical faith in the league's potential to insure "the destruction of every arbitrary power that can separately, secretly, and of its single choice disturb the peace of the world." To the French premier, such misinterpretation of all political experience inspired little confidence.

In the French view, an effective league had to be provided with the instrumentalities necessary for the enforcement of its decisions. This meant that it must have at its disposal an international army, composed of assigned national contingents under its command. The French also proposed that the league's executive council take charge of international arms control and create a permanent organism to "foresee and prepare the military means for insuring the fulfillment of the [league's] obligations." This emphasis on military aspects and sanctions produced a chilling effect on Wilson. His hopes were for a relatively harmless peace institution composed of members who had joined it in good faith, not a league of war. It made little sense to him to substitute international militarism for national militarism. The French conceived the league as an international security alliance dominated by the major powers. They were prepared to submit to international arms control, but few other countries would go along with it. Certainly the United States government could not permit an international organization to require of it what its own Constitution did not allow it to do. The divergence of views was further accentuated by the president's preference for disarmament as the safest road to security. When his draft of the covenant included a provision for the abolition of conscription, the French realized how irreconcilable their opposition to Wilson's league was. Without effective executive power, the league was for all practical purposes reduced to what Clemenceau described as a "super-talky talk" parliament. It would endlessly discuss problems, but would be impotent to make decisions it could impose.

A number of other issues also highlighted Franco-American differences. To improve the chances for Senate ratification of the treaty, Wilson followed former President William H. Taft's advice to include a clause in the league convenant specifically safeguarding the Monroe Doctrine. Originally included in Article X, by which members undertook "to respect and preserve as against external aggression the territorial integrity and existing political independence of all Members of the League," the Monroe Doctrine safeguard caused considerable controversy. Above all else, the French feared the interconnection between Article X and the clause in the Doctrine asserting America's tradition not to take part in wars of the European powers or interfere in their internal affairs. Broadly interpreted, it might be used to excuse the United States from implementation of Article X. It might thus nullify America's obligation to help preserve the territorial integrity of France in case of another German invasion. The separate reference to the Monroe Doctrine in Article XXI did not entirely eliminate this possibility, but it protected regional understandings of France as well. Disinclined to refer to the Monroe Doctrine in an international treaty, the French endeavored at least to circumscribe it in such a way as to deprive the United States of its unilateral interpretations. Wilson's refusal to tolerate this insensitive attempt left a trace of resentment.

In the light of modern European history, and particularly after a protracted war, it was perhaps no surprise to observe the predominance of nationalism in a conference assembled to erect a new international order. The discussion of practically every issue confirmed this tendency. Wilson's call for a "a free, open-minded and absolutely impartial adjustment of all colonial claims" made the Allies uneasy. They felt they had to watch out for the president's essentially anticolonial inclination. The cynical attitude of colonialists was expressed by those "friends of the league" who suggested it would be best to distribute the colonies first so as not to burden the conscience of the league with them later on. The prime ministers of the British Empire and French imperialists did not hesitate to oppose openly the proposal that a system of mandates be set up as a sacred trust under the auspices of the league. They favored outright annexation. The temporary suppression of the King-Crane report on Syria, unfavorable to a French mandate in Syria, and vehement French press attacks against Wilson's defense of the rights and interests of colonial peoples, heated up this issue. Instead of giving in to the imperialists' pressures, the president stood up to them as best he could.

In the end, the mandate system accommodated the colonial ambitions of the various powers, but Articles XXII and XXIII embodied many of Wilson's enlightened safeguards. According to them, "The Members of the League will a) endeavor to secure and maintain fair and human conditions of labour for men, women and children . . . b) undertake to secure just treatment of the native inhabitants of territories under their control." Even though these words expressed merely noble intentions, they were potentially seeds that would ultimately bring forth a more humane governance of so-called underdeveloped societies.[95]

The president also took it for granted that an enlightened mandate system would not allow nations to claim exclusive economic privileges. Before long, however, his alert secretary of state, Bainbridge Colby, had occasion to protest the San Remo Agreement of April, 1920, whereby Britain and France divided the oil resources of former German and Turkish colonies. The United States judged this accord unfair and illegitimate. It claimed in a series of blunt notes that American interests had been intolerably ignored, and demanded equality of opportunity as a global principle.[96]

The bitter feelings engendered by war experiences lingered for some time. To many victims of German aggression, the "Huns" continued to be outlaws, unworthy of membership in the League of Nations. The French government, strongly supported by public opinion, tried to bar Germany's admission by stipulating conditions

95. D. F. Fleming, *The United States and the League of Nations, 1918–1920* (New York, 1932), 107–14, 184–90; Noble, *Policies and Opinions at Paris*, 114–17, 158–59; Georges Clemenceau, *Grandeur and Misery of Victory*, trans. F. M. Atkinson (New York, 1930), 170–78.

96. Herbert Feis, *Diplomacy of the Dollar, 1919–1932* (Baltimore, 1950), 50–55. Secretary of State Charles Evans Hughes ultimately succeeded in winning the battle for American oil companies. With French help, they were by 1922 granted 24 percent of the shares in the Anglo-Persian Oil Company.

it could not possibly meet for years to come. To admit only countries that had no reparations to pay would have excluded Germany for decades. And the French suggestion to require a unanimous vote for admission to the league would have given France a perpetual veto. The sentiments underlying such procedural maneuvers ran counter to what were the president's efforts, if not to bury the past, at least to develop friendlier relationships among nations. Although Wilson's eloquent arguments in favor of less stringent conditions prevailed, it was not until 1926 that Germany was finally admitted to the league, as a by-product of "the spirit of Locarno." Generally, the French have taken pride in their superior sense of humanity. In their dealings with Germany, however, they invariably underrated the psychological importance to Germans of being treated with dignity. It probably would have made a considerable difference if Germany had been encouraged to join the organization of the family of nations as soon as peace was concluded.

In the background of the peace conference loomed the specter of bolshevism. The disintegration of the German, Austro-Hungarian, Russian, and Ottoman empires amounted to a political earthquake, presenting world leaders with great opportunities and also testing their wisdom. The future stability of the world community depended considerably on the reintegration of Germany and Russia into the family of nations. Each of the victorious powers approached this challenge differently. France was determined to hold Germany down and restore Russia's capacity to balance the power on the Continent. For this reason, Clemenceau would have liked to see the restoration of a strong czarist regime controlling all of Russia. The advancement of British interests in the Near and Middle East stood to be facilitated by a government in Russia less inclined to compete with Britain in these regions. A smaller and weaker Russia would therefore open the door to a more flourishing Britain. Since the United States was not greatly concerned with Russia itself, America's main stake in Russia's disintegration was to prevent Japan from moving into eastern Siberia and from improving its strategic position vis-à-vis China, the country in the Far East of special interest to the United States.

Along with issues about the balance of power, the Western leaders at the peace conference were all preoccupied with the possibility that the Bolshevik ideology might infect their populations. Perhaps even more disturbing was the possibility that Germany and Russia, the two "outlaw" nations, would join forces. Guided by fear and vengeance, French policy makers actually contributed to the realization of these prospects while trying to head them off. Their designs for a weakened Germany, whether or not carried out, and their protracted blockade after the Armistice were not likely to be forgotten by Germany. And how could the Bolshevik leaders forget Clemenceau's unwillingness to talk peace with them and Marshal Foch's insistent recommendations for war against them? Lloyd George, who had heard in February of 1919 of "fantastic French schemes to organise an army of Russian prisoners in Germany" along with a variety of mercenaries to invade Russia, wondered who the French thought would pay for these armies. France, he was sure, could not afford to pay.

With the prominent exception of Winston Churchill, then secretary of war and air, the British government was more comfortable with President Wilson's agonizing conclusions on how best to proceed concerning the Russians—to allow them to overcome their internal conflict without outside interference, to invite them to the conference, and to hope for the evolution of democratic institutions in Russia. Wilson welcomed the demise of the old Russian political regime. Tired soldiers, war-weary populaces, depleted treasuries, and indecision on the part of the conference leaders finally left the Russians to work out their own salvation. Whatever the consequences of this decision, they would have to be dealt with in their time.[97]

Reviewing the entire peace conference, one finds that certain paradoxes can sum up how much and how little it accomplished. The major issues it failed to resolve definitely, such as the Russian problem, reparations, and the establishment of a cooperative international economic order, seriously complicated world affairs in the 1920s. Although it was mutual concessions that made the peace treaty possible at all and that accounted for agreements on its more than four hundred articles, "the spirit of Versailles" embraced vengeful, narrow nationalism much more than progressive internationalism. It was extraordinary that President Wilson was at all able to persuade his colleagues to turn a page in the history book and establish a new concert of powers. And as weak as the league

97. David Lloyd George, *Memoirs of the Peace Conference* (2 vols.; New Haven, 1939), 216–50; Mayer, *Politics and Diplomacy of Peacemaking*, 300–42.

turned out to be, at least it provided a ready international meeting ground. In retrospect, world leaders profoundly regretted that such a forum had not existed in 1914, for it might possibly have averted the outbreak of hostilities. Nothing, therefore, gave Wilson more satisfaction than Article XI of the covenant, which provided for exactly such consultation on all kinds of international problems. Whatever the shortcomings of the Treaty of Versailles, the president fought for improvements in the twentieth-century world order as best he could in the politically polluted Parisian environment. His concessions were usually negotiated at the price of counterconcessions, which resulted in a less draconic peace. He had set out to accomplish much more. But fighter that he was, he nonetheless permitted himself to be outmaneuvered.

Interestingly, each power had gone to Paris not just to conclude a peace with its former enemies but to advance its own interests in dealing with its "friends" as well. Nothing illustrated this dual function of the peace conference better than the attempt of the Allies, particularly France and Great Britain, to slip the bill of war costs to Uncle Sam by tying Allied war debts and German reparations together. Certainly the United States was not quite so unselfish as Wilson liked to assert. It advocated the freedom of the seas, open markets, and reasonable access to raw materials because they were vital to America's continuing prosperity. Incidentally they promised to benefit the world economy as well. Implicitly, this way of thinking assumed that the rest of the world, particularly the industrialized European countries, would acknowledge the United States as the new leader in world trade and finance. But the Europeans had no intention of yielding their historic leadership. They looked upon the reduction of their financial and industrial capacities as temporary by-products of the war and not as an indication of the permanent decline of their empires.

The major European powers attempted to reestablish the economic balance with the United States by burdening it with the enormous cost of the war and by linking the reparations with debts to be repaid. Financially embarrassed at the end of the war, France interpreted America's entry into the war as a belated acceptance of its claim that it had all along fought for the sake of freedom and democracy in America as well as in Europe. It also took for granted that the security of France and the United States would eternally continue to be inseparable. Only sentimental oratorical references to their traditional ties lent a degree of reasonableness to these two assumptions. Since the United States was eventually dragged into the originally strictly European war primarily because American interests would not be served by the total victory of one European camp over the other, France could hardly assume an identity of French and American policy objectives. France fought for complete victory and all it would entail. The United States joined the Allies as an "Associate" to prevent Germany from registering a complete victory over France and all it would entail. President Wilson had never left any doubt about this distinction. Despite America's participation in the war, its interests remained distinct from those of Europe, even though its new responsibilities had somewhat modified them. Not having been and not expecting to be a partner in the formulation of European policies, Wilson rejected European attempts to "use" the financial resources of the United States practically as a matter of entitlement. Altogether, the extent to which he involved America in Europe's future fell far short of the Allies' expectations. Their grudging concessions to his pleas for nonimperialistic changes did anything but inspire Wilson's trust in their sincerity to move from the nineteenth into the twentieth century of world politics.[98]

From the start, Clemenceau shrewdly realized that the president's influence would be diminished if he sat in the peace conference as a delegate. As a celebrated outsider, he would have been in a powerful position to assume the role of spokesman for many of the smaller nations. Indeed, by abandoning the principle of equality of nations in international relations when he tacitly accepted the "oligarchy of the Great Powers at the Conference and in a modified form in the Covenant," the president played into the hands of the French premier. By agreeing to the procedures of the conference, he opened the gates for concessions violating his guiding principles and objectives and thus lost his peace at the outset. At the end, in May, 1919, Secretary Lansing deplored that the conditions that had produced the war had not been destroyed. Several young American experts, among them A. A. Berle, Jr., William C. Bullitt, Joseph V. Fuller, and Samuel Eliot Morison, despaired when they found that the proposed German treaty "bartered away our principles in a series of compromises with interests of imperialism and revenge, until hardly a shadow of them remains." They were not consoled by

98. Levin, *Woodrow Wilson and World Politics*, 140–48.

the argument that without concessions Germany would have fared much worse. Herbert Hoover summed up their belief that a steadfast fight for a truly Wilsonian peace, even at the risk of the unlikely collapse of the conference, would have been preferable to arrangements ushering in a new century of war.[99]

The final peace treaty bitterly disappointed many of Wilson's true believers at home and abroad. Characteristically, leftist Allied and American representatives of labor blamed their disillusionment on themselves, saying they should never have assumed that a bourgeois president would honestly spearhead a genuine revolution against international capitalism. It was hardly a surprise when in November, 1917, Trotsky interpreted America's belated intervention in the war "under the influence of a sober calculation of the American Stock Exchange . . . [as a means of] weakening both coalitions and strengthening the hegemony of American capital." Some contemporary German comments expressed similar views. The *Koelnische Zeitung* of January 10, 1918, rejected Wilson's Fourteen Points, arguing that "under the false label of Society of Nations, Anglo-American domination would be permanently reestablished." And a German academician labeled America's foreign policy during the war "a ruthless, purely business policy," formulated by Wilson, an incredibly deceitful and unctuous hypocrite.

Clemenceau, too, was simultaneously attacked from the Left and the Right as either too imperialistic or not nationalistic enough. Although he pressed Wilson unceasingly to accommodate French demands, he was always conscious that he must not antagonize Wilson, because of the value he attached to future Franco-American cooperation. His concessions to the president displeased Foch and French royalists, who counted on a militarily strong France to enable it either to dispense with America's long-term assistance or to obtain such assistance anyway because of France's leading role in Europe. These nostalgic Frenchmen identified permanent peace with French domination. Clemenceau was too much of a realist to embrace such romantic notions in defiance of existing power constellations. The interplay of power deprived both Clemenceau and Wilson of accomplishing all that they sought.

99. Robert Lansing, *The Big Four and Others of the Peace Conference* (Boston, 1921), 12–15, 72–73, 90–91.

Human factors and the perceptions of personalities and policies played their distinct roles in World War I diplomacy. As the advocate of "open convenants, openly arrived at," President Wilson felt very uncomfortable that he negotiated behind closed doors and kept the press uninformed about the internal struggles in the councils and commissions. Although this protection from undue outside pressures was not leakproof in Paris, the confidential leaks from "high sources" could be very annoying. As chairman of the commission drafting the league covenant, the president would have felt more at ease without minutes being taken of the exchanges. The French members, however, insisted on formal proceedings. The pressures resulting from these external formalities merely aggravated the strain showing from hard bargaining sessions. Not much inclined to delegate authority, the president took on more responsibility in Paris than he could physically and mentally endure. Above all, the substantive battles exhausted him. Those with the French, on which this study focuses, constituted only one significant series. Those with Britain, Italy, and Japan also exacted a toll.

Although Lloyd George and Wilson saw essentially eye to eye on many territorial questions, the League of Nations, and the Bolshevik dilemma, they parted ways on the reparation settlement and on planning for economic reconstruction. Aside from somewhat different national interests, their personal temperaments precluded the degree of Anglo-American cooperation and coordination that might have resulted in a more enlightened peace. Wilson's emphasis on moral ideals and abstract principles clashed time and again with Lloyd George's pragmatic opportunism. Wilson's mission would have been made much easier had he and the British prime minister been able to work as a team.[100]

Early in 1919, Clemenceau told President Wilson that, in his judgment, "the grave fault of his [Wilson's] attitude is that he eliminated sentiment and endeavored to efface all memory of the past, a grave, very grave fault it seems to me." Referring to the Franco-Prussian War and the recent conflict, Clemenceau continued: "Mr. President, I speak for our glorious dead who fell in the two wars. For myself, I can hold my tongue, but not for them." As much as the eloquence of this criticism touched Wilson, it did not really address itself

100. Tillman, *Anglo-American Relations at the Paris Peace Conference*, 402–406.

to the question of for what kind of peace these brave soldiers had made their supreme sacrifice.[101] In the past, "peace" had meant victory. In the president's mind, now only "peace without victory" would be lasting and to the glory of all those who contributed to it. On May 15, 1919, Vance McCormick, one of Wilson's peace commissioners, recorded in his diary the innermost feelings of the disillusioned president. In the presence of Herbert Hoover, Norman Davis, and Bernard Baruch, Wilson confided freely his difficulties with his colleagues on the council: "President . . . called them mad men, particularly Clemenceau. . . . He says he has a great pity for them. They have such fear of the Germans and such great self pity." Wilson had developed a certain contempt for Clemenceau, and he disliked Lloyd George. He looked forward to meeting the social needs of the age of industrial capitalism on a global scale and with new, enlightened, and peaceful approaches. But the leaders of the Old World were tradition-bound in thought and policies. They did not keep pace with the rapid changes calling for broader vistas and cooperation. The frustrated president regretted that the statesmen at Versailles did not rise to the occasion.[102]

Contemporaries, preoccupied with their opponents, did not fully perceive the debilitating effects of the war itself on each of their countries. On balance, Germany had been practically untouched, and it emerged as a much stronger entity than victorious but ravaged France. Other paradoxes were no less significant. Europe was in every respect so badly shaken up by the war that, as a power entity, it yielded its preeminent place to America. And nationalistic realists in Europe lived to learn that the idealistic advocate of one interdependent world was not a simplistic dreamer. Both Wilson and the European statesmen in the end awakened to the realization that it was easier to stumble into war and hammer out a peace treaty than to establish a truly lasting peace.

Secretary of State Lansing vividly described the memorable gathering at which the final draft of the peace treaty was handed to the German delegation. The atmosphere was formal and correct. Standing up, though couched and with his gloved hands on the table, the Tiger addressed the Germans. "Dispassionately, he outlined the subjects dealt with in the treaty and told the Germans they

101. Bonsal, *Unfinished Business*, 71.

102. See McCormick, Diary, May 15, 1919, in McCormick Papers.

had fifteen days to consider it,'' Lansing wrote. However disappointed some Frenchmen might have been with Clemenceau's businesslike tone, Lansing observed that Foch was more than disappointed: "I looked at Marshal Foch while Clemenceau was speaking and saw his lips . . . twisted into a sneer. Doubtless he was thinking how he could have flayed the Boches. . . . The Marshal, who dislikes Clemenceau, found it a bitter pill to have the latter the spokesman of France. . . . Yesterday he attacked the treaty at the Plenary Session of the Conference and said it ought not to be signed. . . . Possibly he had . . . in mind an attack on Clemenceau for refusing to listen to his militaristic schemes.''

Count Ulrich von Brockdorff-Rantzau's immediate, largely propagandistic response contained some adroit comments of special relevance to this study. He reminded the world that Germany had agreed to the Armistice on the conditions expounded in the Fourteen Points. He knew enough about the treaty to hint at Germany's feeling of betrayal. The order in which he listed Germany's peace aims assumed special significance: "First the industrial life of Germany is to be restored, and after that reparation is to be made for the Belgian and French industries wantonly destroyed.'' Finally, he appealed for Germany's early admission to the League of Nations, an act that would make it again a respected member of the family of nations.[103] Once the Treaty of Versailles was signed, on June 28, 1919, it was up to the respective parliamentary bodies to ratify it.

On the eve of Wilson's departure for Paris, Theodore Roosevelt warned the Europeans that the election results of November, 1918, had considerably weakened the president's political authority. On December 21, another political foe, Henry Cabot Lodge, Republican chairman of the Senate Foreign Relations Committee, advocated the early conclusion of a peace treaty agreeable to the Allies. The concept of a league of nations could then be leisurely explored in subsequent discussions. Lodge sided with the French, who wished to impose terms that would destroy Germany's military capacity for a long time. "To encourage or even to permit any serious differences to arise between the United States and Great Britain, or with France,

103. Robert Lansing to G. S. Knowlton, May 10, 1919, in Lansing Papers, Princeton. Wilson admitted that the Fourteen Points had been "accepted in principle but negated in detail.'' See Lindsay Rogers, "The Relation of the Armistice and the Treaty,'' *American Society of International Law: Proceedings* (1923), 90–96.

or Italy, or Belgium," he contended, "would be a world calamity of the worst kind. . . . This unity between us and the allies is the first essential condition for a successful peace. . . . As one of the greatest and most powerful of the civilized nations, if we are to have a lasting peace now, we can not avoid the problems which the war has bequeathed to us." Three days earlier, Senator Philander C. Knox of Pennsylvania, secretary of state under President Taft, had enunciated his "American Doctrine" in an effort to head off any concerted international obligations. He deemed it sufficient for the United States to pronounce the new doctrine, which stated: "If a situation should arise in which any power or combination of powers should, directly or indirectly, menace the freedom and peace of Europe, the United States would regard such situation with grave concern as a menace to its own freedom and peace and would consult with other powers affected with a view to concerted action for the removal of such menace."[104]

The European press reported these events. On the whole, they revealed a welcome awareness by Americans of their nation's international responsibilities in the postwar world. They also placed Europe's leaders in a stronger bargaining position. But at the risk of antagonizing the Senate, the strong-minded president went his own way in his effort to secure a lasting peace. The senators, he assumed, would not dare overrule the president, the official authorized by the Constitution and by tradition to conduct America's foreign affairs, though with the consent and advice of the Senate, to be sure. He was determined to prevent parochial domestic politics from seriously interfering with transcendent cosmopolitan desiderata. As a citizen of the world, he endeavored to create a world of peace. And he meant to keep faith with his new world constituency. His assumption that what was good for the United States was good for the world combined sincere naïveté with an appalling misconception of world politics. Worse, it was entertained by a leader who had no organized mass following abroad. Wilson ignored at his own risk the fact that the shifting sentiments of masses offer no substitute for solidly established support. As mankind's crusader for peace, he felt Republican criticism would not get very far, notwithstanding Senator Lodge's round robin of March 4, 1919, defiantly announcing

104. *Congressional Record*, 65th Congress, 3rd Sess., 724–26, 603–607.

certain rejection of the League of Nations "in the form now proposed."

On July 10, the president presented the treaty for ratification. Defending it and the League of Nations as the only hope for mankind, he appealed to the senators to assume the moral leadership this world settlement had entrusted to the United States. America, he emphasized, had not become a world power by design. But in the twentieth century its achievements and principles imposed upon it the new responsibility of lifting mankind to higher levels. No longer isolated or able to pursue a self-centered policy, he urged the senators to understand: "We cannot turn back."

Without adequate explanation, Wilson delayed the presentation of the guarantee treaty with France until July 29. By the terms of this treaty, he was obliged to submit it to the Senate on the same day as the Treaty of Versailles. One can only speculate that, unlike Clemenceau, who valued the guarantee pacts with Great Britain and the United States as essential to French security, Wilson looked upon the world organization as the cornerstone of peace. It was in Clemenceau's interest, therefore, to insist on the simultaneous presentation of the two treaties. He did not want to convey the impression that he agreed with Wilson's order of priorities. The French premier considered the guarantee pact as the ultimate sanction of the peace treaty. Wilson, of course, recommended its ratification. In his words, our "peculiarly sacred" ties of friendship with France since the days of the American Revolution amply justified this guarantee. He dismissed as groundless the argument that this alliance established a balance-of-power combination destined to weaken the effectiveness of the league.[105]

France would obviously have preferred the Roosevelt-Lodge policy of a harsh peace and continuation of the league of allies. But being pragmatic, the French were willing to cooperate with the president to a considerable extent, despite their many objections to his untested approaches to world peace. At the least, it seemed that most Wilsonians and their opponents recognized the necessity for an end to America's political isolation in world affairs. What France dreaded the most was the unthinkable return of the United States to the traditional policy of nonentanglement.

105. Woodrow Wilson, *President Wilson's State Papers and Addresses* (New York, 1918), 547–57.

It was probably the combination of political conviction, partisanship, and personal rivalry that motivated Senator Lodge when he reminded the president that the Senate's constitutional responsibilities in the treaty-making process had to be reckoned with. To shape the course of developments, he had seen to it that the committee over which he presided was largely composed of senators opposed to the league. Preliminary discussions and hearings by the committee deliberately delayed the process before the entire Senate could take up and vote on the treaties. In the meantime, public opinion was mobilized against the break with traditional nationalism and nonentanglement. Despite endorsement of the league by many educated Americans and about half of the country's press, the president faced bitter frustrations. Lodge pigeonholed the guarantee pact in the committee and did not even send it to the Senate floor for a vote. Because he anticipated Senate rejection of the Versailles treaty, he made no effort to expedite the guarantee pact, which was entwined with the treaty. The French were naturally disappointed when the White House failed to urge Senate action on this vital pact.

Not all Senate amendments and reservations to the Versailles treaty were mischievously designed to defeat it. But irreconcilable isolationist Senator William E. Borah of Idaho and some of his like-minded colleagues were utterly opposed to any "political partnership or alliance or league which commits us to meddling in European affairs." In their view, entangling alliances with Europe meant involvement in wars of at best remote concern to the American people. The causes of war, Borah believed, were so deeply embedded in the structure of European society that no written covenant could remove them. Besides desiring to preserve America's complete freedom of action in international affairs, Borah ruled out the possibility of preserving the Monroe Doctrine by reservations in the treaty. American interference in Europe, he feared, would justify European interference in America.[106] Why, he continued to ask, did France and its allies draft the guarantee pact if the league was supposed to insure peace? Didn't they agree on this alliance to take care of the next war? He and many of his Republican colleagues were not opposed to rescuing France in case of another German assault. But should it ever materialize, he wanted the contemporary generation to be free to make its own decision, unfettered by previous com-

106. *Congressional Record*, 66th Cong., 1st Sess., 3143–44.

mitments. Sharing Borah's disdain for the "absurd" tripartite alliance, Albert Beveridge, a prominent progressive Republican who believed in Anglo-Saxon supremacy, prodded the senator from Idaho to reject the security pact. He strenuously objected to involving the United States in French politics.

Other senators opposed the league because it upheld the legality of war and provided for economic sanctions. "Instead of abolishing war," Senator Knox deplored, "it absolutely requires that every future war shall be a potential world war." He went to the extreme of condemning American acceptance of the league, and particularly its Article X, as "national suicide." Several senators took strong exception to this article because its implementation might deprive Congress of its war-making powers. These senators acted as if treaty stipulations were not subject to interpretations that often allowed considerable functional flexibility. What, after all, did the word *preserve* in Article X mean? What constituted "external aggression"? The league's council could "advise," but it could not compel, the United States to take certain actions in the international arena. And in case the league attempted to meddle in the internal affairs of the United States, the federal government possessed the means to react vigorously, if it so willed. Had the president listened to Lansing, the furor over Article X would never have materialized. Instead of the positively stated obligations, the secretary of state would have preferred a disclaimer by each member not to impair the integrity and independence of other states. Such a clause would have safeguarded the prerogatives of nations.

After lengthy debate, the Senate rejected the forty-five amendments proposed by the Republicans. But the Senate appended to the treaty, by simple majority vote, fourteen so-called Lodge reservations. Their thrust reserved the right of Congress to interpret and implement the clauses of the league convenant as it saw fit and declared the Monroe Doctrine to be "wholly outside the jurisdiction of the League." The president was willing to make some minor concessions, but he fought hard to keep the treaty intact. To him, more was at stake than the compromises, principles, and concepts embodied in the treaty. He was determined not to permit anybody to trifle with the honor and prestige of the United States or with its presidency. Tragically, late in September, 1919, the president's attempt to enlist the support of the people by going directly to them ended in his physical collapse. Exhausted and partially paralyzed,

Wilson had to abandon his fight. He left the Democrats and the country practically without a leader.

The French followed these incredible developments anxiously. Originally, their leaders managed to hide their apprehensions by displaying a subtle optimism about America's fundamental loyalty. In their own ratification proceedings, French deputies and senators found the treaty wanting in a number of respects. They did not hesitate to criticize its imperfections. Disillusioned French Socialists labeled Wilson's compromises an abandonment of his noble principles. As they saw it, the league was built "on the principle of the balance of power"; general disarmament and the principles of the freedom of the seas and self-determination of peoples had been victimized. And above all, failure to establish a sound economic world order was destined to perpetuate the anachronistic system of commercial rivalry and capitalistic imperialism. Despite these and other regrets, however, the French Chamber felt compelled to approve the *ensemble*. By their final vote, French parliamentarians hoped to send the message to America that, on balance, one had to judge the treaty as the most feasible compromise.

As Clemenceau's anxiety increased, his optimism for a last-minute change of mind by the United States gave way to the ominous sigh that America's nonratification would be "a singular irony of fate." A few days before the Senate defeated the treaty with the Lodge reservations, the Quai d'Orsay instructed its ambassadors in Washington, London, Rome, and Brussels that, juridically, one could not conceive of a treaty ratification with reservations. Significantly, however, the communication suggested that reservations of a strictly interpretative character would be preferable to outright rejection of the treaty. Such French newspapers as the influential *Journal des Débats* and the sophisticated *Le Temps*, close to the foreign ministry, began to stress the acceptability of the Lodge reservations. A treaty with reservations now appeared less troublesome than none at all. Thoroughly alarmed by Christmas, 1919, Clemenceau found it impossible to fathom how the United States could behave as it was behaving, which he warned would "cause an irreparable wrong."[107]

These French hints did not mollify Wilson. His stubborn refusal to accommodate even mild reservationists in the Senate revealed

107. Georges Clemenceau to Jean Jules Jusserand, December 26, 1919, CPEU, Vol. 38, AMAE.

psychological quirks in his personality. In Paris, he did not fight for his kind of peace to the point of a tough showdown. But in his dealings with the Senate, he displayed an almost irrational inflexibility. With a few compromises, which would have resulted in a few shifts of Senate votes, he could have ended his presidency in a more glorious way than he did. Instead, he defiantly reiterated his defense of the covenant. To him, any League of Nations without Article X amounted to "hardly more than a futile scrap of paper," and failure to accept it "to an act of bad faith." The relative closeness of the final vote on March 19, 1920, indicated that the shift of only seven votes would have been necessary to ratify the treaty. This was the sad climax to all of the president's effort. A little less rigidity in his dealings with the Senate and a little more understanding of foreign affairs on the part of the American people would have held out the promise of a steadier future.[108]

Ahead of its time, Wilson's design suffered a serious defeat. But historically, his world concept was not defeated. He impressed it on the mind and conscience of future generations. According to Benjamin Disraeli's definition of a great statesman, Wilson thus met the essential qualification. Even Clemenceau, who had every reason to regret and resent the Senate's final verdict, acknowledged President Wilson's towering contributions to "the laws of New Europe" and to the search for "a system of justice between nations who up till this time had lived by violence alone." French public reaction was less generous. People who only a year before had worshipped the American president as a savior felt let down when they realized he did not truly represent the views of his countrymen. Henceforth, France accepted official American propositions with skeptical reserve.[109]

In the meantime, America's separate peace with Germany in the fall of 1921 caused painful reactions in France. Without America's full participation in the implementation of the Versailles treaty, the proceedings of the League of Nations, and the economic reconstruction of France, the future looked bleak. Without a system of collective security in which the United States assumed responsibilities commensurate with its resources, the chances of prolonged instability and of war on the Continent appeared to be greatly en-

108. Noble, *Policies and Opinions at Paris*, 408–409.

109. Aristide Briand to Jean Jules Jusserand, January 29, 1921, CPEU, Vol. 39, AMAE.

hanced. From the immediate perspective, the split among the Allies, always a German policy objective, was likely to be exploited by the Germans. By dragging their feet on the payment of reparations, the Germans were likely not only to slow down French recovery but also to gain time for their own recovery. Procrastination, after all, acts as a thief of time. And finally, considering America's well-known interests in Germany's early economic recovery, France faced the future with dismay.[110]

In exchange for concessions with respect to the Rhineland, France counted on the guarantee treaty for its security. The concessions were final, but the guarantee collapsed. In exchange for concessions on the League of Nations, it counted on the United States to help develop it into an effective instrument of international security. But the United States decided not to join the league. France thought it had made important concessions to the United States on the reparations question. It counted on America's active role in the satisfactory solution of this issue; but when the United States did not ratify the Versailles treaty, it vacated its seat on the reparations commission. Having won the war with the much-appreciated help of the United States, France believed it had yielded to America's desire not to cripple Germany. In exchange for this sacrifice, France counted on the continuation of the wartime alliances, but the United States turned its back on such "entanglement." Drawing a balance sheet of these profoundly upsetting experiences, France could not but wonder how much it could rely on the United States, though it found itself in circumstances calling for the closest ties with America. It sought them because of many advantages it could derive from them even without a Franco-American alliance. Up to now, they had not been "partners" consulting each other on international problems. It was remarkable, though, that they managed to maintain frank and useful relations with each other, despite many differences.

110. Tardieu, *The Truth About the Treaty*, 462–73; Thomas A. Bailey, *Woodrow Wilson and the Great Betrayal* (New York, 1945), 284–85, 356–59.

II

Franco-American Frustrations 1921–1932

THE WASHINGTON ARMS LIMITATION CONFERENCE, 1921–1922

When President Warren G. Harding received Clemenceau at the White House on December 5, 1922, he made what was—considering the character and reputation of his distinguished guest—a rather gauche comment: "Germany's defeat might be the greatest tragedy in history." No matter how much the United States desired friendly relations with France, it clearly wished to see Germany restored to a vital role in Europe and in world trade. If these two objectives seemed to be incompatible with each other, American officials were inclined to attribute the major responsibility for this state of affairs to French ambitions and intransigence. Afraid of Germany's resurgence and obstruction of the Versailles treaty, Frenchmen saw no better way to insure their future security than to deal firmly with the Germans. America's refusal to ratify the guarantee pact or to recognize the de facto interrelation between debts and reparations, in addition to its sympathetic attitude toward Germany, left France with a feeling of virtual abandonment. The French were therefore very determined to enforce the stipulations of the Versailles settlement, to collect reparations even at the risk of occupying the Ruhr, and to avoid a sharp reduction of their military and naval strength. With respect to its debt payments to the United States, France was more concerned with keeping solvent than with what it regarded its morally questionable obligations. In any case, unless it received reparation payments from Germany, it pleaded inability to pay its debts to the United States. Washington's "return to normalcy," that is, its apparent unwillingness to become actively involved in Europe's problems, hardly qualified it, in French eyes, to lecture France on its search for survival as a major power.

America's common-sense approach suggested disarmament as a universally desirable solution for peace and economic recovery.

Harding's secretary of state, Charles Evans Hughes, encouraged by Senator Borah to head off a costly naval and arms race, took the initiative in this regard. The Washington Arms Limitation Conference convened in November, 1921, and lasted until February, 1922. The American statesman dropped a diplomatic bombshell when in his opening address he proposed specific reductions for the leading navies of the world in the name of disarmament, economy, and security. Although the accomplishments of this conference impressed contemporaries more than posterity, it indeed evidenced an unusual readiness for cooperation on a global scale. Undoubtedly the most significant development growing out of this conference was the replacement of the Anglo-Japanese alliance by the Four-Power Treaty, in which Great Britain, Japan, France, and the United States pledged to respect one another's insular possessions and dominions in the region of the Pacific. Besides the Nine-Power Treaty, the provisions of which amounted to the internationalization of the Open Door policy in China, this conference put limits on the number of capital ships and aircraft carriers the various powers were allowed to have.

The Washington conference raised some disturbing points for the French government. In the first place, the three major naval powers—Great Britain, the United States, and Japan—did not include France in their preliminary discussions, at which they proposed the relative 5:5:3 ratio for their own capital ships while limiting France and Italy to only 1.75 apiece. Considering its long coastlines and global colonial interests, France found its ratio unsatisfactory, and placing it on a par with Italy amounted to an insult to its dignity. That Great Britain agreed to naval parity with the United States came as a totally unexpected surprise to French officials. In fact, this unprecedented, historic concession appeared to be potentially ominous. The prospect of Anglo-American cooperation and domination in world affairs greatly increased the odds against France because it had to protect itself against the possible pooling of German and Italian naval might.

France resented this attempt by foreign powers to set limits to its naval strength. Since it had a colonial population of fifty-nine million, adequate means of communication and defense for its empire alone called for a military establishment of significant size. As a major colonial power it felt entitled to more than a third-rate navy. While Clemenceau acknowledged heavy French reliance on British sea power during World War I, he and his successors considered the wartime emphasis on armed forces at the expense of French sea power as only a temporary expedient. Even financial constraints following the war were not to stand in the way of again building up the French navy. The postwar political unreliability of Great Britain and the United States prompted the French to think increasingly in terms of relying on their own naval and military establishments. Just before the Washington conference convened, Vice Admiral Maurice Albert Grasset, chief of staff of the French navy, let it be known that his country would not agree to any limitation of armaments unless its navy were allowed to be equal to that of Japan. With respect to capital ships, this meant an allotment of 300,000 tons. France, possessing in 1921 a total of 164,500 tons of capital ships, did not pay much attention to the fact that, unlike Great Britain and the United States, it would not have had to scrap any ships. Its opposition to the projected limit of 175,000 tons threatened to jeopardize the success of the conference.[1]

Such opposition amounted to more than the refusal to accept permanent status as a third-rate naval power. Premier Aristide Briand, who attended the conference for a short time, deplored the lack of support France received from its former allies. Not entirely convincingly, he contended that in its struggle for the maintenance of the status quo France was defending Western interests. He and his colleagues, he stated, were prepared at any time to abandon what appeared to be their tactical demands if Great Britain and the United States would underwrite French security. Since this implied submitting to French domination on the Continent and holding defeated and disarmed Germany down, America's leaders felt they had to disappoint Briand.[2]

Concerned about the French attitudes, Hughes decided to address a personal appeal to Briand. In his lengthy message of December 16, 1921, he tried to soothe the feelings of the French by reassuring them that no final naval limitation would be undertaken without their "appropriate agreement." Inasmuch as Italy's economic constraints moved it to favor the reduction of capital ships,

1. Thomas H. Buckley, *The United States and the Washington Conference, 1921–1922* (Knoxville, 1970), 107–26.

2. Achille Elisha, *Aristide Briand: Discours et écrits de politique étrangère* (Paris, 1965), 113–14; Henry de Béarn to Ministère des Affaires Étrangères, October 14, 1921 (telegram no. 937), CPEU, Vol. 61, AMAE.

"the attitude of France," Hughes stated bluntly, "will determine the success or failure of these efforts to reduce the heavy burden of naval armament." He also pointed out the likelihood, in a continued naval race, of an Anglo-American naval ratio of 6 to 1 in relation to France. He balanced these observations with an allusion to America's willingness to aid France in its economic recovery. "It is not against the interest of France," he lectured the French in closing, "that we express the hope that her industry and resources will be devoted to economic recuperation and the enhancement of her prosperity rather than be expended in the building of fighting ships." If necessary, Hughes was prepared to go ahead without French participation. Leaked indications of stubborn French resistance to significant disarmament had already aroused world opinion against France.[3]

In the course of a meeting with Briand, the American ambassador gained the impression that a final agreement was likely. The premier's personal inclinations with respect to multilateral disarmament were well known. But the obstinate position of the French delegation at the conference could be attributed to two extraneous considerations. First, Briand had to protect himself against the merciless criticism of his political adversaries, and second, he was trying to secure a strong bargaining base for future discussions about smaller ships. In his official response, the president of the French Council of Ministers distinguished between offensive and defensive naval armament. Encouragingly, he promised to instruct "our Delegates in the sense you desire." But, he added, the French Chamber would not accept corresponding reductions of defensive ships. The full significance of this reservation came to light on the afternoon of December 19. At that time prominent French spokesmen disagreed with Hughes's interpretation of Briand's acceptance of the limit of 175,000 tons for capital ships. According to Hughes's construction, the premier's acceptance was unconditional and cleared the road for the discussion of other important naval questions. Hughes regarded Briand's instruction as a fact; he viewed the premier's observation with respect to what the chamber would or would not do as an opinion. Characteristically, the French delegation considered its instruction to be merely a general statement to

3. Charles Evans Hughes to Myron T. Herrick, December 16, 1921, in FRUS, *Diplomatic Papers, 1922*, I, 130–33. See also General Correspondence, Box 4A, Charles Evans Hughes Papers, Library of Congress, Washington, D.C.

cooperate with the other powers as far as possible, "but without being bound to any absolute figure." They held, moreover, that Briand consented to the 175,000 tons "on the express condition that France would keep the tonnage she considered indispensable as to her light cruisers, torpedo boats, and submarines." To Albert Surraut, minister of the colonies, these two aspects of the issue could not be separated. Significantly, the French delegation hinted that they considered 330,000 tons of auxiliary craft and 90,000 tons of submarines to be "indispensable." This amounted to more than three times the tonnage of French submarines existing in 1921. They justified their submarine projection, at least in part, on the ground that no country could be effectively prevented from building submarines secretly. Germany, for instance, could build, ostensibly for commercial purposes, diesel engines capable of being placed in submarines and then acquire the hulls from countries not bound by the Washington treaty.[4]

If the naval experts of the United States found this French submarine projection excessive, the British government, which judged a war between France and England "unthinkable," saw no justification for any French submarines. The British were alarmed by this ambitious tonnage and asked themselves against what nation other than Great Britain the French intended to use their submarines. The size, speed, and range of submarines could be designed for offensive as well as defensive purposes. As far as Britain was concerned, the implication of the French projection appeared ominous. Secretary Hughes also saw it as a tragic omen for the future. Under these circumstances, Britain was not prepared to support any limitation on auxiliary ships. Remembering the havoc caused by German submarines in World War I, the British favored a strong antisubmarine fleet for the protection of their merchant ships. This decision made even more sense when the French refused to ratify the treaty attempting to "civilize" submarine warfare.

Moreover, in view of the fact that at the end of 1921 the French possessed 1,722 military planes, compared with the 2,079 of Great Britain, Italy, and the United States combined, the future of Anglo-French relations gave England legitimate concern. The desirability of the development of commercial airplanes and the fact that they

4. "Memorandum of a Conversation at the State Department," December 19, 1921, in FRUS, *Diplomatic Papers, 1922*, I, 137–41.

could be converted into military aircraft relatively easily puzzled the experts at the Washington conference sufficiently to make them abstain from any attempt to limit the numbers of these potentially dangerous instruments. Before the Washington treaties had been fully ratified, an air rivalry had developed between France and Great Britain, and there was much loose talk of a war between them. The explanation could be found in French dissatisfaction with Britain's enforcement of the Versailles treaty. Like the United States, Britain preferred the gradual recovery of Germany and a balance of power on the Continent instead of French supremacy. But to the French, the whole Versailles system was threatening to fall apart because of lack of Anglo-French cooperation. In the last analysis, the Washington conference confirmed that there could be no meaningful disarmament or arms limitation without prior or simultaneous understandings with respect to divergent political interests.

As at Versailles, Americans found it difficult to do business with the French at the Washington conference. Their tendencies to be overly punctilious and pose as prima donnas could be exasperating. At the beginning, for instance, they were piqued because Briand was seated near the bend of the U-shaped table rather than at the center. At the end of the conference they refused to sign the treaties unless the word *French* appeared before *English* in the statement authenticating both texts. Reacting to this childishness, Elihu Root, one of the American delegates, lost his usual self-control. "To hell with them!" he exclaimed. "Let the whole business go to pot—I would not care!"[5] Secretary of State Hughes, however, decided to accommodate the French in order to salvage the results of the conference. He regretted leaving the floodgates open for an arms race in auxiliary ships below ten thousand tons, submarines, military airplanes, and ground forces. But it was only by leaving these types of armaments unregulated that the Washington conference could accomplish any significant limitation at all.

The dangers of a costly naval race had caused much concern, but the underlying reason for the Washington conference was the alarming prospect of a war between Japan and the United States.[6]

5. Philip C. Jessup, *Elihu Root* (2 vols.; New York, 1930), II, 465.

6. It is noteworthy that the French minister in Copenhagen reported to the Quai d'Orsay that European business circles would welcome such a war in the Pacific as an opportunity to profit sufficiently from neutral trade to restore Europe's economic

Japan's expansionist policy in the Far East in the wake of the Western powers' preoccupations during the World War had signaled a growing challenge to American interests in the region. As important as the defense of the Philippine Islands was, America's protection of China assumed an even larger significance. In the past, at least a precarious balance of power had been maintained by the imperialists' control of certain spheres of influence in China. Japan's advances threatened to upset this balance. Ironically, the Anglo-Japanese alliance of 1902, which added much to Japan's maneuverability, foreshadowed the possibility of an Anglo-American confrontation, an eventuality Canada dreaded as much as the United States. By coincidence, this alliance was due for renewal in 1921. Both Great Britain and Japan wished to renew it. But at the same time they sought to reassure the United States that it had nothing to fear from the alliance. They therefore came up with the suggestion of transforming the Anglo-Japanese alliance into a "tripartite agreement" by inviting the United States to become a party to it. Since this scheme would not have canceled the alliance, Secretary of State Hughes rejected it as unacceptable. In line with President Wilson's emphatic rejection of the system of imperialistic alliances, Hughes proposed a consultative pact among the four powers. The addition of the French, who had been aware of America's opposition to the Anglo-Japanese alliance, was acceptable to the British and Japanese. The French were so flattered by Hughes's adroit maneuver that their chief delegate surprised the unemotional secretary of state with a kiss on his cheek. The truth was that Hughes preferred a fourth party so that the United States could avoid being regularly outvoted by the original allies. He also hoped that this gesture would make France more amenable to the proposed ratios on capital ships. Not the least important consequence of the Four-Power Treaty was a feeling of relief in London, Paris, Ottawa, and Washington. The abolition of the embarrassing alliance promised to bring about greater harmony between the Anglo-Saxons, hardly a goal of French diplomacy.[7]

health. Consult his note of November 10, 1921, in Série "Y" Internationale, No. 503, AMAE.

7. Akira Iriye, *After Imperialism: The Search for a New Order in the Far East, 1921–1931* (Cambridge, Mass., 1965), 13–38. See also William A. Williams, "China and Japan: A Challenge and a Choice of the 1920s," *Pacific Historical Review*, XXVI (1957), 259–79.

While the Anglo-Americans endeavored to maintain the status quo in the Far East, the French colonial empire stood to reap benefits from this policy. With whatever mixed feelings the French evaluated the expanding responsibilities of the American navy in the Pacific (which permitted the British to concentrate their navy more heavily in the Atlantic), France had little choice but to make the most of the American presence in the region. As the champion of the Open Door in China, the United States welcomed the Nine-Power Treaty upholding the "sovereignty, independence and territorial and administrative integrity of China." In the abstract these principles sounded more benevolent than the extent of their implementation warranted. The Wilson administration's concessions to Japan, highlighted by the Lansing-Ishii Agreement and the Shantung compromise at Versailles, had dampened China's faith in America's benevolent protection. A fairly trivial episode, involving the French demand for its Boxer indemnity to be paid in gold francs, delayed French ratification of the Nine-Power Treaty. To the great annoyance of China, the United States sided with France in this dispute, which, like the proverbial horseshoe-nail sequence, delayed the early calling of a tariff conference of crucial importance to disintegrating China. Germany and Russia, whose absence made the Washington agreements problematical, took realistic cognizance of the emergence of a new China. By doing so, they tried to outflank the Nine-Power Treaty.

In March of 1920, Ambassador Jules Jusserand informed the State Department of "the painful impression" the president's description of France as militaristic had caused in his home country.[8] But if anything, French recalcitrance at this conference made a painful impression on American officials and public opinion. Nevertheless, even though domestic politics in France delayed ratification of the Washington treaties until July, 1923, the New York *Times* interpreted ratification "as a somewhat belated but indisputably friendly gesture" to the United States.

The leadership the United States assumed in this international conference deprived the League of Nations of the prestige of accomplishment it needed so badly. It also seemed to contradict America's frequent reiteration of its intention to pursue only nonentangling

8. Jean Jules Jusserand to Frank L. Polk, March 11, 1920, Reel 107, in Woodrow Wilson Papers and Correspondence (microfilm), Library of Congress, Washington, D.C.

policies. But the United States viewed the recent treaties as multilateral understandings to promote peace, not bilateral alliances for war or regional hegemony.

THE RUHR CRISIS

International developments from the end of the peace conference until the invasion of the Ruhr in 1923 demonstrated how little the war had settled and how much the policies of the various governments continued to differ. To complicate matters, such experienced key figures as Clemenceau and Wilson no longer directed the policies of their countries. By 1923 Briand, Lloyd George, and Orlando had also lost their influential positions. But aside from the concern in the West about the Bolshevik danger, the basic foreign policies in the postwar era hardly assumed a new look. Victorious France feared the rapid resurgence of Germany and tried to prevent it. Germany reacted bitterly and strove to regain its status as a major power. Italy aspired to become the leading Mediterranean power, whether France liked it or not. Japan left no doubt about its intention to expand its trade and raw-materials bases. Britain and the United States demobilized quickly and continued to seek a balance of power on the European continent, which would involve an economically healthy Germany, as the surest way of promoting their own prosperity. The expansion of their economic influence promised them financial and political leadership. Their competition for it did not preclude their cooperation in the search for world peace. And finally, it was also true of these years that endeavors aiming at collective security by no means diminished the vitality of nationalism.

America's failure to ratify the Versailles treaty and the guarantee pact with France and its refusal to join the league bewildered the international community. Instead of assuming responsibility for the conditions its participation in the war and the shaping of the peace imposed upon the United States, it confounded the world with a return to its traditional aloofness. At Versailles, France had frustrated Wilson's peace plan for the twentieth century and the president had blocked France from imposing a crushing victor's peace. When the Versailles structure showed signs of crumbling, France fell back on its own devices to protect its security, even though its former allies frowned upon its unilateral actions. It developed a far-flung alliance system, crossed the Rhine under flimsy pretexts, and eventually took the "prudent precaution" of occupying the Ruhr Valley. It justified such occupations as guarantees for reparations and denied any intent to annex these regions permanently.

America's successive ambassadors in Paris, Hugh C. Wallace and Myron T. Herrick, were such Francophiles that they referred to such military actions as short-term defensive measures. President Wilson did not trust similar French assurances. He suspected that Marshal Foch was in fact pursuing the objectives the peace conference had denied France. Pierrepont B. Noyes, the American observer on the Rhineland High Commission, shared Wilson's suspicion. His talks with the French high commissioner early in 1920 convinced him of the French desire for the "wonderfully strong economic unit" of the Rhine and Ruhr.[9] President Harding and Secretary of State Hughes moved cautiously and indecisively when they witnessed France's military moves. For a time, they even contemplated the withdrawal of the American occupation forces. But their commander, General Henry T. Allen, recommended that they be left in the Rhineland as a restraining influence on the two ancient European rivals. Without the American presence in Europe, Allen was convinced, French aggression would be stepped up. France's conduct, he wrote Hughes, "is highly detrimental to the peace in Europe, consequently to our interest."[10]

Displeased with the thrust of postwar French policies, England and the United States began to show increasing concern for the survival of Germany's territorial integrity and economic revival. Such indications, of course, gave Berlin new hope. On several occasions, the Anglo-Americans took parallel steps. When French troops occupied Frankfurt and Darmstadt on April 6, 1920, without prior knowledge of the British, Foreign Secretary Lord Curzon protested sharply. As an official indication of its disapproval, the United States expressed serious concern. Just prior to the occupation of the Ruhr, both England and the United States cautioned Poincaré to consider the far-reaching consequences of such an inadmissible act. But instead of confronting the French statesman with a strong united front, Secretary Hughes actually declined the British suggestion that America send at least an observer to the crucial conference in Paris

9. Dieter Bruno Gescher, *Die Vereinigten Staaten von Nordamerika und die Reparationen, 1920–1924* (Bonn, 1956), 43–48, 132–35.

10. Henry Allen to Charles Evans Hughes, February 4, 1922, in Box 11, Hughes Papers.

at the beginning of 1923. The secretary of state evidently underrated the importance of functional processes in the conduct of foreign policy when he failed to understand that combined Anglo-American opposition to the occupation of the Ruhr would carry much more weight at the conference than Britain's alone. Hughes felt that the initiative for American participation in this conference had to be taken by Poincaré. This was of course the last thing the experienced French leader could have desired. Jusserand's professed ignorance of what lay behind rumors of the impending occupation left Hughes in a state of uncertainty. Poincaré evidently preferred to present the American secretary of state with a *fait accompli*. His evasive reaction to the secretary's call, just prior to the conference in January, 1923, for an expert commission to determine Germany's capacity to pay reparations leads to the same conclusion.

Otto von Wiedfeldt, the German ambassador in Washington, tried his best to convince Hughes that without America's renewed involvement in the dangerous European situation, turmoil—especially disorder inspired by bolshevism—might spread like a plague. But in view of the disappointing results of America's recent efforts to steer Europeans away from their perennial conflicts, the secretary of state hesitated to tip the political scale in Europe one way or the other. In the meantime Lloyd George had consulted with Premier Briand in attempts to tone down French fears regarding Germany's potential revenge. Briand sought a comprehensive alliance with Britain that would not only guarantee French soil against any future German aggression but would also become operative in case of "indirect aggressions" affecting French interests. Although agreeable to a treaty of reciprocal assistance, the British prime minister, keeping the likely attitude of Parliament in mind, declined to assume broader obligations. If nothing else, the Briand–Lloyd George discussions during 1921 at least explored ways and means of improving the unstable situation.

In January, 1922, Raymond Poincaré assumed the direction of the French government. Unlike Briand, he preferred to conduct foreign policy through diplomatic channels, exchange of precise notes, and personal conversations rather than international conferences. Above all, he believed that the interests of France would be compromised if their defense depended too much on cooperation with other powers. While reiterating the sanctity of the Versailles treaty, he was determined to implement it in a way that ran counter to the spirit of

Wilson's Fourteen Points and the league covenant. If Poincaré's policies at this time threatened to reduce Germany to impotence, his ultimate grasp for control of the Continent aroused the fears of both the American and the British governments. French denials with respect to such ultimate designs notwithstanding, the United States, Britain, and Germany believed that these designs were real. It is well to observe that perceptions usually affect history at least as much as verifiable facts. In the past, France had relied on Russia to counterbalance Germany. Now Bolshevik Russia also opposed French predominance in Europe. The rapprochement between Russia and Germany, embodied in the Rapallo treaty of April, 1922, served as a reminder that it was not wise to treat "outlaw" nations as if they possessed no rights. Their cooperation, actual or potential, introduced a new element.[11]

As far as France was concerned, Rapallo posed a potential threat to its security. To defuse it, Germany must not be allowed control over the means to industrial and military power—the iron, coal, and steel plants in the Rhine and Ruhr regions. The goal of attaining their separation from Germany, and possibly also that of Bavaria, therefore dictated the future course of French policy. Poincaré, a former general counsel of the French steel trust, the Comité des Forges, understood the far-reaching geopolitical significance of such a course. Germany's steadily deteriorating financial situation foreshadowed its impending default on reparation payments. If this happened, French retaliation—the occupation of the Rhine and Ruhr districts—loomed on the horizon. Both London and Washington had economic reasons of their own to caution France against such a drastic step. For its part, Germany held out an olive branch to France in the hope of providing time for rational and realistic solutions. The Germans proposed an international agreement not to make war without a plebiscite. As Secretary Hughes read the text of the proposal to Ambassador Jusserand, Germany was suggesting "that France, Great Britain, Italy, and Germany solemnly agree not to resort to war against each other for the period of one generation without being authorized to do so by a plebiscite of their own people. Germany would not hesitate to enter such an obligation." Hughes

11. Maurice Baumont, *La Faillite de la Paix (1918–1939)* (Paris, 1960), 164–67; W. N. Medlicott, *British Foreign Policy Since Versailles, 1919–1963* (London, 1968), 12–17; William A. Williams, "A Note on American Foreign Policy in Europe in the Nineteen Twenties," *Science and Society*, XXII (1958), 1–20.

pointed out the merit of this proposal, particularly in view of a growing popular disposition to oppose war. He welcomed its constructive nature; it could do no harm and might possibly contribute to Europe's stability.[12] Skeptical from the start, Jusserand confessed that France might be interested in such an agreement only if the United States guaranteed it, something the secretary ruled out. Poincaré promptly turned it down because "he did not trust the Germans."

Since France claimed that it was primarily concerned with the collection of reparations, the secretary of state proposed that this question be removed from politics and entrusted to a body of experts. Its findings as to Germany's capacity to pay would then lay the groundwork for a realistic *modus operandi* to finance the German obligations. The United States repeatedly acknowledged France's entitlement to reparations, but it objected to the impending seizure of the coal mines in the Ruhr Valley as a means of collecting them. Such a move, the Americans feared, would poison the international atmosphere without producing any positive results. As early as December 12, 1922, Undersecretary of State W. R. Castle expressed his opinion that French occupation of the Ruhr would be seen as going far beyond seeking financial satisfaction. It would have to be considered an attempt to weaken Germany permanently by placing the German steel industry under French control. If the French thought they could compel German workers to produce for them, Castle believed this to be a gross miscalculation. To minimize the effects of his impending move, Poincaré deemed it prudent to declare that he did not contemplate any "annexation" or "diminution" of German territory but was merely seeking to secure "certain guarantees." This assurance sounded as convincing to Secretary Hughes as Jusserand's denial of any French intention to occupy the Ruhr militarily.[13]

Dramatic events soon shed more light. On January 8, 1923, Ambassador Jusserand still pretended to know nothing about the rumored imminent occupation of the Ruhr. Should it materialize, the secretary of state told the ambassador unequivocally, American occupation troops would be withdrawn. Thinking quickly, the French diplomat asked Hughes at least to postpone such action "for fear it

12. Interviews with ambassadors, France, December 21, 26, 1922, in Box 174, Hughes Papers.

13. Ludwig Zimmermann, *Deutsche Aussenpolitik in der Ära der Weimarer Republik* (Göttingen, 1958), 140–41.

would give a wrong impression abroad." It would not only tend to isolate France but would attach to the occupation, which after all would be seeking only justice, the onus of a military aggression. When, two days later, France and Belgium sent "control missions" into the Ruhr, allegedly in response to Germany's default in its deliveries of wood and coal in 1922, President Harding indeed ordered the complete withdrawal of American troops on the Rhine. These missions, composed of engineers and troops under the command of a French general invested with "full dictatorial powers," were presumably sent to enforce the payment of reparations. Germany promptly protested this "unlawful oppression." Secretary Hughes was so upset that he did not hide his displeasure in his next conversation with Jusserand. In his judgment the occupation was not likely to yield substantial reparations, though it would sow seeds harmful to the peace and recovery of Europe. In principle, though, the United States emphasized its neutrality and, to protect its own interests, issued the reminder that "sovereignty over foreign territory is not transferred by such occupation."

In three fascinating personal letters, Ambassador Alanson B. Houghton tried to enlighten the secretary of state about the recent developments as seen from Berlin. Prior to the occupation of the Ruhr, Houghton observed, the war-weary German people had abandoned the idea of revenge. Wilhelm Cuno, the chancellor of the German Reich, was prepared to immediately offer France a substantial sum in cash and a peace pact. Poincaré's almost contemptuous rejection of such a pact, followed by his seizure of the Ruhr, completely reversed popular feelings. The presence of a French army of fifty-five thousand soldiers, "horse, foot, artillery, with the most modern machines and devices for making war," convinced the German people that domination, not reparations, had prompted the French action.

Ambassador Houghton, a Germanophile, agreed with the German people. In his opinion no amount of reparations would satisfy France. "Her real policy," he asserted, "is based . . . upon fear of what a strong and powerful Germany could and perhaps would do. . . . Because of [this] fear she purposes definitely and systematically to destroy her potential enemy." In other words France was trying "to remove the danger by eliminating the cause." When the German government decided to organize a passive resistance, the whole nation stood behind it. Germans would rather suffer hardships, imprisonment, and even death than help the French succeed. Their extraordinary spirit of nationalism did not bode well for the future of France. By persevering in their passive resistance, for which they had "methodically and in the greatest detail" planned for two years, the Germans hoped to drive the invaders out of the Ruhr. If the French thought that a mere show of strength would lead the German government and the Ruhr population to submit to them, they were in for a rude awakening. The local population took pride in being Westphalians, not Rhinelanders. And they counted on the complicated industrial Ruhr complex, which they knew how to operate, to pose insuperable challenges to the occupiers. More problems awaited the French if they thought the employment of harassing tactics would induce Ruhr companies to liquidate their enterprises and sell them for a song to eager French buyers. To replace knowledgeable technical and managerial personnel promised to be costly and time-consuming. Soldiers could not run the industry. Furthermore, France did not send sufficient numbers of competent engineers—indeed it did not even have them to send—to achieve a satisfactory level of production in the Ruhr. The importation of foreign workers might help to some extent, but their productivity was open to question. It was one thing to develop political plans; it invited defeat, however, to try to implement them without thorough industrial planning. Under these circumstances, a fight to the finish risked a second Waterloo.

For the sake of peace, Germans had been willing to ignore, if not forget, the humiliations they had suffered since the Armistice. They acknowledged the justification of manageable reparations, but they resented the unreasonable amounts imposed upon their impoverished country. As Ambassador Houghton pointed out, the view prevailed in Germany that the loss of colonial and continental territories, as well as resources, markets, and merchant ships, in addition to several milliards already paid to the Allies, amounted to a major penalty. Germans therefore regarded French encouragement of Rhenish separation, with the aim of dismembering the Reich, as an intolerable affront. Who authorized France, they asked, to establish its supremacy on the Continent at the expense of a neighbor that possessed superior manpower and industrial capacity, that excelled in scientific and technological respects, and whose vitality and contribution to civilization were widely admired? And finally, they asked, what was the difference between militarism and imperialism pursued by France and that pursued by Germany? Was the one inherently virtuous and the other inherently evil?

As the French accused the United States of having jeopardized their national security at Versailles and immediately thereafter, so the Germans accused the United States of having contributed to their national helplessness, first by compromising the integrity of the Fourteen Points and then by leaving Germany defenseless. As Ambassador Houghton knew only too well, under these circumstances the German people felt that America owed it some measure of protection against an invader who would never have dared to treat an armed Germany so provocatively. Germans felt betrayed because the United States had not only left them to the mercies of the French but, by removing its troops, had "made a bad situation even more desperate." In a frank and friendly conversation in September, 1923, the German chancellor, Dr. Gustav Stresemann, finally told the visiting chairman of the House Committee on Foreign Affairs: "The United States bore the greatest share of guilt for present conditions in Europe. . . . [Having] decided the war and the peace . . . she left Europe to stew in its own juice." He reminded the American legislator that at the time of the Armistice, the Germans had not made an unconditional surrender but had laid down their arms in response to the definite terms submitted by President Wilson, who was the official spokesman not only of the United States but of the Allies as well. Evasive constitutional arguments, therefore, could not absolve the United States from its moral responsibilities.

In view of all these German arguments, Ambassador Houghton recommended effective intervention. The letter he sent to Secretary Hughes on February 27, 1923, was so strongly worded that only quotations from it can do justice to its forcefulness.

> "Having destroyed any balance of power in Europe and left France for the moment all powerful, we have simply let loose a great elemental force which inevitably seeks to satisfy itself. It *is* a force. It can only be dealt with as a force. And unless it is met by armed force . . . it must be met by economic force in the shape of threatened ruin. . . . France must be met by force. One might as well attempt to reason with the law of gravitation. . . . I believe sincerely if it is to America's interest to save of what is left of German capital and German industry . . . some positive action is required without too much delay. . . . The franc suggests the obvious point of weakness. If it were possible, di-

> rectly or indirectly, for either or both Britain and ourselves, to remove or overcome the artificial support now given the franc, the franc would fall. . . . And France would recognize that while [she] can undoubtedly destroy Germany for a time, she herself may be swallowed up in the resultant ruin.[14]

Aware of Houghton's strong pro-German proclivities, the State Department was inclined to read his reports with caution. Internal French government evaluations of him were severely critical. Pierre de Margerie, the French ambassador in Berlin, accused his American colleague of being a man with "childish conceptions . . . a solemn mediocrity . . . [with] the innate tendency of the American race to preach and even to lecture."[15]

The steady deterioration of the French situation demonstrated the limits of military power as an instrument of policy. Although passive resistance brought financial ruin to their country, the Germans regarded it as a temporary catastrophe, whereas French-imposed national disintegration threatened to be a long-lasting humiliation. Meanwhile the disastrous economic ramifications of the Ruhr crisis increasingly affected the rest of the world. Stresemann, like Cuno before him, was willing to abide by the decision of a commission of experts, and criticized Hughes somewhat for not pushing this recommended procedure more vigorously. The urgency for a resolution of all the interrelated financial and political troubles pressed for early action. According to Stresemann, "the only means of alleviating the situation" was an international loan floated by the United States. The longer the crisis lasted, the more voices called for America's and England's diplomatic intervention to end it. Certainly the League of Nations lacked the means to accomplish such a result.

The knowledge that public opinion in the United States was about equally divided concerning the French seizure of the Ruhr made it more difficult for Hughes to act decisively. Ultimately he had to be guided by an objective analysis of all the ramifications of the deepening crisis. The opinions of private citizens, many of them ill-informed and probably still influenced by attitudes developed during the recent war, commanded attention. But by and large, they ex-

14. Alanson B. Houghton to Charles Evans Hughes, January 29, February 27, March 6, 1923, in Box 4B, General Correspondence, Hughes Papers.

15. Pierre de Margerie to Aristide Briand, March 20, 1926, CPEU, Vol. 6, AMAE.

pressed personal sentiments rather than national interests. Direct and indirect consequences of the Ruhr crisis compelled Hughes to become gradually more actively involved in it. A vicious circle developed. The payment of reparations depended largely on Germany's ability to export its goods. But the strangulation of German credit handicapped its industrial capacities and made prospective buyers hesitant to order goods. Obviously the Ruhr crisis disrupted normal trade. Italy and Switzerland, for instance, depended on German coal. In fact, the economies of all countries trading with Germany, the industrial heart of Europe, soon began to feel the pinch of declining exports and reduced access to German imports. French authorities in the Ruhr did their share to aggravate this situation. American firms suffered long and costly delays when these authorities repeatedly interfered with their transactions in the Ruhr.

Disturbing as these consequences of the occupation were, they paled by comparison with the potential problems growing out of the gigantic struggle for control of the steel industry. As long as neither France nor Germany singly controlled the coal, iron, and steel plants of the Rhine, Ruhr, and Saar regions, their industrial, military, and political power remained limited. As matters now stood, full control of all these resources by France, or by a combination of France and Germany with France in the driver's seat, promised to assure the French the "security" they coveted. For whoever was absolute master of this region was in a geopolitical position to guide the destiny of Europe. Indeed, by seizing the Ruhr, France threatened not only the interests of Germany but those of England and the United States as well. France would be able to compete with their steel industries and act in the world-political arena with greater independence from them than in the past. Henceforth, the policies of Britain and the United States, and those of the American steel industry, would strive to block the emergence of such a colossal competitor.[16]

If some French and German industrialists were tempted to explore the possibility of a European economic union, Charles Schwab, president of the Bethlehem Steel Corporation, also thought big from the beginning. He intended to convince the directors of the German steel industry that, under existing circumstances, it would be most

16. Ludwig Zimmermann, *Frankreichs Ruhrpolitik: Von Versailles bis zum Dawesplan* (Zürich, 1971), 164–65; C. K. Leith, "The World Iron and Steel Situation in Its Bearing on the French Occupation of the Ruhr," *Foreign Affairs*, I (1923), 146–51.

profitable for them to sell their works to him. Failing in such an effort, he would have been satisfied with becoming a controlling stockholder and chairman of their respective boards. The leading members of the Harding administration had been fully apprised of his plans before he traveled to Europe late in February, 1923. Ambassador Wiedfeldt cautioned Schwab not to be too optimistic about gaining such concessions. German industrialists cherished their independence, even from their own government, too much to relinquish it to foreigners. But he saw a certain advantage in signaling Schwab's ambitions to the French.

Although Schwab did not succeed with his plans, various American industries could temporarily take advantage of Germany's inability to protect its world trade. American steel, coal, chemical, leather, and textile companies promptly invaded markets in Europe and South America once dominated by German firms. But the occupation also resulted in economic disadvantages for the United States. Ultimately it was these disadvantages that forced Hughes's hand. Before long, Americans were preoccupied with the loss of the German market. It began to drag down the entire European economy, and the United States felt this enlarged impact. Spokesmen for American agriculture, which was particularly hard hit, pressed Congress to help restore their normal outlets. Various business representatives also grew impatient with the overall decline of the American economy and asked Washington to come up with a speedy diplomatic solution. In the background, moreover, ominous signs indicated the possibility of Franco-German monopolistic combinations in various fields as a price for peace between their two nations. Ever since the end of the war, some Frenchmen, prominent among them Jacques Seydoux, looked upon Franco-German economic cooperation as the best way to promote lasting peace and Europe's viability. They were inclined to hold the view that their politicians' emphasis on political approaches was tragically misplaced.

Any attempt to attach major significance to such enlightened soundings is contradicted by actual developments. Mutual suspicions of long standing could not be easily overcome, particularly under circumstances denying equality to one of the neighbors and implying an attempt at domination. Without first creating an atmosphere of mutual trust, the political and psychological barriers to aboveboard cooperation could not be removed. As the indications of possible Franco-German fusions increased, the time seemed, moreover, ripe for the United States and Britain to cut the Gordian knot.[17]

The Ruhr episode had been costly to both Germany and France. Its economic consequences produced the total breakdown of Germany's financial structure and confronted France with bleak prospects for maintaining the soundness of the franc. Although the franc had been frequently under attack since 1918, the French people displayed great optimism about its resiliency. During 1919 the dollar rate in Paris had moved from 5.45 to 10.87 francs; by the end of 1920, it had reached 16.80 francs; but it had returned to 10.90 francs in April, 1922. By late 1923, however, many Frenchmen found their faith in the franc badly shaken. They felt extremely uncomfortable witnessing not just the decline of their money but, just as serious, the concomitant erosion of old bourgeois values. Neither was it reassuring to find out that the French national debt had risen from 173 billion francs in 1918 to 428 billion in 1924. Realizing now that Germany would not pay meaningful reparations, the French people awoke to the hard fact that they would have to make greater sacrifices, for their own sake and to justify foreign loans. It took Poincaré some time before he was ready to admit that he had overreached himself. Near the end of the Ruhr crisis, it became obvious that only a Pyrrhic victory was in the offing.[18]

When on October 16, 1923, the German chargé in Paris confidentially advised Poincaré that passive resistance had been suspended and that Germany requested "conversation with the French government regarding the commencement of work in the Ruhr," the French premier icily replied that he would take up this question with the German industrialists directly. In the same fashion he disposed of the German offer to make proposals to the reparations commission. Poincaré was opposed to negotiations with the German government directly. Still, the American chargé in Paris believed that "some mild expression of opinion from Washington might sway [the delicate situation] in favor of a constructive line of action."

17. See Werner Link, "Die Ruhrbesetzung and die wirtschaftspolitischen Interessen der USA," *Vierteljahrshefte für Zeitgeschichte*, XVII (1969), 372–82, which is excellent, and Charles S. Maier, *Recasting Bourgeois Europe: Stabilization in France, Germany, and Italy in the Decade After World War I* (Princeton, 1975), 274–75.

18. Martin Wolfe, *The French Franc Between the Wars, 1919–1939* (New York, 1951), 27–32; Tom Kemp, *The French Economy, 1913–39: The History of a Decline* (London, 1972), 77–85.

DEBTS, REPARATIONS, AND TRADE

The largely politically motivated maneuvers to collect debts and reparations gave way to more businesslike methods only after years of fruitless conferences. The developing destabilization of currencies and world trade did not bring the powers involved to their senses until 1924. Although all these powers shared responsibility for postwar instability, three of them—France, Germany, and the United States—contributed to it to a larger degree than the rest.

The decision of the Versailles conference not to set a collectable fixed sum, and instead leave the amount up to the reparations commission to determine, opened a Pandora's box that created troubles for more than a decade. Time and again, simple questions turned into complex disagreements. How much should Germany pay? For what should Germany pay? How could Germany pay? Would Germany pay even if it could? Did France merely want reparations for damages done, or was it determined to use reparations as a means of removing Germany as a rival? How would the rest of Europe and the Anglo-Americans react to French predominance on the Continent? Would the Allies present a united front vis-à-vis Germany on the question of reparations and vis-à-vis the United States on the question of debts? Would the United States ultimately acknowledge a linkage between debts and reparations? Would the whole world drift into a dangerous storm because national leaders lacked the courage and vision to get together realistically on these issues?

The pages of diplomatic exchanges and memoranda are so full of these tediously repeated questions that an integrated focus on the major issues promises a clearer understanding of the frequently confounding technicalities. Lest one get lost in the labyrinth of this technical complex, let it be said at the outset that the reparations commission's 1921 compromise of 132 billion marks was gradually reduced to 50 billion. Altogether, the Reich paid about 20 billion, much of it with money borrowed abroad. In terms of American dollars, Germany made reparation payments to the tune of $4,470,300,000. More than half of this amount, $2,475,000,000, had been borrowed in the United States. In other words, the United States paid over half the reparations bill. Since the Allies had paid to the United States only $2,606,340,000 on their debts, Uncle Sam practically took care of the entire war debt. The United States could hardly have fared any worse, particularly in light of the fact that it denied all along the existence of a linkage between these separate obligations. And evidently, neither France, spearheading the drive for reparations, nor Germany, maneuvering to dodge their payment, anticipated the ruinous consequences of their actions for Europe as a whole. In financial terms alone, the cost of the by-products of their self-centered policies ultimately far exceeded the sums over which they quibbled so much. In the perspective of history, they made the "utopian" Wilson look like an amazingly farsighted realist.[19]

On closer examination, each of the "simple" questions involved intricate complications. While a justifiable fixed amount of reparations might have simplified their payment, each of the concerned parties could also seek advantages from an unspecified amount. If France really intended to cripple Germany's economic and military capacities, it could have imposed capricious penalties for defaults. For its part, Germany saw in this somewhat ambiguous condition an opportunity to haggle down the total amount and, eventually, reduce it to a phantom. And Great Britain saw in it a wedge for eventual revisions.

In regard to the "simple" question of Germany's capacity to pay, it made a difference whether vengeful politicians or financial experts undertook this determination. In his New Haven speech in December, 1922, Secretary of State Hughes proposed that a body of respected experts be named to calculate Germany's capacity to pay affordable annuities over a long period of time. This procedure held out the best hope for solving this pernicious problem once and for all. But Poincaré reacted by showing interest primarily in Germany's immediate capacity to pay. According to Ambassador Jusserand, "Poincaré was anxious to have the cooperation of the United States in such an inquiry." But in view of the volatile situation created by the Ruhr occupation, the secretary of state responded by showing his annoyance at the uncompromising severity France displayed in its dealings with Germany. "If Germany broke up," he asked Jusserand, "would France be secure?" To disabuse France of such an illusion, Hughes ventured to predict that "the Germans

19. Sally Marks, "The Myths of Reparations," *Central European History*, XI (1978), 231–55, and *The Illusion of Peace: International Relations in Europe, 1918–1933* (New York, 1976). See also Marc Trachtenberg, *Reparations in World Politics: France and European Economic Diplomacy, 1916–1923* (New York, 1980).

would come together again in the future and then France would have neither security nor reparations." There could be no recuperation in Germany, he reiterated, if the French government persisted in placing "obstacles in the way of the only avenue of helpfulness that seemed to be open." The reparations question was not a matter for France alone to decide. The United States did have considerable interest in its fair and reasonable liquidation. The different approaches of the American secretary of state and the French premier obviously aimed at different results.

Whatever total amount would be payable, it was generally recognized that most of it had to be earned through German exports. The cost of the war had impoverished Germany, and the peace treaty had curtailed its sources of income. These factors, in addition to its immediate reparation payments in the amount of about eight billion marks, reduced the prospect of its ability to transfer to the Allies sizable amounts of cash. Even if it had been possible thus to gratify the Allies, such action would have ruined Germany's credit and, with it, its capacity to finance the industry that was supposed to produce the earnings to be handed to the Allies. Also, the major industrial countries could not lose sight of the potentially catastrophic effects of such greatly enlarged German exports on their prosperity. For good measure, European and American tariff walls and complications likely to arise from massive currency transfers added to the perplexity of this problem. Neomercantilistic policies could not be easily implemented in the modern industrial age.

In an effort to free itself from burdens imposed upon it, vanquished Germany, like victorious France, continued to fight the recent war by diplomatic means. Germany tried to outmaneuver the victors by pleading inability to pay reparations and by asking for delays, loans, reductions, and revisions. In the last analysis, Germany's willingness to pay depended on its good will. To induce it to make major sacrifices, Lloyd George recommended, at a conference in London on December 19, 1921, that his French colleagues foster "hope of recovery" and promise "to withdraw a part of the Armies of Occupation if she [Germany] paid her installments for two or three years." This understanding attitude fell on deaf ears. As skeptical as ever, Briand and his assistants believed that the leaders of big business in Germany simply did not want their government to pay reparations. Germany's deteriorating condition, the French leaders had concluded, "was not due to the burden of reparations, it was due to bad finance." As they saw it, what was at issue was not Germany's capacity to pay but rather its "determination not to pay."[20] As Colonel George Harvey, America's ambassador in England, wrote to a friend in August, 1922: "The Germans outwitted . . . the segregated Allies. . . . They began to inflate their currency by degrees so slight as to create no particular alarm, but they continued the process gradually with amazing skill and ingenuity, until the Allies suddenly woke to the fact that they had been duped, and that a condition had been created which rendered them powerless." The Germans marshaled all their resources for their speedy recovery. The French feared this development, but they did not succeed in aborting it. On the contrary, they overreached themselves to the extent that they antagonized not only Germany but England and the United States as well. The more they desired a united front against Germany, the more they alienated these friendly powers. And the more divided the former allies were, the greater were Germany's chances to modify, if not entirely nullify, the framework of Versailles.

The United States discovered belatedly that existing conditions did not permit it to be a loner in the interdependent world it had helped into being. Indeed, it could not escape responsibility for the ensuing sequence of events. In the light of European history, one cannot lightly dismiss the frequent charge that victorious France suffered from a Napoleon complex. Its Rhine and Ruhr policy in the early 1920s, its military actions in disregard of its allies, its militaristic posture, and its anything-but-conciliatory attitude toward defeated Germany offered disturbing evidence supporting such a charge. But all these incriminating factors represented only one side of the argument. In many respects physically weaker than Germany, a militaristic power that had several times violated its territorial integrity, France had every right to guard itself against another invasion and the humiliation and suffering it would entail. When the centerpiece of its future security system collapsed with America's failure to ratify the tripartite guarantee pact, what was France to do? In this circumstance it fell back on measures it might possibly have preferred

20. Great Britain, Foreign Office, *Documents on British Foreign Policy, 1919–1939*, ed. E. L. Woodward and Rohan Butler (42 vols.; London, 1967), 1st Series, XV, 764–67.

to avoid. When the United States neither ratified the Versailles treaty, for whatever reasons, nor joined the League of Nations, France nearly panicked and trembled for its future. As was the case with the treaty and the league, the United States did not consider the consequences of its official withdrawal from the reparations commission. It opened the floodgates to waters that ultimately engulfed America as well as Europe. For with the absence of the United States from the commission, France and Belgium could easily outvote Great Britain's moderating proposals.

Aside from speculations about larger French designs, the policies of France with respect to Germany differed in principle from those of Great Britain and the United States. Europe's prosperity before the war depended a great deal on Germany's vigorous industry. The Anglo-Americans did not see how prosperity could return without Germany's vital contributions. These Western statesmen hoped that Germany would also help stem the flood of bolshevism and nip in the bud the as-yet-remote threat of another war, though these were secondary considerations. The speedy removal of the reparations obstacle therefore emerged as a matter of the highest priority for the revitalization of world trade, which America and the entire British Empire desired, preferably with the concurrence of France, but, if necessary, without it. Objectionable as such potential Anglo-American domination appeared to the French, their alternatives were not limited to just being resigned to it. An imaginative political détente with Germany, facilitated by a friendly combination of French and German industrial enterprises, and on a basis of full equality, held out very positive possibilities. But their fleeting shadow usually disappeared in the polluted air of European history.

The direction of French policy in Europe might conceivably also have been different had the United States originally acknowledged the linkage between debts and reparations. Its stubborn insistence that, legally, the one issue had nothing to do with the other could not refute the French argument that, from a practical viewpoint, France could not afford both to pay its debts to the United States and also to finance its reconstruction unless it received reparations. This position *ipso facto* established an interrelationship between the two financial issues. Repeated American intimations that generous downward revisions of reparations would spill over on America's generous treatment of the debt issue certainly implied official acknowledgment of this linkage. Even France hinted occasionally, however ambiguously, that it might go along with reductions, provided the United States translated its intimations into specific proposals.

Uneducated public opinion in France and the United States did its share to persuade their politicians to collect. Although it does not excuse their unbusinesslike treatment of debts and reparations, such ill-advised influence accomplished the opposite of what it sought. The failure of America's leaders to lead public opinion in these matters and to be courageously guided by pragmatic realism evidently reflected their larger failure to assume unhesitatingly the new leadership thrust upon them. The American government simply was not prepared for such a challenging role.

Interestingly, Germany was among the first to grasp the significance of America's key position in the world. To be on the safe side, even during the war, it had left the diplomatic door open to America. It trustfully approached President Wilson for an armistice and counted on the fair-mindedness of the United States to protect it from French excesses and abuses. Unlike Poincaré, who in the early 1920s objected to America's sprawling influence in European affairs, the Germans welcomed its role as an arbiter in them. Frankly, this friendly disposition was in part founded on the realization that only the United States possessed the means to be of genuine help. Walter Rathenau, the highly reputed industrialist-statesman, for instance, contended already in 1921 that the question of reparations could not be resolved without America's assistance. His ingenious scheme combined debts and reparations in a way to satisfy all parties. Germany, he suggested, must seize the initiative and offer to the Allies its readiness to take over their debts to the United States in exchange for being relieved of corresponding reparation payments. Besides demonstrating its good will, such a swap promised to benefit Germany in at least two tangible respects: lower interest rates and more bearable amortizations. But fear of rejection kept the German government from exploring the feasibility of such a proposal.[21] The political leaders of the Weimar Republic, particularly Stresemann and Heinrich Brüning, fully agreed with Rathenau's basic contention that the whole complex of issues growing out of the late war could not be effectively tackled without America's active cooperation. Whether the financial and industrial giant across the

21. Walter Rathenau, *Tagebuch, 1907–1922* (Düsseldorf, 1967), 242.

Atlantic realized it or not, peace and prosperity could no more be separated from each other than interdependent economies. Oceans had always been highways as well as barriers. Inasmuch as the Allies were not inclined to reduce German reparations as long as the United States was not disposed to cancel or reduce Allied debts, Germany had to turn to the United States for relief. For all practical purposes, the United States, not France or Great Britain, held the key to the reparations dilemma.[22]

Despite the difficulty of the Weimar Republic's early years of existence, its leadership blazed the trail toward recovery, treaty revision, and return to great-power status with consummate skill. Stresemann, foreign minister from 1923 to 1929, pursued policies designed to lead Germany along this trail. In his judgment, it was absolutely essential to bring about a lasting conciliation between France and Germany. Without it, another devastating war was a definite likelihood. With it, the close economic ties between them would bring prosperity and Europe's independence. The trouble in the past, he rationalized, had basically not been with Germany, but with French policy toward Germany. Even now, conciliation would require French evacuation of the Rhine and Ruhr regions, abandonment of the notion of a separate Rhenish entity, and reversal of French policies in the East, particularly those concerning Poland, that aimed at weakening Germany. He was aware of strategic conflicts within France and hoped that the economy-oriented groups favoring cooperation would prevail over paranoiac military concerns. As he saw it, France had alternative choices: they boiled down to promotion of a genuine entente or perpetuation of alienating provocations reflecting an abnormal obsession with security. Stresemann had no illusion about the time and tact required to restore trust between the two nations.

To provide the time, moral support, and vitally important finances Germany needed in the meantime, Stresemann also considered it absolutely essential to rely on the United States and, as far as possible, Great Britain. He realized that up to 1923 the Anglo-Americans, while showing understanding for Germany's plight, preferred not to deal firmly with French policies to which they took exception. But when the disquieting ramifications of the Ruhr oc-

22. Heinrich Brüning, *Memoiren, 1918–1934* (Stuttgart, 1970), 78–80. See also the excellent work by Eckhard Wandel, *Die Bedeutung der Vereinigten Staaten von Amerika für das deutsche Reparationsproblem, 1924–1929* (Tübingen, 1971), 166–67.

cupation threatened to affect their own interests, they no longer hesitated to put pressure on France. The world economy registered warning signals, and almost nothing mattered more to the United States and the British Empire than the health of the world economy. When the Western powers seemed substantially inclined to leave Germany to rely on its own devices, that nation frightened them with a renewed emphasis on its historic *Ostpolitik*. Actually, Central Europeans dreaded Bolshevik expansion as much as the West. But the Anglo-Americans were so concerned about a Russo-German understanding that they felt the time had come for overall revision of the Versailles system.

Still, as much as they desired Franco-German conciliation, the central requisite for European stability, they did not at all welcome a Franco-German industrial fusion. From their point of view it was fortunate that neither France nor Germany was ready for this kind of common enterprise, which would have confronted them with undesirable competition. As a German, Stresemann appreciated America's helpful assistance, but as a European, he, like the French, frowned upon the extent of America's ascending influence in the Old World. Since the French, too, valued their ties with America, Stresemann calculated correctly, the United States could use its offices to persuade France to be more conciliatory. More than that, as France intended to use the reparations as a controlling check on Germany, the war debts gave the United States leverage to induce France to let Germany regain a status of equality. Washington could, moreover, exercise its influence to help treat Germany with dignity, as a respected member of the family of nations, a matter of greatly underrated significance both at the time and since.[23]

Stresemann approached Germany's future in the broader setting of contemporary capitalism. Early in 1924 he read a paper that had been prepared in the Auswärtiges Amt, Sonderreferat Wirtschaft. It contended that American banks were much concerned about huge capital surpluses for which they could not find appropriate places for investment. If the United States could somehow be persuaded

23. Eric Sutton (ed. and trans.), *Gustav Stresemann; His Diaries, Letters, and Papers* (3 vols.; London, 1935–40), II, 12–14, 246–47. See also Michael-Olaf Maxelon, *Stresemann und Frankreich: Deutsche Politik der Ost-West Balance* (Düsseldorf, 1972), 95–99, 181–83, 231–41, and Stephen A. Schuker, *The End of French Predominance in Europe: The Financial Crisis of 1924 and the Adoption of the Dawes Plan* (Chapel Hill, 1976), 383–92.

to invest large sums of idle and unproductive money in German industry, not only would Germany's capitalistic system benefit, but its economic recovery and the revision of the Versailles treaty would almost certainly be accelerated. Germany was financially ruined by the end of the war, long before reparations and the Ruhr occupation made it official. Under these circumstances a German-American connection appealed to Stresemann as the best way out. The more heavily America invested in Germany, the greater would be its interest in protecting its investments. In other words, the combination of Germany's lack of financial liquidity and America's surplus of capital held out the promise of extraordinary mutual benefits. As France and Great Britain enlisted American financial aid to win the war, Stresemann set out to enlist it to win the peace.

Although the Republican party had rejected Wilson's international program, it was not prepared to take bold initiatives of its own. It was "concerned" about world trends after 1920, but with the exception of disarmament, it hesitated to become too involved in Europe. Although England understood the need for reviewing the harshest stipulations of the Versailles treaty, it lacked the strength to fight this battle alone. Private hints that only a strong Anglo-American front could accomplish such a feat did not fall on fertile soil in Washington. Like other European powers, Britain endeavored to be on good terms with the United States for several reasons. In the early 1920s, French activities in Germany, the Balkans, Morocco, Egypt, Turkey, and other countries foreshadowed a clash of interests potentially capable of leading to an Anglo-French conflict. Not only French attitudes toward the German question and reparations, but even the general direction of French foreign policy temporarily disturbed Great Britain and the United States. France appeared to be the power to watch if the European equilibrium was to be preserved.

But actually, even at the height of its apparent supremacy, the diplomatic position of France showed signs of erosion. Although Belgium officially stood behind France, unofficially the Belgians, too, would have welcomed America's moderating influence on France. The Italians also had indicated their interest in tightening the reins of French dominance in Europe. Secretary of State Hughes limited himself to speeches until the Ruhr situation and British prodding convinced him that stronger measures had to be taken to prevent the spread of chaos. In the summer of 1923 "the painful impression" made by French responses to British proposals for "a final settlement of German reparations" signaled the approaching end of the period of restraint in British relations with France. Finally, the British chargé in Washington, H. G. Chilton, recorded the British position on reparations in his aide-mémoire of October 13, 1923. Noting that European action to head off the drift into economic disaster was not feasible in the immediate future, he officially advised the secretary of state that "His Majesty's Government have for long entertained the belief that the cooperation of the United States Government is an essential condition of any real advance towards settlement."

In the meantime, the Ruhr crisis had reached a climax. Stresemann, who had assumed the direction of the German government in September, 1923, abandoned the financially ruinous passive resistance. France had by then learned that its stern course did not help collect reparations. This disappointing result and the decline of the French franc began to shake the people's faith in Poincaré's policies. Other powers, moreover, combined to call a halt to further unilateral French interventions in Germany. President Calvin Coolidge made the essential move when he gave the go-ahead signal for private American citizens who possessed the required expertise to participate in drawing up a new reparations scheme.

The prospect of American bankers becoming involved in the restoration of Germany's financial stability and therefore its capacity to pay reparations could not but please Poincaré. But the notion entertained by Jules Cambon, his representative at the conference of ambassadors in November, 1923, that France still reserved the right to take unilateral measures against Germany, exposed France to stiff diplomatic remonstrances. Even the Belgian delegate let Cambon know that, with respect to new sanctions, he was authorized to go along only with a unanimous vote of the conference. It is not clear whether this de facto diplomatic isolation had a sobering effect on Poincaré, but he was too much the realist not to see the advantages of a new reparation study in which American experts participated. His instructions to Jean Louis Barthou, the French representative on the reparations commission, left little doubt, however, that whatever the experts decided to recommend must be within the framework of the Versailles treaty. He would support anything that resulted in improved reparation payments. But the general thrust of his German policy continued to distance him very fundamentally from the Anglo-Saxons.[24]

With constructive input by Charles G. Dawes, chairman of the board of directors of the Chicago Central Union Trust Company, and Owen D. Young, chairman of the board of General Electric, the so-called Dawes Plan was ready by April 9, 1924. Among its more significant recommendations were its provisions for realistic reparation payments during the first five years, an international loan of 800 million gold marks to cover the first year's reparations, supervised reorganization of Germany's financial structures, unanimity in case of any future sanction, and the immediate military evacuation of the Ruhr. Looking ahead, the Dawes Plan wisely provided for the means to implement its provisions. The German railroads were to be restructured into an independent organization, the surpluses of which would be set aside to pay the interest for the obligations. The interest of the five-billion-mark mortgage imposed upon German industry was also to be paid into the Dawes account.

Although the Dawes Plan did not deal with the total amount of reparations, it improved the international atmosphere sufficiently to work out further details with more confident expectations than in the recent past. Several other developments also encouraged the success of the London conference in July and August of 1924, at which the participating powers, including the Germans, were asked to adopt the Dawes Plan. In England the Labour party had occupied the seat of power since the end of January. Prime Minister Ramsey MacDonald had never concealed his friendly leanings toward Germany and his opposition to the French occupation of the Ruhr. Perhaps an even greater impact was produced by Poincaré's fall on May 11. Although he had indicated his approval of the Dawes Plan in principle, his successor, Edouard Herriot, was likely to be more accommodating. Herriot and the Radical Socialists had all along been uncomfortable with Poincaré's Ruhr policy. Nevertheless, Herriot knew very well that if he went along with all the provisions of the Dawes Plan, he would encounter bitter opposition in the French parliament. Expressing this fear to Secretary of State Hughes, who had insistently urged him to carry out the plan at once, Herriot pro-

24. Gescher, *Die Vereinigten Staaten . . . und die Reparationen*, 194–95, 203–13; Jacques Bariéty, *Les relations franco-allemandes après la première guerre mondiale* (Paris, 1977), 262–75, 495–97, 754–55.

tested: "I'll fall! I'll fall!" Whereupon Hughes observed that "the Premier would fall anyway, if he did not carry out the Plan."

MacDonald's skillful contributions to the success of the London conference have been widely recognized. The British Empire had much at stake at this gathering. British leaders sought to restrain French unilateralism and restore Germany as a stabilizing factor in Europe. In response to MacDonald's warning that Great Britain would not sign the London agreements unless France evacuated the Ruhr, Herriot tried to deflect this move by turning to the Germans directly. He seemed disposed to shorten the Ruhr occupation if Germany agreed to armaments control, and he proposed a Franco-German treaty of commerce. But the spokesmen of the Weimar Republic—Stresemann, Hans Luther, and Wilhelm Marx—realized the transcendent value of Germany's reliance on the United States and Great Britain and turned these suggestions down.[25]

By strange coincidence Secretary of State Hughes managed to be in Europe at the time of the London conference. Quite in character, he did not actively participate in its deliberations. He had officially gone to Europe in his capacity as president of the American Bar Association. But his presence on the Continent opened to him many opportunities to lend strong unofficial support to the adoption of the Dawes Plan. It embodied, after all, many of the suggestions he had recommended long ago. In Paris he had a heart-to-heart talk with Poincaré, whose opposition Herriot feared the most. With reference to Anglo-French asperities following the Ruhr invasion, the American statesman reminded Poincaré of the special interest the United States took in British security. The French leader undoubtedly caught the double meaning of the secretary's explanation that "Great Britain was America's best and most honourable debtor." In the course of this after-dinner conversation Hughes confronted the influential French statesman with a choice: "Here is the American policy. If you turn this down, America is through."[26] Similarly, in his discussions with the political leaders in Germany he impressed upon them that there would be no further American aid if they rejected the Dawes Plan or introduced unreasonable amendments and reservations. With the full weight of the United States behind him, Hughes could

25. Pierre Olivier Lapie, *Herriot* (Paris, 1967), 142–45; Zimmermann, *Frankreichs Ruhrpolitik*, 282–91.

26. "The Dawes Plan," Beerits memorandum, March 1, 1928, in Box 172, Hughes Papers.

thus informally exercise pressures of enormous impact. The use of private bankers in these transactions also seemed to him preferable to direct government financing, particularly from the point of view of domestic politics. He evidently was not concerned that the private bankers' enhanced role in international affairs would to some degree diminish the State Department's assumption of responsibility for the conduct of foreign affairs.

The most delicate issues at the London conference concerned the evacuation of the Ruhr and the problem of future sanctions. Any concession Herriot would make in these respects was of course subject to close scrutiny. The likely reactions of the French politicians, press, and public were constantly on his mind. The House of Morgan and the governor of the Bank of England put extraordinary pressure on the French premier when they let it be known that they could not advance sizable loans to Germany unless unilateral sanctions were banned in the future. Following the war, financiers clearly outranked generals. Uncertain political conditions had to be brought under control so as not to interfere with the bankers' business of making profits. With respect to the evacuation of the Ruhr, Herriot found himself facing such a solid insistence on it that he secured the cabinet's approval for advancing the evacuation by one year. It took the diplomatic intervention on the part of MacDonald and Ambassador Frank B. Kellogg to dissuade Stresemann from seeking a still earlier evacuation. This conference accomplished much because of the determination and cooperation exhibited by the major participants, and its achievements held out the promise of a more sensible future. Did they really amount to a turning point?

A major test in the fall of 1925 ended with an affirmative answer. The European powers signed a series of treaties at the small Swiss town of Locarno, hopefully ushering in an era of peaceful cooperation. Germany, France, and Belgium agreed to set up a demilitarized zone along the Rhine, which they pledged never to cross to attack one another. Great Britain and Italy signed as guarantors of this "magnificent and unhoped for" reconciliation. In addition, Germany's arbitration treaties with Poland and Czechoslovakia, providing for peaceful settlements of troublesome boundary disputes, and Germany's admission to the League of Nations created considerable euphoria. That Locarno did not include any German commitment with respect to its eastern frontiers was at the time played down. It is also noteworthy that these forward steps were facilitated by the growing "European idea," which emphasized the need for the unity of Europe as the only effective means of dealing with the political and economic penetration of the Continent by the United States.

Europeans were not bothered by the dichotomy in their dealings with the United states. They liked to make use of America as much as they could, and they tried to minimize its direct influence as much as possible. Stresemann counted on America's high financial stakes in Germany to improve his political maneuverability directly and indirectly. His secret meeting with Briand in the small French town of Thoiry, on September 17, 1926, revealed a great deal more than an extraordinary attempt to put a quick end to the unsatisfactory results of past policies. Its success would have raised Europeans' hopes that they could regain mastery of their continent; its failure signified that, given the postwar constellation of powers, Europe was not yet ready to do so. Stresemann's priorities were the liberation of the Rhine and Ruhr and the return of the Saar at whatever cost, with America's help. Briand's primary concern in 1926 was the declining value of the franc. Conscious that the bargaining value of an advanced withdrawal from the Rhineland would decrease with the passage of time, he was not disinclined to cash in on an early evacuation. It is noteworthy that the two statesmen saw great merit in conversations *à deux,* away from the limelight of the press. Such personal exchanges allowed explorations possible only in an informal atmosphere. In their premature discussion they explored the possibility of a mutual accommodation in which the marketing of German railroad obligations in the United States played a key role. The amounts were sizable enough to stabilize the French budget and the franc. But though the scheme was apparently feasible, it was blocked.

Parker Gilbert, the American agent-general for reparations payments, counseled against it. In the first place, he wanted to reserve these railroad obligations for a final, overall liquidation of the postwar financial issues. Second, President Coolidge and the secretary of the treasury deemed it inadvisable for American bankers to agree to huge financial transactions with France before the Mellon-Bérenger agreement on debts had been ratified. By December, the franc had unexpectedly recovered, and political opposition to the scheme in France shelved it altogether. One of the losers in this aborted scheme was the banking firm of Dillon, Read and Company, which evidently had taken the initiative in promoting it. The commissions to be gained from placing the German railroad obligations appeared as attractive to Dillon, Read as the demonstration that it could compete with J. P. Morgan, the leading American banker in France.[27]

All parties became anxious for a comprehensive settlement. Even Poincaré appeared to be gradually moving in the direction of a conciliatory attitude toward Germany, provided it paid its reparations. The Dawes Plan was meant to serve only as a stopgap measure. Sooner or later it was to be replaced by an overall liquidation of the controversial financial and occupation problems. This legacy of the war called for farsighted political and economic decisions transcending narrow national interests; but it was treated by the Allies, particularly France, as a question of safeguarding their military victory.

Germany's behavior was no better. Hjalmar Schacht, the president of the German Reichsbank, maneuvered Germany's finances in such a way as to impede the payment of reparations. The gradual lowering of the Reichsbank's discount rate starting in January, 1926, had the effect, for instance, of reducing foreign credits. Consequently, Germany's gold and foreign currency reserves diminished to an extent that its reparation transfers were put in jeopardy. Parker Gilbert went so far as to accuse Schacht in September, 1927, of "openly and actively working for a breakdown of reparation transfers."[28]

The governor of the Bank of France also acted at this time in a questionable manner when he threatened the stability of the British pound by steadily withdrawing French gold holdings from London. As he admitted in his diary, he was prepared to play the game of financial diplomacy by using monetary transfers "to further the political objectives of the Poincaré government." Interestingly, as far back as 1922, André Tardieu had charged American and British bankers with aiming at "an imperialism of gold." By returning after the war to so-called free competition under the guise of not-so-open doors, Tardieu believed, the Anglo-Saxons were looking after their selfish interests at the expense of the rest of the world.

The politics of bankers, including the easy money policy of the American Federal Reserve Bank, created situations that discour-

27. Jon Jacobson, *Locarno Diplomacy: Germany and the West, 1925–1929* (Princeton, 1972), 86–90; Wandel, *Bedeutung der Vereinigten Staaten*, 42–77.

28. Wandel, *Bedeutung der Vereinigten Staaten*, 102–109.

aged coordinated international action, which was an overriding need in this period. While American bankers preferred to see the government stay out of the foreign investment process, the Commerce Department, headed by Herbert Hoover, liked to tie it to safeguarding opportunities for American manufacturers. In the general interest of sound international developments, Hoover also argued that bankers should not make funds available for unproductive purposes. In his opinion political instability would be perpetuated as long as financial instability prevailed.[29]

Owen D. Young, chairman of a committee charged with preparing a "final liquidation of the war," presented his compromise reparations plan in the spring of 1929. It asked Germany to pay annuities for fifty-nine years. They were lower than those of the Dawes Plan. To make it easier for Germany to pay them, they were kept below two billion marks per year during the first ten years, a reasonably manageable amount. For the first thirty-seven years the average annuity amounted to $473,700,000, of which France was to receive 52.7 percent. The average annuity for the remaining twenty-two years came to about $381 million, to be paid out of the profits of the Bank for International Settlements (BIS). This bank, located in Basel, replaced the reparations commission and the supervisory structure under the Dawes Plan. It was significant that the BIS freed Germany from foreign controls and helped further its financial autonomy.[30]

The functions of the BIS included disbursing reparations and acting as a link to the various central banks. France looked forward to at least regular reparation payments, despite a further reduction of reparations and guarantees as well as a British-induced early evacuation of the Rhineland. The Hague conference at which the details of the Young Plan were adopted appeared to be another harbinger of more promising developments. Alas, for opposite reasons the Young Plan encountered vociferous opposition in both France and Germany. Many nationalistic Germans took a stand against "fulfillment" of any "tribute" payments. Many Frenchmen spoke up against the gradual whittling down of their fair and legally due claims. Clemenceau himself summed it all up with the comment "From Versailles to the Hague, what a tale of surrenders!" To a large

29. Joseph Brandes, *Herbert Hoover and Economic Diplomacy: Department of Commerce Policy, 1921–28* (Pittsburgh, 1962), 45–47.

30. Ernest L. Bogart, *The Young Plan and Other Papers* (Claremont, Cal., 1931), 11–25.

extent he blamed the United States. Nevertheless, in the end sufficient numbers of French and German deputies swallowed this latest pill in the hope that in the meantime a general cure could be found for the persistent ills.[31]

But the competitive national state system stood in the way. The same officials who called for collective security dared not compromise their own national interests. Several developments between October, 1929, and October, 1933, moreover, exposed them to such severe shock waves that the whole international structure showed signs of crumbling. The collapse of America's unbalanced prosperity following the Wall Street tumble, the attempted customs union between Germany and Austria, the Austrian Kreditanstalt's financial difficulties, the growing political strength of German nationalists, and the dreaded implications of Adolf Hitler's rise to power abetted the deepening economic deterioration. Before long, it resulted in an extraordinary panic, characterized by flight of capital, foreign-currency difficulties, the drying up of credits, and massive unemployment.

The combination of these factors seriously threatened Germany's capacity to honor the obligations it had assumed under the Young Plan. Chancellor Brüning felt he could no longer cope with the impending domestic and foreign political disaster. It was easy enough for him to consider asking Germany's creditors for relief through a spectacular gesture, such as a five-year moratorium on all intergovernmental debts and reparations, but actually to urge them to grant such a breathing spell was much more difficult. Just the news of such a request was likely to compound his problems. American, British, and Italian leaders followed developments nervously and searched for ways to bring this emergency under control. Much depended on the attitude of France.

By coincidence, France was temporarily in a position to weather the crisis unusually well. Its low unemployment, stable currency, and military might were underpinned by gold holdings second only to those of the United States. France used this strength to pursue its own objectives, regardless of the consequences to the rest of the world. This seemed to be the time, at last, to check the role of Germany's benevolent Anglo-Saxon protectors and shape France's re-

31. Clemenceau, *Grandeur and Misery of Victory*, 312–16. See also Etienne Weill-Reynal, *La politique française des réparations* (Paris, 1945), 71–73.

lationship with its neighbor without outside interference. In this process it employed financial weapons rather than military force. In the spring of 1930 and thereafter France made heavy gold withdrawals from London in the vain hope of forcing Great Britain to yield to compromises favoring French views on reparations. At the same time the French succeeded in strengthening their functional control of the Bank for International Settlements by locating it in Basel rather than London and by securing the appointment of the nationalistic Frenchman Pierre Quesnay as its general manager. Furthermore, French banks aggravated the already explosive situation by recalling short-term credits following the announcement on March 21, 1931, of the Austro-German customs union. Hidden from immediate view, this apparent overreaction to a relatively insignificant "violation" of the Versailles treaty actually offered France a chance to develop its financial tutelage over Austria and Hungary, a matter of vital concern to Italy. Speaking with the authorization of Briand and Pierre Laval, André François-Poncet, the French ambassador to Germany, confided to the German ambassador to France that his government did not object to the concept of the customs union per se. "France wants to suggest the application of the same system to all of Europe," he said, "whereby the further pursuit of the Austro-German plan would become superfluous." This European cartelization constituted a recurring theme in long-range French plans to halt and diminish Anglo-Saxon penetration of Europe.[32]

President Herbert Hoover, who had never approved of the Versailles treaty, entertained a longstanding suspicion of France's ultimate political designs. The sequence of events from June, 1931, until the end of that year subjected the treaty to a severe test. Germany's condition had moved so rapidly from bad to worse that its ambassador in Paris alerted the French government to the possibility of an impending request for the temporary suspension of reparation payments within the framework of the Young Plan. The French reacted rather calmly to this alarming news, and they expressed their regret that it would probably hurt Germany's credit. Hoover and his secretaries of state and treasury feared the impact of Germany's financial collapse on American banks so much that independently,

32. Herbert Hoover, *The Memoirs of Herbert Hoover*, Volume III: *The Great Depression, 1929–1941* (New York, 1952), 62–65; Brüning, *Memoiren*, 222–32; Edward W. Bennett, *Germany and the Diplomacy of the Financial Crisis, 1931* (Cambridge, Mass., 1962), 96–112, 132–75.

without the knowledge of the French or the Germans, they debated the best means of heading off such a catastrophe. They would have preferred to see France take the initiative in prompt remedial action. When it was not forthcoming, they decided to move ahead, having gained the approval of congressional leaders, with the proposal of a one-year moratorium on all international debt and reparation payments.

The sympathetic Ramsay MacDonald was the first foreign statesman to be taken into confidence. The French ambassador, Paul Claudel, was vaguely apprised of it when he met Secretary of State Henry L. Stimson at the State Department on June 18. In the course of their conversation, Stimson impressed upon Claudel, with reference to the German debacle, that "unless France would help, we could not help." Stimson did not think much of a moratorium under the Young Plan because it could not provide immediate relief, which was urgently needed. He then referred to "the least objectionable plan . . . of giving time on the part of everybody for one or two years. . . . No plan which would propose that America should give up her debt receipts and leave France and England free to hold on to their receipts from Germany would have any chance of acceptance by this government." When Claudel asked if Stimson meant that the move must come from France, the secretary of state replied, "Yes, we shall certainly make no move nor consent to any move until we are certain what France's attitude is." As blunt as this statement sounded, Claudel, who was on excellent terms with Stimson, was intrigued by America's evident readiness to participate in any truly joint relief.[33]

Without giving the French government a chance to study and respond to these preliminary soundings, and after feverish last-minute internal preparations, President Hoover suddenly announced on the evening of June 20 his proposal to postpone "all payments on intergovernmental debts, reparations and relief debts, both principal and interest," during the year beginning July 1, 1931, "conditional on a like postponement for one year of all payments on intergovernmental debts owing the important credit powers." In his judgment, time was of such essence in this crisis that he expected his initiative immediately to pay high psychological dividends. But

33. "Memorandum of Conversation with Paul Claudel," June 18, 21, 1931, in Henry L. Stimson Papers, Yale University Library, New Haven. See also Stimson, Diary, June 15, 16, 18, 1931, in Stimson Papers.

the unusual speed with which Hoover had proceeded to make this grand gesture not only deprived Brüning of political credit for this rescue operation; it also embarrassed Ambassador Walter Edge and more than irritated the French government.

As soon as he had received word of the Hoover moratorium, Edge, in an effort to save face, rushed to the racetracks at Longchamp, where he knew many French officials and diplomats had gathered, and advised them of it. They made no secret of the fact that they bitterly resented American "shock tactics" of informing them without prior consultation of a measure of vital concern to France. This conspiracy of Anglo-American finance, they suspected, was a brazen attempt to deprive France of its rightful place in Europe. This predictable reaction, however, did not prevent Claudel from conveying the customary diplomatic niceties on the following day. Going overboard, he told the secretary of state: "France appreciates very much what America has done in showing a spirit of solidarity. . . . France will do all that is possible to cure the situation." But when the ambassador asked for a day or two before his government could give a more specific answer, Stimson emphasized the significance of a speedy general acceptance that would leave details to be worked out in the future. "The central thought in President Hoover's proposition," the secretary stressed, "was that a wise creditor gives time to his debtor."[34]

It took two precious weeks for a compromise to be worked out between France and the United States. The loss of time aggravated the situation so much that a total collapse of Germany was feared. It certainly dampened the initially hopeful spirit of the financial world, and it generated anti-French, indeed anti-European, sentiments in Hoover. The president became sick and tired of running time and again into obstructions and procrastinations, despite the enormous sacrifices the American people had been making for the sake of the Old World's well-being. He and his compatriots were approaching the time when they were ready to turn their backs on the apparently incorrigible continent of Europe.

In fairness, one must recognize that, whatever France's ultimate response to Hoover's proposal, it was entitled to be properly consulted in advance. And though France, unlike the United States and Great Britain, was an insignificant creditor of Germany, there were

34. Walter Edge, *Jerseyman's Journal* (Princeton, 1948), 191–96.

major financial and tactical questions at stake that called for internal deliberations before an authoritative reply could be formulated. No wonder the unbridled French press lambasted the United States without restraint. For the moment, Premier Pierre Laval had to wait until its hostile outbursts died down. He also had to consider the strong opposition in the French parliament to a prompt, unqualified acceptance of the moratorium. Talking with Stimson by long-distance telephone, he explained the wisdom of letting the domestic storm die down in France before the United States reacted to his suggested compromise. In essence, this compromise protected the unconditional reparations payments provided for in the Young Plan—payments Germany was obliged to make regardless of economic conditions. There was, however, one difference: Germany would deposit them in the BIS to its own credit rather than that of the Allies. Such an arrangement would at least maintain the principle of continued payments to the end of the moratorium period.

Since the negotiation of such details would cause undesirable delays, Hoover stubbornly resisted it. Ramsay MacDonald and British bankers backed the president's stand, because any concession to France was likely to result in other such requests. Besides, the French compromise, if adopted, would interfere with recently negotiated Anglo-German credit arrangements. In a state of exasperation, President Hoover decided to instruct Ambassador Edge to inform the French that enough governments had accepted the original proposals unconditionally to proceed without France. Such isolation of France was as unacceptable to its government as the uncompromising tone of the messages from Washington. Secretary of the Treasury Andrew Mellon and Ambassador Edge, who conferred with French leaders in Paris and kept in daily touch by telephone with officials back home, had their work cut out for them. Their courteous and pragmatic approach ultimately facilitated an agreement late on the evening of July 6. France agreed to the Hoover moratorium in principle, and the United States accepted the French compromise with respect to the unconditional reparations. Laval, a shrewd politician, could thus face his parliament proud that he had not bowed to America's original ultimatum. Although the Hoover moratorium meant forgoing for a year about $80 million, an amount France needed to help balance its budget, Laval could defend this decision by pointing to the preservation of Franco-American solidarity. The United States made a much greater sacrifice by forgoing

$250 million it would have liked to have to reduce its sizable federal budget deficit.[35]

The moratorium, of course, was not an end in itself. The important task remained the search for long-range solutions. Even the total cancellation of debts and reparations would no longer have been an adequate prescription for a stable and peaceful world. In Chancellor Brüning's view, it might at least have helped lay a foundation for it. As urgent as was the need for short-term credits to prop up Germany's faltering economy, they were only symptomatic of the problem and offered no fundamental solution. Before the French agreed to the Hoover moratorium, they approached Germany, as they had done on several past occasions, to explore the feasibility of direct Franco-German negotiations. Familiar with the Anglo-American attitude toward France at this time, Brüning chose not to follow up on this risky sounding, particularly in view of the French habit of mixing financial discussions with politics.

At a conference in London, Stimson had an opportuity on July 24, 1931, to have a frank exchange with Laval. In the course of this friendly conversation, the wily French premier told Stimson that "the only difficulty in Franco-German relations was the Polish corridor." He assured the secretary that the French people did not want war. Without warning, he also volunteered that, upon his return to Paris, he would do his best to influence the Bank of France to stop withdrawing gold from the Bank of England. Such withdrawals ultimately hurt Germany's finances, the main topic of the conference. Stimson was impressed by Laval's professional skill and cooperative disposition. He felt confident of being able to do business with Laval and his minister of finance, Pierre Etienne Flandin.[36]

Europe's rivalries and financial troubles contributed to the ever deeper depression into which the United States was sliding. When the Central and Eastern European countries could no longer meet their short-term obligations and European orders for agricultural and manufactured American products declined sharply, the United States began to feel the pinch. Its own high-tariff policies, moreover, tended to aggravate the trend climaxing with the Great Depression.

To see these developments in a broader framework, it is essential

35. Stimson, Diary, June 23–25, September 13, 1931, in Stimson Papers.

36. *Ibid.*, July 24, 1931; Hoover, *Memoirs*, III, 72–80.

to trace at least the highlights of related issues. A review of Franco-American tariff and trade relations starting in 1919 shows that they generated almost as many controversies as the debt and reparations problems. Both the American government and individual traders assumed that France would reciprocate America's helpful assistance during the war by permitting the United States to play a considerable part in the rehabilitation of French industries and the reconstruction of the country. Instead, France embittered Americans by barring such American products as tractors and trucks. At the Lyons Fair in 1919, not only were twenty-five American concerns harassed and treated with incivility, but the French rebuffed them by placing not even a single order with them.[37]

Given the structural differences between the economies of France and the United States, it was nearly impossible to satisfy either country's desire to trade with the other most advantageously. America's theoretical formula toward that end stipulated "equality of treatment" and defended open markets. France insisted on "equitable treatment" and defended its two-column tariff of minimum and maximum rates that allowed discriminations as it saw fit. In addition, like the British Empire, France, too, tried to uphold the principle of imperial preference. The situation was further complicated by Americans who favored tariffs to protect their country against inundations of cheap foreign goods and others who realized that, considering America's industrial superiority, foreign competitors might be overwhelmed by the Yankees' aggressive conquest of world markets. The continued existence of these competitors, not their diminution, these Americans believed, offered a better chance of world prosperity. Live and let live was their capsuled viewpoint.

The depression of agricultural prices in 1921 and widespread discrimination against American commerce prompted Congress to pass the Fordney-McCumber Act as a protective measure. Those clauses in the Versailles treaty designed to inhibit the resurrection of Germany's industrial complex also deprived the United States of a promising outlet for its goods. When, at the end of the stipulated five years, Germany was no longer required to grant France most-favored-nation treatment, the two countries initiated negotiations that led in August, 1927, to the Franco-German Treaty of Commerce. This mutually advantageous accord created unfavorable

37. Tampa *Daily Times*, August 13, 1919.

conditions for American exporters because French customs officials did not extend the newly established minimum rates to the United States. As Washington protested against this discrimination and the sudden, in most cases upward, revisions in French rates, France complained about the American customs system. By levying customs duties according to the American value of goods rather than the original French market price, the United States customs administration made these goods more expensive. Even worse, America's "series of regulations of a sanitary or phyto-pathological nature [were] often completely fatal to agricultural exports from France."

It would be a mistake, however, to exaggerate the significance of these charges. Historically, Franco-American trade had never reached its potential, but it was always relatively steady. In 1927 France occupied the fifth place among America's customers, and the United States ranked fourth among France's customers. Following the United Kingdom, Canada, Germany, and Japan, in 1927 France took 4.7 percent of total American exports. This amounted to only 13 percent of the total imports of France; most of them were raw materials. Since a large share of American imports from France were "luxury articles," France ranked only eighth among the raw-materials suppliers of the United States. As a result, the trade balance naturally favored the United States. Altogether, the United States fared well in its tariff negotiations with France at this time. Despite its usual complaints about unfair and injurious treatment, on balance France made substantial concessions by granting most-favored-nation treatment to 471 American products. In return, the United States accommodated France in regard to its dissatisfaction with customs practices. Moreover, as Hoover pointed out, 65 percent of American imports were duty-free.[38]

It must be kept in mind that tariffs are neither the only nor necessarily the most important factor in determining the volume of international trade. Supply and demand, price attractiveness, currency fluctuations, and the political atmosphere play significant roles in it. The occasional weakness of the French franc in relation to the American dollar did not result in an increased French share of the American market. And though in the mid-1920s the accelerated flow of international investments accounted for larger imports by many

38. "Note sur les relations économiques entre la France et les États-Unis," October 12, 1921, CPEU, Vol. 182, AMAE; Parrini, *Heir to Empire*, 220–25, 239–47.

countries, their increased imports were not matched by a proportional expansion of their exports. Governments are in a position to induce export sales. The American government, for instance, decided in 1928 to permit the flotation of French industrial securities, something France had anxiously promoted. The United States was hoping that this would lead to French importation of American automobiles and other manufactured items.[39]

The economic crisis of the late 1920s and early 1930s, accompanied by sharply reduced American purchases abroad and precipitous shrinkage in the supply of dollars, severely aggravated the world situation. The high tariff wall the United States erected with the Smoot-Hawley Act of June, 1930, led to foreign retaliations, including the French quota system. Instead of being remedial, these measures actually fanned the fires of economic warfare, ratifying the bankruptcy of the stubbornly inadequate policies that had been in effect since the end of the war. The world economy demonstrated that it was more integrated than nations and their leaders seemed to comprehend.

An even more nagging issue throughout this decade involved the settlement of the debts France owed to the United States. Of the $10,350,500,000 the United States advanced to foreign governments during and immediately after the war, France received a total of $3.4 billion. Prior to the Armistice it had borrowed $1.97 billion to keep its war machine moving; in the post-Armistice period it had borrowed another billion dollars for badly needed relief and reconstruction. In addition, France had purchased surplus war stocks of the American Expeditionary Force in the amount of $407 million. In the ensuing debate over "war debts," these important, distinct components of the total debt became conveniently blurred.

Emerging from the war financially exhausted, bled in manpower, and faced with the task of massive reconstruction of its devastated areas, France suggested, at first discreetly and then directly, a sharp reduction of these debts and preferably their cancellation. Its central argument rested on the claim that, unlike the United States, France had made its enormous sacrifices for the "common cause" for more than four years. Moreover, since most of the borrowed money was

39. Jules Henry to Aristide Briand, June 9, 1930, CPEU, Vol. 451, AMAE. See also M. E. Falkus, "United States Economic Policy and the 'Dollar Gap' of the 1920s," *Economic History Review*, XXIV (1971), 599–623.

spent in the United States, Americans had profited while Frenchmen died for freedom and democracy. As the dominant world creditor, the United States was therefore morally obligated to share the total cost of the war and help lay a solid foundation for recovery. This line of argument made it practically impossible for French politicians to yield to American demands for repayment without being thrown out of office. Suddenly the savior of France was accused of being a merciless and greedy creditor.

The French government repeatedly acknowledged the debts and professed to honor its original pledge of repayment. But it asked the United States also to act honorably by not forgetting the millions of French soldiers who died or were wounded in the struggle for civilization. As Clemenceau unhappily phrased it in his open letter of August 19, 1926, to President Coolidge: "You are claiming from us payment of a debt not of commerce, but of war. You know, as we do, that our treasury is empty. . . . France is not for sale, even to her friends." References to "Uncle Shylock" and "USury" expressed the depth of resentment against the United States. Its lingering effects could not but compound mutual misunderstandings. Public opinion in France acted as if the United States conducted business with it rather than with the government of France. American newspapers reacted by pointing out that French taxpayers seemed to ignore the fact that they were really trying to shift their own obligations to American taxpayers. But what really annoyed the American people in this unpleasant matter was the attitude of the French government. Instead of countering demagogic public arguments, it used them as a means of refraining for several years from offering a basis for funding negotiations. Many Americans regarded this procrastination as an act of bad faith.

To strengthen the French case, Ambassador Jules Jusserand recalled the fraternal sentiments of American citizens toward France in 1917. They had even offered to raise a private gift of a billion dollars in gratitude for what France had done in America's struggle for independence.[40] But Secretary of the Treasury McAdoo had considered it more expeditious to meet French needs with interest-free government loans, repayable on convenient terms. Such informally

40. Jean J. Jusserand, "Le sentiment américain pendant la guerre," *Revue des deux mondes*, September 15, 1930, pp. 241–73, and October 11, 1930, pp. 511–46.

expressed sentiments and suggestions, however, were one thing; formal contractual agreements were another.

President Wilson had never left France in doubt about its erroneous reference to the "common cause" of the Allied and Associated Powers. The United States was certainly disposed to make generous adjustments through lowering the interest rate on the French debt and through liberal repayment schedules. But it was not politically feasible to cancel or reduce the basic debt. Upholding the traditional concept that a contract is a contract, Presidents Harding and Coolidge defended the universal application of this principle. As Ambassador Herrick explained to the chairman of the French Senate Finance Committee, "Cancellation of debts . . . would make it most difficult for nations to borrow abroad in the event of another war."[41] French attempts to link the payment of these debts to the payment of German reparations were as unacceptable to the United States as the suggested scheme by which Washington's advances to Germany were to be applied to the payment of reparations. Since this simplistic, though devious, scheme would have maintained Germany's dependence and enriched France at the expense of the United States, Wilson and his successors reiterated that Europe itself had to take care of its war debts.

The duration of the war and its aftermath caused enormous financial headaches. But they constituted only one challenge in an immensely complex world situation. The legal right to collect the debts was undeniable. Whether it would be in the interest of the creditor or the world economy actually to collect them was disputable. In an article John Foster Dulles published in *Foreign Affairs* in 1922, he raised this very question. Soon thereafter, Assistant Secretary of the Treasury R. C. Leffingwell made the realistic observation in the *Yale Review* that "a good customer is better than an insolvent debtor." And in a statement before the House Ways and Means Committee in January, 1926, Secretary of the Treasury Andrew Mellon explained more pointedly, "The entire foreign debt is not worth as much to the American people in dollars and cents as a prosperous Europe as a customer."

Such broader views, however farsighted, did not appeal to the

41. Myron T. Herrick to Charles Evans Hughes, December 21, 1923, in Personal Correspondence, Box 25, Hughes Papers.

masses or to those critics who believed that France and its people were trying to take advantage of the United States, both in a commercial and power-political sense. It has been similarly suggested that America's emphasis on the contractual nature of its claim for full reimbursement merely tried to conceal its grasp for power. America's latent "imperialism" and France's desire to play first fiddle on the Continent stood in the way of a prompt removal of the debts as an obstacle to Europe's recovery. Despite America's complicated transition from war to peacetime conditions, it might have been able to forgive the debts in exchange for profitable trade relations. But past experience offered no encouraging evidence that Europeans would limit such released funds to trade and recovery. It was not in the interest of the United States to facilitate Great Britain's competition or to help finance destabilizing French ambitions.

The comments of several prominent Americans concerning French procrastination in settling the debt issue reflected both popular and official viewpoints. Frank B. Kellogg, ambassador to the Court of St. James's, compared England's conscientious efforts to meet its obligations to the United States, despite its industrial depression and high taxes, with the French government's failure to tax its people adequately or to impose rigid economy. "She [France] has maintained a large military establishment, and loaned money to other countries to maintain like establishments," Kellogg wrote. "She has paid her interest out of borrowed money for years; she has shown no disposition to settle her national debts to the United States or to Great Britain." The inference of this critical observation was clear: nothing mattered more to France than its leadership position.[42]

Senator William E. Borah of Idaho elaborated his views more bluntly. He objected to "fattening the bureaucrats and militarists of Europe" at the expense of American taxpayers. In Borah's judgment, by demanding from Germany reparations it could not possibly pay, the vindictive powers of Europe, led by France, were pulling down not only Germany but themselves and the world economy as well. Indeed, the money the French derived from their unmet debt obligations was used to maintain military armaments threatening the future peace. In the historical cause-and-effect relationship, he held, France's treatment of Germany posed a threat

42. Frank B. Kellogg to Charles Evans Hughes, December 5, 1924, in Personal Correspondence, Box 61, Hughes Papers.

that the United States could not possibly underwrite. As he saw it in 1924, the French military establishment and alliances could be justified only for the "sole purpose of a military dominance on the continent." He was sure that American taxpayers wished to support the cause of peace, not grandiose political ambitions. Certainly their government treated the French debt as a contractual obligation, not as a political weapon in its diplomatic arsenal.[43]

Looking at the European scene with the pragmatic sense of a well-meaning American, General Henry T. Allen found that France's fear of Germany's vitality called for coexistence, not perpetual provocation. Facing the facts of life dispassionately, he concluded, "France must in the end recognize the necessity of living amicably by the side of a stronger, antagonistic state just as weaker states have done throughout history." Unencumbered by historically rooted prejudices and rationalizations, he became convinced that France could not obtain security by trying to assert its vaunted superiority.[44]

Secretary of the Treasury Mellon, a banker by profession, would have liked Congress to entrust him with the refunding of the foreign debts. Instead, Congress in February, 1922, created the World War Foreign Debt Commission to collect the loans over the next twenty-five years at an interest rate of 4.25 percent. This commission, composed of Secretaries Mellon, Hoover, and Hughes, as well as a senator and congressman, was specifically instructed to exclude cancellation as a means of "settling" the debts. By mid-1922, Premier Poincaré had established contact with the commission, but only to let it know that the straits of French finances prevented any debt negotiations for the time being. In the meantime the French pleaded every so often for cancellation. Nearly three years passed before France unofficially began to explore solutions, a process culminating in the Mellon-Bérenger Agreement of April, 1926. It took another three years for France to ratify this accord. Underlying this slowness was the awareness of France's limited resources. The cost of the war and reconstruction, the loss of the loans to czarist Russia, and its heavy domestic indebtedness made it press so hard for German reparations. To mortgage its future financially would have risked a relative power-political decline.

To the embarrassment of France, in June, 1923, Great Britain

43. *Congressional Record*, 67th Cong., 2nd Sess., 1684–85.

44. Henry Allen to Charles Evans Hughes, February 4, 1922, in Box 11, Hughes Papers.

reached a debt-settlement agreement with Washington. Based on its capacity to pay, Britain funded its $4.6 billion debt over the next sixty-two years at about 3.3 percent interest. Now that Europe could no longer confront the United States with a united opposition, the debt commission hoped that other debtors would follow suit. In the case of France, the threat of a loan ban late in 1924 signaled American impatience with its delaying tactics. Finally, mildly prodded by Ambassador Herrick, an understanding friend, Finance Minister Étienne Clémentel submitted his government's views. He proposed a ten-year moratorium for the debts, no interest for the following ten years, and an interest rate of 1.5 percent until the year 2015. This unacceptable basis was a fitting prelude for the rather undignified haggling that followed. In a subsequent revision, Clémentel offered a range of interest rates up to 2 percent, adding, however, a "safeguard clause" according to which French interest payments would be reduced if Germany did not deliver on reparations. Since France knew that the United States rejected such linkage in principle, this proposal, too, amounted to little more than shadowboxing. It took another loan ban to make France move closer to a solution. Frequent changes of government personnel also consumed more time in this process.

When, after the fall of the Herriot government, Joseph Caillaux succeeded Clémentel as finance minister, he explored his predecessor's formula once more, with the same result. France clearly misjudged the United States. Instead of accusing America of a "rigid attitude," France could have saved itself much trouble by officially making a realistic proposal with respect to the sole area of discussion that the United States would entertain—the "adjustment of interest payments to economic necessities of France." Such a businesslike approach, the debt commission indicated, would have held out real benefits for France. Contrary to many demagogic insinuations, the United States wished to see France recover its prosperity as quickly as possible.

Finally, several factors motivated the French government to inch closer to an agreement. As Caillaux was fully aware, without it, there was much less chance for obtaining financial aid from the Americans. Foreign Minister Aristide Briand never abandoned his dream of drawing the United States into the French security system. Disagreements with Britain, Italy, and the United States and inability to count on Soviet Russia made security-conscious France feel uncomfortably isolated. This feeling was also nurtured by another observation. France had hoped to emerge from the war as the dominant power in Europe. Instead, it watched with concern the growing cooperation of the Anglo-Saxons. Their surprising agreement on naval parity and their debt-funding settlement seemed to be interconnected acts, suggesting that they had joint control of world trade and political constellations favorable to them. Their parallel attitudes with respect to the recovery of Germany, without enabling it to challenge France again, also seemed to serve this purpose. A balanced and prosperous Europe accommodated Anglo-Saxon strategic considerations that aimed at limiting the influence of France. In light of these observations, France had an interest in weakening any Anglo-American condominium, just as the Anglo-Saxons had an interest in preventing France and Germany from pooling their considerable resources. Although it was only a small step, Briand announced in July, 1925, that a French commission, headed by Caillaux, would soon go to the United States to resolve the debt impasse. He did not spell out the terms he had in mind, and he did not publicly repeat what he had said privately, namely that he would not bring up the question of linkage.

As promising as Briand's move appeared, at the first meeting with the Americans on September 24, Caillaux again offered unacceptably low payments. At least as disturbing, he also resurrected the "safeguard clause." Despite a subsequent offer of higher payments, the discussions ended in failure, essentially because of the disagreements on linkage. But the total amount of $6,220,000,000 Caillaux was willing to have France pay over a period of sixty-eight years did constitute the limit of French capacity to pay. Considering that the Mellon-Bérenger Accord of April, 1926, settled for a total of $6,847,000,000 over sixty-two years, without the safeguard clause, the Caillaux offer deserved more serious consideration than the Coolidge administration gave it. The question of the safeguard could have been more skillfully handled by detaching it from the main body of the agreement and giving lip service to it in an attached note. Such a procedure was adopted in the Anglo-French debt agreement of July, 1926.

Actually, the Caillaux offer greatly advanced the chances of a realistic settlement. In a relatively short time, Henry Bérenger, ambassador extraordinary and plenipotentiary, and Robert Lacour-Gayet, financial attaché at the French embassy in Washington, worked out the details. It was not easy, but they succeeded by April 29 in satisfying the American negotiators. For the first five years no interest would be charged. Thereafter, staggered interest rates ranged from 1 to 3½ percent over a period of sixty years. The average of 1.64 percent gave France a genuine break. It amounted to canceling the French debt by 60.3 percent as compared with 51 percent on all war debts.

As Dwight W. Morrow of J. P. Morgan and Company observed, it was fortunate that this final phase, under Bérenger's guidance, moved expeditiously, for there was always an element of uncertainty in negotiating with the French. Their personnel changed so often. As Morrow noted, "There have been five finance ministers in France in the last eight months." By closing this chapter, Americans anticipated improved international relations. On the recommendation of President Coolidge to ratify this "fair and just" settlement, Congress gave its approval. The Senate deliberately waited for the French parliament to ratify it first.[45] Bérenger confidently expected it. But in France a howl of protest from the press, parades of mutilated veterans, and politically motivated critics dramatized strong opposition to the "unjust and immoral" accord. Their criticism snowballed sufficiently to put ratification in jeopardy. The resignation of the Briand ministry on June 15 did not inspire confidence in early French action. Neither did the return of Poincaré to power at a time when, in relation to the dollar, the French franc had fallen from the usual twenty cents to about two cents. For the next three years, acrimonious discussions held up the ratification process. Embarrassed and frustrated by this impasse, Stimson finally asked the French envoy what the best way would be to defuse the growing irritation. Claudel seriously recommended a kind letter: "You know France values kind words." Claudel displayed great shrewdness with this apparently ridiculous suggestion because, if nothing else, a kind American letter could hardly be followed up with retaliatory measures. In the summer of 1929 Poincaré finally gave the go-ahead signal for ratification because the Young Plan at least implicitly linked debts and reparations. Ironically, only two years after the ratification of the Mellon-Bérenger accord, the Hoover moratorium called

45. U.S. Congress, Senate, *Hearings Before the Committee on Finance, U.S. Senate, June 9, 10, 11 and 18, 1926: French Debt Settlement*, 69th Cong., 1st Sess.; FRUS, *Diplomatic Papers, 1925*, I, 133–54, and *1926*, II, 90–98.

a halt (though supposedly a temporary one) to all war debts and reparations.[46]

Belatedly, Hoover intimated to Stimson his readiness to tackle these two questions "head on." Observing the developing dilemma of the United States, Chancellor Brüning pleaded for an end to the patchwork of short-term credits used for reparations and domestic deficits. Conference after conference had merely postponed a genuine overall agreement. The time was long overdue for statesmanlike action. Laval, too, sensed that it was a propitious time for a decision, in the French style. In a friendly meeting with Brüning, he urged the chancellor to be patient and to realize that the two of them had it in their power to effect a lasting Franco-German understanding. Hinting that a favorable turning point was likely to result from his forthcoming visit to the United States, Laval puzzled the chancellor with his strange request not to show up in Washington at the same time. What was behind this quite extraordinary suggestion? Brüning surmised that perhaps the French premier wanted to convince the Americans not to interfere again with existing reparations arrangements. Abandonment of all efforts to collect reparations, Laval might want to warn, would enable Germany to rearm more quickly. These two possibilities did not bother the chancellor, because he counted on the confidence he enjoyed in official American circles. But when Laval alluded to the growing crisis in America, it dawned on Brüning that France probably intended to use its current gold treasures to set itself up as *arbiter mundi*. By attempting to pressure the United States, now that its financial wings had been clipped, to stay out of Europe's political affairs, Laval evidently hoped to accomplish what Frenchmen had long dreamed about—to lead Europe. But this goal was destined to remain an elusive dream as long as Germany insisted that Franco-German reconciliation could be accomplished only on the basis of equality and the gradual expiration of the Versailles treaty.

Brüning anticipated that Laval was about to overreach himself in his dealings with the United States. He therefore issued official instructions for his government to be silent for a while on the reparations issue so that the impending Franco-American showdown could take its natural course. Both sides started before Laval's ar-

46. For an excellent discussion of the debt question, see Ellen Schrecker, *The Hired Money: The French Debt to the United States* (New York, 1978). See also "Conversation with Claudel About France's Debt," June 29, 1929, in Stimson Papers.

rival in Washington. On October 10, 1931, the American government let it be known that it probably would not insist on the resumption of European payments at the end of the moratorium if the debtors could not deliver them. Applied to reparations, the French obviously would not go along with such generosity. Talk of debt reductions in exchange for disarmament was in the air. According to a published trial balloon, Laval was about to propose the reduction of reparations by 50 percent and defense expenditures by 25 percent. The United States actually declared its readiness to lend active support to the establishment of an international gold fund to help stabilize currencies. The Bank of France promptly opposed such a step; it would have interfered with France's intention to use its gold as an instrument of policy.

France demonstrated this destabilizing policy with its massive gold withdrawals from Germany in July, 1931, from England in September, and from the United States in October. Between the middle of September and the end of November, 1931, France withdrew from the United States $324,609,000 in gold. The Bank of France and the French treasury accumulated more dollars than were held anywhere else abroad. Two French banking experts arrived in New York a week before Laval's visit. They asked for higher interest on official French deposits in the United States, and they also revealed that, to avoid its recent experience with sterling balances, France wanted the par exchange rate of its dollar holdings guaranteed. But the United States rejected the higher interest rates and fought off the threat of further French withdrawals. French monetary policies produced worldwide pressures and dislocations. In some countries, such as Canada, gold exports had to be prohibited or subjected to strict regulations. To put an end to the ensuing panic in money markets, the government and banks of the United States decided to let France know who was stronger. They stood ready to return all French deposits in gold. For the third time in 1931, the French challenge was met and thwarted.[47]

Since the contemporary financial and disarmament problems could not be satisfactorily resolved without prior removal of the political obstacles underlying them, Premier Laval's visit promised to offer an excellent testing ground. As the date of his arrival ap-

47. Stimson, Diary, September 12, 1931, in Stimson Papers; Brüning, *Memoiren*, 412–33; John W. Wheeler-Bennett, *The Wreck of Reparations* (New York, 1972), 118–22.

proached, Ambassador Claudel, probably deliberately, lowered Stimson's expectations. To the secretary's surprise, Claudel suggested an agenda, whereas Hoover and he had envisioned frank, informal conversations. It turned out that many influential people in France were a little anxious about Laval's exposing himself to unfamiliar territory. "They are willing to have matters opened but not finished" in Washington, Claudel said. He also cautioned Stimson not to count on significant progress on disarmament, because "the munition manufacturers in France were very powerful and controlled the Press." Laval could not disarm against their wishes. Besides, the premier looked upon "the French Army as a great safeguard against Communism." If these advance clarifications left little room for removing political obstacles, Laval's negotiating technique in this instance added a touch of mystery. Evidently determined to play his cards close to his chest, he left Briand and Flandin at home, much to their resentment. During the discussions from October 22 through 25, he also disappointed Ambassador Claudel by leaving him out of them. The premier had to be persuaded by Stimson to have his own interpreter. All these procedural details told more about the likely substantive outcome than Americans appreciated. Stimson placed Laval "in a class by himself for frankness and directness and simplicity," quite "different from all other Frenchmen with whom I have negotiated." Laval's obliging and charming manner also endeared him to the American press.[48]

President Hoover introduced Laval to the viewpoint of ordinary American citizens when he plunged into issues about the politics of Central Europe, the trouble spot of Europe and the world. As he summed it up, despite all the contributions and sacrifices America had made, Europe was more unstable in 1931 than in 1914. Unless there would be some improvement, it would make no sense to Americans to continue their assistance. On a broad range of questions, however, Laval showed no willingness to deviate from orthodox French positions. He granted that the Versailles treaty was an absurdity, "but it was a political impossibility now to change it." The Polish Corridor was also an absurdity, but to change the eastern boundary would be a politically impossible undertaking. In matters of naval disarmament he indicated that his hands were tied by the minister of marine and the naval committee in the Chamber

48. Stimson, Diary, October 6, 9, 23, 1931, in Stimson Papers.

of Deputies. And when asked about the size of the French army, he noted that it constituted "after all the defense against Bolshevism." He resumed an old French theme when he alluded to the desirability of a Franco-American consultative pact and said that France could not disarm before its security was assured. When he asked the president what he thought of such a pact, Hoover pointedly responded "that it was a political impossibility." At the heart of preventing a reasonable state of the world was this political blockage. Pressure groups, vested interests, and the public's ignorance and emotional biases blocked the application of analytically sound policies. Even competent leaders could not overcome these obstacles, despite the disastrous consequences they foreshadowed.

President Hoover was extremely discouraged when Laval fell back time and again on conventional arguments to the effect that Germany posed a perpetual danger to France. If this was so, then Laval's notion of a ten-year political moratorium between France and Germany lost its credibility. This moratorium would have perpetuated the Versailles treaty system for a decade, holding out to Germany some hope of major changes thereafter. But if the French believed that Germany constituted a perpetual danger to France, the moratorium was in effect a ploy that would favor France for ten years, without offering a real opportunity for change later.

Laval was receptive to the plan of having a commission determine the immediate capacity of Germany to pay during the depression, as long as it would operate under the framework of the Young Plan. Even though Hoover indicated his willingness to cooperate with the commission's recommendations, subject to congressional approval, Laval left no doubt that he would never be in favor of an entire abolition of reparations: "That would put German industry in such a favorable position compared with France, England, or America that we would all regret it."

On the whole, the Laval visit produced only very meager results.[49] The president noted with regret his visitor's disposition not to budge one inch. As he put it to the secretary of state: "France always goes through this cycle. After she is done and begins to recuperate, then she gets rich, militaristic, and cocky; and nobody can

49. If one of its objectives was, as the German press speculated, to strengthen Franco-American ties to compensate for the growing coolness of Franco-British relations, it clearly failed to achieve it. See "Voyage de M. Pierre Laval à Washington," October 21, 1931, in Série "Y," Affaires Politiques et Internationales, No. 61, AMAE.

get on with her until she has to be thrashed again." In the light of this historical perspective, "Hoover saw nothing in the future but a line-up between Germany, Britain, and probably ourselves against France." Noticing the lack of magnanimity on the part of France, Stimson reminded Laval of the historic oscillations of power back and forth between France and Germany. Any attempt to perpetuate French dominance, history had demonstrated, would meet with failure. He referred to the battle of Jena to illustrate his point with a view to the future: "France had never been so strong nor Germany so prostrate. Yet in eight years had come the battle of Leipzig and the overthrow of France." Without a sense of the past, he intimated, France might regret the final verdict of history because of its treatment of Germany. Nothing could have accentuated these views more dramatically than the friendly after-dinner conversation the secretary of state set up between the French premier and Senator Borah, about whom Laval said, "Why, the man lives on Mars." To Borah, French policies could lead only to disaster.[50]

It took a long time for the final communiqué to be readied for publication. It pointed out the need for some agreement regarding intergovernmental obligations prior to the expiration of the Hoover moratorium. By far the most significant clause in it stated, "The initiative in this matter should be taken at an early date by the European Powers principally concerned, within the framework of agreements prior to July 1, 1931." Although they might have regretted it later, the French got what they said they wanted: all future initiatives with respect to reparations must come from the European states. Hoover's diplomacy frankly succeeded in turning the tables on France, much to the satisfaction of Congress.

The White House was dismayed when in an address before the Chamber of Deputies, late in November, 1931, Laval took the tough line on reparations and made revision conditional on proportional reduction of war debts. To Claudel's surprise, Laval had told him after his talks with Hoover "that there was some understanding as to war debts." Laval's assertion—"We will demand payment of the unconditional annuities, and we will not accede to priority being given to private debts over our reparations"—was undoubtedly reassuring to many deputies. But Stimson deplored putting such

50. "Memorandum of Conference with Laval," in Stimson, Diary, October 23, 24, 1931, in Stimson Papers; Brüning, *Memoiren*, 498–99; Geoffrey Warner, *Pierre Laval and the Eclipse of France* (London, 1968), 46–53.

handcuffs on the Basel committee studying Germany's capacity to pay. And if Laval intended to convey the impression that America had endorsed these conditions, the secretary of state was anxious to dispel such a notion. He had trusted Laval; now he came close to feeling deceived by him.

A particularly interesting discussion with Dino Grandi, Benito Mussolini's foreign minister, enlightened Hoover and Stimson a few weeks after Laval's departure. Asked about France, Grandi explained "that she was difficult. She was suffering from a mystic frame of mind, thinking only of security. . . . On the one hand, Tardieu with his strong armament policy and, on the other hand, Briand with his Pan-European idea both lead to the same end singularly enough, an imperialistic position for France." Because Hoover conjectured that if Germany collapsed, France would be more affected than Britain and Italy, he asked his Italian guest, "Would not France rise to the occasion?" Grandi replied he feared not. "France has no international financial policy such as Britain has. . . . French loans had been purely political, not economic," Finally, the Italian diplomat confided in the course of the very intimate conversation that "France had tried to get Italy to cooperate with them in resisting the Hoover Moratorium. . . . There was no idea of a common cause, which would benefit all. He [Flandin] was merely for pulling selfish benefits at the sacrifice of others." In view of the high esteem in which Grandi was held, these comments confirmed Hoover's own impressions, though Stimson, somewhat more charitably inclined, abstained from generalizations about France and the French.[51]

When the Lausanne conference concluded on July 8, 1932, with a reduction of German reparations to about $750 million, provided the United States canceled Europe's debts, the Hoover administration lost no time in declaring that its debts policy had not changed. It welcomed this strictly European settlement. It thought that, with genuine progress in disarmament, the settlement would contribute to world stability. But America emphasized that it had not been consulted, "is not a party to, nor in any way committed" to the Lausanne settlement.[52] This agreement was never ratified; it had come too late. The reparations issue, which had caused so much trouble,

51. "Conversation Between President Hoover and Signor Grandi," November 18, 1931, in Stimson, Diary, pp. 62–66, Stimson Papers.

52. W. S. Myers (ed.), *The State Papers and Other Public Writings of Herbert Hoover* (2 vols.; New York, 1970), II, 235.

died a natural death with the rise of Hitler. The war-debts questions lingered on. As Congress taught Europeans defaulting on their installments on December 15, 1932, they nurtured isolationist and neutralist sentiments in the United States. On their part, Europeans held that America's rigid war-debts policy and its refusal to make any collective-security commitment were responsible for the politically and financially cancerous development during the 1920s. Underneath the professed unselfishness of the United States, which they originally admired, they detected a not-very-subtle materialism that alienated them from the model republic.

DISARMAMENT AND THE KELLOGG-BRIAND PACT

In Hoover's mind disarmament had a major role to play in the promotion of sound international finance. The positive, though limited, accomplishments of the Washington conference attested to the widespread desire immediately after the war to control future conflicts at the source, through disarmament. The record of the next ten years, however, turned out to be dismal. Fears and ambitions competed with the weapons themselves as sources of conflict. Unless these fears and ambitions were conquered or controlled, stocks of arms looked more reassuring than the hopes entertained by a civilization in search of peace. From the Geneva Naval Disarmament Conference in 1927, "one of the most dramatically unsuccessful gatherings in the 20th century," to the World Disarmament Conference in Geneva in 1932, the trail was marked by merely modest concessions.[53]

Significantly, up to 1932 the conferences concerned themselves with naval disarmament. They set out to maintain a balance of sea power by establishing tonnage ratios with which the participants could live without undue fear. As the dominant military power on the Continent, France was determined not to permit the major sea powers to disturb the status quo in regard to land forces. Reluctantly, it limited its naval strength, but it feared the military potential of Germany too much to risk another German invasion. In principle, nothing mattered more to French leaders than their nation's

53. David Carlton, "Great Britain and the Coolidge Naval Disarmament Conference of 1927," *Political Science Quarterly*, LXXXIII (1968), 573–98.

security, as they conceived it. France regarded disarmament and Franco-German rapprochement as unrealistic ways to peace. It would therefore support disarmament only if Great Britain, the United States, or both guaranteed its security. France let this essential condition be known at every opportunity that presented itself.

The quantity and quality of cruisers and submarines posed the greatest difficulty at these naval conferences. As the London conference of 1930 demonstrated, it was possible to stabilize the relative strength of the three largest navies.[54] The Anglo-French Compromise on the Limitation of Armaments (July, 1928) illustrated the kinds of technical differences that existed and, in this instance, the devious means used to overcome them. Britain and the United States did not see eye to eye with respect to cruisers and their armaments. The British preferred a large number of light cruisers with six-inch guns to protect their commercial sea lanes. But the United States not only set a goal of parity with British cruiser tonnage, it also tried to achieve this goal by building the cruisers with eight-inch guns. In the past France had often sided with the United States in Anglo-American naval differences. Similarly, Britain had taken a stand against French resistance to limiting its trained military reserve manpower. Now France and Britain made a "compromise" that reversed these positions. They pledged in the future to limit heavy cruisers and large submarines and not to place limitations on France's trained reserves. With this understanding, they safeguarded their special interests in light cruisers, small submarines, and military manpower. This deal, secretly negotiated behind the back of the United States and Germany, was substantively less serious than its larger ramifications. The United States was no stranger to European duplicity. But if this obstruction of the disarmament process came as a blow to the United States and American leaders took vigorous exception to it, what was Germany to think? Did this Anglo-French understanding signal the premature end of "the Spirit of Locarno"? Without trust there could be neither understanding nor peace.[55]

A destabilizing factor was introduced by uncertainty about what France meant by its security and how it proposed to maintain it. Was

54. For an excellent account of this conference, see R. G. O'Connor, *Perilous Equilibrium: The United States and the London Naval Conference of 1930* (Lawrence, Kan., 1962), 84–107.

55. Jacobson, *Locarno Diplomacy*, 187–91.

it limited to the legitimate desire to have its territorial integrity respected? Or did it go beyond this to justify extraordinary long-term limitations to its unpenitent neighbor's independence? And did it have to rely on intimidating alliances, military might, and economic sanctions, or could its security not be more lastingly based on friendly political and economic cooperation? Its double standard was provocative and inconsistent. It claimed the right to a strong defensive posture but denied this right to its disarmed German neighbor. Expressing a sense of inferiority, France defended its fear by arguing that equality with Germany in regard to disarmament would in time not amount to equivalent strength. To promote its control of the Mediterranean, it denied Italy's claim for parity in cruisers and submarines. France asserted that in any future military showdown it had to be prepared to reckon with an alliance between Germany and Italy; this possibility called for French superiority. As a major colonial power, moreover, France often referred to its obligation to maintain its bridge of communication with Africa. Whatever merit these arguments had, Secretary Stimson went to the heart of the matter by laughingly questioning their sincerity: "You could not make such a bridge out of submarines."

Not only Briand and Herriot articulated their country's desire for peace. Tardieu, Poincaré, and Laval professed it just as strongly and, undoubtedly, just as sincerely. The perception, however, prevailed in chancelleries around the world that the kind of peace France was pursuing might in time provoke Germany to react with a vengeance. In the words of Stimson, "The key to disarmament . . . lay less in Germany than in France, and it was the French attitudes that were most difficult and distressing to Americans in 1931 and 1932."[56] Not surprisingly, Tardieu asserted France felt no obligation to reduce its armaments, because it had on its own reduced the duration of service and the total number of its effectives. Even Herriot defended the French position, by referring in July, 1932, to current budget reductions of 10 percent for the army and navy and by pointing out that France had already refrained from authorized naval construction. Absolutely opposed to compromising French security, Frenchmen of various political shades rationalized their at-

56. Henry L. Stimson and McGeorge Bundy, *On Active Service in War and Peace* (New York, 1948), 272.

titude by claiming they sought security "not for ourselves alone, but for all nations."[57]

Even prior to 1930, the rocky road of disarmament did not inspire much confidence in the future. Disregarding America's role in Europe's postwar recovery, the European powers rejoiced that they had achieved Locarno without America's help. They thought that perhaps they could also regulate armaments among themselves. Quite inconsistently, they hoped that Europe, still the world's political nerve center, could induce the United States, the world's creditor and modern industrial giant, to help it out financially without interfering in its political affairs. At the same time, France pushed the notion of a security pact with the United States. How unrealistic could France be?

Initially, in June, 1927, Briand proposed a bilateral agreement solemnly renouncing war "as an instrument of their national policy towards each other." J. Theodore Marriner, the chief of the State Department's Division of Western European Affairs, counseled caution. This vague proposal, he concluded from his analysis, might be interpreted by other powers as "a kind of perpetual alliance between the United States and France." It might contravene the neutrality of the United States during a war in which France was engaged, "since France might deem it necessary to infringe upon our rights as a neutral under this guaranty of non-aggression." France, moreover, had certain obligations under the League of Nations convenant to aid in punishing an aggressor state. Certainly the United States cherished its freedom of action outside the framework of the league too much to be drawn into its machinery. Although American pacifists enthusiastically supported such official renunciation of war, Secretary of State Kellogg explained that "this government could not enter into a treaty with France that it would not enter into with other powers." Would not France be aroused, for instance, if the United States entered into a treaty of this sort with Germany alone? He therefore suggested that Briand should endeavor to obtain the adherence of all the principal powers to a declaration renouncing war as an instrument of national policy.

Briand aimed at the *organisation de la paix*, not just a verbal affirmation of peace. Even when he appeared ready to accept a multilateral treaty, he not only proposed that it renounce "all wars of

57. *Le Temps*, November 15, 1930, June 9, 1932.

aggression," but he also wanted France and the United States to sign it first, so as to give at least the impression of an alliance, to be followed by the signatures of all other nations willing to join it. His frequent recommendations of reservations and amendments, all designed to accomplish French security objectives, did not endear him to the secretary of state. Kellogg steadfastly refused to allow interpretations attached to the treaty that would make it more than just a pact renouncing war. It amounted to no more than a commitment to seek pacific means for the settlement of international controversies. But the futility of multilateral renunciation of war was soon demonstrated by Japan's invasion of Manchuria, despite the fact that it was one of the signatories of the peace pact.[58]

On the question of peace through disarmament, France and the United States could not get together. In the years following the Kellog-Briand Pact, France saw Great Britain and the United States patch up their differences on naval matters. It also took notice of the growing friendliness between Washington and Rome. Its increasing isolation made it so touchy that it suspected the Anglo-Saxons of "trying to disarm France to the advantage of Germany and Italy." And when, without prior consultation with the French and British, President Hoover's representative, Ambassador Hugh Gibson, confronted the World Disarmament Conference of 1932 in Geneva with America's proposals for the abolition of all offensive weapons, Tardieu left the conference in a huff. On his return to Paris he immediately called Ambassador Edge to air his resentment: "When would the American government learn that it could not brutalize France into concessions which it was not prepared to make?" he asked.[59]

To understand this outburst, one must place it in the context of contemporary developments. Although psychologically not conditioned for it, some perceptive Frenchmen by the end of the 1920s might have granted that a more conciliatory attitude toward Germany and more sensible cooperation with the United States would have led to more satisfactory results. But France's historical experiences did not favor the demonstration of such political maturity.

58. FRUS, *Diplomatic Papers, 1927*, II, 616–20; L. Ethan Ellis, *Frank B. Kellogg and American Foreign Relations, 1925–1929* (New Brunswick, N.J., 1961), 194–200; Robert H. Ferrell, *Peace in Their Time: The Origins of the Kellogg-Briand Pact* (New Haven, 1952), 263–64.

59. Edge, *Jerseyman's Journal*, 214.

Now that the political leaders and the press in Germany had begun to talk about rearmament, and Prussian militarism and chauvinism had returned to show their all-too-familiar faces, it seemed too late for mere conciliatory gestures. France had to prepare itself in earnest to face the rise of Hitler and the whipped-up masses following him. To listen to American advice to disarm, without firm commitment to stand by France defensively, sounded very unrealistic.

The United States, too, discovered that it could not accomplish much on the disarmament front without French cooperation. It realized much too late that debts, reparations, disarmament, stability, and prosperity were so closely intertwined that by failing to apply timely realism to one issue, one could not successfully resolve the others. Protected by its geographic location, size, and resources, and also by its common market, historically known as the American System, the United States looked to peace as a precondition for growth and for reaching world markets. Disarmament and trade, America believed, would further the cause of peace and perhaps even guarantee it. American leaders saw Europeans, already exhausted by a long and costly war, senselessly spending their treasures on military establishments, with merchants of death rather than their national economies reaping the benefits. Disarmament meant lower budget deficits and less need for American loans. In 1932 Hoover pointed out, "The world is spending $500 million a year on armament . . . [much of it] expended upon fears of invasion." From every point of view, therefore, both Europe and the United States stood to benefit from disarmament. Both European and American leaders were aware of it. And yet, they did not rise to the occasion, in large part out of fear of domestic political repercussions.[60]

In August, 1931, Ambassador Edge thought that a rare opportunity existed for the United States to make a deal with France "buying a reduction in military armament" in exchange for reduction of the French debt. He recommended this action "while our debts are thought to be a real asset." It would soon be clear that "the debts will never be collected," he said, and America's bargaining power would have vanished. Hoover was ready to offer the French exactly such a deal. He was waiting merely for the politically "right mo-

60. FRUS, *Diplomatic Papers, 1932,* I, 180–84; William Starr Myers, *The Foreign Policies of Herbert Hoover, 1929–1933* (New York, 1940), 137–52.

ment" to risk it. But the world situation worsened rapidly. As unemployment rose and France refused even to discuss Brüning's moderate proposals for the revision of the Versailles treaty, time was running out for Germany's highly competent and reasonable chancellor. The demagogic forces, ridiculing democracy and peace, "solving" complex issues with simplistic slogans, and promising work likely to be paid for with blood wages, gained the upper hand in Germany. Lausanne had come too late to halt this political avalanche.[61]

So did President Hoover's memorandum of May 24, 1932, proposing a reduction of battleship and cruiser strength by one third, the reduction of all armies by one third, and the abolition of all aircraft carriers, all submarines, all military aviation, all ranks, and poison gas. If the World Disarmament Conference would not muster the courage for such dramatic action, the president cautioned somberly, it would be a calamity for civilization. It is noteworthy that G. L. Dickinson's classic study, *International Anarchy* (1926), had only recently elucidated the thesis that any massive accumulation of arms always resulted in war. Secretary Stimson agreed with the president's ultimate objectives, but he disagreed with his shock method. The secretary shared the French view that disarmament must be a gradual affair, each successful step leading to the next one. It had to be a continuing process. In his discussions with Tardieu and other French leaders, Stimson softened the original impact of Hoover's massive abolition plan. Tardieu welcomed the assurance that the United States had no intention of depriving Europe, particularly France, of the means of settling its own political affairs. America hoped only to see Europe move toward a constructive settlement based on the realization that military armaments were a cause of insecurity. As far as French ferriage from Africa to Marseilles was concerned, Stimson said, France had to understand that the proposed reductions in naval strength did not apply to it. As long as Great Britain controlled the Mediterranean, "the British navy will control France's tender spot." Tardieu's illness brought Herriot back to the center stage. His agonizing reappraisals moved him a little closer to concessions, but no breakthrough was in sight when Brüning was edged out of office.[62] And the continuing squabbles at the World

61. Stimson, Diary, August 27, 1931, in Stimson Papers.

62. "La situation extérieure de la France en 1932," 1 DA 3, dr. 2, in Papiers Edouard Daladier, FSP; Brüning, *Memoiren*, 600–601.

Disarmament Conference were of absolutely no interest to Hitler. He ratified the failure of this conference by leaving it and leaving the League of Nations.

GENERAL OBSERVATIONS AND A NOTE ON CULTURAL DIFFERENCES

The French were puzzled by Washington's deep involvement in this conference in contrast to its persisting reluctance to underwrite French leadership on the Continent. Actually the Republican administrations of the 1920s abhorred the old alliance system just as much as had George Washington and, more recently, Woodrow Wilson. Besides, Franco-American cooperation was feasible only as long as mutual interests justified it. France frequently misjudged this mutuality by erroneously assuming an identity of interest that simply did not exist as far as the American government was concerned. Convinced of their superiority, Frenchmen tended to patronize the United States. This counterproductive attitude caused as much resentment as self-deception.

The stubborn and often contemptuous manner in which both France and Germany pursued their international goals invited bad feelings against them. Britain and the United States tended to come into the picture because of the adverse effects of French and German policies, not because of any deliberately planned designs for codominion. As a self-appointed guardian of Europe's status quo, France envisioned a nonaggressive Germany as a full member of the European family of nations. But its officials appeared to be more inflexible than this objective warranted. Alas, French politics and public opinion could usually be satisfied only with strongly nationalistic positions. France's obsessive fear led it to treat Germany, particularly up to the time of the Locarno pact, in a way that elevated this fear to the level of a self-fulfilling prophecy. Subsequently, Hitler's rise to power convinced the French of the soundness of their original foresight, because they applied strictly subjective, cause-and-effect interpretations to the events that occurred. Objective historians can, on the contrary, make a convincing case for the unsoundness of French policies vis-à-vis Germany, which accomplished the opposite of what France intended, within the framework of existing realities.

Guided by fear of Germany, France became so accustomed to a

negative attitude toward Germany that it failed to explore alternative policies seriously. This psychologically conditioned shortcoming assumed even greater significance in view of France's simultaneous apprehension of Anglo-Saxon domination. It feared that, should a close Anglo-American entente ever be realized, France would be reduced to an inferior position. Strangely, this twofold anxiety did not lead it to larger conceptions in the formulation of its foreign policy. Logically, a Franco-German political détente, combined with the development of close industrial ties, offered the most promising answer to the competition France faced from both Germany and the Anglo-Saxons. The risks involved in such a positive course were genuine and great. But so were the risks of the traditional policies. The difference lay in the fact that, with vision and courage, the enlightened course offered hope and security; the antagonistic policies perpetuated impasses and insecurity. Such a relationship obviously could not come about or be maintained without mutual trust. The essential precondition for creating the atmosphere in which it could flourish called therefore for enlightened pragmatism, not abusive rivalry.

Another French objective, particularly after America's entry into the First World War, was to perpetuate the perception of close Franco-American ties. The enlistment of America's resources and support promised to solidify the international role to which France aspired. But its ambitions at the expense of other powers, especially Germany, its emphasis on military approaches, and its legalistic and often intransigent attitudes accomplished, once again, the opposite result. For a government in the habit of interpreting contractual obligations narrowly, insisting that others strictly abide by them, the French government displayed a strange inconsistency in regard to reparations and debts. Without considering the damaging consequences for the world economy, it persistently demanded reparations. But for several years it also rationalized the nonfulfillment of its financial obligations to the United States. From the presidency of Wilson to that of Hoover, France lost ground in America, even among its friends.

Neither did the United States accomplish its goals. In the 1920s it appeared to be uninterested in involving itself in European affairs when, in fact, its own economy and world peace required its active participation. Despite isolationist preferences, the interdependence of world trade and the need for stable currencies drew it into the whirlpool of European antagonisms. Its main goal was to minimize the impact of Europe's political and economic conflicts on America. The world paid dearly for the indecision American leaders displayed at crucial moments during the decade from 1914 to 1924. Repeated expressions of "concern" and "neutrality" hardly impressed those bent on empire. And the monotonous rejection of any linkage between debts and reparations not only left the world's economy swinging in the air but, ironically, in the end it helped bury them together.

Upset by America's post–World War policies, France also feared being overshadowed by a combination of the Anglo-Saxons. It noted that in business matters the British and Americans were guided by similar principles and thought processes, whereas the French thought and acted quite differently. But though the French knew they could not definitely rely on Great Britain, they realized that England's geographic proximity and strategic stakes in Europe tied them geopolitically closer to England than to the United States.

Despite common traits and substantial cooperation, Anglo-American global interests differed sufficiently to discount the emergence of an Anglo-American confederation. Indeed, anxious to remain a world leader, Britain sometimes employed divisive tactics. A memorandum of the U.S. Department of State's Division of Western European Affairs, dated September 29, 1931, called attention to the mischievous nature of British diplomacy toward contemporary Franco-American relations. Prior to Laval's visit to Washington, Lord William George Tyrell, the British ambassador to France, endeavored to induce the French premier to ask the United States for a consultative pact that would practically guarantee French military and political security as the price for a successful disarmament conference. Inasmuch as such a condition was foredoomed to be rejected, the State Department cast suspicion upon British diplomacy in respect to Franco-American relations, as it had in fact been doing ever since 1917. The department acknowledged the existence of a deep psychological gulf between France and America but also maintained that there were no fundamental political differences. On the other hand, it also saw the same psychological gulf between France and England and noted that, in addition, these two countries had to cope with "a sharp divergence of political interests." It therefore concluded that, on both these grounds, Britain was not qualified to "interpret" French policy to the United States, although "ever since

America's entry into the World War, the British have endeavored to constitute themselves as the logical interpreters, the diplomatic middlemen, between France and the United States." In view of the fact that, in accordance with traditional balance-of-power techniques, Britain played off France against America and vice versa, the memorandum contended that the British "intensified American suspicions of France and French suspicions of America." Recommending direct and friendly understanding with France, the State Department summed up its somewhat anti-British attitude: "We are quite capable producing our own diplomacy without the suave midwifery of the British Foreign Office."[63]

The perceptive observation of Warrington Dawson, the special assistant of the American Embassy in Paris, concerning Franco-American diplomatic relations is interesting in the light of historical perspective. During his protracted residence in France, he noted that "the French are never on really cordial terms with both Great Britain and the United States at the same time." Strong anti-Americanism in France at the time of the Spanish-American War resulted in closer relations with England. But the Fashoda crisis brought England and France to a confrontation. Faced with this situation, France desired closer relations with America, "until the *Entente Cordiale* was established, when once again France marked her rapprochement with England by cooling off towards the United States. . . . The swing of the pendulum," Dawson observed in 1933, "has continued ever since, even during the whole of the World War when the French could never at one and the same time have equally friendly feelings towards both nations of Anglo-Saxon origin."[64]

Nevertheless, France's desire to maintain a tripartite relationship satisfied its need for equality of status and offered the greatest deterrent against German aggression, whatever differences the French had with their Anglo-Saxon "partners." It also opened up opportunities to influence, if not control, the Anglo-Americans and therefore diminish Anglo-Saxon dominance.

The mutually frustrating Franco-American problems after the First World War were further aggravated by developing cultural differences. Whereas nineteenth-century Frenchmen and Americans had

63. U.S. State Department, Division of Western European Affairs, "Comment," September 29, 1931, in RG 59, Box 57, 033.5111, NA.

64. U.S. State Department, "The French Attitude Towards America," Warrington Dawson's confidential report, March 17, 1933, in RG 59, Box 6068, 711.51/91, NA.

found something appealing in each other's respective civilizations, developments in twentieth-century industrial America tended to widen the cultural gulf between them. The individualistically inclined French increasingly detested America's materialistic practices and rationalizations. For example, standardized mass-production methods and their social ramifications offended the sensibilities of bourgeois believers in the virtues of humanism. The clash between the preservation of traditional social values and the restless exploration of innovative social experiments deepened the erosion of the already tenuous ties between France and the United States. It symbolized more than a tension between cultural nostalgia and the search for a "better" world, between a comfortable, known standard of living and an untested, increasingly fast-paced, modern way of life. As French intellectuals saw it, since France had neither the capacity nor the desire to keep up with this alleged "progress," America threatened not only to overtake France and Europe in a power-political sense but also to undermine the cultural foundation of existing civilization. The fear of the spread of this "cancer" caused much ill will. The French elite was especially worried, feeling that it had the most to lose from creeping Americanization. Expressing various degrees of concern, representatives of the elite sounded the alarm over this gathering challenge.

Near the end of the nineteenth century, Paul Bourget, in his *Outre-Mer* (1895), had already noted striking differences between French and American civilization. Believing in the superiority of French social values, this conservative critic and novelist departed the United States convinced that its people's drive and energy would ultimately result in a democracy with "astonishing inequalities" between competing individuals, unlike democracy in France, which had characteristically led to "perpetual levelling." According to Bourget, in America the formula was equal social opportunity; in France, equal social reality.[65]

Although the antidemocratic nationalists of the Action Française were in the forefront of strident attacks against the political system in the United States, the central arguments of French critics were aimed at America's social and industrial system. In his *Scènes de la vie future*, Georges Duhamel expressed the disdain and disgust with which Frenchmen reacted to America's mass-production system. In

65. Paul Bourget, *Outre-Mer: Impressions of America* (New York, 1895), 416–19.

their view the monotonous work on a Ford assembly line reduced the individual to a collectivist tool. They never tired of condemning the brassy, money-chasing, and wasteful life-style of Americans. Its eroding impact on individual creativity and traditional social values, they believed, threatened to usher in a revolution of illusory progress. As Frenchmen by and large disapproved of developments in the New World, so Americans in turn judged French cynicism, indecisiveness, intellectualism, and lack of discipline to be a drag on modern civilization destined to lead to decline.[66]

Even such eminent Franco-American publicists as Bernard Faÿ and André Siegfried did not feel comfortable with the direction in which American life was moving. In his *Civilisation américaine*, Faÿ referred to "the machine as an integral part of American life, the attribute of its soul." But taking a more positive view than did many of his compatriots, he credited it with contributing to social peace and well-being. Siegfried, who analyzed Franco-American differences dispassionately, traced them to different philosophical and sociological roots. Cartesian philosophy, with its emphasis on logical analysis and its mechanistic interpretation of physical nature, he observed, was fundamentally opposed to Bostonian Puritanism and sentimental Wesleyanism. By inference, he thus confirmed the independent and in many respects unique nature of American civilization. In 1927 Siegfried wrote that whereas Frenchmen feel comfortable only in work "free from strict discipline and organized cooperation," Americans value teamwork and organization as essential for efficiency and productivity. He concluded therefore that America is "a materialistic society, organized to produce things rather than people," whereas "Europe squanders her man-power and spares her substance." Although he saw great risks for the integrity of the individual in America's supercollectivism, he acknowledged that it held out the promise of an unprecedented standard of living, not only for Yankees but for all mankind. Profound reservations, however, raised the troubling question of whether it was worth the price in human terms. After all, comfort alone did not necessarily lead to happiness and fulfillment.[67]

66. Georges Duhamel, *Scènes de la vie future* (Paris, 1932), 208–17. For an excellent discussion of this topic, see David Strauss, *Menace in the West: The Rise of French Anti-Americanism in Modern Times* (Westport, Conn., 1978).

67. Bernard Faÿ, *Civilisation américaine* (Paris, 1939), 87; André Siegfried, *America*

The complexity of these different outlooks becomes more evident when one attempts to place them in a broader context. As the center of political gravity shifted away from the heart of Europe after the First World War, concerned Frenchmen felt practically helpless to cope with what they referred to as the industrial and financial "imperialism" of the United States and the momentum of its modern civilization. But what some Europeans diagnosed as "the American cancer" attracted others with great fascination. It was anything but reassuring to these concerned Frenchmen to discover a certain kinship between the United States and Germany. Both seemed to share the quantitative ideal, emphasis on social discipline, persevering stress on method and organization, and the worship of success. Their citizens also shared the same dynamism and vitality, and they were constantly preoccupied with the future. The past did not interest them as it did the French. This emphasis on "becoming" and "changing" contrasted sharply with the static and enduring values cherished by French civilization, which emphasized the qualitative. When the Germans began to adopt American production methods and to imitate American mass civilization, the French took strong exception to the spread of these alien influences.

To the further discomfort of the French, the Soviets, too, cast their eyes on the workings of American society. In 1928 the writer Luc Durtain expressed the alarming view that Soviet Russia enviously admired America's industrial system. As far as France was concerned, the Soviet Union and the United States constituted two massive entities with like tendencies toward materialism and the colossal. Despite their ideologically different economic and political systems, they had more in common with each other than France had with either of them. Caught between these two giants, a weakened postwar France attempted to do what it could to protect the humane foundation of Western civilization from falling victim to the waves of collectivism encircling it. In this large sense, the American peril disturbed Frenchmen, even though the United States did not set out to imperil France. Altogether, though, during this period the French elite was less interested in the United States than was the French

Comes of Age (New York, 1927), 315–16, 348; Firmin Roz, "L'évolution des États-Unis et l'avenir des relations franco-américaines," *Revue Universelle*, XXXII (1928), 175–203; Max Rychner, "Europa und America," *Neue Schweizer Rundschau*, XXI (October, 1928), 721–22.

government. Obviously, they would not have dreamed of applying America's industrial system as a possible approach to solving their country's staggering domestic and international problems. Their virtually contemptuous attitude toward the march of civilization invited grievous trouble.

III

The Crises of the 1930s

SOME FRENCH VIEWS OF AMERICA AND EUROPE

Throughout the 1920s Great Britain and the United States endeavored to improve Germany's situation through peaceful changes. In pursuing such a course, they were hoping to benefit their own economies and to raise the level of stability on the Continent. Rightly or wrongly, Germans of all political shades looked upon France as the symbol of the misguided policies of the Versailles system. When the inadequacies of the limited modifications of this system manifested themselves by the early 1930s in economic deterioration on a global scale and in German resistance to continuing national degradation, the entire world found itself in a quandary.[1]

In 1917 Wilson and Lenin had offered new approaches to the fundamental problem of how to enable the masses to live in peace with dignity, and in 1933 Franklin Delano Roosevelt and Adolf Hitler also appeared on the political scene with new concepts and methods. While the dynamism of Roosevelt and Hitler restored the hope of their peoples, France was politically too divided to produce a resourceful national coalition capable of coping with the profoundly disturbing challenges. The urgency for effective solutions became the more pressing as the French and the Americans, with their democratic and pacifistic proclivities, found themselves vis-à-vis the fascist dictators, with their warlike tendencies.

The unsolved problems of the 1920s—debts, reparations, credits, world trade, disarmament, and security—preoccupied the various powers also in the 1930s. In the meantime, however, power constellations had changed. Within a dozen years victorious France had lost its relative position of strength; Germany had skillfully man-

1. Werner Link, *Die amerikanische Stabilisierungspolitik in Deutschland, 1921–32* (Düsseldorf, 1970), 621–30.

aged to reorganize itself; Britain's desire to head off a violent showdown on the Continent inclined it to dilatory tactics; Italy's territorial ambitions introduced a very disquieting element; Stalin's Russia remained a feared enigma; and Roosevelt's America, a key factor in world affairs, chose not to treat Europe's troubles as matters of truly serious consequence to itself. Indeed, when Hitler and Roosevelt came independently to the conclusion that the European imperial powers were too set in their accustomed ways of conducting their affairs, the two new leaders fell back on selfishly national preferences. Neither the concert of powers of the League of Nations nor various collective-security schemes seemed flexible enough to procure and maintain world stability. Unkept promises of general disarmament led to the failure of the Geneva World Disarmament Conference. Unwilling to be tied down in the web of international monetary agreements insisted upon by France at the London World Economic Conference, President Roosevelt suddenly decided to preserve his freedom of action. The soundness of a nation's internal economic system, he contended, took priority over international currency stabilization. This controversial statement led to the failure of the World Economic Conference, itself a tragic illustration of the apparent inability of France, Great Britain, and the United States to form a solid democratic front. FDR's change of mind in this instance was largely prompted by the prudent precaution not to fall into the clutches of "those crafty Europeans."

Important as the respective domestic policies of the various countries were, France feared above all the consequences of Hitler's threat to tear up the *Versailles Diktat*. In interviews before his assumption of power Hitler stated that he reserved "a fitting place" for France, provided the French bourgeoisie and military would cease encircling Germany. But in one of these interviews he also said, "Joffre did not win the Marne battle nor Foch that of Verdun; our senior commanders were incompetent and incapable of appreciating the advantages of the brilliant Schlieffen Plan." France naturally feared this mentality, without, however, taking protective measures commensurate with the potential peril.[2]

In the checkered record of Franco-American relations, France oscillated from staying close to the United States to maintaining merely

2. Edouard Calic (ed.), *Secret Conversations with Hitler: The Two Newly Discovered 1931 Interviews* (New York, 1971).

peripheral contacts. Individuals in and out of the French government proposed various schemes to block America's penetration of Europe through a European combination of national states. Aristide Briand dreamed of a "United States of Europe." But some nationalists preferred the notion of a "United States of France," or "Greater France," composed of metropolitan France and its colonial empire as the way to counterbalance the United States. Others, like the Comte Edmond de Fels, thought in terms of this French federation as the nucleus of a European Atlantic bloc from which the United States would be excluded. Not the least important objective of this great coalition would be an attempt to draw England away from the United States. Whereas the utopian socialists Robert Aron and Arnaud Dandieu believed the rebirth of France to be possible only by rejecting industrial capitalism of the American variety, André Siegfried, more realistically, believed that Europe could hold its own against the onslaught of American civilization by consciously relying on its considerable creative genius. Unwilling to accept the unalterable fact that in many respects America had overtaken Europe, many Frenchmen treated the United States as if it were a foe. They misjudged realities all around.

The publicist and diplomat Wladimir d'Ormesson took a much broader view. To him, since the World War the United States had occupied the place in world affairs that England had held in the late nineteenth century. The major contemporary economic and financial problems could not possibly be solved without its active participation. Beyond this necessity he saw merit in a European federation as a means of establishing an equilibrium between Europe and America. He judged such a federation even more useful as a means of stemming the eventual offensives of the Soviet Union.[3]

Pierre Etienne Flandin, the prominent conservative political leader, also acknowledged the usefulness of Franco-American cooperation. In his reservations, however, he frankly criticized the United States for not helping Europe as much as was incumbent upon it. He looked upon the United States as if it were Europe's keeper. In addition to the need of liberal American credits, tariffs, and trade policies, Flandin reminded Washington that until passage of the immigration restrictions of the 1920s it had greatly re-

3. Walter Sommer, *Die Weltmacht USA im Urteil der Französischen Publizistik, 1924–1939* (Tübingen, 1967), 124–44. See also Pierre Étienne Flandin, *Politique française, 1919–1940* (Paris, 1947), 81–89.

duced the seriousness of Europe's demographic problems. America's new immigration policy had worsened Europe's housing and employment situations. In international affairs Flandin liked to see the United States assuming more responsibility, whatever his misgivings about certain specific policies. Like many of his compatriots, the total panorama of foreign policy in the 1930s convinced him of the need for a close Anglo-French entente. As a realist, he also understood that in turn the security of the British Empire, notably in the Pacific, depended on Anglo-American cooperation. But the French often indulged in extravagant hopes with respect to America's solidarity with the Western democracies. Helpful as its moral support might be, the United States could at best only strengthen the desirable perception of solidarity.

Undoubtedly, President-elect Roosevelt's conversation with Ambassador Paul Claudel gave rise to high French expectations concerning relations with the United States. The president's genuine sympathy for France and his comprehension of its difficulties was a welcome change from the attitude of his predecessor. Indeed, Roosevelt's assurance that in world affairs he intended to collaborate closely with France seemed to be a return to policies that had been suspended since Wilson's presidency. His promise, in response to the ambassador's urging, to admit, under favorable conditions, all French products not in competition with American products was especially appreciated by French wine producers.[4]

In his confidential instructions to Claudel, Foreign Minister Joseph Paul-Boncour detailed his positions on several urgent issues with which he wished to familiarize the incoming administration. They included the implementation of the Lausanne accords, the stabilization of currencies, the return to the gold standard by those who had abandoned it, an international monetary fund to help countries in temporary need of assistance, the removal of trade barriers, and the restoration of business confidence through the voluntary cooperation of France, Great Britain, and the United States. But to create the atmosphere of confidence needed for the two countries to work together on such issues would take time.[5]

France had every reason to be pleased with President Roosevelt's

4. Paul Claudel to Joseph Paul-Boncour, February 23, 1933, in *DDF*, 1e Série, II, 684–86.

5. Joseph Paul-Boncour to Paul Claudel, February 27, 1933, in *DDF*, 1e Série, II, 700–701.

change of America's policy toward Nazi Germany. In contrast to the frequent support the United States had in the past extended to Germany, the president lectured Hjalmar Schacht, the president of the Reichsbank, whom he saw in mid-May, 1933, that nobody could trust Germany any longer, that it posed a threat to its neighbors, and that he favored the disarmament by the other powers rather than German rearmament. If Germany was seriously concerned about its security, the president would be glad to assist in facilitating a ten-year peace guarantee. André de Laboulaye, the new French ambassador, to whom FDR confidentially relayed this conversation, grasped immediately that the president had gone to the limit. It was up to France now, he advised his superiors, to walk the extra mile for peace. Without such a demonstration, FDR might be compelled to retreat to a more aloof position. In international affairs he was far ahead of American public opinion, the press, and Congress in 1933. Unless the president could convincingly demonstrate that his broad-minded approach served the best interests of the United States and world peace, Laboulaye speculated, he would not be able to withstand public pressures.[6]

THE GENEVA DISARMAMENT CONFERENCE

Both Presidents Hoover and Roosevelt considered disarmament an urgent solution to many of the world's troubles. But Hoover's disarmament proposals had disquieted the major European powers and Japan. He saw clearly that without sharp reductions of weapons, Germany would soon claim the right of self-defense and rearm, regardless of protests and treaty provisions. The choice was clear: the only alternative to disarmament was rearmament and increasing chance of war. Under President Hoover and Secretary of State Stimson the United States had inched closer to cooperation with other nations than it had been before. But cooperation meant neither coordination nor a blank check. The cornerstone of American foreign policy was the Kellogg-Briand Pact, which provided for peaceful approaches to all conflicts. Despite endless French efforts, the United States refused to commit itself "before the event to any form of concerted action or consultation." American public opinion

6. Edouard Laboulaye to Joseph Paul-Boncour, May 16, 20, 1933, in *DDF*, 1e Série, III, 492–500, 542–44.

and such influential leaders as Senators William E. Borah and Hiram Johnson were utterly opposed to any binding participation in a collective-security system. In the course of lengthy arms-embargo deliberations Borah and Johnson went so far, to the annoyance of America's munitions industry, as to insist on its impartial application to both sides in a conflict.[7]

At the Geneva World Disarmament Conference the participating nations essentially stuck to their own viewpoints and found it impossible to arrive at a workable consensus. Time-consuming plans and procrastinating tactics soon exasperated the Germans. On December 11, 1932, England, France, and Italy promised them "equality of rights in a system which would provide security for all nations." What they meant by equality of rights and what Germany understood by it brought out the complexity of this principle. Actually, French officialdom was inclined to deny Germany's legal right to equal treatment in armaments, especially in view of its provocative preparation for another war. In contrast, American officials were concerned about the undesirable consequences of trying to keep Germany in an apparently permanent condition of inequality.[8]

Governments found it easy to be for disarmament in general, but differences over details led to countless arguments. Britain and the United States, for instance, differed in that Americans preferred limitation of the number of ships, whereas the British preferred limitation by ship size. The French did not want to hear of disarmament unless it was preceded by security guarantees. Under both Hoover and FDR the United States was anxious to help bring about disarmament, stressing particularly the urgency of abolishing aggressive weapons, such as heavy tanks, and prohibiting air bombardment. But America steadfastly refused to become involved in strictly European political problems. And contrary to the contentions of those who accused the United States of being an imperialistic warmonger, FDR was not tempted to overcome the hardships of the severe economic depression by activating the war industry.

Britain, too, disappointed the French with its deliberate decision

7. Robert A. Divine, "Franklin D. Roosevelt and Collective Security, 1933," *MVHR*, XLVIII (1961), 42–59.

8. On disarmament see Box 65, Foreign Policy—General, 1934–45, Cordell Hull Papers, Library of Congress, Washington, D.C.; and Edward W. Bennett, *German Rearmament and the West, 1932–33* (Princeton, 1979), 95–96.

not to assume definite commitments in Europe beyond those it had pledged as a member of the league and a signatory of the Locarno treaties. On the question of land armaments, the French proposed in a "maximum plan" the creation, under the auspices of the League of Nations, of a nonprofessional militia army throughout Europe that would halt aggression at its source by removing offensive capabilities. Proponents of this plan saw in this collective-security arrangement the most effective protection of France's frontiers. A "minimum plan" provided for national forces to be at the league's command whenever it appeared necessary to prevent or stop aggression. General Maxime Weygand, chief of the French army's general staff, made himself the spokesman of those professional soldiers for whom the militia system offered too many pitfalls. In any event, the Germans argued that "the defensive or aggressive character of an army depended more upon the arms and war material at its disposal." They were more interested in the nature of armaments than in the size and type of the forces they would be permitted. With such a mix of arguments, prospects for genuine disarmament did not look promising, something the United States deplored deeply.[9]

Few contemporary French statesmen appreciated good relations with the United States as much as Edouard Herriot. Soon after President Roosevelt assumed office, Herriot, then chairman of the Chamber's Foreign Affairs Committee, went to Washington. In mutually informative meetings he brought the president and a number of senators up to date on French views about disarmament. FDR seemed particularly impressed by Herriot's observation that the British navy and the French army maintained peace in Europe and the world and that the French army offered the British navy essential protection. The distinguished Frenchman felt in several respects reassured when he returned to France. The president had indicated his lively interest in world peace by his willingness to help organize it on a global scale. Provided substantial progress was made at Geneva, he held out the hope of relaxing America's neutrality by passively cooperating in the application of sanctions against a European aggressor. He also went along with France's firm insistence that

9. Memorandum from Berlin dated January 19, 1934, in *DDF*, 1re Série, V, 508–12; Stephen Roskill, *Naval Policies Between the Wars* (2 vols.; Annapolis, 1976), II, 140–43.

Germany should not be provided with modern weapons until an overall disarmament agreement had been reached.[10]

On May 16, 1933, President Roosevelt urged the disarmament conference to eliminate all offensive weapons and to take the first definite steps immediately. He also asked the assembled representatives, in addition to solemn reaffirmation of "the obligations they have assumed to limit and reduce their armaments . . . individually to agree that they will send no armed force of whatsoever nation across their frontiers." On May 22, Norman Davis, the chairman of the American delegation, announced his country's willingness "to consult the other states in case of a threat to peace, with a view to avert conflict," and "to refrain from any action tending to defeat" any collective effort of other states to restore peace. But when France attempted to translate such general declarations into a more concrete commitment by linking the United States with the league's machinery against aggressors, the United States, which had gone as far as it possibly could, pulled back.

In an extraordinarily conciliatory speech before the Reichstag, Chancellor Hitler welcomed FDR's proposed method of overcoming the international crisis. At this early stage of his leadership he was "prepared to renounce offensive weapons if the rest of the world does the same [and] to agree to any solemn pact of non-aggression." Was this declaration merely a tactical move to induce others to believe in his reasonableness, thus gaining time for Germany's massive rearmament? Contemporaries could not be sure. We know now that on February 3, 1933, a few days after his assumption of power, the Fuehrer addressed the commanding officers of the army and navy. Concerning his principal objective—building up Germany's military power—he was aware of the enormous hazards he faced in the immediate future. "If France has statesmen," he said, "it will not give us time, but rather attack us."[11]

Hitler's defiant threats during his rise to power to tear up the "so-called peace treaty of Versailles" and his feverish militaristic activities in Germany did not inspire French faith in his pacific assurances. France declared itself willing to disarm drastically after a

10. Edouard Herriot to Joseph Paul-Boncour, April 26, 1933, in *DDF*, 1e Série, III, 326–27.

11. Thilo Vogelsang, "Neue Dokumente zur Geschichte der Reichswehr 1930–1933," in *Vierteljahrshefte für Zeitgeschichte*, II, (1954), 434–36.

transition period of at least ten years if during this time Germany was not permitted to rearm. The French insisted on a system of supervision, control, and sanctions in case of violations. Although Great Britain and, remarkably, the United States would go along with supervision and control, sanctions were completely out of the question. Quite aside from insurmountable political obstacles at home, fundamental differences between the Anglo-Saxons and the French ruled out compromises on the question of sanctions. In September, 1933, Norman Davis explained to Joseph Paul-Boncour that "the Anglo-Saxons were not disposed to define in detail what they would do in future contingencies whereas the French desired to attempt such a definition."[12]

As the impasse at Geneva began to appear hopeless, Davis theorized that a preventive war setting out to crush Germany at once would be an alternative to disarmament. Some French officers considered it seriously, and members of the Second International urged it strongly. But the people and government of France wanted to live in peace with Germany. War was odious to them. Davis, too, counseled against it. At this time France possessed military superiority over Germany and could therefore overrun it. But, Davis cautioned, Germany and its people would not disappear, and the German problem would once again baffle the world and its economy.

In an eloquent speech in the early fall of 1933, Edouard Daladier, president of the council and minister of war, assured Germany of its right to exist as a great nation. He warned, however, that an armaments race would ruin Europe and a war would destroy it. Perhaps steering the French people toward some substantial compromises on armaments, he argued that "national defense is inseparable from a balanced budget." If Germany forced heavy military expenditures upon France, he asked his countrymen to "reject easy and lazy solutions." As American leaders had repeatedly pointed out, heavy military spending seriously interfered with economic recovery.[13]

The longer the Geneva conference lasted, the more obvious it became that mutual mistrust had erected irrational barriers between France and Germany. Without confidence in one's neighbor there

12. "Note de la délégation française à la conférence du désarmement," December 12, 1933, in *DDF*, 1e Série, V, 216–18; "Conversation du ministre avec M. Norman Davis," September 9, 1933, in *DDF*, 1e Série, IV, 389–91.

13. *Le Temps*, October 9, 1933.

could be no feeling of security, and without such security there could be no disarmament. As Schacht had bluntly impressed upon FDR in the course of his discussions in May, the endless disarmament talks at Geneva had convinced Germany of the fundamentally dishonest treatment it received at the hands of the armed powers. When the highly regarded German ambassador, Hans Luther, saw the secretary of state on October 9, he charged France with merely paying lip service to disarmament. Probably in an effort to break up the fairly solid front of France, England, Italy, and the United States, Luther unalterably refused to accept a trial or transition period at the end of which France *might* consent to reduce its armaments and allow Germany a larger military establishment without, however, clearly and publicly spelling out details about this "concession." To him, this proposal amounted to a "thinly veiled disguise" to keep Germany under control. Luther also defended his country's insistent demand for modern sample arms. Since the heavily armed powers were not really disarming, Germany's security demanded equality, he argued. President Roosevelt, as he had previously indicated, remained dead set against any sample weapons for Germany. As to the transition period, he thought in terms of a shorter period with satisfactory arrangements to foster mutual confidence.[14]

As it turned out, the German ambassador's arguments were precisely those Foreign Minister Konstantin von Neurath made on October 14 in his telegram to the president of the Geneva conference advising him that, because Germany's claim to equality of rights was not being satisfied, "the German Government is accordingly compelled to leave the Disarmament Conference." The consequent collapse of the disarmament discussions confronted the world with a new armaments race. The French general staff was in favor of a military response, possibly the occupation of the Rhine provinces. Many economic and political factors, however, persuaded the civilian government to abstain from such action. FDR decided to continue with further disarmament explorations. But following the failure of the London Economic Conference and the virtual collapse of the talks at Geneva, his disappointment came through clearly: "We are not interested in the political element or in the purely European aspect

14. Nancy H. Hooker (ed.), *The Moffat Papers: Selections from the Diplomatic Journals of Jay Pierrepont Moffat, 1919–1943* (Cambridge, Mass., 1956), 98–105.

of peace. . . . We should stay out of relations relating to European peace." Henceforth it was up to Europe to decide whether further disarmament efforts would make any sense. Evidently incapable of managing its affairs in a cooperative way, Europe turned the United States off.[15]

As usual, the situation going into 1934 involved more than the Franco-German differences. Norman Davis was convinced that the best course France could pursue was to control German rearmament with the help of England. But in the same way that France could not count on meaningful cooperation from the United States, neither could it count on the definite guarantees it sought from England. Daladier found England's hesitation incomprehensible. At least theoretically, if by any chance France and Germany should suddenly enter into an agreement, they could, if they wished, divide up continental Europe. The inherent danger of such a policy, he reasoned, ought to make Britain realize the stakes it had in the prevention of a solid Franco-German understanding.

Regarding itself a friend of France, Britain saw contemporary Franco-British differences in quite another light. As Sir John Simon, the British foreign secretary, phrased it, "It was impossible to cooperate with the French unless you agreed with them on everything." England and America, he noted, had their occasional differences, but they did not prevent the two countries from cooperating in other respects. Furthermore, Britain did not intend to sit idly by watching Germany rearm while France was trying to complete its eastern alliances before daring to disarm. Simon hinted that, unless France acted promptly to salvage the disarmament conference, England might decide to head off an unacceptable deterioration of European affairs by making a deal with Germany and Belgium.[16]

France exposed itself to Anglo-American criticism for still another reason. The protection of its vital interests in the Far East had long benefited from the strong presence of American and British sea power in the region. For some time Great Britain had looked upon France as an unreliable ally in the Far East. When the Japanese government announced its intention to terminate the Washington Na-

15. Aide-mémoire of December 13, 1933, and memorandum of December 18, 1933, in Papiers Edouard Herriot, AMAE; FRUS, *Diplomatic Papers, 1933*, I, 273–98.

16. Norman Davis to Cordell Hull, May 29, June 2, 4, 1934, in FRUS, *Diplomatic Papers, 1934*, I, 76–77, 94–97.

val Treaty of 1922, the practical identity of views in Tokyo and Paris on this matter came, in Cordell Hull's words, as "a source of surprise and disappointment" to America and Britain. Referring to the Anglo-Saxon principle of equality in security, in contrast to equality of armaments, Ambassador André de Laboulaye used it to justify the need for revising the 1922 treaty. More concerned about German than Japanese naval expansion, he pleaded on grounds of equality of security for the expansion of French naval defenses. This argument satisfied neither London nor Washington. In fact, it cast doubt on France's dependability as a partner in the Far East.

The fundamental differences distinguishing British policy from that of France were also shared by the United States. Disarmament questions could not be solved without political accommodations. Britain disagreed with France's unyielding determination to maintain the status quo established by the Versailles treaty. It recognized the need for meeting Germany's grievances before Germany would take the law into its own hands. It also disagreed with the French tactic of constant delays accompanied by fine words and holding out hope of indefinite improvements in the future while in the meantime trying to build a ring of alliances around Germany.

Hitler's decision to leave the Geneva conference and the League of Nations marked the beginning of the end of the conference. After a brief postponement it ended in the fall of 1935 in dismal failure. Soviet Ambassador Maxim Litvinov's last-minute proposal to convert the disarmament conference into a permanent peace conference, with American participation, ran counter to basic foreign-policy tenets of the United States. Even the minor agreements of the Second London Naval Conference in 1936 could not help but acknowledge the fact that the dynamics of contemporary power politics had doomed disarmament as an engine of peace.[17]

FRANCO-AMERICAN TRADE RELATIONS AND MONETARY QUESTIONS

Roosevelt's pragmatic economic policies left doors wide open for flexibility, including opportunistic reversals. It was his way of doing business.

17. Memorandum of Jesse I. Straus, January 30, 1935, in FRUS, *Diplomatic Papers, 1935*, I, 182–85.

Historically, Franco-American trade had never developed the volume both countries considered feasible. Their protectionism reached new heights in the early 1930s and contributed to declining imports and exports. To make matters worse, the French market was blocked off by quotas, high quota license fees, sales and turnover taxes, and outright discrimination against American goods, which were placed at a distinct disadvantage compared with those of a number of European countries. Agricultural interests in both countries fought vigorously to protect their markets. California apple and pear growers and southern rice producers complained bitterly about discriminatory duties that made it nearly impossible for them to compete with much lower prices charged in France. American automobile manufacturers and film producers, among others, joined the American chorus against French protectionism. By the same token, French commercial interests were dissatisfied with the limited sales opportunities they found in the United States for champagne, wine, and cheese, and they protested against the often exorbitant tariffs on lace, gloves, and other specialties. When in mid-1934 Cordell Hull launched his crusade for international peace and prosperity through trade on the most-favored-nation principle, the time seemed right to negotiate a liberal trade treaty with France.[18]

Unlike such negotiations in the past, which took years and decades, this time the will existed on both sides to proceed expeditiously. Accompanied by Herbert Feis, economic adviser to the Department of State, the second secretary of the embassy in Paris deliberately cautioned Robert de la Baume, the chief of the Commercial Section of the Ministry for Foreign Affairs, not to build up an artificial bargaining position prior to official trade negotiations. On the contrary, he told Baume on August 29, 1934, he hoped for generous considerations in the interim, without resort to quid pro quo demands. The chief assented in principle but hinted that a quid pro quo would most likely be asked for substantial tobacco purchases, which France could make more cheaply in the Near East, particularly Greece, than in the United States.

The United States wanted a comprehensive treaty, not just partial adjustments. Ambassador Jesse I. Straus, being close to the political machinery of the French government, counseled not to rush into a

18. Pierre Laval to André de Laboulaye, November 5, December 15, 1934, in *DDF*, 1ᵉ Série, VIII, 36–39, 386–87.

treaty or "to waste our best ammunition" until "the French are really prepared to make . . . genuine concessions." It certainly appeared encouraging when the French government held out the possibility of conceding minimum tariff rates throughout their schedule. No doubt France's difficult economic situation dictated a broad search for relief through exports. The United States found itself in a similar situation.[19]

Politicians in both countries did not ignore the domestic political dividends that might derive from improved international trade. In this connection it was noteworthy that diplomatic officials often had to convince their colleagues in the Departments of Commerce and Agriculture of the merit of making certain concessions. In essence, the United States offered France an enlarged market and a position of protected equality. In return it asked for nondiscrimination and lower tariff rates and turnover taxes. When in the preliminary discussions French vested interests resorted to old-fashioned tricks, an official from the French Foreign Ministry confidentially suggested to the Americans that his hand would be strengthened if proposals for concessions as yet withheld would emanate from Washington rather than from him. Why, for instance, should minimum tariffs be applied to German chemicals but not to the American chemical industry?

Table 3

United States Trade with France, 1921–1945
(in millions of dollars)

	1921–25 average	1926–30 average	1931–35 average	1936–40 average	1941–45 average
U.S. Exports	265.2	244.6	117.5	172.4	98.6
U.S. Imports	147.9	152.7	58.5	58.7	4.0

Sources: U.S. Bureau of the Census, *Commerce Yearbook, 1930*, p. 129; U.S. Department of Commerce, *Foreign Commerce and Navigation of the United States, 1935*, p. 701, and *1946*, p. 4.

Between 1929 and 1934 American exports to France declined from $265,591,895 to $115,706,656. During the same period, French exports to the United States fell from $171,485,155 to $57,326,673.

19. Memorandum of Harold L. Williamson, August 31, 1934, Cordell Hull to Jesse I. Straus, October 13, 1934, Straus to Hull, October 14, November 22, 1934, all in FRUS, *Diplomatic Papers, 1934*, II, 176–84.

Clearly, this sorry state of affairs called for corrective action.[20] In May, 1935, Cordell Hull officially announced the opening of Franco-American negotiations for a trade treaty. The French government stood ready to extend conditional most-favored-nation treatment predicated on reciprocity. With few specific exceptions, it was willing to accord minimum tariff rates in bilateral commercial treaties. It was justly concerned, however, with fluctuations in currency exchange and their consequent impact on cost and price levels. Stabilization of currencies, France urged, ought to precede any serious effort to break down trade barriers. Inasmuch as the French were contemplating replacing their quota system with more desirable all-around tariff procedures, Americans had to keep their eyes on the rate changes this process was likely to produce. To safeguard whatever concessions the United States made, Washington endeavored to include in the trade treaty a provision for automatic cancellation under certain conditions. The United States saw this provision as a means to discourage the unfavorable unilateral revision of concessions received. On the whole, the French went to their extreme limit to facilitate possibilities for trade expansion between the two countries. As a sine qua non, however, they insisted on large tariff reductions on laces, wines, and cigarette paper.[21]

In the treaty concluded on May 6, 1936, both sides indeed lowered many tariffs as much as 50 percent. The United States granted France most-favored-nation status, and France generously agreed to reduce even its minimum tariff on a number of important American items. As Georges Bonnet, the minister of commerce, declared, "With this treaty the two great republics of America and Europe demonstrate to the world their faith in the promise of liberalism." American public opinion welcomed this step toward détente and underscored it with a revival of tourism to France.[22]

Subsequent minor difficulties in the implementation of the treaty were promptly worked out. It soon became evident that Bonnet actually wished to enlarge the scope of the trade agreement. What he

20. Jules Henry to Pierre Laval, May 14, 1935, CPEU, Vol. 452, AMAE. See also FRUS, *Diplomatic Papers, 1934*, II, 185–95, 214–21.

21. Jesse I. Straus to Henry Morgenthau, Jr., March 22, 1935, in Paris Cables, Henry Morgenthau, Jr., Papers, FDRL.

22. Antoine Touche, "Les relations économiques entre la France et les États-Unis—Le traité de commerce du mai 6, 1936," *France-Amérique*, May–June, 1936, pp. 101–104. See also, Georges Bonnet to Yvon Delbos, April 23, 1937, CPEU, Vol. 454, AMAE.

had in mind was to enlist the United States as an important link in France's grand strategy. He inquired "whether the United States would agree in principle to a plan to provide economic outlets for Germany if the French government should . . . develop a large scale comprehensive plan for this." Ambassador Bullitt reminded the minister that, in principle, the United States never accepted vague commitments: "Americans were not in the habit of promising to get married until they had seen the face of the lady." But the serious nature of this inquiry deserved a more thorough exploration to determine whether Germany's legitimate needs could be met through such economic cooperation. After all, if it could contain Germany's ambitions and check its rearmament, the United States would benefit as much as France.

As a rule, the operations of French business enterprises in the United States were infinitely less encumbered than those of American interests in France. One of the most troublesome complaints of American business concerns operating in France through French subsidiary corporations involved a so-called double-dividend tax. In addition to the regular French taxes imposed upon the income and dividends of the French subsidiary, the American parent corporation's dividends were also taxed "on the theory that a portion of the earnings and profits out of which such dividends were paid were derived from French sources." By a convention signed at Paris on April 27, 1932, and ratified by President Hoover July 25, France gave up its right to collect this double tax. The businessmen concerned, however, were extremely irritated when the Ministry of Finance refused to submit the document to parliament for ratification. When the Chamber of Deputies and the Senate finally considered action on it, they took their time because they felt America's advantages by far exceeded its concessions. They also thought the convention could be used as leverage in future debt and trade negotiations. It took the threat of American retaliation and practically the full weight of the entire French government to persuade the minister of finance and the chairman of the Senate finance committee to complete the ratification process. After three years, the ratifications were finally exchanged on April 9, 1935.[23]

23. For the text of the convention, see *Senate Documents*, No. 134, 75th Cong., 3rd Sess., 4184–87. See also Cordell Hull to Franklin D. Roosevelt, January 17, 1935, in folder labeled "France, 1940–45" POF; Jesse Straus memorandum October 25, 1935, in RG 59, Box 6298, 851.00/1441, NA.

Another issue also illustrated the frustrations Americans experienced doing business in France. After they had obtained twenty-year licenses, American oil interests invested about fifty million dollars in France for import facilities and refineries. But in 1933 they were suddenly confronted with the possibility of a French government oil monopoly. If it was true that France intended to rely heavily on Russian oil, such a shift would jeopardize the Americans' operations and investments. Regardless of whether such a shift would be made for economic or political reasons, the American oil companies concerned would be hurt. For they had "so developed crude oil production in this country [the United States] as to meet the requirements of their French refineries." Naturally they enlisted the aid of the State Department to make official representations with a view toward protecting them whatever the French government decided to do.

The French admired Roosevelt's resourcefulness. Beset by internal economic and political troubles and the possibility of war, they appreciated FDR's belief that the solution for the deepening world crisis must be cooperation among the major powers. Such an international outlook augured well for heading off what looked like a wholesale collapse of the world's economic and financial system. Because Roosevelt realized the seriousness of the situation, he was a man in a hurry. Early in April, 1933, he invited many leading statesmen to visit him to lay the groundwork for the world economic conference that Hoover and Stimson had planned for the spring of 1933. After consultation with Prime Minister MacDonald and Premier Herriot, Roosevelt agreed that it should convene in London on June 12.[24]

In the meantime, Roosevelt's still indefinite policies underwent successive changes resulting in a shift from international interdependence to an emphasis on intranationalism. Although originally he was agreeable, given a tariff truce that lasted until the end of the London Economic Conference, to liberal trade provisions, stabilization of currencies, and maintenance of the gold standard, the president, a pragmatist rather than an ideologue, then moved away from these positions, at least temporarily. His abandonment in April

24. For a general discussion of the London Economic Conference, consult Raymond Moley, *The First New Deal* (New York, 1966), 393–496, and Elliot A. Rosen, *Hoover, Roosevelt, and the Brains Trust: From Depression to New Deal* (New York, 1977), 369–80.

of the gold standard, his devaluation of the dollar, and his retreat from monetary stabilization followed the recommendations of his advisers who believed that the restoration of America's economic and financial strength must precede its cooperation in international affairs. Indeed, these advisers considered America's recovery unlikely if it permitted Europe, which was much less self-contained than the United States, to slow it down by exploiting it. In his first inaugural address, FDR had already revealed his general direction: "Our international trade relations, though vastly important, are, in point of time and necessity, secondary to the establishment of a sound national economy. . . . I shall spare no effort to restore world trade by international economic readjustment, but the emergency at home cannot wait on that accomplishment." From Roosevelt's point of view, price inflation and public works, in the United States and in all other countries, held out the best promise for stimulating the world economy.[25]

France's priorities put monetary stabilization and related credit questions at the top of the list. Like Great Britain and the United States, France had by now come to the realization that high tariffs, quotas, and other impediments to international trade no longer protected its interests. But it saw no profit in such trade as long as volatile currency fluctuations created an intolerable instability. The devaluation of the British pound and the American dollar, France feared, might sooner or later compel it to devaluate the franc again, jeopardizing the maintenance of its gold standard. An agreed-upon stabilization of currencies was its sine qua non for any meaningful concessions. It also continued to press for the final liquidation of the destabilizing debts and reparations issues. Already before the world economic conference Bonnet, the chief French delegate to it, predicted its failure if it did not resolve these issues. When FDR instructed his delegation, headed by the secretary of state, to bar any discussion of debts and disarmament and to concentrate on ways to expeditiously restore health to the world economy, the French were upset.[26]

By early July the London Economic Conference had reached a crisis point. France, taking the lead on the issue of the gold standard, proposed: "(a) That it is in the interest of all concerned that stability

25. Franklin D. Roosevelt to Cordell Hull, May 30, 1933, in FRUS, *Diplomatic Papers, 1933*, I, 622–27.

26. 1 DA 3, dr. 4, April 13, May 13, 1933, in Papiers Daladier.

in the international monetary field be attained as quickly as practicable; (b) that gold should be reestablished as the international measure of exchange value." In the meantime, all governments, whether on the gold standard or not, were asked to pledge to adopt measures limiting exchange speculation. FDR doubted that immediate stabilization in the international monetary field would create permanent stability. In any case, he wanted to preserve his freedom to follow his method "of stabilizing our own domestic price level in terms of the dollar regardless of foreign exchange rates." Rejecting "the specious fallacy of achieving a temporary and probably an artificial stability in foreign exchange on the part of a few large countries only," he advocated the replacement of "old fetishes of so-called international bankers" by national currencies with a steady purchasing power. He did not mind letting France know that the original purpose of the conference had been to find permanent solutions to world economic problems, not to search for answers to the domestic economic problems of one nation.

Although Hull was bewildered by the president's shift toward national priorities, he also deplored the conference's undue emphasis on monetary issues. He tried to fight off French attempts to disrupt it in response to FDR's rejection of their recommendations. Ambassador Bullitt, the executive officer of the American delegation, found France's obstruction to the continuation of the conference so obnoxious that he described Bonnet as being about "as cooperative as a rattlesnake." Bullitt evaluated the failure of the conference from a broader perspective. In a personal letter to FDR, dated July 8, 1933, he recommended a reappraisal of America's relations with France. Its uncooperative and negative policies with respect to disarmament, debts, and now world economic questions, he wrote, showed such a contempt for our collaboration with them in foreign affairs "that the time has almost come for us to make it clear to the French . . . by appropriate actions . . . [that] our personal affection for them will not prevent us from refusing to support them" in future exigencies.

Under the competitive national state system, each nation had the right to pursue its own policies. At least in principle the obstructiveness of the United States seemed as "justified" as that of France and the other gold bloc countries. Erroneously, each side assumed what was appropriate for itself was also desirable for the other. But the interests of the United States and France were not identical, though they were sometimes critically interrelated. As Great Britain had the habit, often trying to others, of deliberately postponing decisions, and as the United States was usually reluctant to be Europe's "generous Uncle Sam," so France, unyielding on its course of foreign policy, not only overplayed its rather weak international cards but also employed bureaucratic negotiating methods that led to counterproductive results. The breakdowns at London and Geneva exposed the disunity among the great democracies. Evidently they did not grasp the full significance of this division, but the dictators took notice of it.

During the next three years, conditions forced London, Paris, and Washington to review their positions on monetary stabilization. In addition to the devaluation of the dollar, the pound had fallen from 124.21 francs in 1931 to about 75 francs in 1935. The resulting trade disadvantage seriously hurt the French economy. The riots of 1934 and the aggravating consequences of Gaston Doumergue's deflationary policies, which culminated in the budgetary crisis of 1934–35, were warning signals that neither Frenchmen nor the international financial community could safely ignore. The lack of confidence in the franc was illustrated in 1935 by the central bank's loss of gold reserves in the amount of sixteen billion francs, an amount equal to about 20 percent of its holdings in the banner year 1932. Although under these circumstances devaluation of the franc might have been an appropriate remedy, most French politicians regarded it as an unmitigated social catastrophe. An "ultra-confidential" informal exploration in March, 1935, by the Bank of France sought the United States Treasury's cooperation for a joint offer to Great Britain of "a credit of very large proportions" to halt the further decline of the pound. Robert Lacour-Gayet, speaking in behalf of the Bank of France, made this defensive sounding to avoid, as he explained, "an international race in currency depreciation." The U.S. Treasury's negative response obviously made it unnecessary to inquire about Britain's likely reaction to such a proposal.[27]

By now President Roosevelt did not mind considering de facto stabilization if it would help to avoid another devaluation. Signifi-

27. Jesse Straus to Henry Morgenthau, Jr., March 7, 1935, in Paris Cables, Morgenthau Papers.

cantly, he put Henry Morgenthau, Jr., the secretary of the treasury, rather than Secretary of State Hull, in charge of stabilization. More than differences of opinion between the State Department and the Treasury Department motivated FDR in this choice. Hull's conservative monetary views and way of doing things simply were no match for Morgenthau's resourcefulness and competence in international finance. Besides, Roosevelt's and Morgenthau's minds usually clicked, and this, too, facilitated their working relationship. Jacob Viner, the able young economist in Treasury who had recently acquired firsthand knowledge about conditions in Europe, impressed upon his superiors the view that without exchange stability there could be no realistic hope for recovery.

Early in April, 1935, Morgenthau decided to strengthen the troubled franc by allocating $5 million for France from his stabilization fund. In this move he was guided by considerations of self-protection. The gloomy situation in France convinced French capitalists that it would be prudent to convert their francs to gold, buy dollars with it, and invest them safely in the United States. The final outcome of this process, besides accelerating international monetary disorder, threatened to be France's departure from the gold standard. Should this come about at a time when the United States held large amounts of francs, American losses could be very heavy. Prudence therefore required that the Bank of France guarantee that any acquisition of francs by the stabilization fund would be promptly convertible into gold. France accepted this condition and on May 29 asked for a credit of $200 million.

With the object in mind of involving Britain in the evolving de facto stabilization process, Morgenthau suggested to the French that they ask the British for $50 million of this amount. Since the British had indicated that they were not interested in preserving the stability of the franc, the French were unwilling to follow up on the secretary's recommendation. Morgenthau therefore provided, with FDR's approval, the total amount. It was a lifesaver for the Bank of France. Following the fall of the conservative Flandin government on May 31, the franc was under siege. But America's credit prevented a panic and enabled France's political leaders to contemplate eventual devaluation in an orderly fashion. When the secret of this "miracle" became known, the French were immensely grateful for Morgenthau's "broad understanding." He had not only "protected the franc from the erosions of fright and the raids of international speculators," as the governors of the European central banks gladly acknowledged at Brussels, but he had also begun to engage the United States in the important process of de facto stabilization.[28]

If this process was to progress effectively, Morgenthau sensed, Britain's participation in it would be absolutely essential. Although British exporters who sold their goods primarily in sterling markets were not overly preoccupied with currency fluctuations, there existed enough sentiment in Britain favoring de facto stabilization, provided the United States took an active part in it. In fact, the real issue—an incredibly delicate one—was not American participation, but Anglo-French cooperation. When Léon Blum became premier on June 4, 1936, the deterioration in his country had reached dangerous proportions. The German occupation of the Rhineland in March, the prospect of another war, the unrest on the part of the demoralized French working class, bourgeois fears of the socialist regime, and the likelihood of devaluation produced a massive flight of capital from France. The prompt devaluation of the franc became a matter of urgency. But the Blum government—or any other, for that matter—could not dare to proceed with it, because it would be political and social dynamite unless, Morgenthau speculated, Great Britain and the United States could give the assurance that they "would not devalue further if the French devalued twenty to twenty-five percent." The secretary of the treasury tried his best to persuade Britain to join in the effort not only to save France, but to prevent a catastrophic smashup in Europe. He succeeded, but only under the procedural condition that France approach London directly.

When Emmanuel Monick, French financial attaché in London, arrived in Washington on June 20 to explore confidentially the possibility of a tripartite currency agreement, he was pleased to find that Morgenthau had already laid out the preliminary steps for it. Among them was the requirement that France take the initiative in soliciting Britain's support. Ironically, the French reluctantly agreed to take this step only after FDR explained to them the propriety of paying respect to Britain's "amour propre." In the course of their frank dis-

28. John Morton Blum, *From the Morgenthau Diaries* (3 vols.; Boston, 1959–67), I, 130–38.

cussions Monick assured his American colleagues that the profits from the contemplated devaluation would go to a French stabilization fund rather than to meet the budget deficit.

After Monick's unexpectedly promising mission, the French government attempted to go far beyond the accepted limits of Anglo-American cooperation, something France had typically and unsuccessfully done so often in the past. The French draft agreement that reached the Treasury Department on September 9 contained a number of unacceptable provisions. It called for fixed rates to be maintained, the management of the currencies to be entrusted to the three central banks, the eventual return to the gold standard, and details on the monetary rates to be embodied in a tripartite treaty. Although the Americans and the British had spelled out the limits to which they were prepared to go, namely, flexibility of rates on a twenty-four-hour basis only, no return to the gold standard, management of the currencies by the treasuries of the three countries rather than private financiers, and the format to be a gentlemen's agreement, it "pained" President Roosevelt that the second French draft did not differ much from the first. Exasperated by this clumsy conduct, Morgenthau simply advised the French government to "read our note very carefully because we have stated our ideas." The French leaders understood this final message and accepted the American draft in toto. On October 1 they devalued the franc by about 25 percent. This announcement was accompanied by the publication of the Tripartite Agreement, a limited technical monetary device to maintain short-term stability of rates. This *modus vivendi*, subsequently adopted also by Belgium, the Netherlands, and Switzerland, helped at least for the time being to delay the introduction of exchange controls. Not least important, the French hailed it as a welcome manifestation of solidarity by the three major democracies.[29]

The political connotations of this overstatement may have temporarily improved the morale of some Frenchmen. To skeptics it amounted to wishful thinking. Actually, until the defeat of France in 1940, Great Britain and the United States stood by the Tripartite Agreement at considerable costs and risks to themselves. But France faced economic disaster long before Hitler delivered the coup de grâce. Several factors contributed to it. While other countries began

29. New York *Times*, September 27, 1936, Sec. E, pp. 1, 3.

to recover from their depression, France's deepening economic deterioration shook the franc again. The deflationary policies of the period from 1932 to 1936, combined with declining exports, increased defense expenditures, and the rising national debt, weakened confidence in the franc. Strikes, disorders, and costly social reforms further worsened France's situation. The lack of patriotism, furthermore, on the part of those bourgeois capitalists who, with the connivance of bankers and financiers, took their fortunes to safer depositories abroad, did incalculable damage. Already by the end of January, 1937, the gold deposited with the French stabilization fund was no longer sufficient to halt the flight of capital and the consequent slide of the franc.[30]

Under these circumstances, Socialist Finance Minister Vincent Auriol began to grasp at straws to avert total financial collapse. Through Jacques Rueff, a highly capable official in the Ministry of Finance, he reached out for several American rescue possibilities. First he inquired whether the American stabilization fund would be willing to purchase francs and hold them "without conversion into gold for a few days." Then he expressed the naïve belief that "France's financial difficulties would be completely ended" if it were announced that the American stabilization fund had made some five billion francs available to the French stabilization fund "for the period of six months or a year." When told that such transactions would violate the spirit of the Johnson Act—which barred American loans and credits to governments and governmental subdivisions defaulting on their debts to the United States—Auriol and Rueff came up with another scheme, inquiring whether the City of Paris or the French government railroads could obtain a loan on the New York market. Ambassador Bullitt quickly dashed such hopes. Even if the Johnson Act were not in existence, he pointed out, the risks would be much too high to grant such a loan to a country burdened with enormous military expenditures and budget deficits. Significantly, European countries were also reluctant to come to France's assistance. Even the governor of the Bank of France soberly asked himself why should foreigners "buy francs and lend money to France when Frenchmen themselves will not hold their own currency or subscribe to securities of the national government?" Seeing these

30. Shepard B. Clough, *France: A History of National Economics, 1789–1939* (New York, 1939), 316–19; Wolfe, *The French Franc Between the Wars*, 73–79, 113–43.

possible escape routes blocked, the trapped finance minister finally suggested the most objectionable of all "solutions": since the Anglo-American partners in the Tripartite Agreement did not want to be bound by a fixed gold value, he suggested, they should agree to an understanding that if one of the three currencies "should slide the other two should move correspondingly and simultaneously."[31]

Between October, 1936, and the end of 1937 the downward spiral of the franc took it from the minimum rate of 4.33 to a quotation in New York at about 2.62. This seemingly endless spiral became a matter of serious concern to Morgenthau. Since France would not, and perhaps could not, stabilize its finances, he felt that somebody should "tell the French they were a bankrupt, fourth class power." How much longer could the United States afford to support the Tripartite Agreement? Morgenthau was prepared to recommend to the French temporary exchange controls, despite their disruptive global repercussions. In the end, he and the British supported the Tripartite Agreement for political reasons. Within the political constraints imposed upon FDR, he found it convenient to pay the price for it, but with some misgivings. Such French foibles as wanting to live well without working hard, waving the tricolor but evading taxes and exporting capital, and acting like a great power when France could not even satisfactorily manage its own internal affairs raised the question in Washington whether one could really help a nation that does not help itself.[32]

THE LINGERING DEBT QUESTION

No issue poisoned Franco-American relations as much as the debt settlement. Although it is clear that the consequences of France's failure on December 15, 1932, to honor its debt obligations to the United States far outweighed the financial significance of the amount due, the circumstances surrounding the drawn-out history of this embarrassing episode are easier to record than to comprehend.

Ignoring Premier Herriot's appeal to pay the installment, the French chambers voted decisively to turn it down. Herriot consid-

31. William C. Bullitt to Henry Morgenthau, Jr., January 25, February 15, 1937, Paris Cables, Morgenthau Papers.

32. William C. Bullitt to Henry Morgenthau, Jr., January 25, 1938, in *ibid*. See also Blum, *Morgenthau Diaries*, I, 456–76.

ered the default as irreconcilable with his personal and national honor. At this critical moment in world history he thus felt compelled to step down as premier, although he ranked among the few farsighted statesmen the postwar political system had produced. In the cooperative spirit of the recent Lausanne "settlement" of reparations, Herriot had proposed to the American government a new examination of the debt question. He hoped to close the books on it with a generous overall settlement.

In both France and the United States the legislative branches and public opinion hamstrung the executives, who were dependent on them whether they liked it or not. These political aspects clearly prevented an early settlement. Neither side tired of reiterating its standard arguments. Procedurally, the United States steadfastly refused to follow the French proposal that it deal with the European debtors as a unit. The Americans assumed that such a European front would put them at a disadvantage, whereas dealing with each debtor separately would put competitive pressure on the Europeans. Competent French analysts countered this superficially convincing argument by insisting that any definite debt settlement could be accomplished only within the framework of an overall international economic accord. Bilateral arrangements, they contended, would fail to provide the depressed world economy with the stimulus it needed. Americans cautioned the procrastinators that should they ever again need huge American credits their default would necessarily bar them. In principle, the Americans continued to reject the linkage between debts and reparations and still refused to acknowledge that the original financial arrangements had been anything else but business transactions. The Mellon-Bérenger accord of 1926 had already cut the total French debt in half, and the devaluation of the dollar in 1933 had reduced it by another 40 percent. Why, then, did the French resist an honorable liquidation of the debt?[33]

All the French governments of the period pleaded temporary inability to pay, but actually they feared that any attempt to settle the debts would drive them from office. This political dynamite would "pulverize" them. They also claimed that the Hoover moratorium and the Lausanne agreement did assume the linkage between debts

33. Alexandre Gauthier, "Les Etats-Unis et l'Europe," *Revue d'histoire diplomatique*, LI (1937), 241–65.

and reparations, whether or not the United States officially admitted it. Without the resumption of German reparation payments, an illusory hope in the 1930s, France decided to take care of its debts to America in its own way. It acknowledged its obligation and gave assurance that it would not contemplate unilateral violation of the agreement concerning the debts. But its delaying tactics cast such doubts on the sincerity of its intentions that the United States in April, 1934, responded with the Johnson Act. After the long years of Franco-American debt negotiations in the 1920s, the long-delayed ratification of the Mellon-Bérenger accord, and its barren implementation, the patience of the American Congress had finally come to an end. French actions had contributed prominently to the resentment that led to the passage of this punitive measure. Those American politicians who did not want to see the United States assume an active role in international politics exploited the foreign-debt question to the hilt, and so did the Hearst press, which was of the same persuasion. During these turbulent years the Johnson Act hurt not only France, but international trade and finance as well. For good measure, it was evident that the democratically oriented *Vossische Zeitung* had a point in its incisive comment on the French Chamber's original failure to appropriate the money for the American installment: "If France is not morally obliged to reimburse America, then the moral basis of the Versailles treaty has been completely destroyed and Germany is no longer obliged to be bound by it."[34]

In December, 1932, to soothe the sensibilities of the French, President-elect Roosevelt preferred to use temperate and informal methods to coax them into payment of the installment. General agreement, however, existed that a silent reaction to the default might be misinterpreted as acquiescence. Frequent allusion to it kept it politically alive. The amounts due were relatively small and would not have caused any hardship. The roughly nineteen million dollars due on December 15, 1932, had only a year later risen to eighty-two million dollars. Owen Johnson, the playwright and novelist, who had frequent access to the higher echelons of the French power structure, reported to President Roosevelt that the "extremely anti-American" André Tardieu had done his utmost to block the Decem-

34. Vol. 32, November 11, 23, December 6, 15, 1932, in Papiers Herriot; New York *Herald Tribune*, December 3, 1936.

ber 15 payment. It was noteworthy that the British and French treasuries acted more nearly in concert than their respective political colleagues.[35]

The French press welcomed the news of the British decision to join other defaulters on June 15, 1934. In the opinion of several writers and parliamentarians, both the Johnson Act and this lapse of existing debt agreements called for a realistic revision of the agreement, taking into account the changed economic and political conditions. At the meeting of the Bank for International Settlements in April, 1934, central bankers expressed extremely critical views of the Johnson Act. In their judgment, debtors were not likely to step up their payments to the United States as a result of it, and European financial centers rather than American international bankers stood to benefit from it. But its most serious consequence—practical exclusion of American capital—would lead to a tendency "to revert to the undesirable practice of European capital countries making loans individually to nations within certain spheres which reciprocate with political views." Finally, American export trade, so vital to recovery, was expected to suffer. On balance, the Johnson Act would hurt the United States more than its debtors.[36]

In the mid-1930s, as long as Laval held key positions, Ambassador Straus feared the debt question would be held in abeyance. In addition to his inflexible objections to its liquidation, Laval was too preoccupied with European affairs to devote much thought and time to American problems. Among the French statesmen who had the courage to denounce such shortsightedness, Herriot and Blum stood out. In an election speech former Premier Herriot delivered at Lyons on April 9, 1936, he reminded his audience that he had been forced out of office in 1932 because of the American debt question. Soon after FDR's first inauguration he invited Herriot to Washington to discuss ways and means of settling the debt question. President Roosevelt urged Herriot, then president of the Radical Socialist party, to "make a gesture . . . give me something on account. . . . I shall be only too glad to assist you, if I can, in all international affairs." The French leader appreciated Roosevelt's friendly disposition to-

35. André Laboulaye to Joseph Paul-Boncour, December 28, 1933, in *DDF*, 1e Série, V, 373–75; "Problèmes des dettes," in *DDF*, 1e Série, III, 458.

36. U.S. Embassy in Paris to Henry Morgenthau, Jr., April 10, June 5, 6, 1934, in Paris Cables, Morgenthau Papers.

ward France, as he indicated when he told his audience at Lyons, "Who knows whether one of these days we shall not see at the White House some German-American." Significantly, he also said, "Oh! if we were sufficiently wise not to forget our friendships!"

Concerned about his country's increasingly precarious position in foreign affairs, Herriot urged the leader of the French Socialist party, Léon Blum, to develop the closest possible ties with the Americans. A few weeks before Blum became premier he publicly denounced France's unilateral abrogation of its solemn contract with the United States. This act, he said, "had offended America's sense of moral and commercial honesty." Ambassador André de Laboulaye also urged his government to break with the recent custom of periodically sending courteous notes but not the money due. Such a gesture, he did not doubt, would be interpreted as tangible proof of a new spirit in Franco-American relations. When Blum took steps in this direction, as much as President Roosevelt welcomed them, he nevertheless made it clear that France should not make small payments to the United States in the expectation of then being in a position to float or obtain large loans.[37]

Owen Johnson's trial ballons led him to speculate that France might go as far as to pay one billion dollars to get rid of the American debt. FDR doubted that this amount would satisfy Congress. When Ambassador Straus discussed the matter with a high official of the Bank of France, he was told that the payment "must be small, and it must be in a lump sum without instalments." Straus himself suggested, on a strictly personal and informal basis, a method of payment that Foreign Minister Louis Barthou considered ingenious and workable. Ambassador Paul Claudel was also impressed by it. According to this scheme, the French government would deliver to the American treasury bonds for the full amount of the French debt. They would run for a very long time, one hundred years or more, and carry interest at between 1 and 2 percent. American businesses and tourists requiring French exchanges would buy bonds from the treasury with dollars and pay their expenses in France with these bonds. Finally, the French treasury would pay French holders of such bonds in francs, thus avoiding all currency transfer problems.

37. Jesse Straus to Cordell Hull, April 17, May 14, 19, 1936, in FRUS, *Diplomatic Papers, 1936*, I, 579–83; André de Laboulaye to Yvon Delbos, November 18, 1936, CPEU, Vol. 361, AMAE.

In the end, though, this scheme and many others remained just an idea.[38]

It took the dramatic political developments of the second half of the 1930s to bring the French government to the realization that it had been a bad mistake to treat the irritating debt question so nonchalantly. This lingering obstacle to better relations with the United States, it admitted by the end of the decade, could no longer be tolerated. Faced with grave dangers in the winter of 1939, France wanted to make sure that the United States would stand by its side, whatever possibly legitimate grievances had tended to drive them apart since the last war. On February 21, 1939, Paul Reynaud, minister of finance in the Daladier cabinet, telephoned Bullitt to arrange an early meeting for the discussion of "a matter of the utmost importance." The following day he told the ambassador of his conviction "that France must make immediately a settlement of her debt to the United States." Going straight to the point, he was prepared to hand to the United States an initial ten billion francs in gold as "sufficient evidence of good faith to relieve France from the restrictions of the Johnson Act." Although amounting to only about $300 million, this was an enormous sacrifice at that time. Bullitt responded that Congress would regard this sum as totally insufficient to settle a debt of many billions but that it might be more inclined to consider it if France also yielded some of its possessions of strategic interest to the United States. Reynaud did not hesitate to react favorably. At a luncheon with Bullitt on April 4, 1939, attended by Daladier, Reynaud, and Jean Monnet, Daladier confirmed his readiness to turn over to the United States as many islands as necessary, "if only the [debt] question could be settled."

Encouraged by Winthrop Aldrich's assurance that the Chase National Bank would extend sizable credits to France if not forbidden by the Johnson Act, the French leaders hoped to remove this restriction with their offer. Anticipating the outbreak of a general war in Europe, they were "most anxious to act quickly." They could not finance such a war without America's help. Monnet, introduced to President Roosevelt as an "utterly honest-minded and utterly discreet" figure, was sent to Washington to explore these possibilities.

38. Jesse Straus to Cordell Hull, September 4, 1934, in FRUS, *Diplomatic Papers, 1934*, I, 570–73; Paul Claudel, *Cahiers Paul Claudel: Claudel diplomate* (Paris, 1962), 262–66.

Alas, it was now too late to hastily rectify a problem that should never have existed in the first place.[39]

GATHERING WAR CLOUDS: ITALY AND SPAIN

Issues concerning armament and the world economy consumed much of the attention America gave to foreign affairs in these years, but it would be erroneous to assume that global diplomatic questions, which were more in the limelight, left the United States untouched or unconcerned. Until 1935, Japan and Italy had upstaged Hitler by going on warpaths Americans watched disapprovingly.

For decades Italy had shown interest in East Africa. When its peaceful penetration of Ethiopia did not yield the desired results, its fascist government prepared for more militant action. With the rise of Hitler, France and Italy found it mutually prudent to build diplomatic bridges. Initially, the German dictator's repudiation, on March 16, 1935, of the disarmament provisions of the Versailles treaty alarmed Rome as well as Paris. A rearmed Germany also constituted a potentially serious threat to Italy's vital interests. Mussolini not only wanted to hold on to South Tyrol but also ensure the independence of Austria.

In April, 1935, it appeared that the Stresa Conference, denouncing "any unilateral repudiation of treaties which is liable to endanger the peace of Europe," had established an Anglo-French-Italian front. Britain endeavored through collective security to induce Italy and France to seek peaceful accommodations with each other with respect to both Ethiopia and Germany. Actually Stresa played into Mussolini's colonial hand by at least diminishing the likelihood of active Anglo-French intervention in his planned Abyssinian campaign. And to Hitler's delight, this diplomatic front against him fell apart when England's appeasement policy led to an agreement with Germany on naval matters. This Anglo-German rapprochement upset France and Italy so much that Paris and Rome were persuaded to reinforce each other despite their historic rivalries in the Mediterranean.[40]

Whereas England's orientation was global, France was preoccupied with Europe and the Mediterranean. Both endeavored to avoid

39. William C. Bullitt to Franklin D. Roosevelt, February 22, April 4, 1939, in File No. 43, "France, Bullitt," PSF.

40. "Abyssinia and Italy," in *Survey of International Affairs, 1935*, II, 30–39.

a major war. England tried to remove the causes for it by accommodating Germany's desire to be an important equal in the family of nations. France tried to shore up its diplomatic network and to rely on the league covenant to maintain the status quo. In this process France encountered one disappointment after another. The very prospect of a Franco-Soviet treaty and doubt about France's ability to stand by a beleaguered Poland induced the government in Warsaw to sign a nonaggression treaty with Germany. Followed by Britain's naval agreement with Germany, France deemed it essential to move closer to Italy and to secure a reinsurance treaty with the Soviet Union.

Despite France's facade of strength, Alexis Saint-Léger, the general secretary of the French Foreign Office from 1933 to 1940, saw great potential risks in this policy. As much as possible, he asserted his independence from the eight foreign ministers under whom he served. To him, only close Anglo-French ties constituted a realistic approach to the volatile political situation of the 1930s. If France's reliance on treaties at best offered "paper guaranties," its deliberate failure to arrange meaningful military staff coordination with Great Britain, the Soviet Union, Poland, or other friendly powers sharply reduced the effectiveness of these treaties. As long as the military strength of pacifist France was insufficient to back up its extensive diplomatic commitments, its network of alliances was destined to break down under stress. After all, it has been axiomatic in diplomacy that a country courts disaster when it extends itself diplomatically without possessing correspondingly adequate military means.

As soon as Louis Barthou became foreign minister in February, 1934, his conservative instincts guided him toward a grand alliance against Nazi Germany. He clearly saw the strategic significance of an alliance with Italy with respect to both Mediterranean and continental issues. But Mussolini was more concerned with his own needs than with those of the French. Although not rejecting Barthou's overtures, he took his time to work out a Franco-Italian understanding. In the meantime, in the fall of 1934, Barthou was assassinated.

His successor, Pierre Laval, was intimately familiar with Mussolini's ambitions in Abyssinia. Premier Laval had discussed them with the Duce as far back as 1931. When, at the end of December, 1934, Mussolini had made up his mind to go ahead with his Abyssinian war plans, he considered it the opportune moment for a political alliance with France. The ensuing Rome Agreements of January 7, 1935, satisfied France by providing for consultations if the independence of Austria was endangered or if Germany unilaterally violated existing disarmament obligations. French military leaders welcomed these understandings because instead of stationing seventeen divisions along the Italian frontier, they could release them, if necessary, to man lines against Germany.

Mussolini was satisfied because Laval had orally agreed to give him "a free hand" in Ethiopia. Although the Duce interpreted this phrase as a tacit French approval of his contemplated conquest of Ethiopia, Laval's shifty mind might have limited it to merely economic penetration. Only a few months before the invasion, the British and French governments counseled Mussolini to negotiate with Emperor Haile Selassie rather than engage him in war. But, confident that his modern war machine would achieve a quick and glorious victory, the Duce disregarded such advice and invaded Ethiopia on October 3, 1935.[41]

What followed had far-reaching significance for the developments leading to World War II. In the larger perspective of history, Anglo-French differences with respect to policies concerning Italy were probably more important than the Ethiopian war. While Britain considered strong measures, including sanctions under the auspices of the League of Nations, that would leave no doubt in Mussolini's mind that the war he planned would be very risky for Italy, France preferred not to commit itself. Whether Laval or Flandin directed French foreign policy, they did not dare offend either the French Right, which favored close cooperation with the fascist regime, or the Radicals, who on the whole supported collective security. Whatever happened to Abyssinia, French politicians and military leaders worried much more about what was going on in Germany. This priority blinded the French government's vision to a degree that it failed to see the immense, worldwide complexity of Mussolini's drive toward war. What was at stake was not only Abyssinia but Italy's Mediterranean designs at the expense of France, the fate of the league, the effectiveness of collective security, and the solidity of Anglo-French determination vis-à-vis aggressively inclined dictators—in short, the future peace of the world.

41. R. A. C. Parker, "Great Britain, France and the Ethiopian Crisis, 1935–36," *English Historical Review*, LXXXIX (April, 1974), 293–332; Auswärtiges Amt, *Akten zur deutschen auswärtigen Politik*, Series C, IV-2, October 3, 1935, pp. 675–79.

Between July, 1935, and the outbreak of the Ethiopian war in October, the British cabinet reiterated several times that without French cooperation in applying Article XVI of the league covenant, which required action against league members who disregarded the covenant, Italy could be neither frightened nor stopped. The British government tried time and again to establish certainty about French policy. It wanted Mussolini to know definitely that France would retaliate against his breach of the peace. The British also felt they were entitled to know whether they could count on unequivocal French support in case they took the lead in league actions. Up to the beginning of the invasion, Laval managed to keep Great Britain in the dark. If anything, his comment to Foreign Secretary Anthony Eden that the "best solution would probably be for Italy to have some form of protectorate over the whole of Abyssinia" suggested a pro-Italian bias. In this instance, France practically exercised a veto over firm British measures.

Even before the conflict began, Hitler had welcomed it. And when its military phase started, he did what he could to keep it going. Despite their ideological kinship, the Fuehrer and the Duce originally had not been on close terms. A conflict of interest in southeastern Europe kept them at a distance. Since Mussolini, moreover, dreaded the prospect of a militarily strong Germany, Hitler calculated that the highest price he could exact for his cooperation with Italy would be when its dependence on Germany's might would be most acute. Initially, he assured the Italian leader of his benevolent attitude. Quite cynically, he also boosted Haile Selassie's fighting spirit by honoring the emperor's request in July for a loan needed for the purchase of weapons and planes. Above all, the Ethiopian conflict promised to and did divert attention from Germany's rearmament and remilitarization of the Rhineland. The German government further anticipated such other dividends as a shift of Italy's attention from the Danubian region to East Africa and frictions between Italy and the British leading to the breakup of the Stresa front and the weakening of the league, France's favorite foreign-policy instrument to maintain the status quo. For good measure, the Reich also believed that it ultimately stood to benefit from the renewed focus on colonial issues.[42]

42. Manfred Funke, *Sanktionen und Kanonen: Hitler, Mussolini und der internationale Abessinienkonflikt, 1934–1936* (Düsseldorf, 1971), 42–47, 176–77; Serge Groussard, "Entretien avec Haile Sélassie," *Figaro*, March 25, 26, 1959.

One has to keep this general background in mind to evaluate the relative effectiveness of American policies with respect to these developments in Europe. Since he was opposed to war and fascism, FDR's sympathies leaned toward Ethiopia's cause. Secretary of State Hull and the State Department, though, preferred not to become entangled in the approaching conflict. In the months prior to the outbreak of hostilities, Ethiopia made several requests for some American gesture. All it asked was that the United States remind the signatories of the Kellogg-Briand Pact of their obligations. Hull rebuffed these requests as inappropriate because the league had the issue before it. But he did remind the French and British ambassadors that the Kellogg-Briand Pact was not dead. He also gave Mussolini to understand, in the name of President Roosevelt, "his earnest hope that the controversy between Italy and Ethiopia will be resolved without resort to armed conflict." This message of August 18 indicated in a general way America's concern that the "outbreak of hostilities would be a world calamity the consequences of which would adversely affect the interests of all nations."[43]

Despite the fact that the American government was willing, independently, to support the peace efforts of England, France, and the league, Hull was careful not to coordinate such efforts officially. He wanted by all means "to avoid accusations by the isolationist elements that we were willing to follow the League." America's desire for peace and a short war prompted it to issue the arms embargo two days before the league invoked Article XVI of the covenant. Similarly, three days before the league's sanctions were to go into effect, notably omitting oil from the sanction list, the American government proclaimed its moral embargo of certain commodities essential in the prosecution of the war, including oil. The implementation of the moral embargo, however, proved to be a net with large holes in it.

Usually France acted as the energetic defender of the league. In this instance it was Britain that was prepared to mobilize strong league action against the Italian aggressor. But Laval explained his opposition to oil sanctions by the league on the ostensible ground that "they would undoubtedly result in a general European war." Britain was bitterly disappointed that France did not give its assurance of unreserved assistance in case of rash Italian military action

43. Cordell Hull, *The Memoirs of Cordell Hull* (2 vols.; New York, 1948), I, 418–42.

against its Mediterranean forces. Britain did not want to take on Italy alone. On November 27 Anthony Eden concluded, "France is clearly unreliable, to put it mildly." Sir Robert Gilbert Vansittart, the permanent undersecretary of state for foreign affairs, distrusted the French so much that he feared practical politicians in Britain might reluctantly have to "write France off for keeps."

In search of a compromise that would end the war, keep Italy in the front against Hitler, and prevent a lasting estrangement between Britain and France, Foreign Secretary Sir Samuel Hoare and Laval drafted on December 8 the Hoare-Laval plan. It granted Italy considerable concessions at the expense of Ethiopia's territorial integrity. After forthright deliberations, however, the plan was deemed unacceptable by the British cabinet because its terms were incompatible with its pledge to support the league covenant. Although Laval was "much perturbed" about this British reaction, in both London and Washington the plan's all-too-generous award for aggression seemed completely out of order.

Hull, who referred to Laval as "one of the most sinister figures of my time," believed that the Ethiopian war would have come to a quick end if Mussolini had confronted unmistakable Anglo-French solidarity. Instead, French sympathies permitted the Duce to drag out the war when a prompt and decisive victory eluded him. This prospect concerned Hull deeply because he diagnosed the potential ramifications of the Italo-Ethiopian war more clearly than his European counterparts. He identified it as "the most serious single factor in precipitating the Japanese-Chinese crisis." In addition to attributing to the war damaging consequences for the restoration of international finance and trade, Hull deplored the encouragement that the league's failure and Anglo-French differences were likely to give to Nazi Germany and Japan. As Anthony Adamthwaite has persuasively observed, "The failure to restrain Mussolini did not make a European war inevitable, but it did make war highly probable."[44]

Still deluding themselves that Italy, despite the Duce's contempt for the "decadent" democracies, might be enticed to join the forces against Hitler, they ultimately recognized his conquest. President Roosevelt preferred to invoke America's nonrecognition principle,

44. Anthony Adamthwaite, *France and the Coming of the Second World War, 1936–1939* (London, 1977), 36. See also Brice Harris, Jr., *The United States and the Italo-Ethiopian Crisis* (Stanford, 1964).

but he continued to do business with Italy. He accredited America's new ambassador, Undersecretary of State William Phillips, to "the King of Italy," but accepted the credentials of Italian representatives who represented "the King of Italy and Emperor of Ethiopia."

On the heels of this tragic episode, civil war erupted in Spain on July 17, 1936. It deprived Europe and the United States of the longed-for breathing space to develop a more peaceful world order. Now, the Western democracies' most urgent concern was to confine the strife to a struggle between the Loyalists and the rebels. Even so, its outcome was likely to produce considerable ideological and strategic effects. What appeared most ominous was that the involvement of outside powers in this internal clash might ignite a general war with incalculable consequences in Europe, Asia, and the Western Hemisphere. American policy regarding this war followed the lead of France and Great Britain. Their policies and motivations, in turn, were largely determined by the moves and aims of Hitler and Mussolini; nor could they ignore Stalin's intentions. The civil war in Spain thus assumed from the start an international character of unpredictable dimensions.

Léon Blum, the premier of the Popular Front, a somewhat shaky coalition of bourgeois Radical Socialists, Socialists, and Communists, assumed power in June, 1936. Sympathizing with the democratically elected Spanish government, he was initially disposed to lend assistance to his friends across the Pyrenees. But a multitude of domestic and foreign political restraints diminished his freedom of action to the point of indecision. That he was a statesman and intellectual with a conscience complicated his agonizing search for responsible solutions.

France's excessively factional political system, as well as its inefficient and depressed economic system, did not provide him with the tools he needed to restore his country's vitality. Nevertheless, guided by his optimistic disposition, he admired Franklin D. Roosevelt's experimental New Deal so much that he hoped his own similar social reforms would lead France out of its depression. Since his early political life, moreover, he had entertained strong views about the political and moral value of the solidarity of the three great democracies—France, Great Britain, and the United States. Upon his election, he considered cooperation with the British a keystone of his foreign policy. But he was also solicitous of American cooperation in the pacification of Europe. Interestingly, rumors persisted in the lobbies of the French Chamber that premier-elect Blum would like to borrow a billion dollars from the United States to support his Socialist government.[45] Although in 1932 he had voted against Herriot's attempt to settle the debt question with the United States, he now regretted "this dramatic misunderstanding between our two countries." Counting on Roosevelt to stand by France in financial and security matters, he was prepared to reopen the debt question. For the same reason, he had been prepared to accept the Hoover moratorium, provided it engaged the United States in an ensemble of policies aiming at Europe's stability. Roosevelt's disarmament initiatives and his sympathetic acceptance of nonintervention in the Spanish Civil War pleased him. He admired FDR, above all, for his readiness to bridge capitalism and socialism within the framework of democracy.[46]

Turbulent conditions did not favor the success of Blum's social experiments. Continually plagued by deflationary developments and the enormous cost of armaments, France faced one monetary crisis after another. The stabilization of the franc, even with the help of the United States and Great Britain, remained an illusory goal as long as, in Morgenthau's words, "the cost of arming" was "breaking down the Treasuries of the World." Blum would undoubtedly have gone along with Roosevelt's notion in 1936 to boycott economically any nation that refused to comply with the stipulations of a general disarmament conference that he intended to organize. But while drastic disarmament would logically have reduced budgets and the chances of war, the dictators' militaristic designs destroyed any real hope that the Western democracies might be able to follow their preferences to disarm. Time and again, circumstances forced Blum to make decisions that were distasteful to him.[47]

The Spanish Popular Front government appealed to him for planes and weapons in sufficient quantities to subdue the relatively weak

45. New York *Times*, May 16, 24, 28, 1936.

46. Léon Blum, *L'Oeuvre de Léon Blum* (9 vols.; Paris, 1954–72), III, Pt. 2, 305–12, 421–28, 531–34, 552, IV, Pt. 1, 371–72, 403. See also Pierre Renouvin, "La politique extérieure du premier gouvernement Léon Blum," in *Léon Blum: Chef de gouvernement, 1936–1937*, Cahiers 155, Fondation nationale des sciences politiques (Paris, 1967), 329–75, and Jasper Glenn Grayson, "The Foreign Policy of Léon Blum and the Popular Front Government in France" (Ph.D. dissertation, University of North Carolina, 1962), 154, 170–71.

47. Blum, *Morgenthau Diaries*, I, 457.

rebel forces before Italy and Germany could reinforce them. A prompt positive French response might have enabled the legitimate government to crush the rebellion, which was spearheaded by the army. But when the news was leaked in Paris that Blum intended to aid the Loyalists, chain reactions at home and abroad compelled him to move slowly. In the meantime, while uncertainty prevailed in France, the scope of support Italy, even more than Germany, extended to Franco not only kept the rebels in the field but enhanced the danger of a wider European war.

"Extremely worried" about the rumored French decision to strengthen the Loyalist forces militarily, particularly about sending them planes, the Conservative government of Stanley Baldwin invited Blum and Yvon Delbos to London for general consultations. When the premier and his foreign minister returned to Paris on July 25, they informed the cabinet council that Britain's attitude with regard to any intervention in the Spanish Civil War was a cautious one. Foreign Secretary Eden apparently had advised Blum in an informal private discussion to weigh Spanish aid very carefully. Against the recommendation of Air Minister Pierre Cot, but after full discussion, the cabinet heeded this advice. Daladier, the Radical minister of national defense and war, joined Blum and Delbos in support of the decision to observe strict neutrality in the Spanish conflict. Explaining this policy which had been so reluctantly arrived at, to the Foreign Affairs Committee of the French Senate, Blum reserved the right to reconsider it, "depending upon the attitude of other foreign governments."[48]

This reservation was typical; France usually sought the collaboration of other powers in the pursuit of its policies. The decision to remain neutral was complicated by different schools of thought within the French government. The keenly analytical and experienced secretary general of the Quai d'Orsay, Léger, did not entertain the slightest doubt that, whatever other allies France might be able to count on, its interests were best secured by the closest possible entente with Great Britain. Delbos, Daladier, and, on balance, Blum shared this view. The widely respected Radical Socialist Edouard Herriot and the French ambassador to Moscow, Robert Coulondre, leaned strongly toward a close entente with the Soviet

48. FRUS, *Diplomatic Papers, 1936*, II, 450–51.

Union. Blum was not opposed to it. A third group, representing the moderate French Right, preferred the Stresa front combination: Pierre Laval, Pierre Etienne Flandin, and the French ambassador to Germany, André François-Poncet, believed strongly in Franco-German-Italian understanding as the safest road to peace. And to the extreme Right, Franco-German collaboration offered the best protection against the communist peril. Considering that French capitalists held 60 percent of foreign capital invested in Spain, it was not surprising that the far Right rooted for General Franco's victory.[49]

On a variety of diplomatic and social questions the extreme Left and Right in France were so far apart that Blum could not preclude the frightening possibility of civil war in France. It was enhanced by the reportedly "great number of potential Francos with a partiality for facism" in the French army. The likelihood of an approaching European war had already created a devastating fear complex. As important as it was to prevent the division of Europe into competing power blocs, it was even more urgent to halt the dangerous polarization threatening France.

In January, 1936, Ambassador Jesse Straus sent observations to FDR that did not portend a brilliant future for France. It was widely known that the press was "almost without exception" venal, and many politicians were reputed to be intellectually and morally dishonest. The sorry state of the French parliamentary system spawned demoralizing cynicism. The members of the Chamber of Deputies, Straus commented, "behave like a lot of naughty children in a nursery. . . . Their acrimonious, vituperative and unwarranted attacks against the government were often made for purely personal satisfaction and aggrandizement. . . . Many of the deputies hold four or five jobs." France's budget continued to be unbalanced, despite official denials. Widespread tax evasion, abetted by inadequate audits and bribable agents, was tempting under a system of crushing taxes on the one hand and wasteful governmental largess on the other. France's air force, Straus called to FDR's attention, was "poorly equipped and unprepared with modern machines, compared to Germany." Even a Jeanne d'Arc could not have performed miracles under these conditions. There was an unwillingness to ad-

49. Richard P. Traina, *American Diplomacy and the Spanish Civil War* (Bloomington, 1968), 28–30; Hugh Thomas, *The Spanish Civil War* (New York, 1961), 224–58.

mit internal error and to seek to correct it. Blum had little choice but to act in a way that would not give either extreme justification for a violent reaction.[50]

Caution was also necessitated by the knowledge that active support for the Loyalists would be opposed by the French Right and by Great Britain. Vice Admiral Jean Darlan's conversations on August 5 with First Sea Lord and Chief of Naval Staff Lord Alfred Chatfield made it clear that Britain intended to stay out of the Spanish imbroglio. It feared that a French decision to tip the scales in favor of the Loyalists might bring about an international war for which it was not prepared. Its "no risk" policy found overwhelming public support. Among other reasons, Britain suspected the Soviet Union's motives for helping the Popular Front. The British did not consider it inconceivable that Stalin might like to see the Spanish Civil War trigger a war in Europe that he would like to watch from the sidelines. They sought to maintain peace through appeasement.

Under these circumstances the French government determined to contain the civil war by proposing, early in August, a nonintervention agreement. When the various European governments accepted it with mental reservations, it remained to be seen whether the agreement would actually accomplish its objective. In the meantime each power continued to consider the likely impact of the war on its own interests. In their speculative analyses, it would make a considerable difference whether the Nationalists or the Loyalists won. A victory by Franco, which was likely to be followed by Spain's close cooperation with Germany and Italy, would threaten to encircle France with unfriendly neighbors. This scenario would not only have required France to station troops along the heretofore unprotected Spanish frontier; much worse, it potentially threatened the communication lines between France and its North African empire. France's ranking military and naval leaders, despite their differences with the Popular Front at home and despite their professional regard for their rebelling Spanish counterparts, did not for a moment question that French security interests had to favor the Loyalists. While Great Britain was much less concerned than France about the implications of a rebel victory, the British were not unaware of the detrimental effects it might have on their stakes in the

50. Jesse Straus to Cordell Hull, April 15, 1936, in RG 59, Box 6298, 851.00/1501, NA. See also "Warrington Dawson Report," No. 1686, April 23, 1936, in RG 59, Box 6298, 851.00/1502, NA.

Mediterranean region. The Anglo-French naval patrol against U-boats and planes that attacked non-Spanish merchantmen in the Mediterranean, which had been created by an agreement reached at the Nyon Conference in September, 1937, attested to this awareness. But England assumed that even a Spain under Franco would not become an integral part of the Rome-Berlin Axis.[51]

From the early 1930s the Soviet Union participated actively in the international chess game. In the view of Foreign Minister Maxim Litvinov, a victory by Franco would weaken France's strategic position so much that it might encourage Hitler to attack the Soviet Union. To protect itself Moscow therefore decided to help the Popular Front in Spain with weapons and planes. But it sent few soldiers. To be sure, the opposite development from a Franco victory—the transformation of Spain into a communist state closely aligned with France's Popular Front—would have been the most desirable outcome from the Soviet point of view.

Precisely this contingency brought Hitler onto the stage. His determination to fight the bolshevization of Europe guided him in his declaration to the French ambassador in Berlin that "no Bolshevik government could be countenanced" in Spain. He had already been disturbed by the recent Franco-Soviet alliance, which to his mind not only aligned France against Germany but might facilitate the bolshevization of Europe. Nevertheless, he told the French ambassador at a reception on January 11, 1937, that "Germany had no territorial or political aspirations whatever in Spain or Spanish Morocco." This did not mean, however, that his long-range plans for a new order in Europe had not already taken into account the valuable contributions a friendly Spain could make. Like Mussolini's, Hitler's support of Franco was a calculated investment. Although originally he looked upon the civil war as an unwelcome interference with his own timetable, he soon sensed its exploitative value. The large-scale fighting in Spain provided an excellent military training and testing ground. In case of a future war in Europe, he expected Franco at least to be benevolently neutral and perhaps to grant access to military and naval bases. He furthermore valued Franco's ideological solidarity with him, which could not but be a psychological blow to the western democracies. Nor did he under-

51. Edwin C. Wilson to Cordell Hull, August 20, 1936, in FRUS, *Diplomatic Papers, 1936*, II, 502–504; Adamthwaite, *France and the Coming of the Second World War*, 450–52.

estimate trade advantages, particularly access to Spain's iron ores and other raw materials. Commercial transactions involving such goods, carried out on a barter basis, promised to alleviate Germany's severe foreign-currency difficulties. As German archival records have since confirmed, by this time the Fuehrer's grandiose designs had already taken him far beyond Spain. For Hitler, it was by now merely a question of timing: what he wanted was to execute his plans under the most propitious conditions.[52]

Mussolini's motives coincided with Hitler's except for his comparatively more limited plans for expansion. Control of the western Mediterranean with the help of a friendly Spanish government was what he desired. It would be a symbol of fascist dynamism. Officially explaining his massive military assistance to Franco in terms of an anticommunist crusade, he and Count Galeazzo Ciano really set out to establish Italy's predominance in the region. A revived Spain under Franco's leadership would compel France to shift some of its troops from the Italian frontier to the Spanish border thus weakening its offensive capacity. Moreover, in case of a Franco-Italian war the movement of French troops from Morocco to metropolitan France would under these circumstances be hazardous, if not altogether barred.

Eventually it dawned on the Italian leaders that the high cost of their Ethiopian and Spanish adventures had weakened Italy so much that it had become uncomfortably dependent on Germany. Despite Germany's willingness to go along with Italy's dominance in the Mediterranean in exchange for its recognition of Germany's vital interests in the Danubian region, the Italian leaders tried to keep their diplomatic options as open as possible. Just as during these years Hitler kept his hopes alive for an understanding with Great Britain and did not foreclose a tolerable relationship with France, so the Duce was prepared to shuffle his diplomatic cards, with Britain and France remaining in his deck.

By the same token, England and France tried repeatedly to draw Italy away from Germany and, for the sake of peace, to offer the totalitarian leaders accommodations. By 1937 the French had inched closer to the British view that, if expediency required it, they would deal with Franco. Like the British, French leaders speculated that

52. Funke, *Sanktionen und Kanonen*, 478–81; M. Merkes, *Die deutsche Politik gegenüber dem spanischen Bürgerkrieg, 1936–1939* (Bonn, 1961), 26–27.

Franco might prefer not to become a full partner in the ideological and strategic offensives of the Fuehrer and the Duce. The nuances of a centrist Spanish government, whether Loyalist or Nationalist, also concerned the United States much less than Spain's independence from the fanatic dictators. All the powers concerned subordinated their principles to their interests. Once the prospects for Franco's victory looked promising, even Herriot did not want to see France dragged into an ideological crusade. Expediency demanded that France's future interests be looked after, regardless of who was in control of Spain.

Although one cannot fairly judge American policies with respect to the Spanish Civil War by looking in retrospect at the web of the European powers' interplay and the results to which it led, neither can a professional analysis be limited merely to explaining the State Department's rationalizations within the framework of contemporary American politics. From the beginning, American officials treated the upheaval in Spain as a local and European affair. They took it for granted that the Spanish people, with the help of their neighbors most directly concerned, would resolve this unfortunate crisis. Since it seemed to be of only remote interest to the United States except for its impact on Latin America, Washington relied on France and Great Britain to exercise a moderating influence. Although he followed developments closely, prior to the presidential election of 1936 FDR chose not to take a public stand on the ideological stakes in this conflict that Ambassador Laboulaye had called to his attention.[53]

Essentially, the United States shared the Western view that their transcendent objective must be to prevent the Spanish imbroglio from spreading to the rest of Europe. For this reason it welcomed Blum's "statesmanlike" decision, for which Baldwin could claim much credit, to reverse course and not aid Spain's republican government. The subsequent formation of the nonintervention committee in London, initiated by France and accepted by most governments, including Germany, Italy, and the Soviet Union, promised to contain the Spanish fire. Claude Bowers, the United States ambassador to Spain, belonged to the minority of American officials who protested: "This policy, whatever its intent, will operate solely

53. André Laboulaye to Yvon Delbos, September 8, 1936, in *DDF*, 2e Série, III, 346.

in the interest of the rebels," he warned. But Bowers did not carry sufficient weight to exercise a decisive influence.[54]

The United States government found the European response sensible, but it declined unofficial French soundings as to whether it would be willing to join the London committee. It had no difficulty with adopting a parallel, but independent, policy. Its fundamental principles of nonintervention and noninterference in the internal affairs of sovereign nations philosophically facilitated its scrupulous abstention from taking sides. According to Ambassador François-Poncet, the Europeans, particularly Germany, waited for precise clarification of America's attitude before accepting the French proposal of nonintervention. America's "moral embargo" of war matériel to Spain persuaded the fascist leaders to accept the French proposal. From then on, they knew that they had nothing to lose and much to gain. The subsequent brazen hypocrisy of these totalitarians in their violation of their pledge of nonintervention was highlighted by their early recognition of the Franco government.

By the end of 1936 the British Foreign Office "did not consider the Spanish situation likely to lead to an international conflict." It also ventured to believe that it could do business with a Franco government should it emerge as the victor. To keep all options open, it therefore considered the recognition of a state of belligerency in Spain. It realized that Blum would reject such a move out of hand to avoid domestic complications. When the British saw that the United States would also reject it, they had to give up the idea. Recognition of belligerency would have amounted to the acknowledgment of a state of war between two opposing national entities at a time when the United States' *de jure* relationship continued to be only with the legitimate government. The government in Madrid, though disappointed with America's embargo restrictions, was nevertheless grateful that America did not oppose it. Neither were the insurgents unfriendly toward the United States, but they were bitter toward the French government.[55]

As much as the Roosevelt administration would have liked to see

54. Claude Bowers to Cordell Hull, January 12, 1937, in FRUS *Diplomatic Papers, 1937*, I, 223–26. See also "U.S. Policy in Spain, 1936–39," in Box 86, Hull Papers; Bowers to Hull, December 1, 1936, in RG 59, 852.00/4063, and February 2, 1937, in RG 59, 852.00/4692, and March 3, 1937, in RG 59, 852.00/4958.

55. See Sumner Welles, memorandum of conversation with the Spanish ambassador, October 18, 1937, in FRUS, *Diplomatic Papers, 1937*, I, 425–27.

the civil war come to an early end, it declined English, French, and Uruguayan initiatives for the president to mediate the conflict. On November 28, 1936, Delbos asked Bullitt unofficially whether FDR would not lend his support to a French mediation proposal that, to be effective, required the prestige of the president of the United States. If England, France, and the United States acted in unison, the French foreign minister contended, the pressure would be great on Germany, Italy, and the Soviet Union to join them in a *démarche* "to Franco and the Madrid Government that they should accept mediation at once." In his personal opinion Bullitt felt constrained to respond evasively. At a time when FDR was promoting peace and solidarity in the Western Hemisphere, he argued, "it might be most prejudicial if he should at this moment involve himself in rearranging the affairs of the continent of Europe."

The pivotal policy that guided the leading democracies in this tangled affair revolved around nonintervention. All three claimed that nonintervention helped to prevent a general war. They also rationalized that, despite shameless infractions, especially by the totalitarians, at least the semblance of a concert of powers was kept alive. This strange self-deception ignored some basic realities. When, in October, 1936, Cordell Hull told the Spanish ambassador, Fernando de los Rios, that "the French Government, the neighbor and special friend of the Spanish Government, has taken the very lead" in the nonintervention movement and that the United States followed its lead, he disregarded the origin of this "movement." Having had much more at stake in the outcome of the civil war than Great Britain, France had originally decided to honor Madrid's urgent request for crucially needed war supplies and planes. But in its anxiety about its own future security it yielded to British pressures not to send these shipments. Against its intuitive judgment, France therefore fell back on its alternative line of defense, general nonintervention. The French domestic scene also weighed heavily in this decision.

Militarily and psychologically unprepared for war, the United States could not convincingly stiffen France's initial determination not to allow itself to be surrounded by three unfriendly dictators. Anglo-French nonintervention therefore offered Hull an appealing excuse for conveying the appearance of cooperation. Since inaction constitutes a form of action, it followed that Hull's policy of scrupulous impartiality could not but have the practical effect of benefiting the rebels. The Department of State was evidently not overly concerned with the consequence that a legal and democratic government might fall victim to rebelling militarists who were massively aided by foreign mercenaries, military hardware, and planes. The scope of this foreign intervention clearly transformed the original civil strife into an ominous international conflict. In addition, the State Department did not see or did not want to see that the longer the Spanish Civil War lasted, the more its immediate international by-product, the ominous growth of the dictators' role in Europe, transcended the war in significance.

In philosophy, false premises lead to a wrong conclusion. In diplomacy, faulty assumptions and diagnoses may lead to a catastrophe. In this instance, the democracies were humbled, and they revealed an appalling lack of vital power. Taking measure of them, the dictators concluded that they could intimidate them. In retrospect, FDR admitted to Ambassador Bowers his "mistake" of not having listened to him. His undersecretary of state, Sumner Welles, went a step further, later calling the nonintervention policy a "cardinal error."[56]

In September of 1940 Hitler observed, "There would be no Franco without German and Italian help." He and the Duce had extended aid to Spain, but in so doing they had intended to advance their own fortunes. By the irony of history, however, the extension of America's neutrality law of 1936 to the Spanish Civil War was a "gesture" General Franco did not forget. Although it was unforeseeable in the mid-1930s, during the Second World War the memory of the gesture evidently helped to take some of the wind out of the Axis leaders' Spanish sails.

THE UNITED STATES, FRANCE, AND THE COMING OF WORLD WAR II

In the 1930s American foreign policy toward Europe was dominated by several tendencies: not to become involved in European political affairs; in general to follow the lead of the Western democracies in issues of wider concern; to assume that Great Britain and France were strong and wise enough to cope with potential disturb-

56. Merkes, *Die deutsche Politik,* 172–76.

ers of the peace in Europe; and to trade with all. How sensible was it to leave Europe to the Europeans?

As late as the summer of 1933, an extraordinarily generous European settlement, replacing the so-called peace treaty of Versailles, might have satisfied Hitler as concrete evidence of the acceptance of Germany as a major power. This was the best result that could have followed from leaving Europe to the Europeans. Barring this unlikely development, Hitler was fanatically determined to put Germany in a state of preparedness adequate to the gigantic task of changing the map of the world by resort to overwhelming force. Until he was ready to strike, he successfully lulled his future enemies into believing that he was open to compromises and concessions in the traditional manner. He skillfully camouflaged his ultimate objectives by taking one step at a time, followed by assurances of his peaceful intentions. Despite the fact that his testing challenges gradually increased his risks, Western reactions were so restrained and outright fearful that they encouraged him to become ever more daring.

In his aggressive moves Hitler was cunning and outwardly defensive. His provocative restoration of conscription in March, 1935, followed, rather than preceded, the intensification of French conscription. And his remilitarization of the Rhineland followed the Franco-Soviet Pact of May, 1935, and the breakdown of the Stresa Front. Ostensibly justifying Germany's rearmament as being in the interest of all powers opposed to bolshevism, the Fuehrer nonetheless did not shrink from according financial credits to the Soviet Union in order to promote commercial ties with it.[57]

The cynical encirclement game the various powers played prior to World War II made a mockery of their professions for peace and collective security. In its desperate attempt to assure its national survival, France turned to any and all powers potentially capable of contributing to that goal, including Germany. Hoping against hope that Hitler would not punish them for Versailles and their postwar policies toward Germany, many Frenchmen were nonetheless haunted by the fear of such an unthinkable madness. Almost paralyzed by this fear, they witnessed only few leaders trying to organize energetic countermeasures. Before his assassination in Oc-

57. André François-Poncet to Pierre Laval, November 27, 1935, CPEU, Vol. 377, AMAE.

tober, 1934, Foreign Minister Louis Barthou was busy engineering a series of accords and rapprochements with such nations as Great Britain, Italy, the Soviet Union, and the members of the Little Entente. In his judgment only a powerful coalition could deter German aggression. He was most keenly working on an eastern Locarno pact as a block to Germany's penetration of the Danubian sphere. Although he temporarily raised French prestige, his legacy underlined the difficulties France faced. The Franco-Soviet rapprochement cooled Franco-Polish relations and opened up possibilities for improved German-Polish relations. It also aggravated Franco-German relations. Italy feared that a Franco-Soviet alliance would downgrade Franco-Italian ties. And the Franco-Italian rapprochement made the Yugoslavs unhappy. These results typified future complications and contradictions and exposed the inadequacies of the alliance approach to security.[58]

The Soviet Union watched the political maneuvers on the Continent with the legitimate concern of a country that was clearly distrusted by its capitalistic antagonists and in some cases was the declared target of countries that viewed it as a mortal enemy. Like France, it saw itself threatened and concluded that a Franco-Soviet pact would be of mutual advantage. As logical as such an arrangement appeared, its ultimate implementation and ramifications led to an incredible degree of confusion. In the summer of 1933 the Soviet Union had taken the initiative to sound out France on the chances of cooperation. Although Daladier favored it, he was skeptical of Soviet military effectiveness and suspicious of possible Soviet attempts to infiltrate France politically. When France and the Soviet Union announced their pact in May, 1935, they meant to give Hitler food for thought and worry. But the Fuehrer defiantly called it a violation of the Locarno agreements. It threatened to upset Europe's balance of power in a way contrary to his own plans for Germany's future.

Anything but enthusiastic about the Franco-Soviet "front," Laval looked upon it as an expedient designed more to satisfy leftist political groups than to be a real guarantee against Germany. In a conversation with Hermann Göring he said it was "practically meaningless." The Soviets, on the contrary, became suspicious when the

58. Pierrepont Moffat to Cordell Hull, October 9, 1934, in RG 59, Box 6297, 851.00/1362, NA. See also William E. Scott, *Alliance Against Hitler: The Origins of the Franco-Soviet Pact* (Durham, N.C., 1962), 173–74.

French did not promptly schedule arrangements for military staff coordination. They began to doubt France's sincerity when they became aware of Premier Flandin's direct and private discussions with Hitler early in 1935. And it chilled them when France was willing to accommodate Italy at the expense of Ethiopia. Could this possibly be a precedent, they wondered, for the Western powers to accommodate Germany at the expense of the Soviet Union? From the French point of view there was another possibility that could not be excluded. As Sir John Simon told the American attaché to the United Kingdom, Litvinov, in the preliminary discussions that led to the Franco-Soviet pact, had implied that his government would approach Germany if it could not negotiate a satisfactory agreement with France. Preferring to ignore this hint, the Quai d'Orsay did not take it seriously, though it was known that certain influential industrial, military, and political figures in Nazi Germany and the Soviet Union were well disposed toward close German-Russian relations in spite of their mutual exchanges of insults and threats.[59]

The Soviets were also exploring possibilities for closer cooperation with Great Britain. But the British disliked continental power blocs and preferred their traditional role as mediator between them. This honest broker role used to pay them handsome dividends. Some even thought that the cynical Joseph Stalin was capable of stringing France and Great Britain along to provoke a war between Nazi Germany and the Western democracies that would exhaust both sides sufficiently to make the Soviet Union safe. In his brilliant analysis of the European quagmire in February, 1936, Permanent Foreign Undersecretary Sir Robert Vansittart considered the haunting possibility that "Germany's policy of expansion in the East might be carried on not against Russia, but in co-operation with Russia." The most significant objective of the Franco-Soviet Pact was therefore the attempt to diminish the likelihood of German-Soviet cooperation.

Persuaded that Hitler was bent on unleashing a European war, Vansittart argued that it was not sufficient for Britain and France to keep Germany and Russia apart, but that they must do everything possible to draw Hitler closer to the Western powers. Although Munich later made the term *appeasement* synonymous with abject

59. Ray Atherton memorandum, February 5, 1935, and John C. Wiley to Cordell Hull, January 19, 1935, both in FRUS, *Diplomatic Papers, 1935*, I, 188–92, 176–78; Louis Barthou to Jules Henry, September 6, 1934, in *DDF*, 1e Série, VII, 375–76.

surrender, historically it had been a perfectly acceptable method in overcoming impasses and crises. Unlike France's ineffectual scramble for collective security, Britain's systematic pursuit of peace through appeasement seemed responsible until realities proved the opposite. The Anglo-German naval agreement of June, 1935, and Britain's awareness of Germany's critical need for economic expansion were safety valves to avoid a military explosion. As the British explained to their French friends, the time for legalistic arguments and public opinion–imposed inflexibility was rapidly dwindling away. Positive action, not negative measures, held out the best hope for peaceful solutions. France's main fear—that the Anglo-German naval agreement might weaken the Anglo-French entente—was theoretically understandable but, as far as the British were concerned, completely unfounded.[60]

Rarely had an American ambassador in Paris been taken into confidence by the French government. William C. Bullitt, formerly the United States envoy to Moscow, enjoyed this exceptional privilege. Blum and Delbos treated this friend and representative of President Roosevelt with an extraordinary frankness. To be sure, his closeness to FDR and their desire to enlist the United States in the steadily deteriorating situation in Europe facilitated his special status. His experience in Moscow, his cosmopolitan outlook, and his imaginative, though at times emotional, comments made listening to him worthwhile. Obviously he could only report to FDR and submit ideas; he could not determine policy. Following a conversation with Alexis Saint-Léger in May, 1936, Bullitt came to the conclusion that "the French Foreign Office has in fact no constructive ideas whatsoever" to preserve the peace in Europe; it could only criticize the British and others for insufficiently supporting France's policies.

This negative impression expressed the frustration he felt because the Quai d'Orsay, the generals, and the entire political system did not demonstrate the resourcefulness and urgency needed at this juncture. Several months later Delbos confided to Bullitt in strictest confidence a step that he and Blum were considering that they had not even discussed with other members of the cabinet. It involved the creation of consortiums for the development of regions in Africa. England and France, and perhaps the United States, would provide the money, and Germany would contribute machinery.

60. Oswald Hauser, *England und das Dritte Reich* (Stuttgart, 1972), 288–94.

Germany would be given a colony, probably the Cameroons, that would become part of the international consortium. In preliminary discussions, Hjalmar Schacht, who was more inclined than Hitler to seek peaceful avenues of economic expansion, saw merits in such a scheme. When asked, Bullitt thought FDR would look upon it as a move in the right direction. It would channel German energies in the direction of peace rather than war. And that would be to the good.

Adolf A. Berle, the assistant secretary of state, took exception to the scheme. He held the view that "fundamentally colonies are not a solution; great free trade areas of middle Europe are." He therefore faulted France for posing so many obstructive objections to "any settlement of middle Europe." While the people of Britain seemed more inclined than their government to offer some colonial concessions if they would preserve peace, by November, 1937, Hitler's global *Programm* had been set in motion. He was no longer interested in Western attempts to divert him. Once he had successfully executed his designs, he intended to be in a position to include quite a few colonies in Germany's world empire.[61]

France greeted FDR's reelection in 1936 with a wave of enthusiasm. In a display reminiscent of President Wilson's reception, the French people looked to FDR, an understanding friend, as a miracle man who would "somehow manage to keep Europe from plunging again into war." Contrary to a general perception, confirmed in a private conversation between Bullitt and Neurath, that Hitler was no longer interested in Franco-German reconciliation, Bullitt continued to believe that, realistically, only such a reconciliation could maintain the peace. The development of Germany's economic relations with Central Europe and the Balkans, he argued, constituted its most essential need for growth and development. Whatever French business interests might think, Blum and Delbos were at last prepared to support it.

For various reasons, however, Great Britain, Italy, and the Soviet Union did not favor a Franco-German rapprochement based on such an understanding. They feared that "economic domination will lead to political domination and the realization of the old Berlin-to-Baghdad bloc." For this reason, Bullitt alerted FDR, the British would

61. Memorandum of November 30, 1937, A. A. Berle Diary, Container 210, in Adolf A. Berle, Jr., Papers, FDRL. See also Klaus Hildebrand, *The Foreign Policy of the Third Reich*, trans. Anthony Fothergill (Berkeley, 1970).

verbally favor Franco-German rapprochement but actually sabotage it. The ambassador despaired when he saw no sign of an outbreak of common sense at a time of intellectual chaos and impending doom. The airplane, he thought, had made the "dinkey little European states" an absurdity. Unless they acted as a reasonably united entity, he feared, they would destroy themselves and hand the continent over to the Bolsheviks. But Bullitt did not abandon his zeal. He continued to urge FDR to help lay the foundation for genuine Franco-German cooperation. And if we "see a fair chance of success," he zealously added, "you could then come forward with some tremendous public announcement," probably a fair and meaningful world economic plan.[62]

In the diversity of American views about European affairs, Breckinridge Long, ambassador to Italy, represented a minority opinion. The St. Louis lawyer-diplomat believed that the peoples in the East and Southeast of Europe would eventually accept German rather than French leadership: "The French domination is of military and political alliances. The German infusion is of blood and race. It runs all through Poland, Czechoslovakia, Hungary, Yugoslavia, and Austria." Since he considered only Germany and Russia capable of emerging as victor in the inevitable war over this regional dominance, he preferred that Germany, with its culture akin to America's, dominate Europe and serve as a bulwark against the Soviets' westward expansion. Like prominent American leaders at the time of the First World War, Long discounted France as a potential candidate for the leadership of Europe. Unlike Germany and Russia, it did not possess the requisite qualifications for maintaining it.[63]

By 1937 France's priority was honorable survival rather than aiming at leadership. As the durability of its far-flung alliance system came under question, next to Great Britain it sought stronger ties with the United States. It somehow did not want to believe, much less accept, that the American neutrality legislation, overwhelmingly backed by the people and supplemented by the Johnson Act, was as inflexible and impenetrable as it appeared. This legislation's

62. William C. Bullitt to Franklin D. Roosevelt, November 8, 24, 1936, in Container 43, PSF; André Laboulaye to Yvon Delbos, November 4, 1936, in *DDF*, 2ᵉ Série, III, 673–74.

63. Breckinridge Long to Franklin D. Roosevelt, April 19, 1935, in Edgar B. Nixon (ed.), *Franklin D. Roosevelt and Foreign Affairs* (3 vols.; Cambridge, Mass., 1969), II, 486–88.

original failure to distinguish between aggressors and victims caused as much apprehension in Paris as it did satisfaction and encouragement in Berlin. It tied the hands of the president, contradicted previous American positions with respect to collective security, and ran counter to America's trade principle of the Open Door. For a business country actively pursuing trade and international investment opportunities in Europe since the end of the nineteenth century and particularly since the end of the First World War, the United States obviously promulgated the Johnson Act and its neutrality legislation out of line with its larger economic aims. The "cash and carry" provision in the revised act of 1937, moreover, added the ironic twist of favoring such sea powers as Britain and Japan, which would enjoy ready access to American war supplies.[64] This so-called compromise served neither the cause of peace nor strict neutrality. The self-interest of the United States would not allow it to watch France and Great Britain go under in a European war. Georges Bonnet, then envoy to Washington, feared that the first few months in such a war would be crucially important to France. Unless the United States could strictly enforce its neutrality laws, France would be better off if they did not exist at all. Bonnet expected a lively battle between American advocates and adversaries of intervention in the event of a future military showdown in Europe.[65]

In the meantime, the United States government complicated matters by making foreign-policy statements designed to appease isolationists and pacifists, reassure internationalists at home, warn dictators and militarists abroad, and keep the Western democracies guessing. Although Cordell Hull's citation of America's fine policy principles was applauded around the world, they did not actually address themselves to the provocative challenges that defied these principles.

President Roosevelt's often oracular speeches were at least more specific in nature, though often nebulous in applicable meaning. A case in point was his famous "quarantine address" in Chicago on October 5, 1937. In it he decried that "the peace, the freedom and the security of ninety percent of the population of the world is being

64. Pierre de Lanux, *La neutralité américaine en 1936* (Paris, 1936), 43–59; Oswald Hauser (ed.), *Weltpolitik 1933–1939: 13 Vorträge* (Frankfurt, 1973), 110–45, 146–66; Sommer, *Die Weltmacht USA im Urteil der Französischen Publizistik*, 170–72.

65. Georges Bonnet to Yvon Delbos, March 3, June 15, 1937, in *DDF*, 2ᵉ Série, V, 80-82, VI, 122–26.

jeopardized by the remaining ten percent who are threatening a breakdown of all international order and law." To raise the American people's international consciousness, he reminded them, "There is a solidarity and interdependence about the modern world . . . which makes it impossible for any nation completely to isolate itself from economic and political upheavals in the rest of the world." He concluded the address with a clarion call: "There must be positive endeavors to preserve peace."

Speaking for the government and people of France, Yvon Delbos hailed this "magnificent" speech as "an act" of the highest importance. Its timing was perfect, because France and England just tried "to deal with the blackmailing tactics of the dictators." Newspapers throughout France welcomed what they interpreted as the end of America's long isolationist period. Such French appeasers as Camille Chautemps and Georges Bonnet banked on America's ability to help lead the dictators to the conference table. Resisters, like Blum and Delbos, believed that with the active help of the United States the concert of Western democracies would make the dictators hesitant to undertake a war against them. Whether such opinions and expectations were warranted remained to be seen. FDR refused to be pinned down when questioned about what he concretely meant by such phrases as "concerted effort of the peace-loving nations" and "positive endeavors to preserve peace." Were they just calculated rhetoric to caution the dictators, persuade the democracies not to give in, and to educate the American people? Moral support alone, without the military capability to back it up, amounted to a palliative Hitler was likely to dismiss as being inconsequential.[66] As long as the United States gave no indication of abandoning its passive foreign policy, Hitler was not to be bluffed out of his predetermined course. By 1938 he felt militarily strong enough to disregard even the assessment of his ambassador to the United States, Hans Dieckhoff. "In a conflict in which the existence of Great Britain is at stake America will put her weight into the scales on the side of the British," Dieckhoff believed. By not including France in this observation, the ambassador evidently implied that the United States placed it in a different order of priority.

A few days following the quarantine speech, Assistant Secretary

66. John McVickar Haight, Jr., "France and the Aftermath of Roosevelt's 'Quarantine Speech,'" *World Politics*, XIV (1962), 283–306.

of State George S. Messersmith submitted his evaluation of the world situation to Hull. FDR and Hull respected the brilliant assistant, who had been consul general at Berlin from 1930 to 1934 and subsequently had served as minister to Austria. As early as 1933 Messersmith had alerted the State Department that the highest echelons of Nazi leaders were "capable of actions which really outlaw them from ordinary intercourse." Now, in October, 1937, he tried to cut through the verbal fog that was misguiding America's self-deceiving foreign policy. With remarkable foresight and insight he sounded the general alarm: "The United States are the ultimate object of attack of the powers grouped in this new system of force and lawlessness." The United States, and for that matter the European democracies, he incisively observed, was conducting foreign policy and preparing for the impending war as if the old procedures, tactics, and weapons were still guiding the destiny of the world. But what had happened under Hitler's leadership, most fundamentally, was the complete breakdown of international morality. Taking a long-range view, Messersmith was convinced that the United States must face up to the clash of ideologies by ceasing to "follow a temporizing policy which will almost certainly bring war in the end." His analysis led to the conclusion that the ultimate aim of the dictators was "the disintegration of the British Empire, the consequent weakening of England in Europe and the opening of the way to attack the United States." The fascist states, he warned, were deliberately playing on the democratic peoples' fear of war and "on the lack of complete unity of action" to paralyze their resistance. It was high time for Americans to awaken to the realization that they could no longer risk ignoring the inexorable truth that the conquest of the European democracies by force would ultimately endanger the vital interests of the United States. Unless America belatedly decided to forge a mighty concert of the democracies, for peace if possible, for war if necessary, it would in time have to face the ruthless dictators alone.[67]

According to Messersmith, those isolationist pressure groups that handcuffed the president in his conduct of foreign policy were evidently too blind to see that though European affairs were indeed Europe's business, Europe's fate was economically and strategically

67. George S. Messersmith to Cordell Hull, October 11, 1937, in FRUS, *Diplomatic Papers, 1937*, I, 140–45.

also America's concern. This did not necessarily mean that the United States must become politically entangled with France or any other European country, but it did mean that America should be in a financial and military position to actively and independently protect its interest in maintaining a power-political equilibrium abroad. This stability could not be achieved by standing passively on the sidelines. In a world of power, not law, at least the existence of a substantial American deterrent was an absolute necessity to deter an unscrupulous upstart from destroying this equilibrium. Many Frenchmen believed, furthermore, that a firm and concerted effort by the United States, though late, perhaps too late, might yet help avert a human tragedy.

Camille Chautemps, the Radical premier whose skill in arranging political compromises made him an attractive figure in France's ministerial merry-go-round, was familiar with the isolationist arguments that kept FDR from throwing America's full weight into the battle for the prevention of war. Chautemps accepted these arguments as an explanation, though not a justification, for America's aloofness from the rising tide of war. The premier understood why the American government could not take what he considered the only effective measure against the outbreak of a European war, namely, a declaration by FDR that "the United States would take up arms against an aggressor or at least . . . send supplies to any nation attacked." Nevertheless he was convinced that such a statement would discourage aggression and "end the risk of the United States being involved in war." The isolationist approach, he had no doubt, would, ironically, draw the United States into a war soon after it began.[68]

In the 1930s the European powers were too preoccupied with developments in Europe to be more than "concerned" about those in the Far East. Even in Europe, they concentrated more heavily on each crisis as it developed than on the potential cumulative effects of successive crises they could sense were in the making. The European democracies and the United States were always inclined to worry about the "next crisis," which, they fearfully charged, would be merely another stepping-stone in Hitler's global design. But even as each new totalitarian advance reduced the strategic advantages of

68. William C. Bullitt to Cordell Hull, January 4, 1938, in FRUS, *Diplomatic Papers, 1938*, I, 1–3.

the democracies, they continued literally to gamble with their individual and collective security.

In *Mein Kampf* Hitler had outlined his world program. Afterward, he sporadically sketched it a little more distinctly. It was so much conceived in his own mind that even as chancellor of the Reich he took very few people into his confidence, not even his key generals. On the whole, foreign reaction did not take his fanatic goals seriously. And on his way to fulfilling them, step by step, his future victims still thought they could do business with him in the old-fashioned manner. Little did they understand that the Fuehrer did not feel bound by past standards of conducting diplomacy. Despite the practice of clever maneuvering in the past, it had long been understood that civilized society did not condone violations of international law and morality.

Hitler insisted on being in absolute control of shaping Germany's future. The "Thousand Year Reich" meant nothing less to him than world supremacy. To reach this pinnacle he was mentally prepared to gamble everything. WELTMACHT ODER UNTERGANG,—to be master or perish—was his capsuled slogan, his battle cry.

One has to pause and look closely at his strategy to see how wrong, almost suicidal, were the arguments of European appeasers and American isolationists. Briefly, he expected to execute his plans in phases, with each successful advance contributing to the next one. From 1933 to 1937 he concentrated on massive preliminary military and industrial war preparations. During this period he appeared to be open to negotiations, first, to gain time for these preparations and, second, to throw his future victims off balance. In January, 1934, he concluded a nonaggression pact with Poland to assure that nation that it had nothing untoward to fear. In the following year he deemed it politically useful to agree to the Anglo-German naval accord, although Admiral Erich Raeder, the commander in chief of the German navy, was not entirely satisfied with the relative apportionments. In the year of the Rhineland liberation the minister of war, General Werner von Blomberg, issued instructions "for the unified preparation for a possible war." They were renewed on June 24, 1937, with a two-front war in mind.[69]

As German scholarship has solidly established, in 1937 Hitler as-

69. Gerhard Meinck, *Hitler und die deutsche Aufrüstung, 1933–1939* (Wiesbaden, 1959), 125–30.

signed priority to the building up of the German navy, including the construction of several big battleships. This truly extraordinary order, by which he stood until the end, revealed his ultimate strategic objective. His annexation of Austria and Czechoslovakia, his intimidation of France, Germany's former "archenemy," and his violation of Belgian and Dutch neutrality if necessary to eliminate the western front, constituted the second phase of his grasp for world rule. In alliance with England, he hoped, but if necessary, without it, he would then launch his third phase, which would achieve the deep penetration of Eastern Europe, including the Soviet Union. Once German hegemony on the Continent had been secured, he anticipated the final showdown between the two remaining major powers, to wit, Greater Germany and the United States. Until 1939 the Fuehrer believed it feasible and in accord with "historical logic" that England would help him fight the Soviet Union and, ultimately, the United States. He had repeatedly given instructions that his American plan should be shrouded in secrecy and silence so as not to arouse the slumbering trans-Atlantic giant's fears. But there is no doubt that his program to build the big battleships, scheduled to be completed by 1944–1945, though they might possibly prove useful against Great Britain, was undertaken primarily with the United States in mind. In Hitler's opinion the kaiser and Tirpitz had been on the right course, but they had lacked the determination and willpower to follow it all the way. Since 1918 the United States had replaced Great Britain as the greatest rival. As he conceived it, his control of Europe was not an end in itself. The conquest of the continent was the essential preliminary in his ultimate challenge of the United States.

With regard to the Soviet Union and the United States, Hitler realized that Japan could play a significant auxiliary role. He used the formation of the Berlin-Rome-Tokyo Axis in 1938 as a diversionary tactic and psychologically intimidating weapon. In the light of Hitler's scenario, the scope of which obviously was not known to his future victims, the squabbles and rationalizations of democratic Europe and America suggest a slightly enlarged Biblical admonition: "Where there is no vision [or courage], the people perish." The democracies made it so easy for Hitler to exploit their fears, hesitations, and disbelief in international Darwinism. Their collective lack of resolution to stand up to even the more limited danger they clearly perceived made him look like a genius.

At this stage it seems appropriate to catch up with Far Eastern developments. The European possessions in the Far East automatically signified an inseparable link between Europe and Asia. Rather intriguingly, French diplomacy endeavored to engage America in the defense of French Indochina and the conflict between China and Japan as a roundabout way of mobilizing it for the defense of metropolitan France. Once the United States ceased being a merely passive force in world affairs by assuming a leading role in the Far East, the French logically expected it to spill over into European affairs. They cited such attractive considerations as the potential Chinese market and the value of strategic and geopolitical bases in the region as essential assets that the Western powers should retain.[70]

The hostilities that developed between Japan and China during Hoover's administration were the beginning of Japan's drive for a new order in Asia that would later join forces with Hitler's new order in Europe. France was in no position to cope with this menacing situation unless the United States and Great Britain threw their weight onto the scales. But though the United States was sympathetic toward China, Great Britain, and France, it was determined not to be pushed to pull their chestnuts out of the fire. It was simply not prepared for such a task. Except for an interest in Far Eastern trade and culture, it showed no real understanding of the emerging new China and had not conceived a constructive plan to provide Japan with the peaceful alternatives it badly needed for its economic survival. When Japan's disregard of treaty obligations manifested itself in violence against China, the Japanese discovered that they had had practically a carte blanche to proceed along this road. The League of Nations proved to be an impotent organization. The Western democracies talked about slapping Japan on the wrist. But they decided that a boycott and economic sanctions during a period of depression would be ineffectual weapons. And as Ambassador Claudel wrote to Tardieu, "America's threat not to recognize Japan's puppet state of Manchukuo is ridiculous."[71]

As usual, complexity took no holiday. The fact that France did not lend support to America's nonrecognition doctrine put its pro-Japanese policy in opposition not only to the United States but to the Soviet Union as well. For Japan's control of Manchuria raised seri-

70. Conversations and memos, 1929–1932, Box 235, Folders 6–8, in Stimson Papers.

71. Paul Claudel to André Tardieu, March 3, 1932, in CPEU, Vol. 380, AMAE.

ous questions about the security of the Trans-Siberian Railway and Soviet interests in Outer Mongolia. Undoubtedly, French munitions manufacturers liked to reap profits from sales to Japan. More far-reaching in French policies vis-à-vis Japan was the concern over French Indochina's future security. On its part, Japan was anxious to be on cooperative terms with at least one of the Western powers. The Franco-Japanese treaty of commerce with respect to Indochina, signed on May 13, 1932, indicated that Japan did not mind paying a price in return. It had gone so far as to offer definitely and formally "to make an alliance with France, agreeing . . . the Manchurian market would be open to France and that Japan would do all in its power to throw Oriental business into the hands of France." Because France turned down this offer of a military and economic alliance, the French felt they had a claim on the United States to help protect their colonial possessions in the Far East. In essence, though, Franco-American views with respect to Japan continued to differ significantly. FDR recognized the Soviet Union not only in the hope of developing promising trade relations with it but in part also as a check on Japan's imperialism. While his administration did not entirely follow Ambassador Joseph C. Grew's advice to block Japan's program in Manchuria with "superior physical force," it continued to exert diplomatic pressures.[72]

In the estimate of the French government, America's ambiguous policies toward Japan offered insufficient protection. If anything, America's retreat in the Philippines, the inability of its Asiatic squadron to offer serious resistance to any Japanese surprise attack, and its inadequate financial assistance to bolster China's independent strength would most likely stiffen Japan's expansionists. Under these circumstances, France tried to maintain great friendliness toward Japan and, as Ambassador Grew reported, supposedly assured Japan's political leaders that it "would not alienate Japan out of consideration for the United States."[73] America's ambiguity could in part be traced to the fact that in the mid-1930s it exported three times as much to Japan as to China, and the trade balance favored the United States. Their cotton-silk trade was especially significant

72. W. R. Castle, "Memorandum of a Conversation with Claudel," October 10, 1932, in FRUS, *Diplomatic Papers, 1932*, IV, 295–96.

73. Joseph C. Grew to Cordell Hull, March 12, 1934, in RG 59, Box 6069, 711.51/106, NA. See also "Évolution de la politique japonaise en 1934," CPEU, Vol. 381, pp. 74–79, AMAE.

because closing the Japanese market to American cotton would have produced catastrophic effects in the South. American financial investments in Japan, moreover, were twice as great as in China—by about $400 million to $200 million respectively. Still, sentimentally China and France occupied a special place in Yankee thinking.[74]

Developing the habit of keeping pace with the European dictators' successful acts of aggression, Japan in the summer of 1937 became engaged in an undeclared war with China highlighted by a frightful slaughter in Shanghai. This violation of the Kellogg-Briand Pact and the Nine-Power Treaty prompted the United States to accept the League of Nations' invitation to the Brussels Conference (November 3–24). American leaders hoped that the participating powers would take joint action against this kind of international lawlessness and, perhaps, find solutions eliminating the underlying causes of the ongoing conflicts.

The United States was by no means united on Far Eastern policies. The State Department's political adviser on the Far East, Stanley K. Hornbeck, recommended firmness. Pierrepont Moffat, primarily concerned with European affairs, counseled strongly against it. He wanted the United States to be on guard against European attempts to entangle it in the Far East. Such entanglements, Moffat feared, would cost America its freedom of action in Europe. The conference was doomed from the beginning because Japan did not show up. It was nevertheless of great interest to observe France's ambivalent attitude at the conference. If the United States and Great Britain did not provide firm guarantees, meaning "physical support," against Japanese aggression in Indochina, France was prepared, as demanded by Japan, to cut off transportation of essential supplies to China. But if these guarantees were given, the French would let the supplies go through. This political oscillation represented just another variation of the tireless efforts by the French to induce the United States to fight the military aggressors and preferably take the lead in stopping them. In the end, the outcome of the Brussels Conference confirmed Japan's belief in the disunity of its antagonists.

The United States steadfastly refused to be drawn into a foreign war. Neville Chamberlain refused to underwrite sanctions against

74. Jules Henry to Yvon Delbos, September 10, 1937, CPEU, Vol. 381, AMAE; Charles Corbin to Yvon Delbos, September 28, 1937, in *DDF*, 2ᵉ Série, VI, 878–79.

Japan. France insisted on maintaining its unacceptable bargaining proposition. The Soviet Union would have liked to see Japan exhaust itself in its conflict with China. Apparently thinking in terms of America's being an ally without a formal alliance, FDR sought to keep French hopes alive, whatever the outcome of the Brussels conference. On November 6 he asked Jules Henry, the French chargé d'affaires: "Doesn't France consider that a Japanese attack against Hongkong, or Indo-China, or the Dutch Indies would also constitute an attack against the Philippines? In such an eventuality our common interests would be menaced and we would have to defend them together." It sounded as if the president wanted to tell the French: "Don't always ask others to help you in advance of an attack. Take your chances. We cannot pledge commitments, but we will act when circumstances warrant it."[75]

This sounded more reassuring than the passing hint Norman Davis had dropped at Brussels, to the effect that the day might come when France would want to adopt toward Indochina the attitude the United States had arrived at in regard to the Philippines. That Davis thought of this anticolonial retreat from French Indochina as a viable alternative raised some Frenchmen's eyebrows.

The American attitude toward an entirely different problem also made French leaders wonder where the United States really stood. For years France had generously given asylum to political refugees. In the 1920s some 200,000 went to France, and in the 1930s several hundred thousand more found a haven there. There seemed to be no end to this human tragedy. By the end of the 1930s France had reached a saturation point. Throughout this period the United States, proudly symbolized by the Statue of Liberty, enforced highly restrictive immigration quotas. It seemed to the French that the United States, a country that spanned an entire continent, had a moral obligation to rescue the uprooted, at least until sanity had returned to civilization. France was willing to be a transit station. But it could not manage such multitudes for any length of time. Daladier was also afraid that so-called fifth columnists might be deliberately disguised as refugees to infiltrate French defenses.

Pointing out that the unprecedented magnitude of the refugee

75. Jules Henry to Yvon Delbos, November 7, 1937, CPEU, Vol. 382, AMAE. See also Dorothy Borg, *The United States and the Far Eastern Crisis of 1933–1938* (Cambridge, Mass., 1964), 411–28, and J. J. Smith, "FDR and the Brussels Conference, 1937," *Michigan Academician* XIV (1981), 109–22.

problem required global cooperation and planning, President Roosevelt took the initiative in calling an international conference, which was held at Evian-les-Bains in France. From July 6 to July 15, 1938, representatives from thirty-one nations and thirty-nine private organizations sought workable solutions. Henry Bérenger, experienced in politics, finance, and refugee problems, chaired the conference. He severely criticized the Anglo-American countries for their callous reaction to a massive human calamity and singled out the United States as the country best able to take care of the problem. But the Americans resisted this suggestion and recommended instead that the Latin American and Caribbean states be approached to open their doors. The upshot of thus going through the motions of doing something for the refugees without accomplishing anything meaningful left a bad mark on history. Contemporary Frenchmen were disappointed that the president of the United States talked compassion but did not assert his influence to organize a large-scale rescue operation to meet the urgent need. The refugees were victims of a war not understood.[76]

Hitler's relentless pressures to satisfy his territorial ambitions made the refugee problem look relatively less weighty. For a long time, Britain, France, and Italy had cooperated in maintaining the independence of Austria. On January 7, 1935, an official Franco-Italian communiqué reaffirmed their determination to preserve Austria's independent status. Both France and Italy had vital interests of their own at stake in retaining the status quo in Austria. The Duce's government actually attempted to persuade Hitler that an independent Austria on friendly terms with Germany would be a more effective link in Germany's economic penetration of the Danubian and Balkan states than an Austria that was merely a part of the Reich. Although the Austro-German accord of July 11, 1936, which upheld Austria's sovereign existence, removed some of Mussolini's concerns, the less-than-satisfactory course of the Ethiopian war drove the Duce into Hitler's arms and, consequently, compelled him to lessen his interest in Austria's autonomy. The gradual consummation of the Rome-Berlin Axis could not but accentuate this tendency.[77]

76. Timothy P. Maga, "Closing the Door: The French Government and Refugee Policy, 1933–1939," *French Historical Studies*, XII (1982), 424–42.

77. Rudolf Lill, "Italiens Aussenpolitik, 1935–1939," in Hauser (ed.), *Weltpolitik*, 78–109.

France and Great Britain had no contractual obligation to come to Austria's rescue in case of another German attempt at *Anschluss*, and they left it vague as to precisely what they would do. As important as economic considerations were, neither the entente powers nor Hitler underestimated Austria's obvious strategic value to Germany, especially given the Fuehrer's designs on Czechoslovakia. The encirclement of Czechoslovakia would make it much more difficult for France and England to implement the guarantees they had given that nation. Hitler considered the course of the Ethiopian war and the Spanish Civil War, and the democracies' wavering reactions to both conflicts were sufficiently reassuring for him to dare the annexation of Austria in March, 1938. The cynical manner in which this coup was carried out dejected the democracies as much as the coup itself. It was a great psychological blow to them. Even the "isolationist" United States did not conceal its disgust.

Hitler's antagonists in Europe and America condemned his use of political intimidation and military force, and they despaired that his tactics and goals meant that civilization was destined to go through a period of darkness. They took it for granted that his dream of a Greater German Reich threatened their own dreams of greatness and foreshadowed a nightmare they could not allow to materialize. It is noteworthy indeed that, at least with respect to Germany's annexation of Austria and its demand for the Sudetenland, one prominent American official presented to Roosevelt a dissenting point of view. Assistant Secretary of State A. A. Berle, Jr., deplored the democracies' emotional approach to Hitler's demands. Analyzing these demands from a historical perspective, he could logically justify them without in the slightest degree trying to be an appeasing mollifier. He recalled that the American delegation at the Versailles peace conference was not happy with the clauses that forbade *Anschluss*. Historically, American opinion had generally favored it up to the fall of the Weimar government. "Union of German-Austria with Germany," he reminded his superiors, "was regarded as a legitimate aspiration of both countries, blocked by the peace treaties . . . solely to maintain France in a superior military position." Long-range policy, he contended, should not be formulated on the basis of dislike of a mortal dictator. According to Berle, "the splitting up of Central Europe into a series of highly nationalistic small states tends to paralyze commerce and development," whereas the development of a larger unit constituted a favorable economic factor. As a highly organized industrial country, Germany required economic expansion, raw materials, and markets. Its strangulation could only produce war. *Anschluss* was primarily a German question and, in Berle's judgment, the attempt to make of the enlarged Reich "an international outlaw which must expect to fight at every turn" might set in motion a chain reaction leading to world war.

Instead of making futile disapproving gestures, he recommended turning acceptance of *Anschluss* into an opportunity for an accord on disarmament, free commercial relations, and racial and religious tolerance. Although it was late, perhaps too late, he did not exclude the chance that if Germany's justifiable aspirations were legitimized, it might respond favorably. Had it not been for French fears, such intelligent treatment of Weimar Germany, Berle strongly implied, would have never produced Hitler in the first place.[78]

When the Czech crisis reached its climax a few months later, Berle again submitted a memorandum to FDR. Reaching back into history, he defended the reconstitution of the self-supporting area of Germany plus Austria-Hungary as a positive goal. Instead of worrying about its threat to Western Europe, he argued, it would be instructive to recall that this unit of sovereignty, which had existed for centuries, "was principally occupied in maintaining its own organization and putting off the Turks." Berle believed that the new empire would most likely find itself occupied with the Slavs. In any case he recommended that American policy should be guided by historical logic, not emotion: The United States should combat Hitler's atrocities, not the Greater Reich. Under no circumstances, he counseled, should America enter a general war to perpetuate the untenable situation created by the Versailles and Saint Germain treaties. Finally, he asked FDR to be on the alert lest French and British diplomats make the United States substantially "an associate power" before the Americans knew it.

On April 2, 1939, Berle developed these thoughts to their logical conclusion in his diary. Looking ahead to the peace that would follow the impending war, he did not think that much "would be gained . . . if central Europe were saved from efficient Nazi tyranny and cruelty and were turned over to an equally cruel Russian tyranny. . . . Rational settlement of the East European problem was

78. Adolf A. Berle to Cordell Hull and Sumner Welles, March 16, 1938, in Berle Diary, Container 210, Berle Papers; Berle to Franklin D. Roosevelt, September 1, 1938, in Container 95, folder labeled "A. A. Berle, Jr.," PSF.

denied Stresemann and even to Bruening by both British and French diplomacy less than ten years ago. Have we any guaranty that a more realistic approach would be taken today?"

Telescoping Anglo-French diplomatic maneuvers from March to September, 1938, one can understand why in the end Hitler acted on the assumption that the entente powers would, in practical terms, do nothing to defend Czechoslovakia. Their eager search for a diplomatic solution clearly indicated to him that they were not willing to fight for it, unless a grand coalition of England, France, and Russia, aided and abetted by the United States, could be organized to stop him. In this respect, realities spoke for themselves.

Contrary to their declarations, neither France nor Great Britain were willing or even able to fight Hitler's modern military war machine in 1938. The British Empire did not want to become involved in a general war on account of Czechoslovakia. In the course of his devious dealings with Paris, Prime Minister Chamberlain did not hesitate to let France, very unsure of itself, make its own decision. There was little doubt that, without British participation, the French would not dare meet their treaty obligation to defend Czechoslovakia. The Soviet Union would not go to the rescue of this "neighbor" without the entente powers' cooperation, and even then it would do so only if Czechoslovakia were invaded by a foreign power and French and Russian assistance could occur at the same time. And, overestimating the military strength of the entente powers, the United States suggested to them at the time of the Munich crisis that they resist Hitler. But it failed to issue simultaneously an unequivocal public warning to him to expect serious consequences if he violated Czechoslovakia's territorial integrity. Despite their apprehensions, Americans simply did not want to be involved in this European crisis. The most FDR was prepared to do was participate in an international conference seeking peaceful solutions for the world's troubles, provided an invitation to it would be unanimously endorsed by the participating powers.[79]

Under these circumstances France was weighing various diplomatic compromises that would permit it to extricate itself without losing face, honor, and self-respect. To have FDR call a conference

79. Edwin C. Wilson to Cordell Hull, March 14, 18, 1938, in FRUS, *Diplomatic Papers, 1938*, I, 35–40; Jules Henry to Yvon Delbos, February 23, 1938, in *DDF*, 2ᵉ Série, VIII, 506–13; René de Saint Quentin to Joseph Paul-Boncour, March 26, 1938, in *DDF*, 2ᵉ Série, IX, 111–14.

or perhaps secretly urge Berlin and Prague to settle their differences peacefully, such possibilities as a plebiscite, Czechoslovakia's neutralization, and its voluntary cession of the Sudetenland seemed worth exploring. When Bullitt asked Daladier in May whether he could confirm a report that he had decided to go to war with Germany if it should attack Czechoslovakia, he tartly replied, "With what?"

Inasmuch as Czechoslovakia's dissolution seemed inevitable, it displeased the French and British that Czech President Eduard Beneš, at the height of the crisis in September, would rather have provoked a general war than yielded the Sudetenland. The French were incensed about indications of Czech mobilization without prior consultation with them. Having decided by the time of the Munich meeting that the choice boiled down to general war or general peace, Daladier and Chamberlain chose peace. As the British prime minister proudly referred to it, they chose "peace in our time." But the French found it painful and foreboding to join Great Britain in the urgent advice to the Czechs to give up the Sudetenland.

The very procedure Chamberlain followed—holding a private discussion with Hitler in Berchtesgarden, leaving the Fuehrer to draw from Daladier's absence the inference of a substantial lack of Anglo-French harmony—was a dead giveaway. It evidenced a weakness that only a general conference of all concerned parties might have been able to overcome. Although Hitler had made up his mind as early as May 30, 1938, "to smash Czechoslovakia by military action in the near future," he did not dare strike until he was "firmly convinced that France will not march and therefore Britain will not intervene either."

Prior to Munich, the makers of French foreign policy had attached undue weight to every hint that America should not be counted out as an important factor in the balance of world developments. But despite FDR's readiness to serve as a catalyst in the exploration of peaceful solutions, Secretary of State Hull went out of his way to deny the rumored existence of a London-Paris-Washington axis. He frowned upon ambassadorial statements implying more forthcoming assistance than Washington intended. To boost the morale of the French, Ambassador Bullitt sometimes went out on a limb from which Hull forced him to retreat. In fact, Bullitt advised FDR before Munich "that we should not permit ourselves to be drawn in." Observing how hard the British and French tried to make the United States share the responsibility for the "sellout" at Munich, Moffat, too, hoped they would not succeed.[80]

Although President Roosevelt's public and private comments conveyed the impression that he desired to act as a major figure on the international chessboard, his silence about his eventual moves diminished his effectiveness abroad. His last-minute messages to Hitler, essentially harmless peace appeals, were either ignored or sarcastically rejected. His known anti-Nazi attitude and his pointed assurance in his recent Kingston address that "the United States will not stand idly by if domination of Canadian soil is threatened by any other Empire" hardly qualified FDR in Hitler's mind to assume the role of impartial peacemaker. But from the French point of view, FDR's public exhortations constituted helpful signs of "courageous statesmanship" and perhaps a harbinger of closer identification with France rather than merely a straw in the winds.

Roosevelt's comments and actions behind the scenes seemed to justify such wishful thinking. Secretary of the Interior Harold Ickes recorded in his diary on September 18 that, given the chance, the president would have taken a tougher stand against Hitler's demands than had France and Great Britain. Privately FDR had encouraged them to expect from the United States "everything except troops and loans." Although he thought that in case of a war, which he did not want to see break out, France would not be able to penetrate the German frontier, he rather rashly assumed that Germany could be effectively blockaded. The European democracies, more realistic, welcomed the tangible assurance found in America's decision to build up its navy and air force. After the shock of the capitulation at Munich it became clearer than ever that time must be gained to narrow the existing military gap as quickly as possible. The Fuehrer evidently respected only force.[81]

In view of Germany's frightening superiority in air power, France's top priority called for the utmost effort to catch up with it. This inferiority was more easily recognized than remedied. Since in the spring of 1938 France lacked the industrial capacity, competent management, engineers, tools, experienced workmen, and pilots to increase its production rate of forty-five planes a month, about one-tenth of the German rate, it tried to "harness American industry to

80. Hooker (ed.), *Moffat Papers*, 198–208.

81. Harold L. Ickes, *The Secret Diary of Harold L. Ickes* (3 vols.; New York, 1954–55), II, 467–69.

the French war machine." Initially, France intended to place orders for a thousand high-speed military planes, preferably the latest American models. And ideally, it would have liked a very early delivery. In general, the United States government was sympathetic, but it had to overcome many legal, political, and industrial hurdles before being able to bolster the French air force. For one thing, American airplane manufacturers had to expand their facilities to accommodate the growing volume of foreign orders. Provisions of the Espionage Act interdicted the export of the latest models. The American army and navy objected to any interference, such as foreign orders might occasion, with their own delivery schedules. Among many other complications, the French wanted their workers and pilots to be trained in American airplane plants and their pilots to test the planes before delivery.

Such an operation could hardly be kept secret, and the stubborn opposition of the army to the sale of the P-40, the newest and best pursuit plane in the world, reached the proportions of public scandal. In the end, the commander in chief had to assert his authority to stop the army's obstructions and shenanigans. Secretary of the Treasury Morgenthau asked for common sense, not jealous intrigues, to decide the vital issue: "If your theory [is] that England and France are our first line of defense, let's give them good stuff or tell them to go home," he advocated. Jean Monnet, the highly competent and trustworthy French negotiator, and FDR were grateful to Morgenthau for resourcefully steering the difficult negotiations to a successful conclusion. By the time the United States entered the Second World War, the French airplane connection had earned it an extra dividend. French orders had given the American aircraft industry a precious head start of two years, facilitating the Defense Department's speedy acceleration of its huge wartime requirements.[82]

Altogether the description of Roosevelt's foreign policy prior to World War II as one largely limited to moral support for the democracies, expressed in equivocal statements and minor tangible assistance, underrates its immensely important economic policy. Far

82. John McVickar Haight, Jr., "Les négotiations relatives aux achats d'avions américains par la France pendant la période qui précéda immédiatement la guerre," *Revue d'histoire de la deuxième guerre mondiale,* LVIII (April, 1965), 1–34; Military Intelligence Division Reports, G-2 Report No. 24, 759 W, January 16, 1939, in Container 186, Harry Hopkins Papers, FDRL.

from being aloof and passive, as Frenchmen felt he was, FDR actually did more to undercut Nazi Germany's preparations for war than his French critics did. The president and his secretary of state gave priority to economic approaches in efforts to overcome pressing political perils. They could thus unobtrusively pursue anti-Nazi policies in defense of America's worldwide economic interests without opening themselves to the charge of engaging in objectionable entanglements with manipulating French and British politicians. The foundation for these policies had been laid with Hull's reciprocal trade policy and its most-favored-nation principle. Their adoption promised a restoration of the world's economic health that would substitute enterprising competition for costly rivalries and obviate an unsound armaments race. Such bilateral agreements, open to all nations willing to participate in them, produced a multilateral web that not only reinforced America's "Open Door" interests but also offered hope for world peace and prosperity.

In contrast to this "economic appeasement" that extended benefits on a global scale, Germany aimed at bilateral agreements to secure raw materials and control markets within an autarchic framework. Even worse, it endeavored to exclude the United States from the European market, especially in Southeastern Europe, and to cut sharply into America's Latin American trade. The use of these weapons in its ideological, political, and economic battle against the overseas democracy became more extensive when the United States retaliated by going on the offensive. Unlike Britain's attempt since the mid-1930s to appease Germany in economic and naval matters in order to motivate it to change its political course, American policy makers reacted to the inordinate German challenge with the resolution at least to blunt it with their still superior economic arsenal. It should be noted that the United States took up the German gauntlet to protect itself and not France or the Western democracies generally. Naturally the democracies could not but benefit indirectly.

Specifically, while in the 1920s German-American trade relations reflected both nations' mutual desire, out of political and economic motives, for steady improvement, their respective import-export trade alone declined by roughly 80 percent in the decade from 1928 to 1938. This steady deterioration was underscored by Germany's notification in October, 1934, that it would not renew the German-American trade treaty of 1923, which embodied the most-favored-nation principle. It was less important that Hull denounced this attack against America's trading system than that Hitler, by ignoring the express advice of his trade experts, critically undermined the economic foundation of his extremely demanding war machine. As the best-informed officials of the German Foreign Office perceptively assessed the consequences of the nonrenewal of the treaty, the loss of most-favored-nation status would increasingly weaken Germany's position in the world market and eventually lead to its economic encirclement. Germany's steadily declining ability to raise foreign exchange for the import of great quantities of raw materials posed a major handicap. It slowed down the preparations for war and, in effect, compelled Hitler to undertake his planned aggressions before he was fully ready. He did not want to give his opponents a chance to match Germany's arsenal and thus cancel his military superiority. The full impact of the decision not to renew the treaty was to work like a delayed time bomb. Already on August 22, 1939, he told his military officers: "Due to our limitations our economic situation is so that we can hold out only a few more years. We have no choice but to act." The early slowdown forced upon him later made a crucial difference.

Under the determined guidance of Messersmith and Moffat, Washington's trade-agreement program was conceived as an automatic economic pressure against Germany to behave reasonably in the international arena or pay a steep price for destabilizing it. That this was not idle talk was attested to by the "Anglo-American trade treaty" of November, 1938, a euphemism for something that German publicists preferred to call by its right name—an Anglo-American front. So as not to arouse public fears, the Nazi government ordered the press to tone down the meaning of this politically foreboding combination.[83]

All along, Roosevelt's "good neighbor" policy toward Latin America had tried to build a dam against the spread of fascist ideology in the Western Hemisphere, erect barriers against Germany's penetration of the Latin market, and organize a hemispheric defense system well in advance of potential hostilities. FDR's determination to frustrate Hitler's aggressive plans was also manifested

83. Consult the enlightening work of H.-J. Schröder, *Deutschland und die Vereinigten Staaten 1933–1939: Wirtschaft und Politik in der Entwicklung des deutsch-amerikanischen Gegensatzes* (Wiesbaden, 1970), 178–95, 278–87.

by his tripartite currency accord, the demonstrative stationing of a battleship near the Thames River for the purpose of removing gold from Europe, the contemplated special fund for the safekeeping of French and English gold, and the threat to Germany of countervailing duties. FDR's policies were not enough to stop Hitler, but they hurt him over the long run.[84]

The world did not trust the German leader. When he violated the Munich accord and annexed all of Czechoslovakia in mid-March, 1939, it knew beyond the shadow of a doubt that he was not an honorable man. Foreign Minister Bonnet surveyed the damage done by this latest coup. Still talking bravely about the defense of Poland, Bonnet and other leaders of the European democracies had long ago come to the conclusion that peace at any price was morally more defensible than a terrible war over Czechoslovakia. France alone was neither psychologically nor militarily in a position to fight it. Great Britain lacked the ground forces to help cut down the massive casualties modern warfare would exact. The alternating hot and tepid statements issuing from Washington were hardly enough to ascertain America's prompt change of attitude in case of war. In fact, Bullitt reiterated to Bonnet that FDR had no choice but to implement the existing neutrality legislation. Deeming it therefore prudent to initiate a last-minute Franco-German accord, the French government hoped that once it was made public, the United States would publicly approve it. But on November 30 Sumner Welles informed the French ambassador that its strained relations with Germany made it impossible "to express approbation of an official act on the part of the German Government." Still believing in February, 1939, in the possibility of reconciliation with Germany, England and France regretted the absence of an American ambassador in Berlin. Instead of strengthening their efforts in Berlin, the United States seemed to complicate matters with its unreconciled attitude.

The United States could afford to be less frightened by Hitler than neighboring France, and it saw no reason to behave like it. In reaction to the Nazis' "flagrantly illegal" violation of truncated Czechoslovakia's independence, it promptly retaliated by depriving goods of Czechoslovakian origin of most-favored-nation treatment and by raising duties on German products. These measures were in a way

84. Adamthwaite, *France and the Coming of the Second World War*, 310–15; *Le Populaire*, April 20, 1939, 2 BL 10, dr. 2, sdr. a, in Papiers Léon Blum, FSP.

America's response to Hitler's declaration that Germany must export or perish. Secretary Morgenthau once again urged the treasuries of the democracies to stay in close contact. As another reminder of America's interest in peace, FDR on April 15 sent appeals to Hitler and Mussolini to offer guarantees against aggression in Europe and the Near East. But the German chancellor, now more arrogant and defiant than ever, was clearly unimpressed by messages without teeth in them.

With Danzig and Poland his next obvious targets, the Fuehrer's prime concern was temporarily to neutralize the Soviet Union. Although the entente powers did not coordinate their efforts adequately, they turned to Moscow for assistance in this imminent crisis. Without tracing the tortuous details of these efforts between April and August, 1939, it should be noted that even at this late hour Paris preferred a military pact with the Soviets rather than a military alliance.

Daladier, who since the recent betrayal of Czechoslovakia had taken much firmer control of foreign affairs, was absolutely certain that President Roosevelt's attitude during the last few months had restrained Hitler from attacking France and England. In his opinion, "the fact that the United States had become an enormous question mark in Hitler's mind had been sufficient to prevent war which otherwise would have been inevitable." He was grateful for the astonishing clarity and ability with which the president labored tirelessly to prevent war in Europe. It went without saying, however, that a change in America's Neutrality Act that would restore access to arms and ammunitions would be a large factor in deterring Hitler from making war in the future, just as withholding them from the democracies would encourage him to attack them.[85]

As in the summer of 1939 French statesmen became more pessimistic about the chances of peace, they saw the urgent need for more tangible American involvement. The French ambassador in London suggested one way of bringing it about. For too long, he argued, Americans had entertained the illusion that Nazi Germany's ambitions were limited to Europe when in reality they encompassed the world. Instead of talking to Americans about the Balkans and Danzig, which did not interest them very much, it would be much more

85. William C. Bullitt to Cordell Hull, June 5, 1939, in Department of State Confidential File, RG 59, 741.61/673, NA.

effective to talk with them about the problems the Axis powers were stirring up in the Pacific and Latin America. Such a shift in arguments, he thought, might well result in a shift of policy. But time for testing this approach had run out.[86]

In the summer of 1939 France faced the unnerving decision whether to stand by the pledge it had given Poland to defend its territorial integrity and independence. The task had been operationally made more difficult, perhaps impossible, by Belgium's neutrality and the defensive mentality of France's military establishment. To give the reputedly excellent Polish army a realistic chance to defend its homeland against the Nazis, the French army had to "retain on the French frontier at least two-thirds of the German army." Even making the dubious theoretical assumption that it could meet this condition, the French government found it absolutely essential that the Soviet Union occupy the first line of resistance to Hitler. This critical requirement was blocked by Poland's decision, understandable in the light of history, to allow neither German nor Russian troops on its soil and by Soviet designs on the Baltic states.

The announcement on August 22 of the Nazi-Soviet Pact came as a shock to the whole world. At the time both Hitler and Stalin gained important strategic advantages that, in their thinking, crowded out all other considerations. Devastating as this dramatic demonstration of cynicism was from a practical point of view, the fact that the French and British had been completely hoodwinked by the Soviets in their long discussions about a united anti-Nazi front added insult to injury. Aside from British and French differences over how far to go with concessions to Moscow, France's lukewarm implementation of the Franco-Soviet Pact and mutual suspicions, accentuated by Moscow's exclusion from the deliberations leading to Munich, evidently influenced Stalin. If he could not fully rely on the capitalistic democracies in case of a German aggression against the Soviet Union, why, he must have asked himself, should he have any compunction to join Nazi Germany in a division of spoils? The enhancement of the Soviet Union's security through its westward expansion seemed worth a political marriage of convenience with "the assassin of the workers."

With war imminent, Bonnet's appeasement policy came to an inglorious end for him and France. Even now he still hoped prayer-

86. Charles Corbin to Georges Bonnet, July 25, 1939, in CPEU, Vol. 319, AMAE.

fully "that the President of the United States would attempt in some way to preserve peace." The socialist French labor movement implored FDR to use the authority of his high office to make a supreme effort for the sake of millions of human beings and the defense of civilization. Believing that Mussolini was close enough to Hitler to help avert war, FDR sent an urgent message to the king of Italy. A day later, on August 24, Roosevelt adjured the German chancellor and the president of the Polish Republic to settle their differences by means of direct negotiation, arbitration, or conciliation with outside neutral help. To make these appeals more worthy of consideration he promised to contribute to peaceful solutions in every possible way. When a few days later Hitler's bombers attacked unfortified centers of Poland's population from the air, FDR made a final vain attempt to stop such unconscionable barbarity. It was the voice of humanity in a lawless international jungle.

As hopeless as winning a war against the Nazi war machine then looked, France and Great Britain opted for declaring it. If they could not save Poland, at least they could save their honor and perhaps miraculously survive the ordeal.

It would be unfair to make Bonnet the scapegoat for a development he strove earnestly to avert. French society as a whole paid a terrible price for its lack of civic responsibility. Political leaders had long shown a lack of courage to do what was necessary to keep France's domestic front in a tolerably strong condition. Its military leaders had failed to maintain an adequate modern military posture or to entrust younger officers with command positions. Although the diplomatic bureaucracy gave the appearance of continuity while foreign ministers did not stay in office long enough to put their own stamp on well-formulated policies, the entire conduct of French diplomacy, procedurally and substantively, showed almost unbelievable weaknesses. For want of the self-reliance a major power must possess, France literally scrambled for alliances, which soon turned into liabilities and exposed serious contradictions. Equally noteworthy, it tended not to carry its preferred policies to their conclusion. Afraid of losing out in an experiment of friendly economic and political cooperation with Germany, it was also afraid to deal sternly with Hitler before he amassed superior military might. It considered Franco-Soviet cooperation as a vital insurance policy, but its reserved treatment of the Soviet Union and its military did not create the necessary atmosphere to reassure Moscow of France's reliability. Afraid or unable to take strong positions alone, it constantly pressed for more guarantees than England and the United States were willing or militarily prepared to provide. Its overemphasis on conferences and paper pacts, moreover, deprived it of the flexibility a confident power knows how to use advantageously. The amazing incoherence of French diplomacy during these years resulted in a harvest of antagonists who were basically disinterested in France and of friends who were often exasperated with its behavior. France wanted to be a major power, but it lacked many requisites for being one. Enamored with the obsolete ways of the past, it evidently ignored the fact that the world was in a constant flux.

America's frequent references to nonentanglement also ignored the truth that the place of the United States in world affairs had drastically changed in the twentieth century. The naïve assumption that by turning its back on European affairs it could not be entangled in them could be sustained neither in logic nor in practice. America's dollars, raw materials, and manufactured goods helped the world turn its wheels. When they slowed down, the world economy turned down. And when that happened, opportunities for domestic discontent and international frictions increased by leaps and bounds. In an age of economic and financial interdependence even geographically separated national entities had to interact to survive. In both France and the United States the masses and most of their leaders showed little or no grasp of global geopolitical conceptions. Because of this serious shortcoming, during the 1930s the United States did not know how to act like a major power, though it was one. The realities of power constellations in this decade made it mandatory for the United States to defend democracy and peace with every means at its command. Its applied alternative policy—neutrality and isolation—did not preserve peace. In reality it was the road to war. But Congress and the people did not see it that way. Unlike their president, they approached the question of war and peace from a very parochial angle and without a sense of history.

IV

The Collapse of France: FDR, Vichy, and de Gaulle

THE OUTBREAK OF WAR AND THE SUMNER WELLES MISSION

According to Hitler, France and England had actually facilitated the Nazi-Soviet Pact by stiffening Poland's sense of independence. Thereafter, Germany found it impossible to negotiate a peaceful solution to the problems of Danzig and the Corridor. On his part, Stalin, unsure of Western guarantees to Russia, preferred to swallow the deal with Germany rather than expose the Soviet Union prematurely to a war with Hitler. In fact, by extending his frontiers westward, he placed himself in a better defensive military position. Equally important, the pact promised to reduce the likelihood of a two-front war, which in the summer of 1939 looked like a distinct possibility. On the other side of the ledger, Anglo-French support for Finland seemed to justify Stalin's suspicion of the capitalist ruling classes. Distrusting Hitler also, he deemed it expedient to remain neutral and prepare for any eventuality.[1]

What amazed the Germans when they quickly overran Poland was the inactivity of the 110 French and British divisions. As General Alfred Jodl testified at the Nuremberg war-crimes trials, at the time Germany had taken the chance of keeping only twenty-five divisions along its western frontier.

Hitler was surprised that the Western democracies declared war against the Reich. His transcending ambition involved the defeat of the Soviet Union. He did not expect war against Britain and France before 1944 or 1945 and even then only if they did not fall in line with his new order on the Continent. Their inclination not to make large military and economic sacrifices in the defense of Poland prompted

1. Adolf Hitler to Edouard Daladier, August 27, 1939, 2 DA 7, dr. 3, sdr. a, in Papiers Daladier; Adrien Thierry to Paul Reynaud, April 8, 1940, in Etats-Unis–Russie 1932–40, Vol. 377, AMAE.

the Fuehrer to order abstention from any offensive action against France as long as it did not engage in hostile acts.[2]

The ensuing lull proved to be deceptive. Cheerful about it, Bonnet drew the extraordinary conclusion from it that "Germany had no chance of winning the war." Indeed, England and France, he predicted, would defeat it, and in the end both Germany and the Soviet Union would collapse. In the meantime Chamberlain and Daladier urged President Roosevelt to induce Congress to modify the existing neutrality legislation. In a statement to the French Foreign Affairs Committee, Daladier called for America's moral and material support in the common struggle against dictatorship. Combined with the democracies' existing mastery of the seas, the prospect of gaining, with America's help, superiority in air power inspired much hope.[3]

Personally in accord with the Anglo-French request, FDR nevertheless realized that Congress and the American people were not ready, however sympathetic they were toward the cause of the Western democracies, to assist them materially. The best chance for the repeal of the arms embargo and its replacement by a cash-and-carry system, as adopted and signed early in November, 1939, lay in presenting this change solely in terms of the security interests of the United States.

On October 4, FDR had already manifested the essential identification of the United States with certain French war needs. He confidentially advised Daladier that, at least for the time being, the United States would not treat armed French merchantmen as warships.[4] The president activated his country's international role quite ostentatiously. In December, twenty-one American republics signed the Declaration of Panama, which barred military operations by belligerents within three hundred miles of American shores. Disregard of this protective measure invited retaliatory sanctions. When, soon after the outbreak of war in Europe, German commercial ships in the Western Hemisphere sought refuge in Mexico to be in a position to conduct maritime war, the United States made every effort to shift Mexican-German trade to the United States.

2. U.S. Navy Department, and Kriegsmarine, Oberkommando, *Führer Conferences on Matters Dealing with the German Navy. 1939–40, 1942–45* (7 vols.; Washington D.C., 1946–47), 1939, pp. 3, 6, 24–28.

3. William C. Bullitt to Cordell Hull, December 14, 1939, in Box 26:7, PSF.

4. "La neutralité Américaine," 3 DA 3, dr. 4, sdr. 3, in Papiers Daladier.

Unlike General Maxime Weygand, who was not convinced that air power could win a war, Daladier was certain that France and England could win this war only if they possessed absolute domination in the air. He counted on the United States to supply France with ten thousand airplanes in the near future, whatever the cost. The orders flowing into American plants for tools, engines, and planes clearly exceeded production capacities. It required a great deal of planning, coordination, and cooperation to speed up the process of industrial expansion in the United States. Daladier suggested that the great automobile manufacturers might be able to use their productive capacities to help accelerate plane production. Unlike Britain, France was from the start anxious to place huge defense orders. To correct its resulting unfavorable trade balance with the United States, it hoped to step up its exports to America under most liberal conditions.[5]

The so-called phony war, from the collapse of Poland until the invasion of the Low Countries, stirred some leading Americans to explore the possibility of achieving a peace before unimaginable damage had been done to civilization. Not discouraged by previous failures of international conferences, such officials of the State Department as Sumner Welles and Adolf A. Berle believed that a peace conference with the goal of preventing war might on balance produce positive results. To determine whether it was feasible, Welles persuaded President Roosevelt to send him to Europe to gather information and to hold out the promise of substantial economic aid if peace could be attained.

The English reaction to this "awful, half-baked idea" was that no settlement with the Hitler regime was worth signing. Anthony Eden, who saw Welles and Ambassador Joseph P. Kennedy on March 12, 1940, went a step further. He maintained that to allow Hitler once more to demonstrate that aggression did pay would be a blow to all Europeans who treasured freedom. For democratic America even to entertain the thought of coexisting with Hitler's lawless dictatorship raised eyebrows. Lord Halifax, the foreign secretary, was by now convinced that no lasting peace could be accomplished as long as the Nazis were in power.[6]

A French background paper about Welles's mission not only de-

5. FRUS, *Diplomatic Papers, 1939*, II, 496–99, 521–27.
6. Anthony Eden, *The Memoirs of Anthony Eden: The Reckoning* (Boston, 1965), 104.

plored that its failure might put the blame for the continuation of the war on the European democracies, but, quite intriguingly, it alerted Daladier to the underlying cynical nature of the mission. It contended that the ambitious American undersecretary of state had surrounded himself with isolationists who would prefer Hitler's domination of Europe to the risk of their country's entry into the war. It suggested, moreover, that the peace mission was more an election gimmick than a serious diplomatic effort. At his meeting with Welles, the French premier let it be known that neither France nor England could accept "any peace which did not provide for the restoration of an independent Poland and for the independence of the Czech people." Otherwise he was willing to grant Germany reasonable concessions. He was also prepared to go far to appease Italy if it would not join the war on the side of Germany. While Welles's observations about Mussolini's apprehensions with regard to Germany's domination in Europe were welcome news to Daladier, they were evidently based on misinterpretation of the Duce's ambivalent policies. Much worse, Welles undermined his peace mission when he stated unequivocally that the United States would not assume any responsibility "which implied as a potential obligation the utilization of American military strength in preserving the peace of Europe."[7]

Guided by past experiences, the presidents of the French Senate and Chamber of Deputies explained to Welles that they saw no solution other than a military victory for France. Edouard Herriot, who had devoted much of his life to promote lasting friendship between the French and the Germans, traced his disillusionment to repeated deceptions on the part of German statesmen. He recalled, for instance, that at a secret meeting in London in 1924 Gustav Stresemann had tried to persuade him to enter into an alliance with Germany. He rejected this proposal because he detected in the exclusion of England a highly objectionable power game. The outlook of leading French parliamentarians precluded peace at this time. Nevertheless, such prominent Frenchmen as Chautemps, Bonnet, and Reynaud were agreeable to the negotiation of any practical scheme that would obtain security for France. It seemed to them preferable to the continuation of a war likely to result in ruin.[8]

7. "Origine du voyage Sumner Welles, Les États-Unis, February 24, 1940," 3 DA 5, dr. 7, sdr. b, in Papiers Daladier.

8. Report by Sumner Welles on his Special Mission to Europe, March 7, 9, 1940,

Perhaps resenting Sumner Welles's intervention in Europe during his temporary absence, Ambassador Bullitt subsequently reported to FDR the unfavorable impression the mission had made. Apparently Daladier and his colleagues gathered from Welles's presentation that the president believed in Germany's invincibility and thought that it would be wise to use Mussolini's good offices to arrange a compromise peace. Bullitt tried his best to enlighten French leaders that neither FDR nor Welles "had the slightest intention of using Welles's visit to persuade the French and British to stop fighting and leave the fate of Europe to Mussolini as arbiter."

As a peaceful gesture, the German chancellor had received Welles on March 2. He insisted that the entente powers had declared war against his country not to protect Poland but to annihilate Germany. He boasted that he was thoroughly prepared to meet this challenge. It was out of the question at this stage to call off the impending showdown.[9] In the same vein, Vyacheslav Molotov, the Soviet commissar of foreign affairs, had asserted in October, 1939, that the real reason for the Western bloc's war with Germany was not the professed restoration of Poland or the defense of democracy, but "their profoundly material interests as mighty colonial powers. . . . The possession of these colonies, which makes possible the exploitation of hundreds of millions of people, is the foundation of the world supremacy of Great Britain and France. It is the fear of Germany's claims to these colonial possessions that is behind the present war." Still confident of achieving victory, each side treated Welles's peace mission with a certain contempt and as an unwelcome intrusion into European affairs. Consequently, FDR yielded for the time being to the existing realities.[10]

FRENCH APPEALS TO THE UNITED STATES AND THE COLLAPSE OF FRANCE

When in April, 1940, Hitler violated Norway's and Denmark's neutrality and soon thereafter showed his disregard of international law in the Low Countries, the world asked itself, what next? The

in FRUS, *Diplomatic Papers, 1940*, I, 59–71.

9. Hans-Adolf Jacobsen, *Der Weg zur Teilung der Welt: Politik und Strategie 1939–1945* (Bonn, 1977), 60–64.

10. Jane Dregas (ed), *Soviet Documents on Foreign Policy, 1917–1941* (London, 1953), 388–92.

invasion of France began on May 10, and by mid-June the German war machine had obtained its objective. The tragic events moved so fast that they seemed unbelievable. The French system of defense and the alliances designed to strengthen it fell apart as the crisis reached a quick climax. Once it became obvious that France's defeat was imminent, its troubles multiplied, hastening the humiliating end. On May 15, Daladier was stupefied and incredulous when General Maurice Gamelin reported to him the collapse of the Belgian army. Simultaneously, Belgian railroad workers went on strike and refused to transport French troops. Belgian officials, however, refused to accept any blame for the northern defeat and emphasized that "it was not the Belgian line that had broken, but the French line, at Sedan." German tanks crossed French antitank defenses, railroad rails sunk deep in concrete, as if they were straw. As in other instances, moreover, the French general staff had not carefully worked out mutual defense plans with the Belgian general staff, largely because of the reluctance of the Belgian government.[11]

On May 28 the king of Belgium took it upon himself to order his armies to cease fire, endangering British forces. They escaped the trap of Dunkirk only by a masterful evacuation from the Continent. Under these circumstances Britain decided not to risk its small air force in a battle that was lost for all practical purposes and instead to preserve them for the expected Nazi attack against England. Although the promise of ever-increasing American aid would not by itself be sufficient, France, practically abandoned, still hoped against hope to have a chance to resist the Nazis as long as Italy would not stab it in the back.

President Roosevelt and his advisers followed these breathless developments with intense concern. For that matter, Daladier and Reynaud, as well as Winston Churchill, unceasingly implored FDR to throw the full weight of the United States into the battle before France and England went under and America would have to face Germany alone. Although they knew that, under the American Constitution, Congress alone had the power to declare war and that the president could not on his own promise military intervention, to which the public was in any case opposed, they nevertheless pleaded for it. They also knew that at the height of the developing

11. "Memorandum of Conversation with Belgian Ambassador," May 28, 1940, in Container 211, Berle Papers.

catastrophe the United States did not possess the thousands of planes they requested for immediate delivery. As the French later blamed Belgium and England for having contributed to their military disaster, their political and military leaders evidently regarded America's relatively passive attitude as a convenient alibi for events culminating in France's saddest hour.

With less reserve and more dramatic flair than is customary for diplomats, Ambassador Bullitt relayed these requests. In close contact with Paris, Churchill stood behind the French requests in a common effort to draw the United States into the war. Their appeals ran the whole gamut. First they urged the immediate transfer of ships, planes, weapons, and tools. They soon asked the United States to promise eventual participation in the conflict. Such a promise would boost the sinking morale of the French and strengthen those leaders who were thinking in terms of carrying on the fight. They asked the United States to make a declaration of nonbelligerency so as to leave no doubt with respect to neutral America's real intentions. They even asked the president to call on Congress to declare war. In May and June they repeatedly suggested the dispatch of American warships to the Mediterranean, not only as a friendly gesture but also to warn Mussolini against giving wounded France a coup de grâce. A courtesy visit of the Atlantic fleet to Portugal, they believed, would make Mussolini think twice before attacking France. As Reynaud saw it, if such limited American intervention was not forthcoming promptly, the United States would in a few months face alone a joint attack by Germany, Italy, and Japan.[12]

With the focus on Italy, the French urged the United States to show their strong disapproval of any Italian military collaboration with Hitler by threatening to block all Italian assets in the United States. The British joined them in their delusion that a direct peace appeal by Roosevelt to the Duce might sway the Italian dictator. The offer of generous colonial concessions, the implementation of which would be guaranteed by the United States, they hoped, might induce Mussolini to come to a conference. But as the Germans expected, the fascist leader would not be tempted by this bait. As Count Ciano summed it up, "Fascists did not break faith." It also occurred

12. William C. Bullitt to Cordell Hull, May 14, 20, 25, 1940, in Box 26:8, PSF; Edouard Daladier to French ambassadors in London and Washington, May 28, 1940, 3 DA 9, dr. 3, sdr. a, in Papiers Daladier.

to the French that the president should use whatever influence he possessed with the pope to persuade him to threaten excommunication and perhaps to establish himself in the United States in case of war. This latter suggestion of course amounted to unthinkable political dynamite in America.

All these appeals reflected the desperate situation in which France found herself. It simply refused to accept the American promise of material aid as an adequate response to the urgent needs of the hour. The French dismissed the notion that the president of the great American republic had his hands constitutionally tied at a crucial moment in history. They ignored the reality of America's military unpreparedness, which ruled out forceful policies fraught with potentially disastrous consequences. The secretary of state and Congress were utterly opposed to any rescue operation for which the United States was not physically ready. Also, psychologically and politically the country was not prepared to intervene in Europe's disgusting power struggles. Somehow Americans did not yet understand that the war in Europe threatened the balance of power throughout the world. After the defeat of France the United States rushed to step up its military preparedness by planning a two-ocean navy and a powerful modern air force. In the course of the discussion of preparedness one could even then hear in the halls of Congress voices opposing the draft as a step that would destroy "personal freedom of our young men and adopt the Hitler policies of continental Europe" by instituting "autocratic military conscription."[13]

All along, America's explanations for its nonintervention in Europe had to be taken seriously. Vague American hints at support were never a basis for realistic appraisals of international policies. Certainly Hitler dismissed Roosevelt's rumblings as being no imminent danger to his schemes. The most they did was to pressure him to execute his plans as fast as possible. Charges that the United States abandoned France as it was going down demonstrated the unrealistic extent to which France assumed it could count on effective American assistance. As late as June 14 Reynaud let his agonizing emotions inform FDR that "if you cannot give France in the coming days a positive assurance that the United States will come into the struggle within a short space of time . . . you will then see

13. *Congressional Record*, 76th Cong., 3rd Sess., 10478–80.

France go under like a drowning person after having thrown a last look towards the land of liberty from where she was expecting salvation."[14]

Believing that their fate would ultimately be that of England and the United States, skeptical Frenchmen were too preoccupied with their daily discouragements to attach much weight to optimistic Anglo-American long-range speculations. That they might benefit France in the long run was of no immediate consolation. In essence, the long view envisioned a protracted struggle between Germany, the dominant land power in Europe, on one side, and the British Commonwealth and the United States, the dominant sea powers in the world, on the other. Given their industrial and military productive capacities, the Anglo-Americans had little doubt about the final outcome of such a confrontation.[15]

To carry on their fight, even if France should go under, demanded hard decisions, however unpleasant, on the part of the British government. The 366,162 men who had been saved at Dunkirk lived to see another, more promising battle. As Lord Alexander Cadogan noted in his diary, it made no sense for Great Britain to uncover itself "to help a helpless France." It would be fatal for Britain, he thought, to send its fighter protection to an expiring France. "Instead of dribbling away to France all that we have that is good . . . let us concentrate on our own defense and the defeat of Germany," argued the British permanent undersecretary of state for foreign affairs. Rightly or wrongly, the French took the position that, as their ally, the British could not honorably withdraw their planes. In their despair they clung until the last moment to the opinion that the battle for France could yet be won. The British had become so disgusted with the military chaos in France that as early as May 26 Churchill aired his temporary exasperation with the personal comment that Britain might be better off without France.[16]

Before long the British statesman went to the other extreme. In order to keep the French empire and fleet out of Hitler's reach and to bolster the morale of French leaders on the brink of asking for an armistice, he proposed a Franco-British union. The details of this spontaneous historic proposal had not been the result of careful An-

14. Paul Reynaud, *In the Thick of the Fight, 1930–1945* (New York, 1955), 508–10.

15. Stimson, Diary, May 15, 1940, in Stimson Papers.

16. David Dilks (ed.), *The Diaries of Sir Alexander Cadogan, O.M., 1938–1945* (New York, 1972), 294–97.

glo-French deliberations. Although the French cabinet as a whole did not take this imaginative idea seriously, to Reynaud and de Gaulle it sounded "splendid" and "stupendous." On June 16 Reynaud described it as the only possible solution for the future—if it were done on a large scale and very quickly. At one point, in the course of a telephone conversation between Bordeaux and London, he gave de Gaulle half an hour to consummate this union in principle.[17]

The unprecedented French defeat caused much bitterness. Whatever justifications existed for recriminations against the British, Belgians, and Americans, the French people now blamed themselves and their politicians and military leaders for the debacle. The blitzkrieg of Hitler's "superior" war machine offered a convincing explanation for what had happened. Nevertheless, contemporary critics considered it an immense mistake that General Gamelin had sent his reserves to Belgium. American military intelligence traced the inadequacies of the French air force to a belief on the part of the French prior to the war that war would not come in their time. Interservice rivalries and a tendency to procrastinate exacted a high price.

More recent studies have focused on the comparative strength of the German and French military machines in World War II. Surprisingly, they found no quantitative or qualitative French inferiority. The record of French tank production by 1940 was so remarkable that the modern French mechanized divisions were "as powerfully equipped as any of the famed German Panzer divisions." The strategy of defense and faulty timing by the French high command evidently dissipated the effectiveness of French "armoured divisions in several hasty and ill-coordinated attacks." By taking the offensive, the Germans gained the advantage of utilizing their air-tank combination infinitely more effectively than the French.[18]

When despite great courage the French armies were smashed and the French government was compelled to leave Paris for Tours and Bordeaux, the crucial question was which of the several possible alternatives for future action France would adopt. It could ask for an

17. Pierre Renouvin, *World War II and Its Origins*, trans. Rémy Inglis Hall (New York, 1969), 219–21.

18. R. H. S. Stolfi, "Equipment for Victory in France in 1940," *History*, LV (1970), 1–20.

armistice, sue for peace, or save the fleet and empire by continuing the fight from North Africa. Its decision would certainly affect the immediate military situation. But much more was at stake from the point of view of future power constellations and their impact on the world economy.

The choice of Marshal Henri Philippe Pétain to direct his country's affairs during this trying period seemed to be reassuring. He and General Weygand, the commander in chief, considered an armistice absolutely essential to save France from sliding into anarchy. Unlike Reynaud, who frantically pleaded for some magic American pronouncement, Weygand regarded symbolic American gestures as totally insufficient to keep France in the war. With the United States refusing to be dragged into the war and Great Britain refusing to release France from the pledge not to make a separate peace, the wavering French leaders resigned themselves to an armistice.[19] Instead of staying with the withdrawing French government in an effort to influence its decisions, Ambassador Bullitt remained in Paris, hoping to be able to help protect the capital from being wrecked by the Germans. As de Gaulle said in his memoirs, this noble but not really vital gesture conveyed "the impression on our officials that the United States no longer had much use for France."[20]

The collapse of France after five weeks of fighting stunned the world. It made an indelible impression on FDR. Great Britain and the United States felt left in a lurch. They had expected France to hold off the Germans for at least a year, time enough to build up their massive striking force. As much as President Roosevelt liked France and its people, like other American statesmen before him he was enormously disappointed to see France not function reliably as one of the great powers.

THE UNITED STATES AND VICHY: THE EARLY PHASE

Henceforth the fate of the French navy constituted the most pressing issue. Should it be combined with the German and Italian navies, the democracies' control of the Mediterranean and Atlantic

19. Paul Baudouin, *The Private Diaries (March 1940 to January 1941) of Paul Baudouin*, trans. Charles Petrie (London, 1948), 76–100; A. D. Biddle to Cordell Hull, June 17, 1940, in FRUS, *Diplomatic Papers, 1940*, II, 455–56.

20. Charles de Gaulle, *War Memoirs* (3 vols.; New York, 1955–60), I, 61.

would be in such jeopardy that the strategic and political ramifications would be incalculable. The British offered the French fleet asylum in the United Kingdom. Talk about sending it to Canada or the Western Hemisphere seemed somewhat less realistic than moving the government and the navy to North Africa.

As attractive as the North African alternative sounded, it was not without serious drawbacks. Marshal Pétain expressed the sentiments of those who were determined to remain in France despite terrible hardships. They could not bring themselves to abandon the *patrie* in order to continue the war. Admiral Darlan was convinced that "the departure of the navy would have made the armistice impossible, the war would have continued, and the *Wehrmacht* would have landed in Africa." Aside from the vengeance Germany would wreak on France in case it continued the struggle from Africa, it was not out of the question that the enraged French people, feeling betrayed and deceived by their past masters, might rise up upon the news of the practical abandonment of metropolitan France. Finally, the very human question about the morale of French soldiers evacuated to Africa and concerned about the fate of their families under Nazi rule could not be ignored. Still, Allied strategists obviously would have liked to see the French, British, and American navies combined, to enhance the prospect of an early victory over the Axis.[21]

Soon after President Albert Lebrun had asked Pétain to head the ninety-ninth government of the Third Republic, the aged marshal assured Deputy Ambassador Anthony Biddle of his desire "to cooperate in every way with us. The friendship of the United States is one of the few assets left to France." There was no reason to doubt the sincerity of this personal statement, regardless of the future circumstances that made it difficult for him to live up to it.[22] As early as May 26 President Roosevelt advised the French government: "If worst comes to worst, we regard the retention of the French fleet as a force in being as vital to the reconstitution of France and of the French colonies and to the ultimate control of the Atlantic and other oceans and as a vital influence towards getting less harsh terms of peace. . . . The French fleet must not get caught bottled up in the

21. Louis-Dominique Girard, *Montoire, Verdun Diplomatique* (Paris, 1948), 33: Anthony Biddle to Cordell Hull, June 15, 1940, in FRUS, *Diplomatic Papers, 1940*, I, 256–57.

22. Anthony Biddle to Cordell Hull, June 19, 1940, in FRUS, *Diplomatic Papers, 1940*, I, 262.

Mediterranean. . . . If the Germans held out alluring offers to France based on the surrender of the fleet . . . these offers are of ultimately no value." On June 17, Cordell Hull instructed Biddle to reiterate this view in interviews with Admiral Darlan and Foreign Minister Paul Baudouin. In extraordinarily strong language, Hull warned the new French government, "Should . . . [it] permit the French fleet to be surrendered to Germany, the French government will permanently lose the friendship and good will of the Government of the United States." Baudouin promised in the most solemn manner that the French fleet would never be surrendered to the enemy: "La question ne se pose pas," he said. He could not refrain, however, from stating that the final sentence in the American message had "deeply pained" the French government.[23]

Indications that the Franco-German armistice agreement permitted a major portion of the French fleet to pass into German hands dismayed Washington. Discounting solemn German assurances not to use it during the war, American officials were equally disturbed by claims to the French fleet that Germany reserved to make at the conference that would write the final peace treaty. Welles termed this provision a direct violation of pledges France had previously given the United States. The secretary of state told the French ambassador that should this arrangement become a reality, it would be tantamount to handing Germany a cocked gun to shoot at the United States. Somewhat later, Hull ridiculed as "wholly fallacious" the assertion that Germany could never get the French fleet. The Nazis, he pointed out, would not find it difficult to charge France with violations of the armistice agreement, if they so desired, to justify their seizure of the fleet in Toulon. And was the French government so naïve, he inquired, as not to anticipate that the Nazis could compel the French government to turn the fleet over to them in the final peace?[24]

Such arguments might possibly have swayed the leaders of a France that no longer existed. But Ambassador Bullitt was shocked following discussions he had on July 1 with Lebrun, Pétain, Darlan, and other high officials. He found that they had cut loose from their

23. Cordell Hull to U.S. consul at Bordeaux, June 17, 1940, Anthony Biddle to Hull, June 18, 1940, in FRUS, *Diplomatic Papers, 1940*, II, 456–57. See also FRUS, *Diplomatic Papers, 1940*, II, 458–62.

24. "Memorandum of Conversation—Hull and Ambassador Henry-Haye," September 11, 1940, in Box 58, Vichy, France, Hull Papers.

past social and political system and foreign political associations to become Germany's favorite province. As to the fleet, Pétain wished Bullitt to know that he had given the orders to sink the ships rather than to permit them to fall into German hands. Although Darlan agreed with Pétain that Hitler would conquer Britain within the next few weeks, a prospect he gleefully anticipated, he took exception to American messages regarding the fleet. He had notified its officers, before the armistice, that if the Germans demanded the French fleet, it would be sent to Martinique and Guantanamo. In any case, absolute orders had been given to scuttle the ships if the Germans should attempt to seize them. In addition, under no circumstances were the French ships to be sent to Great Britain. In Darlan's bitter judgment, the British at the end of the war would accord the French fleet no better treatment than the Germans. Such sentiments were obviously reinforced when, on July 3, a powerful British squadron opened fire on French warships anchored at Oran, near the naval base of Mers-el-Kebir. Their officers had ignored the ultimatum either to join the British fleet or scuttle their ships.[25]

The United States and Great Britain obviously preferred France's order to scuttle the French fleet over giving the fleet to Nazi Germany. But it implicitly indicated the gulf that now separated France from its recent allies. It no longer thought and acted like an ally of long standing. The concept of the community of Western democracies had for all practical purposes ceased, as far as Vichy France was concerned.

When it became an open secret in the fall of 1940 that France might provide assistance to Germany and her allies in the war against the British Empire, FDR informed Pétain that the use of the French fleet against the British fleet "would constitute a flagrant and deliberate breach of faith with the United States." To Churchill's satisfaction, FDR made it unmistakably clear that such Franco-German cooperation "would most definitely wreck the traditional friendship between the French and American people, [and] would permanently remove any chance that this government would be disposed to give any assistance to the French people in their distress." To make his warning even stronger, he bluntly told Pétain "to forget any Amer-

25. William C. Bullitt to Cordell Hull, July 1, 1940, in FRUS, *Diplomatic Papers, 1940*, II, 462–69. See also Russell Brooks, "The Unknown Darlan," *U.S. Naval Institute Proceedings*, LXXXI (1955), 879–92.

ican assistance when the appropriate time came to help insure to France the retention of her overseas possessions."[26]

Hitler's restrained moves with respect to the French fleet were largely determined by his overall strategy. His immediate objective was to remove England—peacefully, if possible, by force, if necessary—as an obstacle to his ultimate goal of crushing the Soviet Union. With England on his side, he anticipated that the United States would recognize the futility of challenging his new order. As Count Ciano recorded it, Hitler was prepared to offer France lenient armistice terms "to avoid the French fleet joining with the English fleet." In the massive attack against England that he was contemplating, he intended to make use of French bases and whatever other direct assistance France could render. Very confident that he could accomplish this feat, he nevertheless noted in the summer that England's initial apprehensions had given way to an extraordinary spirit of defiance. He conjectured that Stalin may have buoyed it. The Soviet leader had indeed been concerned that France had collapsed so quickly. There had been no exhausting struggle such as he had expected.[27]

Nature also interfered with the Fuehrer's program. He waited in vain for the four to five days of good weather he needed for his relentless bombardment of England to soften it up for the all-out assault. Rejecting Hitler's interspersed peace soundings, England rather decided to gird itself for battle. Throughout this period, and contrary to Admiral Raeder's more aggressive attitude, Hitler had given instructions not to provoke the United States. As a safeguard against American intervention he relied on the tripartite pact with Italy and Japan. Signed on September 29, 1940, the pact was as much directed against the British Empire as it was designed to give the United States second thoughts. The message was clear. America's interference in Europe might confront it with a two-front war. But instead of intimidating the United States, the Axis pact produced the opposite effect: it stimulated greater Anglo-American coordination and gradually transformed the European war into a world war.[28]

26. Cordell Hull to H. Freeman Matthews, October 25, 1940, in FRUS, *Diplomatic Papers, 1940*, II, 475.

27. Hugh Gibson (ed.), *The Ciano Diaries, 1939–1943* (New York, 1946), 265–66.

28. Franz Halder, *Kriegstagebuch: Tägliche Aufzeichnungen des Chefs des Generalstabes des Heeres, 1939–1942*, ed. Hans-Adolf Jacobsen (3 vols.; Stuttgart, 1962–64), II, 48–49, 98–99. See also Andreas Hillgruber, "Der Faktor America in Hitler's Strategie,

Practically prostrate France was caught in the gathering of these global forces. At the same time, the rest of the world found it increasingly confusing to deal with "France," because different groups now claimed to represent it. Vichy France, headed by Pétain, Laval, and Darlan, insisted that it was the legitimate government. General Charles de Gaulle proclaimed that in the name of France he would continue to fight the Nazi curse until, with the help of the Anglo-Americans, the enemy had been destroyed. Although Pétain and de Gaulle respectively looked upon each other as traitors to French unity, they and other, less unbending, Frenchmen really yearned for the same national goal, namely, the restoration of France as a free and independent world power. They might differ with respect to reborn France's political system, but they could not conceive of its existence without dignity and honor. By chance this ultimate unity of purpose was furthered by their different alignments. Should Germany win the war, with the help of Vichy France, or should the Anglo-Americans win the war, with the help of de Gaulle's organized resistance, or should Frenchmen subtly cooperating with the Allies and simultaneously maintaining their loyalty to Pétain successfully bridge the Pétain–de Gaulle gulf, in the end France nonetheless stood to benefit from such unplanned orchestration of policy.

The factionalism that had plagued French politics in the thirties also characterized French conduct during the war years. At times it interfered with efficient prosecution of the war. Fortunately for France, the Allies did not permit the aberrations of the Vichy leaders and the frequent antics of de Gaulle to divert them from the basic consideration that only the defeat of the Nazi regime could make possible the rebirth of France. Despite incredible frustrations, the quite deliberate interplay between London and Washington succeeded in overcoming the Pétain–de Gaulle feud. Originally, Great Britain assisted and financed de Gaulle while the United States kept its distance from him. The reverse relationship existed with respect to Vichy.

Britain's attacks against the French fleet resulted in Vichy's severance of diplomatic relations. Deploring this political alienation, London appreciated the close contact the United States maintained

1938–1941," in Wolfgang Michalka, *Nationalsozialistische Aussenpolitik* (Darmstadt, 1978), 506–11.

with Vichy until the North African invasion. This contact enabled messages of mutual importance to be passed among the countries and factions. Despite his strong anti-British leanings, Pétain, too, counted on FDR to relay Vichy's desire to keep on friendly terms with England. Regardless of public statements to the contrary, Pétain's personal attachment to the United States and Britain rested on the combination of past ties and the realization that a Pax Britannica or a Pax Americana would be infinitely preferable to a Pax Germanica. Although Laval and Darlan did not share this view, they nevertheless deemed it essential for France not to alienate the United States.[29]

De Gaulle and his supporters, as well as ideologically inclined Americans, thoroughly disapproved of the president's official dealings with the Vichy regime. They did not seem to understand that he was guided by strictly pragmatic factors. Prompted by wartime conditions and the awareness that the war had to be won militarily before freedom and democracy could again be enjoyed by the French people, FDR did not hesitate to do business with Vichy. This did not imply approval of Vichy's foreign and domestic policies or continued support of its leadership upon termination of the war. Uppermost on the president's mind was his transcendent concern about the fate of the French fleet and empire bases. To keep them out of German reach was a matter of top priority. It was useful to know what was going on in occupied and unoccupied France and to be in a position to influence policies as much as possible. Furthermore, assuming that the majority of the French people would continue to favor the traditional values of Western civilization, FDR wanted to let them know that the United States cared about their fate and would neither abandon nor forget them. Whatever degree of accomplishment resulted from this interaction, it precluded any reproaches that would have been made for not having tried it.[30]

When Hitler came to the conclusion that Vichy could play an im-

29. Great Britain, Prime Minister's Office, Operational Papers, January 31, 1942, PREM 3/187 (microfilm); R. T. Thomas, *Britain and Vichy: The Dilemma of Anglo-French Relations, 1940–42* (New York, 1979).

30. For FDR's elaborate defense of his Vichy policy, see his letter to Edwin C. Wilson, U.S. representative to the FCNL, January 5, 1944, in "France, 1944–45," PSF. According to William Langer, *Our Vichy Gamble* (New York, 1947), the United States gained from it valuable diplomatic and military intelligence that made it worth temporarily ignoring ideological differences.

portant role in his attack against England and in his strategic plans in the Mediterranean, he sought its collaboration. Should France accommodate him, he would consider it a master stroke because such a development would definitely result in terminating Franco-American ties. News of a secret meeting on October 24 between the Fuehrer and Marshal Pétain created a sensation. The public later learned that Foreign Minister Joachim von Ribbentrop and Vice Premier Pierre Laval were present when "the Marshal was received with honors due his rank." Pétain's communiqué described the atmosphere at Montoire, the small community where the meeting took place, as one of "high courtesy." Little, however, was revealed about the substance of their conversation. Initiated by the German chancellor, its main purpose was to probe the feasibility of Franco-German collaboration in the fight against England and in the implementation of Hitler's African designs. In exchange, France expected release of its prisoners of war, reduction of occupation payments, and more favorable peace terms. Laval and Darlan favored collaboration as long as the war situation warranted it and provided the price was right. Pétain officially went along with it, but slyly, he underwrote it only "in principle." Even so, at Churchill's emphatic requests, FDR reacted to this ominous prospect in terms designed to make collaboration appear too costly for the future of France.[31]

The change of the political climate that had taken place in France since July accounted at least in part for the Franco-German soundings. Keenly aware of the hardships and indignities their people were suffering the Vichy leaders tried to put an early end to them. Convinced of Germany's invincibility, it made sense to them to shorten the war. The upper levels of France's economic and social hierarchy bought the Nazi thesis that Europe's choice boiled down to German dominance or bolshevism. For the industrialists and for the remnants of the French aristocracy, who felt more comfortable with "order" than with popular front–type democracy, the choice created no problems. Leaders like Laval and Darlan saw a future for France if Hitler conceded to it a positive role in the new Europe. With the passage of time, they counted on their gift to "outwit their blundering and less civilized neighbors." In the meantime, Laval saw utter ruin for Europe if the war dragged out for several years, no

31. Pierre Laval, *The Diary of Pierre Laval* (New York, 1948), 60–65; Eberhard Jäckel, *Frankreich in Hitlers Europa* (Stuttgart, 1966), 118–23.

matter who won. If he could help mediate a negotiated peace, in his judgment everybody would be a winner.

Unlike America, which, he deplored, did not comprehend the political revolution that had occurred in Europe since Hitler took office, Laval looked upon that revolution as a potential harbinger of permanent peace. Europe simply could not afford the luxury of a war every twenty years. He professed not to be the tool of Hitler or Mussolini but rather to be concerned with what was best for France, eternal France. Nothing could have pleased him more than to persuade the United States of the virtue of collaborating with the new Europe. Little did he understand Roosevelt's determination to help Britain defeat dictatorship and autarchy in Europe. When in a lengthy conversation on November 15 the American chargé indicated to Laval that his collaboration policy might easily lead to a Franco-American rupture, the vice premier reacted with horror. This did not prevent him, Georges Bonnet, and others from spreading the word that the United States, long an advocate of a United Europe, favored the creation of the new order in Europe. Presumably, because it meant peace, the United States would eventually cooperate with it. After all, Laval asked, what good would Europe be to the United States if its prewar best customer became nothing but a cemetery? American aid to Britain, which could never hope to conquer the Continent even if Hitler did not smash it, he argued, would only prolong the war and delay the solution of Europe's problems. In any event, he stood by his assertion that friendship with America "would always be a cornerstone in France's foreign policy." But for untrustworthy Britain, which, according to a widely held French view, had pushed France into a senseless and unnecessary war, he reserved his contempt.[32]

Whereas Laval's personal ambitions and close German associations gradually lost him Pétain's confidence, Admiral Darlan's standing rose steadily. The commander in chief of the French fleet, who thought more in global than continental terms, enjoyed considerable respect. In his analysis late in 1940, Germany would probably win the war and the British Empire would cease to exercise the

32. H. Freeman Matthews to Cordell Hull, November 14, 15, 1940, Robert D. Murphy to Hull, December 9, 1940, in FRUS, *Diplomatic Papers, 1940,* II, 403–11, 414–17. In later years Laval exploited the factionalism among collaborationist groups to prevent ultrarightists from establishing a totally fascist regime. See Bertram M. Gordon, *Collaborationism in France During the Second World War* (Ithaca, N.Y., 1980).

influence it had wielded for generations. The resulting drift of Canada and probably Australia and New Zealand toward the United States meant to him that "the future of Europe will be governed by collaboration between the United States and France." Such a development, along with inherent German weaknesses, he estimated, held out the real chance that France would eventually become the dominating continental force. That is why he believed that France had less to fear from a German victory than from a revival of British power.

Although Darlan admitted that the Germans had informally expressed their interest in the French fleet, he reiterated France's opposition to turning it over to them. Both at this time and afterward, the United States resorted to the technique of extracting such French assurances every so often. Darlan also wanted to leave no doubt that Vichy would defend its colonial possessions against any attacker. Should the British, moreover, attempt to enforce a complete blockade against France, the consequences would be far-reaching. He hoped that the United States would see "the wisdom of supplying France's North African colonies with much needed sugar and gasoline and avoid the necessity of seeking them from Germany." It is noteworthy that Vichy's leaders saw a certain advantage in being on bad terms with Britain. The more they verbally condemned Britain and de Gaulle, particularly after repulsing de Gaulle's attempt to bring Dakar into his fold, the more Vichy improved its standing with the Germans.

As captives of their conquerors, the Vichy leaders were obviously not in a position to protest too much. But they could and did play for time before making any irreversible commitment either to Germany or to the United States and Great Britain. Darlan left his options open, leaning whichever way the military pendulum was swinging. Laval's opportunism led him too close to Germany to retain Pétain's trust. Laval was condemned in the end because he was willing to lose France's soul in order to safeguard its existence. Notwithstanding his advanced age and the almost unbearable burden of his office, Pétain tried to hold on to France's traditional Western ties more honorably than the ministers around him. While outwardly submitting to Germany, he prayed fervently for an Allied victory. The Germans had acted miserably toward France. In the marshal's judgment, they had demonstrated their inability to administer a foreign people and had therefore "missed their great chance of rapprochement with France."[33]

Germany exploited France without any consideration for the most elementary needs of the French people. It compelled French industry and labor and the French government to contribute to Germany's war economy. It took advantage of the advanced state of France's aviation industry and forced it to deliver thousands of new and repaired airplanes, engines, and helicopters. In both the occupied and unoccupied zones, French enterprises worked almost exclusively for the occupation authorities. The leather, shoe, and textile industries delivered the great bulk of their production to their German masters. Regardless of the repercussions on local economies, coal, hydroelectric power, and wine supplied fuel for the Axis war machine. Wine was distilled, turned into alcohol, and mixed with the gasoline used in tanks and trucks. German tanks were literally drinking French wine. Bauxite, nickel, rubber, and olive oil, among many other items, were drained from France to reinforce the German war machine. As demoralizing as this situation was, it could not be effectively sabotaged.[34]

As FDR had feared since the collapse of France, the Greater Reich also began to lay the groundwork for long-range control of French industry. Beginning in the summer of 1941 negotiations were under way to form a Franco-German dye trust, to be composed of the I. G. Farbenindustrie and leading French dye producers. The objective of this trust, to be called Francolor, was "to bring the major dye producers in Europe . . . into the orbit of German control." Instead of continuing the previous competitive cartel arrangements that had existed between I. G. Farben and the French dye industry, the German dye trust was now reaching out for absolute domination. The

33. Leland M. Goodrich and Marie Carroll (eds.), *Documents on American Foreign Relations, 1939–1946* (8 vols.; Boston, 1940–48), III, 392–95. See also FRUS, *Diplomatic Papers, 1940*, II, 411–20.

34. "German Intervention in French Economy, July and August 1941," in William D. Leahy to Cordell Hull, December 1, 1941, Records of OSS, No. 7763, RG 226, NA; "Note Concerning the Part Unoccupied France Plays in German War Economy," in Ray Atherton to William J. Donovan, February 2, 1942, Records of OSS, No. 11261. See also Peter F. Klemm, "La production aéronautique française de 1940 à 1942," *Revue d'histoire de la deuxième guerre mondiale*, CVII (July, 1977), 53–74, and Patrick Facon and Françoise de Ruffray, "Aperçus sur la collaboration aéronautique franco-allemande (1940–1943)," *ibid.*, CVIII (October, 1977), 85–102.

prospect of a European economic bloc directed from Berlin intensified FDR's determination to do what he could to help defeat the Reich.

Pétain realized how vital it was not to alienate the United States if France was to throw off the German yoke. But he pleaded with the Americans to understand that unpleasant appearances in French policy should be judged by the necessity to pursue a course of many tracks.

This uncertainty led to numerous misunderstandings and occasional irritations. The National Assembly's overwhelming vote in July establishing a dictatorship headed by Pétain, now the chief of state with full executive and legislative powers, constituted at least a symbolic identification with the new order in Europe. Whether or not this act was of dubious constitutionality, at this time America was less concerned with ideology than with the course of the war. The United States recognized the Vichy regime primarily to keep it from joining the enemy camp.

As much as Vichy appreciated this gesture, it realized that recognition did not protect it from nagging Franco-American differences. Upon the collapse of France, for instance, the United States had frozen all French government and private assets, which amounted to about a billion dollars. Being in dire financial straits, Vichy made repeated efforts to unfreeze some of these funds to pay its diplomatic representatives around the globe. Robert Lacour-Gayet, who talked with Assistant Secretary Berle about this matter, thought it might help to remind him that "France was France, and was going to continue to be." But whether it involved these funds or food and medicines, American officials did not want to see them get into German hands. As Berle phrased it, "We could never quite tell whether Vichy was talking the language of France or of the Armistice Commission where the German masters at Wiesbaden issued their orders."[35]

Jacques Rueff, a prominent official of the Bank of France, frankly admitted that "Germany was annoyed at the wrangling methods of the French and their insistence on details." This habit explained at least in part the slow progress in creating the new Franco-German financial arrangements following the armistice. They involved such

35. Berle Diary, October 10, 1940, in Container 212, Berle Papers.

matters as the removal of the economic and financial barriers between occupied and unoccupied France, and Germany's demand for control over French foreign trade. The Germans exhibited an early interest in the gold reserves of France. Fortunately, most of them had been taken to the safe shores of the United States and Canada. Sizable French, Belgian, and Polish gold holdings had also been removed to Dakar. Unofficially, the Nazis inquired about the possibility of unfreezing French dollar balances in the United States in order to use them for substantial purchases of American cotton and petroleum. Naturally Washington reacted negatively to such maneuvers.[36]

What irked the United States as much as specific grievances were the contradictions between French professions of friendship for America and the apparently growing Franco-German cooperation, which often went beyond the stipulations of the armistice. Worse yet, Vichy had neither informed nor consulted Washington prior to its Montoire discussions. Cordell Hull expressed his annoyance to the Vichy ambassador, Gaston Henry-Haye, about the lack of candor and normal contacts with high-ranking French officials. Only Tokyo, Berlin, Rome, and Vichy, he complained, withheld from him legitimate information. If Vichy wished to retain America's sympathy, it must be disposed to confer back and forth in a thoroughly accurate and candid manner.[37]

To head off an undesirable break, FDR chose Admiral William D. Leahy as his ambassador to France. Close contacts between Pétain and Leahy, he hoped, might restrain Vichy from moving too close to Hitler. They would at least make certain that vital information Laval was suspected of withholding from the marshal would be promptly brought to his attention. The friendly personal relationship between Pétain and Leahy would provide the marshal with the unadulterated viewpoints of the Roosevelt administration with respect to the French fleet and bases. It was also deemed useful to emphasize the inevitability of the dismemberment of the French empire in case of a German victory. Perhaps most important, through

36. American embassy, Vichy, to Treasury Department, July 30, November 17, 1940, in Folder 213, Morgenthau Papers.

37. "Memorandum of conversation—Hull–Henry-Haye," November 4, 1940, in Box 58, Folder 208, Vichy, France, Hull Papers. See also Henri Philippe Pétain to Franklin D. Roosevelt, November 2, 1940, in Container 41, PSF.

this personal contact France could be reminded time and again that the Anglo-Americans were absolutely determined to carry on the war to the bitter end.

Pétain invited Leahy to make frequent visits. He seemed to be pleased "to have somebody to whom he can tell his manifold troubles." Surrounded by disloyal ministers, the aged marshal felt free to speak his mind to Roosevelt's representative. In Leahy's estimate, Pétain would have preferred to resign than move his government to North Africa or "direct General Weygand to join the cause with the Democracies." Very alertly, however, the marshal anticipated a clash in the near future between Germany and Russia. And perhaps remembering the national reaction Napoleon's conquests had stirred in Europe, Pétain perceptively believed that "Germany in the future faces trouble in all the occupied countries because of its wide dispersion of force."

While patiently watching developments, he depended heavily on America's good offices to help ease British blockade restrictions on essential foodstuffs and on the American Red Cross's expansion of its relief work. But fearing that such shipments would ultimately reach the Germans, the British were not at all disposed to make exceptions.[38] Darlan's extensive collaboration with Germany made America's task as middleman between France and Great Britain ever more difficult. What were the British to think, for instance, when over Weygand's protest Darlan supplied General Erwin Rommel's Cairo-bound forces with hundreds of trucks, and the Italian navy with petroleum? What were they to think of Darlan's cooperation with the Nazis in Syria and his agreeing to cooperate if necessary in Tunisia?[39]

During the six months after the armistice, Laval was in the driver's seat of the French government. He had no difficulty rationalizing his acceptance of the new order as being in the best interest of France. Still, he did not go so far as to conclude a military alliance with Germany. Upon his dismissal, Marshal Pétain entrusted Admiral Darlan with the practical direction of the French ship of state. When on February 9, 1941, Etienne Flandin, a moderate collabora-

38. William D. Leahy to Franklin D. Roosevelt, 1941, in Container 41, "France 1941," PSF.

39. Franklin D. Roosevelt to Winston Churchill, May 3, 1941, in Container 1, FDR-Churchill Correspondence, January–June 1941, Vol. 2, Map Room Collection, FDRL.

tionist, resigned as foreign minister, Darlan became, in addition to being the head of the navy, vice premier and foreign minister. Designated as successor to Pétain in case of the marshal's incapacity to carry out his official duties, he assumed a commanding position in 1941. It must be noted that Vichy's greatest concessions to Hitler were made during Darlan's stewardship. He revealed himself as a most calculating political poker player. Noble principles meant even less to him than to the machiavellian Laval. He considered minor alleviations of the oppressive conditions Germany had imposed upon France as fairly insignificant. On the other hand, full restoration of France as a vital power in Hitler's Europe, "guaranteed" by a definite peace treaty, would have been worth full collaboration to him.

At the same time, he watched the military tides and changing international constellations. Reputedly very anti-British, he was too much a pragmatist to let his private opinion interfere with hard realities. Believing in 1940 that Britain would be defeated, he put no stock in its future and felt free to abuse it. When it tenaciously resisted Hitler and when Russia and the United States began in the second half of 1941 to cast doubt on Hitler's victory, Darlan did not hesitate to reevaluate his estimates. In August of that year he made the characteristic statement to Admiral Leahy: "When you have three thousand tanks, six thousand planes, and five hundred thousand men to bring to Marseilles, let me know. Then we shall welcome you." He intended to be on the winning side.

His military collaboration with Germany constituted a new development that was disturbing to Pétain and unacceptable to the United States. Darlan's cryptic statement in July, 1941, that "so long as political relations . . . are based on the Armistice, permission will not be given to anybody to occupy or use the African base," deceptively concealed the fact that he was in the process of trying to replace the armistice with the Paris Protocols, a far-reaching Franco-German understanding. Without binding counterconcessions, they facilitated German and Italian penetrations into the Near East and West Africa. Most disturbing was the agreement "in principle" to open up Dakar to German warships and airplanes. Long concerned with Dakar's strategic proximity to South America, President Roosevelt reacted to these potentially dangerous developments with his declaration of a state of unlimited national emergency. Darlan's policies helped to move the United States closer to war.[40]

The periodic assurances FDR gave Marshal Pétain with respect to the restoration of France and its empire were largely of a tactical nature. He wanted to stiffen Pétain's determination to resist German pressures. This attempt was made more meaningful with the destroyer-base deal with Britain in September, 1940, and the Lend-Lease Act of March, 1941. Making America "the arsenal of democracy" gave convincing evidence prior to the entry of the United States into the war that FDR meant to have the last word in the showdown with Hitler.

Given Germany's expansionist tendencies and Nazi commercial strongholds in South America, American strategists had to assume that the Fuehrer would sooner or later direct his attention to the Western Hemisphere. He looked upon the Canaries, the Portuguese Azores, and Dakar as desirable air bases from which to reach South America, the Panama Canal, and eventually the United States. In recognition of this potential danger, Congress adopted a resolution on June 18, 1940, shortly thereafter embodied in the Act of Havana, reiterating the principles laid down in the Monroe Doctrine. It warned that the United States would not recognize the transfer of existing colonies in the Western Hemisphere of any European power to another non-American power. Under certain circumstances, moreover, the United States was prepared to constitute a temporary inter-American trusteeship for the French possessions in the region.[41]

Notified to that effect, Berlin and Vichy feigned they could not understand the necessity of such a communication. And de Gaulle used the occasion to assert his authority in defense of the sovereignty of France's ancient colonies. In a cooperative spirit he advised the American government that France would resent the unilateral occupation of its colonies even by a friendly power. Inasmuch as he considered the Vichy government neither constitutional nor free, he proposed that in an emergency situation the recently estab-

40. "Memorandum of Conversation—Hull–Henry-Haye," June 9, 1941, in Box 58, Folder 208, Vichy, France, Hull Papers; William D. Leahy to Cordell Hull, July 16, 1941, in FRUS, *Diplomatic Papers, 1941*, II, 394.

41. Norman Rich, *Hitler's War Aims* (2 vols.; New York, 1973, 1974), II, 416–19.

lished Council of Defense of the French Empire would administer the colonies. This council would be prepared to grant to the United States air and naval bases. To de Gaulle's regret, this back-door attempt at quasi recognition did not elicit a positive response. Secretary of War Stimson expressed the view of how best to protect Latin America: "The whole menace of Germany to South America via Dakar-Natal requires that the hold by American seapower upon the South Atlantic be so strong as to be unchallengeable." The increasing number of appearances of German submarines in the Caribbean led Secretary of State Hull to recommend strong measures against French bases that probably lent aid to such submarine activities.[42]

Germany did not pose the only danger to peace in the Western Hemisphere. After the encounter between the French and British naval forces at Oran, General George C. Marshall, chief of staff of the American armed forces, began to wonder about what might happen at Martinique, where three French and at least two British warships were present. To head off a clash between them, American diplomats tried to secure firm assurances from the British. Since the French authorities would not consider letting their warships, including an aircraft carrier with 106 American-made planes on board, join the British navy or be interned in a United States port, the solution finally agreed to was their immobilization. But the failure of Vichy to find a way to resell the planes to the American manufacturers annoyed Washington more than Vichy apparently realized. Incredible as it seemed, these planes, originally diverted to France from the American military establishment, were permitted to rot.[43]

At least drawn-out discussions with Admiral Georges Robert, the French commander at Martinique, ended with promises not to move the $245 million in French gold stored on the island. The admiral stubbornly enforced the neutrality of the French Caribbean empire until his "abdication" in July, 1943. He defied both German and Vi-

42. See Guerre 1939–45, Politique extérieure, Etats-Unis, No. 211, October 27, 1940, AMAE; and Charles de Gaulle to Franklin D. Roosevelt and Cordell Hull, October 28, 1940, in RG 59, 811.34511 B/3, NA.

43. "Memos of Conversations—Sumner Welles–René de Saint-Quentin," July 8, 20, 24, 30, 1940, in FRUS, *Diplomatic Papers, 1940*, II, 506–13. See also Charlotte Girard, "The Effects of Western Hemispheric Issues upon Franco-American Relations During the Second World War" (Ph.D. dissertation, Bryn Mawr College, 1967), 46–63, 245–88.

chy orders to destroy the ships and the gold, he resisted de Gaulle, and he remained on guard against any possible American annexation.

FDR'S REACTIONS TO DE GAULLE

If foreign policy were guided by logic, one would reasonably assume that General de Gaulle, who rallied French resistance to Nazi and Fascist aggression, would have been as welcomed by the United States as by Great Britain. In his appeal to the French people on June 18, 1940, he tried to strengthen his bold decision by telling them that France did not stand alone: "Like England, she can draw unreservedly on the immense industrial resources of the United States." Naturally he was disappointed when Britain's formal recognition of the Free French National Committee on August 17 was not also extended by the United States. Having chosen to work with Vichy, which controlled substantial assets of France, Washington could not simultaneously officially recognize de Gaulle's movement.

Almost from the beginning, FDR developed an antipathy for the resistance leader. Surprisingly few prominent Frenchmen answered de Gaulle's original call for duty. No massive support gave the self-appointed leader of France the momentum and stature he needed to overcome his position as a rather obscure figure. As time went on, not only American observers, including Ambassador Leahy and H. Freeman Matthews, first secretary of the American embassy at Paris, but also prominent Frenchmen, such as Alexis Léger and Camille Chautemps, came to distrust the general's ultimate objectives. FDR therefore chose to be cautious and to adopt certain principles in dealing with de Gaulle. Foremost among them was "the belief in the right of the French people to choose their own government after they were freed from Nazi domination." Second, the prosecution of the war had to take precedence over French politics. The president feared that de Gaulle as a symbol of French resistance might abuse this psychological advantage to lay the groundwork for a personal dictatorship at the end of the war. These principles and apprehensions motivated Roosevelt to search for more acceptable, less politically oriented leaders. Generals Maxime Weygand and Henri Giraud, both anti-Nazi soldiers inclined to concentrate on military aspects, looked like promising candidates. Needless to say, only wartime conditions and France's disarray could have possibly excused such interference with strictly French prerogatives.[44]

In the meantime, de Gaulle moved fast to make his position secure. Encouraged by his quick successes in the French Cameroons, most of French Equatorial Africa, and the New Hebrides, he embarked at the end of September on a campaign to bring Dakar into the fold of Free France. The failure of this enterprise temporarily diminished his reputation. But throughout his remarkable public service he usually managed to overcome setbacks.

De Gaulle had many outstanding attributes. Anyone familiar with his extraordinary feat of establishing in a short time an administrative and political network around the globe must acknowledge his superior executive ability. He knew what he wanted and tenaciously persevered until he obtained it. His dedication to the cause of France and his sense of mission knew no bounds. To him, whether victorious or terribly humiliated, France never ceased to exist. Its roots were so deeply embedded in the history of Europe that a temporary setback did not seal its fate forever. In his vision France was unthinkable without greatness. Ultimately he inspired a vast number of Frenchmen to devote their lives to achieving this patriotic objective.

The manner in which he pursued his goals antagonized even many who respected him. But according to his philosophy of life it was logical to test one's most powerful friends more harshly than the weaker ones. Too proud to receive alms from the Anglo-Americans, or Anglo-Saxons, as he preferred to call them, he often treated them in a haughty, intransigent, and contumacious manner. They in turn called him an obnoxious, self-styled dictator, a prima donna and upstart driven by a messiah complex. Whoever had to do business with him found him overbearing and difficult. In view of the embarrassing weaknesses under which he labored, he used his unyielding attitude as a weapon of strength. Amazingly, it produced results in his case.

HITLER'S HESITATIONS

Defeated France was not out of the international picture. It still had a significant role to play, both actively and passively. To be sure,

44. "President Roosevelt's Policy Towards de Gaulle," June 21, 1945, in Box 3, George M. Elsey Papers, Truman Library, Independence, Mo.

the divided authority between Vichy and Free France deprived it of the maneuverability a united France in full control of its colonial and naval trumps would have possessed. But even this division could in limited ways be exploited. As Darlan once remarked, if de Gaulle did not exist, he would have been invented to ease Vichy's lot. The clash between Vichy and de Gaulle served as a constant reminder to the Germans that they had more to gain from a cooperative France than from a fiercely antagonistic one. Their callous insensitivity, however, hardly recognized this distinction as a justification for lifting the hardships of the French people.

The scope of France's international role depended largely on Hitler's overall strategy. At different times the Fuehrer considered different alternatives. His failure upon the collapse of France to follow through with the contemplated all-out attack against England, and his failure to persuade France and Spain to become his allies in the destruction of the British Empire, affected not only the course of the war but the fate of France as well. Instead of realizing his dream of controlling the Mediterranean and North Africa, and thereby consolidating the hegemony he saw within his reach, he decided first to invade and annihilate the Soviet Union. Confident that he could defeat it in a few weeks, he chose temporarily to postpone the conquest of the Mediterranean region. His hatred of the communist system and his racial contempt for the Slavs propelled his crusade against Russia as much as did the attraction of rich spoils. He lived to regret his rejection of Admiral Raeder's suggested priority of peripheral conquests before attacking the Soviet Union.[45]

Although Hitler appeared to the outside world as a decisive leader who went resolutely after his objectives, his hesitations in the six months following his triumph in France turned out to be fatal in the long run. He fully agreed with Raeder that he must wage war against England before the United States could effectively intervene and that he must prevent an Anglo-American bridgehead in the Mediterranean. Such a program called for the prompt acquisition of Gibraltar and the Canary Islands and for German control of the bases in French West Africa and the port of Dakar. Toward these ends Hitler sought alliances with Spain and France. Both General Franco and Marshal Pétain were "in principle" not opposed. But following Hitler's meetings on October 23 with Franco at Hendaye and the next day

45. Halder, *Kriegstagebuch*, III, 226–29, 337.

with Pétain at Montoire, it became obvious that both had asked for prices the Fuehrer judged excessive. When Franco's price included a good deal of French territory, Hitler hesitated to make up his mind whether France or Spain was more essential to him.[46]

There were of course other reasons for Germany's failure to enlist these two countries as full partners in the war. They feared for their own independence in a Europe dominated by the Reich. They also noted that, for whatever reasons, Hitler had not attacked Britain immediately after the French armistice and that Britain had withstood the brutal bombardment to which it was subjected far longer than anticipated. And as long as Britain was not defeated, Spain preferred neutrality.

To help keep Spain out of the war, London and Washington made joint efforts, despite vociferous antifascist objections, to prop up the Spanish economy. These critics evidently did not understand that by permitting Hitler's Mediterranean strategy to succeed, his ultimate victory and the destruction of European democracy would have been practically assured. Despite some serious violations, French and Spanish neutrality was crucially important to the Allies. It also paid off for the Latins. Franco and his people welcomed American edibles, wheat, cotton, oil, and other goods, which alleviated their economic difficulties. One of the most farsighted Allied policies during the war was the Anglo-American preemptive purchasing program of strategic minerals from Spain such as wolfram, strontium, and fluorspar. With the approval of Franco's bureaucracy these minerals, previously bought by Germany, were permitted to be purchased by the Allies. The longer the war lasted, the more doubtful became Hitler's victory. Although not sure whether the victorious Allies would not in the end topple his regime, Franco specualted that his neutrality might save him.[47]

FRANCE, JAPAN, AND THE UNITED STATES

From the beginning of the war in Europe, Japan expediently tried to advance its influence in the Pacific area. The greater the calamities of France and Great Britain on the Continent, the more Japan pressed its designs in Asia. In part it did so also out of fear that a

46. U.S. Navy Department, *Führer Conferences*, I, 69–73, II, 17–24; Rich, *Hitler's War Aims*, I, 166–75.

47. "Our Spanish Policy," May 26, 1943, in Box 86, Hull Papers.

victorious Germany might try to include East India and Indochina in its world empire. French Indochina became one of Japan's major targets. Never having possessed sufficient strength to defend this colony against serious aggressors, France depended on the United States and Britain to assist it in times of crisis. Unfortunately these powers were at this time tied down in Europe. The complexity of the developing crisis therefore posed the question whether it would not be more desirable to appease Japan than to rely on the Soviet Union to help check its designs. As far as conservative groups in France were concerned, the Nazi-Soviet Pact removed any doubts about Soviet unreliability. Soon, however, these circles also learned that the extent of Japanese ambitions went far beyond their expectations. Japan's "Greater East Asian Co-Prosperity Sphere" was intended to establish a vast new empire under its control.

The Japanese government found it almost hopeless to restrain its military leaders, who, to stop such essential supplies as trucks and gasoline from reaching Chiang Kai-shek, bombarded the French railroad from Indochina to Yunan. They thus threatened to cut off all trade with China. The French protested against this violation of international law. Too weak in the summer of 1940 to react resolutely, they approached the United States to render "tangible assistance." Although anxious to maintain the status quo in the Pacific, the Roosevelt administration declined under existing circumstances "to assume any additional responsibilities in the Far East." It was not militarily prepared to force a showdown with Japan, a party to the Axis pact of September, 1940.[48]

Nevertheless, Secretary Hull took strong exception to Vichy's "political agreement" of August 31, under which the French government recognized the "preponderance of Japanese interest" in Indochina and assented to supplementary economic and military accords yet to be formulated that would grant Japan a "privileged position" in Indochina. As Leahy described the situation, "Here endeth the French colonies in Asia." From Darlan's point of view, it was better to save something in Indochina than to lose the colony in a hopeless fight. The fact that Vichy merely informed Washington about this *fait accompli* and did not consult it in advance typified

48. "Memorandum of Conversation—Hull–Henry-Haye," September 11, 1940, in FRUS, *Diplomatic Papers, 1940*, IV, 106–107; "Aide-Mémoire" from French embassy in United States, September 20, 1939, in Box 58, Folder 207, Hull Papers.

the lack of frankness that it had chosen to adopt in its relations with the United States.[49]

By demonstrating its inability to defend its possessions in the Far East, France failed at a crucial moment in history to maintain its share of regional stability. FDR looked upon this breakdown as the springboard for "the Japanese attack on the Philippines, Malaya, and the Dutch East Indies." This view substantially strengthened his vision of independence for French Indochina.[50] To Francophile Walter Lippmann this situation would not have developed "had we in June and July of 1940 allowed ourselves to send a few warships to Indo-China and a few to Casablanca, along with pledges of help." Such actions, he admitted, would have involved risks, but they would not have been comparable to the risks the United States faced later. "Our isolationist policy in 1940 compelled us to let the French empire go by default," he wrote in 1942.[51]

The State Department interpreted the Franco-Japanese protocol of July 29, 1941, which provided "common defense" of French Indochina, as an agreement virtually turning over to Japan bases for military operations vitally affecting American security. It certainly emboldened the Japanese military. Reacting to America's tightening of the economic noose and to the dead-end status of Japanese-American diplomatic negotiations, Japan decided to strike at Pearl Harbor on December 7. Neither Hitler nor Mussolini welcomed this premature war between continents. As late as June 22, General Franz Halder, chief of the German General Staff, had alluded to the desirability of keeping both Japan and America out of the war. Count Ciano also feared their entry would prolong the war, strain Axis resources to the limit, and complicate the final peace.

Hitler was not obligated to declare war against the United States. He did so very reluctantly, because his original plan envisioned the showdown with the United States at a much later date. Still, he now expediently did what he could to help Japan pin the United States down in the Pacific and thus blunt its intervention in Europe. Strangely, even when his war machine had bogged down in Russia, Hitler opposed his advisers' suggestion to have Japan open up a

49. William D. Leahy to Cordell Hull, August 1, 1941, in Container 4, "Safe File, France," PSF.

50. Hull, *Memoirs*, II, 1595.

51. Walter Lippmann, "We Pay for Our Mistake," New York *Herald Tribune*, July 29, 1942.

second front against the Soviet Union. He still had not given up his goal of being the sole master of the East European land mass.[52]

In an enlightening comment, Assistant Secretary of State Berle credited Cordell Hull's wisely drawn-out deliberations with Japan for timing the outbreak of the war at the strategically most opportune moment. Until the summer of 1941 it would have been rash to force a showdown with Japan. The collapse of France, the possible defeat of Britain, the unavailability of British naval assistance, and the unknown factor of Russia's ability to repulse Hitler's attack, in addition to the time the United States needed to mobilize its overwhelming striking capacity, called for statesmanlike restraint. Not until the autumn of 1941, when Britain had reasonably safeguarded the Suez Canal and its Near Eastern lifeline, when Germany's military power was immobilized and crippled on the Russian front, and when, with America's substantial help, the Atlantic had become secure, could the United States confidently take on Japan. As Berle has pointed out, history cannot be just "what happened," because alternative choices could have drastically changed what happened. For instance, had the United States pressed Japan into war in the early spring of 1941, Hitler, instead of attacking Russia in June, would probably have concentrated his entire might in the Atlantic, "at a time when both we and the British were under maximum strain in the Far East, when the Near East defenses were still incomplete, and when German striking power was at its level maximum." Hull's diplomatic delays contributed to the separation of Germany's military operations from those of the Japanese. The combination of these factors profoundly affected the outcome of the war and the future of France.[53]

In the context of overall war strategy, one of the truly important decisions was FDR's and Churchill's early understanding of the virtual necessity to concentrate on the war in Europe before going all-out against Japan. Underlying this decision was the realization that Hitler represented the greater danger. Whereas the defeat of Japan would still have required a herculean effort to destroy the Nazis, the

52. Halder, *Kriegstagebuch*, III, 353; Hildebrand, *The Foreign Policy of the Third Reich*, 102–17.

53. Adolf A. Berle to Cordell C. Hull, December 15, 1941, in Berle Diary, Container 213, Berle Papers; Louis Morton, "Germany First: The Basic Concept of Allied Strategy in World War II," in Kent R. Greenfield (ed.), *Command Decisions* (Washington, D.C., 1960), 11–47.

defeat of Germany, once accomplished with the massive help of the Soviet Union, held out the hope of ending the war victoriously shortly thereafter. Japan was clearly the lesser threat.

The resistance and resilience of the Soviet Union's armed forces astonished Hitler and the rest of the world. The widely held assumption in mid-1941 that they would be crushed within six to eight weeks turned out to be a fatal miscalculation. Every month Soviet forces continued to hold out compelled the modification of political assessments. By the time the United States actively joined the conflict, the combination of Great Britain, the Soviet Union, and the United States threatened to overwhelm the Fuehrer. He could not match their combined resources in a drawn-out war. He had recklessly gambled on a daring blitzkrieg; but he was confronted with a devastating counterattack that might last for several years.

If America's relations with Vichy were clouded by doubts and uncertainties, those with de Gaulle suffered from mistrust, misunderstandings, and mutual irritation. Seen in the perspective of history, the St. Pierre–Miquelon episode soon after Pearl Harbor was blown up out of all proportion to its significance. FDR looked upon it as a "teapot tempest" even at the time. But Hull was extremely upset by what he considered a breach of faith committed by the so-called Free French, who took control of the islands in violation of solemn pledges and international law. The international repercussions gave him serious concern. For one thing, the South American republics might doubt the sincerity of the United States in preventing the forcible transfer of territories in the Western Hemisphere. Also, Darlan mentioned that Germany had already used de Gaulle's seizure of St. Pierre and Miquelon "as an argument for the entry of Axis troops into Africa in order to be protected against a similar invasion." And last but not least, the United States had promised to respect Vichy's rights in the Caribbean in return for its assurance not to surrender its fleet or its North African ports to the Germans. Washington's temporary embarrassment could not be hidden. But Hull's lasting resentment seemed somewhat out of place.[54]

The protection of the radio station on St. Pierre, which in unfriendly hands could have caused havoc by transmitting shipping information, could be achieved through diplomatic channels. By not

54. FRUS, *The Conferences at Washington, 1941–42 and Casablanca, 1943* (Washington, D.C., 1968), 106, 382–88; Dorothy Shipley White, *Seeds of Discord: De Gaulle, Free France and the Allies* (Syracuse, 1964), 12–13, 209–17, 322–23.

standing by his given word, de Gaulle lost credibility. The nasty St. Pierre incident haunted him for a long time.

VICHY'S PRIDE AND THE NORTH AFRICAN CAMPAIGN

It calls for keen discrimination to judge the often contradictory statements and actions of American and Vichy officials during World War II. Regardless of the resulting confusion that contemporaries were asked to cope with and that put Vichy-Washington relations on practically a day-to-day basis, certain fundamental considerations exercised a steadying influence. Despite the sometimes patronizing attitude of the United States vis-à-vis Vichy France, which was under the heel of a ruthless conqueror and anxious about the fate of 1.5 million of its young men in German prison camps, the United States continued to think of France as a handicapped ally. And despite many American doubts, France's genuine sympathies tilted toward the Allies.

Some political dreamers speculated that if Hitler could not inflict a decisive defeat upon Russia in the summer offensive of 1942, France and America would be useful intermediaries in bringing about a negotiated peace. As unrealistic, moreover, as was Laval's eagerness to serve as a mediator between the United States and Germany, it rested on his fear of a Bolshevik Europe. To prevent such a disaster, he would rather have seen Germany win the war. To his mind, this preference made him neither pro-Nazi nor a fascist; it was a choice of the lesser evil. His goal and hope centered around the welfare of France. Like General de Gaulle, he deeply believed in France as one of the indestructible and essential pillars of European civilization. He desperately longed for America's understanding of his vision of how to achieve lasting peace. Instead, Americans looked upon his reinstatement as chief of government in mid-April, 1942, as an ominous turn of events. FDR recalled Admiral Leahy for consultation and left the embassy in the hands of a chargé d'affaires until the break of diplomatic relations in November. To Pétain, who had done a magnificent job of stalling for two years, German pressures left him no choice but to reappoint Laval with great reluctance. Perceptively, several contemporary observers, including the British foreign secretary, interpreted Laval's reinstatement as a sign of German weakness. In the words of the widely respected journalist Anne O'Hare McCormick, "Laval is the symbol of Hitler's defeat, the sign not of cooperation, but of French refusal to cooperate."[55]

With Hitler in a quagmire in Russia, with Anglo-American military strength mounting steadily, and with the Free French expanding their hold, Vichy was compelled to juggle its neutrality according to the drifting prospects of the moment. Nevertheless, to save face it acted as if its sovereignty were beyond question. America's approval of Britain's temporary occupation of Madagascar and Washington's stern warning that any warlike act of retaliation would "of necessity have to be regarded by the Government of the United States as an attack upon the United Nations as a whole," elicited Laval's almost pathetic protest that his government rejected as inadmissible Washington's pretension "to forbid France to defend herself when her territory is attacked."[56]

The rapid advance of General Rommel's army in the summer of 1942 drew attention to the fate of the French naval squadron at Alexandria. Vichy instructed Admiral René Emile Godfroy, in case Britain evacuated Alexandria, to reach a French port if possible. Should this prove impossible, he was to remain at Alexandria under the French flag. He was furthermore instructed neither to follow the British in their retreat, should it take place, nor to permit the ships to fall into foreign hands. The German and Italian governments found these instructions to be in conformity with the armistice convention, and they gave assurances to respect its provisions. When Laval officially apprised President Roosevelt of these arrangements, the president promptly responded that in view of Germany's untrustworthy record he did not discount the likelihood that the Germans might take control of the ships. Since the British would under no circumstances permit the ships to return to French ports, FDR offered asylum for them in neutral ports in the Western Hemisphere. But Laval formally rejected this proposed solution "as being contrary to the honor and interests of France." Akin to General de Gaulle's posture, he labeled it "a slur on the dignity of France." As the offended party, he finally insisted, "France has a right to be respected." Believing in the fiction that Vichy could speak with the

55. New York *Times*, April 15, 1942.

56. Cordell Hull to S. Pickney Tuck, May 4, 1942, in FRUS, *Diplomatic Papers, 1942*, II, 698–99.

undiminished voice of sovereign France, Laval simply closed his eyes to the tragic realities.[57]

One of the few Frenchmen on whom FDR counted for substantial cooperation was General Weygand, delegate-general in French Africa. His anti-German attitude and his realization of America's indispensability to France's recovery singled him out as the most reliable French leader of stature. He appreciated the Franco-American economic agreement providing for the importation of such crucially needed essentials as food and gasoline into North Africa. It considerably strengthened the general's political relations with the Arabs and undercut those of the local Nazi sympathizers. Interestingly, the British did not put much faith in Weygand, because he seemed to lack the boldness required for independent leadership. He was more a staff officer than a fighting man. They also feared that a strengthened French force in North Africa might attack rather than help them.

Weygand strongly opposed the Paris Protocols and kept insisting that in all its important decisions France must not ignore the attitude of the United States. In overall strategic terms, he understood that opening French Africa to Germany would be the ultimate disaster for France and Europe. On the other hand, without control of the vitally important maritime highway, the Mediterranean, Hitler would find it impossible to organize a Germanized Europe.[58]

His conviction of the wisdom of playing the American card conflicted with that of Franco-German collaborators. Darlan and several ministers resolved this collision course by intriguing against Weygand. On November 18, 1941, he was relieved of his post by the devious device of abolishing the post of delegate-general in Africa. That this step was taken at a time when doubts about Germany's triumph over Russia were mounting accentuated Roosevelt's sharp reaction to Vichy's latest unfriendly act. Pétain, greatly distressed, yielded to the invaders, who had threatened him with the occupa-

57. S. Pickney Tuck to Cordell Hull, July 2, 1942, "France, Disposition of French Ships," in Container 35, Special Files, Map Room, FDRL; Franklin D. Roosevelt to Winston Churchill, telegram of July 8, 1942, Churchill to Roosevelt, July 9, 1942, both in Container 311, Hopkins Papers.

58. Weygand's memorandum, transmitted November 18, 1941, in FRUS, *Diplomatic Papers, 1941*, II, 161–63. See also William D. Leahy to Franklin D. Roosevelt, July 28, 1941, in Leahy Diary, William D. Leahy Papers, Library of Congress, Washington, D.C.

tion of the rest of France unless Weygand was completely removed. What was the United States to do? If it slammed the door in the face of France, Admiral Raymond A. Fenard, who was friendly toward the United States, believed, "France will surely and inevitably be thrown into the German camp." Reluctantly the United States kept in touch with Vichy and, after a brief interruption, resumed its shipments to North Africa.[59]

Another consideration weighed heavily in this decision. In December, 1940, FDR had sent Robert D. Murphy, a State Department official with expertise in French affairs, to French Africa to act as his personal representative to General Weygand. In connection with the Franco-American economic agreement Murphy worked out, America was permitted to increase the number of its vice-consuls in French Africa, ostensibly to supervise the correct implementation of the economic accord. But in practical terms they were intelligence agents who gathered invaluable information and made personal contacts that late in 1942 facilitated America's temporary occupation of the region.[60]

Rumors of German and American designs on Africa intensified their mutual distrust in 1941. According to Darlan, the Germans had no immediate interest in that area, though "it would have been simple enough for [them] to take a force to Morocco." His son, who had recently returned from Spain, had counted 120 batteries of artillery directed against Gibraltar. The Germans feared a move by the Allies. They particularly dreaded an American occupation of African bases, because it would affect the outcome of the battle of the Atlantic and possibly lead to the opening up of a "battle front running from the sands of the Sahara through Russia to the White Sea." For the moment, however, the Germans were preoccupied with Russia. They had no choice but to seek an open break between France and the United States so that France would not, directly or indirectly, assist in an American invasion.

Pétain and Darlan repeatedly warned in the most categorical manner that they would defend French North Africa against any attack. They took it for granted that outsiders would understand if in relatively small ways they yielded to German pressures. Admiral Leahy certainly was not overly alarmed about Vichy's limited assis-

59. Milton Viorst, *Hostile Allies: FDR and de Gaulle* (New York, 1965), 60–65.

60. Michael Howard, *Grand Stategy: History of the Second World War* (6 vols.; London, 1964–72), IV, 146–47.

tance to Germany. But he thought that the publicized threat of strong American countermeasures in case of unacceptable German demands might provide the Vichy government with an effective tool of resistance.[61]

In response to threats of German penetration of French North Africa in the winter of 1940–1941, Anglo-American understandings helped lift the British blockade sufficiently to stiffen General Weygand's determination to react firmly. Shipments of badly needed supplies to Morocco and trade with Spain were designed to block German advances. For good measure Marshal Pétain was again confronted with a possible break with the United States unless he threw his full authority behind Weygand's resistance. At the same time the United States pleaded for Vichy's abstention from attacks against the Free French forces in Africa. Disagreements between the two groups were bad enough; to allow them to escalate to civil war would be intolerable.

Typical of the period of deliberate Franco-German collaboration, the Vichy government did not object, much less offer resistance, to Germany's movement toward Iraq, Egypt, and the Suez Canal, which used Syria as a convenient base. Disquieting evidence indicated the connivance of French authorities in Syria in this operation. The successful British counterthrust against German moves in the Near East found Vichy up in arms. It suspected Britain of wanting to annex Syria permanently. Ironically, Darlan boasted that he had refused Germany's offer of military aid for the defense of Syria against the British. Evidently he at least made a distinction between Germany's and Britain's long-range use of Syria as a springboard for, respectively, the destruction or the defense of the British position in the Middle East.

When Roosevelt and Churchill met at the Washington Conference of 1941–1942, Darlan inquired whether he would be accepted into the conference. As the minutes of their meeting on January 12 record, FDR had, probably unwisely, responded: "Not under present circumstances. . . . If he brought the French fleet over to the Allies, the situation would change."[62]

The two Allied statesmen decided that it was of vital importance

61. Henri Philippe Pétain to Franklin D. Roosevelt, September 17, 1941, Container 41, "France 1941," PSF; William D. Leahy to Cordell Hull, September 25, 1941, in FRUS, *Diplomatic Papers, 1941*, II, 436–39.

62. FRUS, *Conferences at Washington and Casablanca*, 185–86; William D. Leahy to

to the successful prosecution of the war to bring the North African shore, including the Atlantic ports of Morocco and Dakar and other French West African ports, under their control. This strategy in no way implied the permanent conquest of the French possessions. If Vichy cooperated by not offering resistance to the Allied forces, perhaps a reconciliation between Vichy and de Gaulle might have a chance. But if in this acid test Vichy actively favored Germany, the Allies' task would be much harder. Correspondingly, so would be the fate of France. Pétain was bluntly told that he must keep French Africa out of German hands and that at the slightest sign of German aggression the United States would take preemptive measures. An inquiry to General Weygand whether he would be willing to assume leadership in such an action produced a polite, but totally negative, response. In fact, he felt "honor-bound" to inform the marshal of this secret sounding.

Vichy's admission that food supplies and trucks had been shipped from France to Tunis in French vessels for delivery to German forces in Libya heightened American apprehensions. To deny Germany control of the area and to use it as a strategic base for future Allied operations, President Roosevelt on July 25, 1942, approved the invasion of North Africa. This projected attack against a technically neutral country, unprecedented in American history, was undertaken in the hope that Vichy would understandingly condone it and offer only nominal resistance or none at all. To encourage such a course, the Americans, who enjoyed considerable prestige in the region, were to spearhead the assault, to the exclusion of British and Free French forces, who were the target of much local bitterness. Their presence, it seemed likely, would incite spontaneous opposition. Regular French army officers, loyal to Pétain, regarded de Gaulle as a disloyal upstart. Indeed, London and Washington thought it most prudent not even to inform General de Gaulle about Operation Torch.[63]

Murphy's discreet preparations did not long remain a secret. The Germans wanted him and American consular officers in North Africa withdrawn. But he had already gathered sufficient information about the likely attitudes of French officers to enable America's mil-

---

Cordell Hull, December 11, 13, 14, 1941, in FRUS, *Diplomatic Papers, 1941*, II, 198–203.

63. "Relations with France," February 10, 1942, in Container 311, Hopkins Papers.

itary leaders to take the considerable chance of testing them. He considered General Giraud as the best-qualified leader to play a key role. General Charles E. Mast, commander of the French Algiers Division and representative of General Giraud in French Northwest Africa, had assured Murphy of the army's loyalty to Giraud. Prior to the invasion, both General Alphonse Juin, commander of the French forces in Africa, and General Mast were especially anxious to know whether American forces would land in Africa on a scale capable of repulsing any Axis attack. Without such a commitment the risks for France and for themselves would have been unacceptable.[64]

General Mast distinguished himself as the most cooperative French officer. He gave General Mark Clark exact details regarding the location of troops, batteries, and installations, and he specified the places at which American forces would not encounter resistance. As usual in such a situation, the dividing line between patriots and traitors was a thin one, and those in either camp might be inspired by equally noble motives. Murphy had prudently cautioned General Eisenhower that the Allies would run into stiff resistance in French Morocco, where General Auguste Paul Noguès held the post of foreign minister to the sultan, and they did.

While the question of who was to command in the North African campaign was likely to cause more than arguments, the campaign's objective to restore France to its former position promised to help overcome this stumbling block. It was also assumed that quick military success in North Africa would silence in short order the expected resistance of the French navy. From Eisenhower's point of view, the less the French resisted, the more quickly he could move toward Tunisia and attack Rommel from the rear.[65]

Although upon Laval's return to power in the spring of 1942 Darlan's civil power was curtailed, at Marshal Pétain's insistence the admiral retained absolute authority over the navy, army, and air

64. "Memorandum of Talk with Robert D. Murphy," September 2, 1942, Stimson Diary, in Stimson Papers; Robert D. Murphy to Cordell Hull, September 26, 1942, "American Policy Regarding French North Africa," in Box 65, France—General 1937–43, Hull Papers; Tyler Thompson to Cordell Hull, August 1, 1942, in Confidential File, RG 59, 711.51/261, NA.

65. Dwight D. Eisenhower to George C. Marshall, October 29, 1942, in George C. Marshall Papers, General George C. Marshall Research Library, Lexington, Va. See also Dwight D. Eisenhower, *Crusade in Europe* (New York, 1948), 71–108.

force. Soon after America's entry into the war, Darlan authorized his son Alain and his friend Admiral Fenard to keep channels open to Robert Murphy, observing strictest secrecy, of course. During a dinner with Murphy on April 11, these two Frenchmen alerted the American diplomat to Darlan's desire for secret conversations with the Allies.[66] French secret agents found Murphy's absence from North Africa between August and October frustrating. In a mysterious message on October 17, Darlan indicated his willingness to join the Allies in heading off the imminent Axis invasion of North Africa, provided he would be the commander in chief of the French armed forces in North Africa and could count on massive economic aid.[67] General Giraud claimed that he, too, could rally French troops in Africa to the Allies if he were entrusted with supreme command of the rumored American expedition. Since key Americans and Frenchmen trusted Giraud more than Darlan, arrangements were made for Giraud to go by submarine from Marseilles to Gibraltar to work out details with General Mark Clark. Initially, Giraud entertained grandiose plans of using his position as supreme commander to invade southern France. In the end, he yielded to the necessities of first securing the North African base and of Eisenhower's directing the campaign.

Coincidental with the landing of American forces, President Roosevelt sent reassuring messages to Marshal Pétain, General Franco, the president of Portugal, and the sultan of Morocco. He pledged that the landing in North Africa was in no way directed against their territory or overseas possessions and that he sought no French territory. But Pétain reacted to the news of American landings "with stupor and grief." He felt that the honor of France called for resistance to the "cruel initiative" of the United States. The old marshal realized that the loss of French Africa would deprive Vichy of whatever little power it had left. There is also some ground for believing that publicly he had to protest but that privately he found hope in America's powerful intervention. How else could the report of the American chargé, who saw Pétain on November 8, be interpreted? "As I rose to take my leave," Counselor S. Pickney Tuck recorded, "he took my hands in his hands looking at me steadfastly and smil-

66. Arthur Layton Funk, *The Politics of TORCH: The Allied Landings and the Algiers Putsch, 1942* (Lawrence, Kan., 1974), 36–37.

67. Eden, *Memoirs*, 399.

ing. He accompained me to the antichamber and turned briskly back to his office humming a little tune."[68]

Laval promptly announced the severance of diplomatic relations with the United States. For several months prior to this break, contact between the two governments had been hardly more than fictional. In a press release FDR exploited this latest development in a genial manner. No puppet of Hitler, he retorted, "can sever relations between the American people and the people of France. We have not broken with the French. We never will."[69] By avoiding reference in this statement to the government of France, he acted as if it did not exist. Even in case Vichy declared war against the United States and Canada, both governments intended to ignore such a declaration. Inasmuch as in their judgment Vichy had ceased to be a legal entity, no French government existed to declare war. For Mackenzie King from Canada this scheme looked to be the most promising way to get around complications with his French population.[70]

On the afternoon of November 8, the German minister in Vichy informed Laval that Hitler did not regard its severance of diplomatic relations with the Anglo-American aggressors as going far enough. The latest developments required a declaration of war against them. Mussolini fully supported this demand. Should France adopt such a policy, Laval was told, "Germany is prepared to march side by side with France through thick and thin." Summoned to see Hitler at Munich the following day, Laval was advised by Otto Abetz, the high commissioner of occupied France, who accompanied him, to expect the Fuehrer's displeasure in case he equivocated. Having discussed the situation with Pétain, Laval indeed exposed himself to Hitler's anger and threats by evading a clear-cut response. The Fuehrer's patience came to an end when the French premier declined to make binding agreements with respect to Axis access to Tunis and Bizerte. In the end Vichy appeased him by authorizing the use of Tunisian airports.

Pétain, essentially neutralist at this stage, won out with his de-

68. S. Pickney Tuck to Cordell Hull, November 8, 1942, in FRUS, *Diplomatic Papers, 1942*, II, 432; Goodrich and Carroll (eds.), *Documents on American Foreign Relations*, V, 545–51.

69. Statement by the president, November 9, 1942, in Container 203, "France, 1940–45," POF.

70. Stimson, Diary, November 10, 1942, in Stimson Papers.

termination not to go to war against the United States, France's ultimate liberator, whatever the cost to the French people in the near term. By not opening up French Africa to the Americans and not fully cooperating with Hitler, the Vichy regime reaped a harvest of bitterness. It should be noted, however, that on balance Vichy's negative attitude toward both belligerents hurt Germany more than the United States. Its basically similar treatment of both did not lead to equal results.[71]

The excellent detailed accounts of the initial military operations have highlighted the volatility of French conduct.[72] General Giraud not only appeared a day late in Algeria and turned out to lack initiative, but much worse, many French officers in Africa looked upon him as unworthy of their confidence. As anti-Nazi as he was, he had, on his personal honor, pledged his fealty to Marshal Pétain, a fact unknown to Murphy and other high American officials. By far the majority of French colonial forces continued to be loyal to the marshal, their supreme commander. Giraud's orders not to resist the invaders meant little to them. In his defense of Algiers, General Juin illustrated his pro-American leanings by merely trying to maintain "elastic contact without aggressivity." Some of the stiffest fighting took place in Casablanca. It subsided only when General Noguès, to whom General Eisenhower referred as a "sail-trimmer," realized that his best interest paralleled those of the Allies. Assuming that Darlan was a prisoner of war, Pétain had appointed Noguès as his representative in North Africa. Before long, however, Noguès relinquished this post to Darlan, whom he willingly accepted as his superior. He knew that the Americans would not recognize his authority, and he loathed the idea of the dissident General Giraud being in a supreme command position.

The presence of Admiral Darlan in French Africa at this chaotic time proved militarily decisive, once the political uncertainty had been removed. This process was for a while complicated by the unwillingness of differing high-ranking French officers to talk or shake hands with one another. The mutual distrust between Darlan and Giraud constituted a major hurdle. Overcoming the many petty intrigues of conceited French officers strained Eisenhower's patience. In his first conference with Ike, Giraud even made a point of his rank.

71. Laval, *Diary*, 130–35.

72. Foremost among them are Funk, *The Politics of TORCH*, and Viorst, *Hostile Allies*.

"Can you beat it?" asked Eisenhower rhetorically. Giraud's nerve was not very different from that of the chief of de Gaulle's military mission in Washington, who in August, 1942, described General Marshall as a sensible person, but totally lacking in imagination. The colonel reported to de Gaulle that Marshall, Eisenhower, and other high American officers "would probably have made good division commanders in 1914/18."[73]

Presumably, the serious sickness of his son had taken Darlan to Algiers. It is impossible to prove that his being on the spot at this critical moment had been secretly planned. Unquestionably Pétain was glad about his being there, and he wired Darlan upon receiving reports about fighting in Algiers: "You can thus act and keep me informed. Stop. You know you have my entire confidence." Typically, Darlan at first hesitated to give the cease-fire order. Wearily sitting on the fence, he did not order an all-out resistance either. He played for time to determine the size of the American forces and to see how Hitler would react to the invasion. Once Germany occupied all of France and thereby deprived Vichy of even the shadow of independence, and once Darlan was presented with a stern half-hour ultimatum by General Clark, who had confined him to protective custody, he "surrendered." At least he could console himself with having acted in accordance with Pétain's order "to continue hostilities for as long as possible." Along with Pétain, in whose name it was generally believed he made this very difficult decision, Darlan still occupied a place in the hierarchy of French officers that commanded respect. But his attempt to bring the fleet from Toulon to North Africa came too late to be executed successfully. The ships were scuttled, including three battleships, seven cruisers, thirty destroyers, and sixteen submarines. Those at Dakar, however, eventually augmented the Allied fleets.

Anxious to seize the ground around Tunis, Eisenhower was "absolutely furious" because of the time he had to spend negotiating with French officers. Every minute lost meant a week spent reorganizing. It also irritated him that ammunition needed against the Axis had to be senselessly expended against the French. By November 13 the "Darlan Deal" had at last been consummated. General Clark and Admiral Darlan signed the agreement at Algiers on No-

73. Eisenhower, *Crusade in Europe*, 677–79; "Mission Militaire, CNF," August 11, 1942, in Guerre 1939–45: Politique Extérieure Etats-Unis, No. 211, AMAE.

vember 22. As high commissioner in French Africa, Darlan was placed in charge of the civil functions of local government. As a political compromise, Giraud was made commander in chief of all French military and naval forces. All these French elements and the American military authorities agreed to join forces in expelling "from the soil of Africa the common enemy, to liberate France and to restore integrally the French Empire." As a safeguard Darlan was not left in doubt that his authority and title extended only to French North Africa. Claiming that patriotism, not personal ambition, guided him, Darlan pledged scrupulous implementation of this limited military agreement.[74]

While it came too late for the 1,404 American casualties, which included 526 dead, it made an important difference in future operations. Continued active and passive resistance in the region would have claimed additional victims, not to mention delays in the pursuit of the enemy. The implementation of the agreement envisioned the building up of an army of several hundred thousand French soldiers capable of reinforcing Allied strategic plans. One of the immediate dividends the Allies collected was the decision of Pierre Boisson, governor general of French West Africa and high commissioner in Togoland, to cooperate with the United Nations in the war against the Axis. He placed himself under Eisenhower's command, but only through Admiral Darlan and no one else. No wonder Eisenhower gratefully acknowledged that the source of all practical help in the region had been Darlan. He lived up to expectations by ordering substantial units of French forces to fight side by side with the Allies in Tunisia. Airfield facilities, railroads, trucks, and everything else needed in the prosecution of the war were freely made available. Although Darlan's credentials as a trustworthy partner were widely questioned, General Eisenhower, impressed with the admiral's cooperative performances, came to the conclusion that "both Boisson and Darlan have committed themselves irrevocably to an Allied victory."[75]

74. "Minutes of a Meeting," Algiers, November 13, 1942, in France: Darlan File 34, Dwight D. Eisenhower Pre-Presidential Papers, Dwight D. Eisenhower Library, Abilene, Kan.; Aaron S. Brown, summary of a telephone conversation by Hull with Walter Lippmann and a Free French Delegation, November 14, 1942, in France—General, 1937–43, Hull Papers.

75. Draft agreement, December 2 or 3, 1942, in Darlan File 45, Eisenhower Pre-Presidential Papers; Dwight D. Eisenhower to George C. Marshall, December 7, 1942,

Charged with conducting a war, not French domestic policy, Ike was not to be deterred by ivory-tower ideological arguments. He would use the means that in his responsible judgment promised the earliest possible victory. As far as he was concerned, the morality of peace and saving lives simply took precedence over premature speculations of a political nature. Tainted as Darlan's political background was, would it have been moral to sacrifice men and time by not enlisting his positive contribution? Liberals everywhere, particularly in America and England, puzzled the supreme Allied commander with their surprising response: "Absolutely." Foreign Secretary Anthony Eden eloquently defined their opposition when he protested, "We are fighting for international decency and Darlan is the antithesis of that." It also seemed to him all too risky to arm "turncoats and blackmailers" with modern weapons. Labor leader Clement Atlee expressed his anxiety about the demoralizing political consequences that the United States completely ignored in its deal with Darlan. The British hoped that the appointment of Harold Macmillan as minister of state at Algiers would remedy this deficiency. The Foreign Office went so far as to recommend getting rid of Darlan as soon as possible.[76]

At home, Walter Lippmann deplored the administration's misguided association with Vichyites. Secretary of the Treasury Morgenthau, among many others, was utterly disgusted, finding the price of the deal totally unacceptable. "There is," he argued, "a considerable group of rich people in this country who would make peace with Hitler tomorrow." And once the working men and women, who were serious about fighting for democracy, concluded that we "favor these Fascists, not only in France but in Spain," Morgenthau worried, "they might question the justification of the war, presumably a crusade for ideals."[77]

General Eisenhower had the last word. In salty language he responded, "I am sick to death of the God damn question. I played ball with Darlan because it would take me ten divisions to hold my

---

in Marshall Papers.

76. For Eden's objections to Darlan, see Britain, Prime Minister's Office, Operational Papers, November 21, 1942, PREM 3/442/10, and Llewellyn Woodward, *British Foreign Policy in the Second World War* (5 vols.; London, 1970–76), II, 375.

77. Blum, *Morgenthau Diaries*, III, 368–75. For a thoughtful critical comment, see Louis M. Gottschalk, "Our Vichy Fumble," *Journal of Modern History*, XX (1948), 47–56.

lines of communications open if I didn't. And I could not get ten divisions here in a year while I am fighting this war." The president and General Marshall supported Ike's temporary military expedient. Winston Churchill, though somewhat reluctantly, and Joseph Stalin also approved the deal. Stalin found it "perfectly correct." Military diplomacy, he ventured to contend, must not hesitate to use the Darlans for military purposes. Referring to a Russian proverb, he believed that war conditions justified the temporary alignment with "the devil and his grandma." The starry-eyed critics of the "Darlan Deal" evidently did not scrutinize the democratic credentials of the cunning dictator of the Soviet Union.

Generals Marshall and Eisenhower did not believe it was fair to treat somebody who was trying to be helpful like an orange peel one discards after squeezing it. The secretary of state, moreover, did not quite understand why the idealists were so concerned with Darlan's hypothetical political future. If the French people did not want him at the end of the war, it was up to them to make the decision. Hull agreed with the secretary of war that "we cannot be made a party to any transition of this war measure into a permanent settlement for France." Indeed, it seemed legitimate to question the motives of such critics as Eden and de Gaulle. It was no secret that the British statesman was pushing de Gaulle's leadership as being in the best interest of England's future ties with the Continent. It was, furthermore, one thing for de Gaulle to reject America's deal with a "traitor" as irreconcilable with the honor of France and as an indication of America's ambitious global designs. But it was quite another matter for him to seize the opportunity created by Darlan's assassination on December 24 to solidify his leadership.[78]

FDR AND DE GAULLE: MAJOR POLICY DIFFERENCES

On October 27, 1940, General Charles de Gaulle pledged from his own radio station at Brazzaville that he would direct "the French war effort in the name of France and solely for its defense." He was driven by the conviction that France had to find its soul again and that it could do so only by its own efforts. Taking a long view of likely developments, he was convinced that France must continue the fight

78. H. Freeman Matthews to Cordell Hull, December 25, 1942, in Confidential File, RG 59, 851R.00/121, NA.

on the side of the Allies to establish its right to participate as an equal in shaping the eventual peace. Because his means in no way corresponded with the goals he set for himself, he hoped very much for positive support from President Roosevelt.[79]

The evolution of FDR's decision to recognize de Gaulle, from its humble beginnings to full acceptance, revealed the two-track course the president had adopted. He had no objection, he once remarked, to the general's becoming the emperor of France, as long as the French people made the determination. But he deemed it his duty to prevent anyone who merely symbolized liberation from claiming to represent the popular will. That the prolonged absence of a unified French authority opened the possibility to FDR of channeling the future of France in the direction he wanted to see it develop can hardly be denied. But while rejecting de Gaulle as the central authority of France, FDR could see the value of his actual and potential contributions. Jean Monnet's skills, in particular, helped overcome many of Roosevelt's objections to de Gaulle.[80]

Step by step FDR therefore increasingly accepted the Free French, a process greatly furthered by the exigencies of war operations. On March 1, 1942, the United States recognized "the French Islands in the Pacific . . . under the effective control of the French National Committee." In April, America recognized the authority of Free France in Equatorial Africa and appointed a consul general to Brazzaville with authority to deal with de Gaulle's committee. On October 6, Fighting France was authorized to arrange for Lend-Lease aid directly. On August 26, 1943, the government of the United States welcomed the establishment of the French Committee of National Liberation (FCNL), but it still qualified its acceptance of the FCNL as the body capable of administering and defending French interests. The United States officially recognized the FCNL only as the administrator of those French overseas territories that acknowledged its authority. By the fall of 1944, once Allied forces had entered France, not only Stimson and Eisenhower but even Hull realized the urgency of making the French responsible for their internal affairs and allowing the supreme Allied commander to concentrate on military affairs. FDR changed his mind on this issue only slowly.

79. Charles de Gaulle to Jacques de Sieyès, July 25, 1940, in Guerre 1939–45: Londres CNF, No. 309, AMAE.

80. André Kaspi, *La mission de Jean Monnet à Alger, mars–octobre 1943* (Paris, 1971), 226–40.

His old reservations, however, became obsolete when the Provisional Consultative Assembly in Paris passed a vote of confidence in General de Gaulle. On October 23, 1944, the United States, Great Britain, and the Soviet Union at last recognized him as the head of the Provisional Government of the French Republic. In a press conference four days later, de Gaulle characteristically cherished his acknowledgment: "The French Government is pleased that it is to be called by its name." He found it equally gratifying that his countrymen accepted him enthusiastically as an "instrument of destiny."[81]

In the past, historians have emphasized the personality clashes between Roosevelt and de Gaulle. This dramatic aspect of their relations has been unduly exaggerated. Had the two men come to know each other early in the war, it is conceivable that their mutual personal respect would have made it easier for them to avoid many later frictions. Behind de Gaulle's calculated outward stiffness was a personality with a keen sense of humanity. And FDR's charming superficialities concealed the aristocratic country squire who appreciated the finer tastes and standards of civilized society. Both possessed a broad vision of the world.

Central to the understanding of FDR's attitude toward France was the clash of policies between him and de Gaulle. In Great Britain, though Churchill and the Foreign Office had their differences over de Gaulle, they agreed on the necessity of restoring a strong France that would keep the peace at home and relieve Britain of undesirable responsibilities on the Continent. In the United States, the president and the State Department differed less over de Gaulle than over the future role of France. In contrast to the State Department, FDR was opposed to treating France as a major power. On the basis of past French performances, he had little faith in France's ability to establish political stability at home unless it underwent a drastic institutional reorganization. In world affairs, he observed, the collapse in 1940 merely climaxed a long period during which France did not qualify for the stabilizing leadership position to which it aspired. In Indochina, he further noted, the French had neither improved the living standard of the masses nor undertaken substantial measures to provide safety valves for the growing national aspirations of the native population. Whereas de Gaulle fought for

81. Goodrich and Carroll (eds.), *Documents on American Foreign Relations*, V, 543, VI, 668, VII, 867–68. See also Viorst, *Hostile Allies*, 192–96.

the complete restoration of France and its empire as one of the great powers, FDR favored only the restoration of an independent France with a reduced rank in the family of nations.

Such was the president's intent and vision. But the immediate pressures of the war tended to compel his postponement of final decisions until after it would be over. His collision course with de Gaulle was accentuated by his apprehension that the general might in the end emerge as France's dictator. As FDR saw it, de Gaulle's national pretensions were destined to create trouble for a stable order in the postwar world.

De Gaulle had all along interpreted the Allies' failure to consult or inform him as directed against France rather than himself. And he correctly believed that FDR was the driving force behind this deliberate policy to downgrade France as a world power. His exclusion from conferences discussing European questions of vital interest to France amounted to a painful blow to French interests and prestige. To be sure, the Big Two or Big Three found it easier to make their already difficult decisions without the claims and objections of still another national interest. Roosevelt's pronounced view of placing the leadership of the world in the hands of the Big Four—Great Britain, the United States, the Soviet Union, and China—spoke for itself. His exclusion of France from this world role was intentional. So was his decision not to assign to France a seat on the United Nations Security Council. The original failure to entrust France with an occupation zone in Germany also suggested that it did not count. And America's preference for dealing during the war with local French officials rather than with a central authority was more than a snub.[82]

In a conversation with de Gaulle in the fall of 1944, Harry Hopkins, Roosevelt's confidant and roving ambassador, explicitly confirmed the president's reservations with respect to France. Asked to explain the unfortunate state of Franco-American relations, Hopkins frankly replied:

> "The cause is above all the stupefying disappointment we suffered when we saw France collapse and surrender in the disaster of 1940. Our traditional conception of her value and her energy was over-

82. Claude Mauriac, *Diaries, 1944–1954: The Other de Gaulle*, trans. by M. Budberg and G. Latta (New York, 1973), 44–45. "France is allied to no one," de Gaulle said at one point.

thrown in an instant. Add to this the fact that those French military and political leaders in whom we successively placed our trust . . . did not show themselves worthy of our hopes. . . . Judging that France was no longer what she had been, we could not trust her to play one of the leading roles. . . . Knowing the political inconsistency that riddles your country . . . are we not then justified in using circumspection as to the share we expect of France to bear of the burden of tomorrow's peace?"

Having heard this explanation directly from Roosevelt when he visited him in Washington not long before, de Gaulle noted his awareness that America was counting on France "only as a subordinate." But he could not comprehend how the United States could "no longer consider the greatness of France necessary to the world."[83]

Despite the long series of disagreeable exchanges between them, a story historians have related in detail, de Gaulle's letter to FDR dated October 6, 1942, suggests that the two leaders could at least have avoided many later controversies had they established personal contact at the very start of the general's mission. In this letter he made a noble effort to explain his true objectives and to refute the charges of Vichyites and others who, for selfish reasons, had set out to discredit him. Maintaining to the president that "only Frenchmen can be the judge of their national interests" and that "France still represents a power in the world which must not be ignored," de Gaulle argued for his right to be consulted on all matters affecting the immediate and future interests of France. In his eloquent explanation of why the role of temporarily speaking for France fell on him, he acknowledged the complete failure of France's leading classes. None of them came forward to carry on the fight. "I was alone. Ought I to have kept silent?" he asked. By the force of his will he rallied the people and tried to unite all the elements of resistance. To think that he aimed at "imposing upon France some regime of personal power, as some people, chiefly abroad, are suggesting," he pointedly rebutted, displayed complete ignorance of the French people. "The French nation is in character the most deeply opposed to a regime of personal power."[84] It was erroneous and unfair to ac-

83. De Gaulle, *War Memoirs*, III, 92–95; Brian Crozier, *De Gaulle* (New York, 1973), 170–71.

84. Charles de Gaulle to Franklin D. Roosevelt, October 6, 1942, in RG 59, FW 851.01/400-3/6, NA. See also Department of State, Division of European Affairs, "Memorandum," October 26, 1942, in RG 59, 851.01/722-1/3, NA.

cuse him of aspiring to dictatorship, he claimed. Those persons who continued to entertain this suspicion did not know that in his correspondence of 1942–1943 with Léon Blum, the Socialist leader, the general had emphasized his awareness that historically France had consistently chosen liberty and the republican form of government.[85]

Echoing the thoughts expressed in the general's plea for understanding, Walter Lippmann regretted America's folly in not using "the military genius of this extraordinary man" regardless of the specious political arguments made to deny him recognition. Particularly ever since the successful campaign in North Africa, Lippmann called for a revision of FDR's doctrine that France did not need a recognized government until after peace was restored. On the contrary, he argued, "France cannot fight the war or re-establish constitutional order without a provisional government."[86]

By now FDR's objections to de Gaulle had been so firmly embedded in his mind that he continued to brush aside recommendations for strengthening the general's authority. He put his money on General Giraud, with whom he found it personally easier to get along and whom he could influence politically. It did not make much sense to Roosevelt to build up a sizable French army only to find out at a later stage that its French commander would decide to employ it the way he saw fit, rather than integrate it into the Allied war effort. FDR felt confident with Giraud. He simply did not trust de Gaulle's reliability on this question.

Attempts to bring about French unity by entrusting de Gaulle primarily with political and administrative responsibilities and Giraud with the post of supreme commander of French forces appeared to offer a reasonable compromise.[87] But the arrangement under which Giraud and de Gaulle were to serve as co-presidents of the newly formed FCNL did not last long, because these two Frenchmen represented two entirely different personalities. Giraud's political ineptness disappointed his American friends. De Gaulle, on the other hand, could not be stopped from brilliantly outmaneuvering Gi-

85. Léon Blum to Charles de Gaulle, November, 1942, de Gaulle to Blum, February, 1943, both in 3 BL 1, dr. 5, sdr. a, Papiers Blum.

86. New York *Herald Tribune*, December 29, 1942.

87. John C. Wiley to Cordell Hull, May 6, 17, 18, 1943, in FRUS, *Diplomatic Papers, 1943*, II, 108–23; Arthur Layton Funk, *Charles de Gaulle: The Crucial Years, 1943–1944* (Norman, Okla., 1959), 180–89.

raud. His struggle for power culminated with the elimination of Giraud from all political participation in the affairs of the FCNL. His perseverance and craftiness finally secured him the sole authority to stand up for France, initially only as a symbol shrouded in mystique, but ultimately as its legitimate leader. His position changed and improved with the passage of time. To increase the support of his countrymen, he did not hesitate to appeal to their hypersensitivity by holding the United States responsible for the prolonged diplomatic humiliation of France.[88]

It is not necessarily a retrospective assessment to find it peculiar that Roosevelt stubbornly refused to have an open mind toward de Gaulle and the FCNL. The man filled a crucial vacuum that nobody else on the horizon could fill. Psychologically, the French people were ready to accept any liberator, whatever his name and background. De Gaulle's tireless efforts on their behalf earned him their respect and support. They identified with his cause and admired his genuine ability to advance it. When they recognized and accepted him as the man of the hour, he no longer had to plead for America's recognition. Contrary to FDR's fears, on the whole, de Gaulle cooperated with Supreme Headquarters. In fact, Ike and General de Gaulle developed a remarkable working relationship.

The failure to deal wholeheartedly with de Gaulle and his FCNL at an early stage was not only illogical, but it also unnecessarily complicated General Eisenhower's task and produced resentments destined to linger long after the war. If one can defend the expediency of the Darlan Deal, it is difficult to justify FDR's treatment of the French problem. In any case, it accomplished the opposite of what the president desired. FDR and de Gaulle were both strong personalities and virtuoso politicians who respected each other personally, but ironically, they were driven apart by apparently irreconcilable policy differences.

In time of war, when conditions and rumors subject public opinion to frequent changes, it is hazardous to speculate about it. Under these circumstances it is not easy to adjust to shifting developments or wise to base policies on questionable estimates.[89] In May of 1942

88. U.S. State Department, Division of European Affairs, "Summary of Selden Chapin's Despatch No. 371," July 8, 1944, in RG 59, 851.01/7-844, NA.

89. U.S. embassy in Madrid, "Franco-American Relations," August 13, 1941, in RG 59, 711.51/168, NA.

a Gallup poll found that 63 percent of Americans did not know who General de Gaulle was, but 75 percent of those who did believed that he truly represented the French people. Marshal Pétain, they felt, represented only a small minority. From a practical point of view American politicians were encouraged to extend Lend-Lease aid to de Gaulle's forces, since 74 percent of those polled indicated approval of such assistance. Indicative of the public's low opinion of France at that time was its response to the question: "In case of an Allied victory what place should France occupy in the peace conference?" A total of 27 percent responded that it should be on a par with the great powers; 20 percent assigned it to a somewhat subordinate place; 28 percent, to an insignificant role; and 25 percent had no opinion.[90]

When in September, 1944, Parisians were asked which nation had contributed most to Germany's defeat, 61 percent responded the Soviet Union, 29.3 percent the United States, and 11.5 percent Great Britain, and 3.5 percent credited all three. But 69 percent expected the United States to help France recover after the war. And 73.2 percent wanted to see President Roosevelt reelected.[91]

Such opinions fluctuated considerably. Immediately prior to the liberation and shortly thereafter the French people expressed their implicit faith in America. In contrast, they doubted Britain's disinterestedness and feared the Russians. Before long, however, France made the United States the scapegoat for practically all its troubles. America was criticized for not sending enough food, ships, and rolling stock. Presumably the United States had not acted fast enough to help the French government establish communications with the provinces or to get French divisions ready for combat. Five months after D-day there were still no French correspondents accredited to the Allied armies. Failure to recognize the provisional French government and German- and Communist-inspired rumors that American imperialists were maneuvering to control France economically were accepted as proof of Roosevelt's intention to keep France weak. To add insult to injury, Frenchmen reacted with bitter indignation against American "coddling" of German prisoners of war. Seeing

90. "La France Devant L'Opinion Américaine," May 6, 1942, in Guerre 1939–45, Politique extérieure: Etats-Unis No. 213, AMAE.

91. *Libération*, September 7, 1944.

the prisoners receive far better rations than the average Frenchman was incomprehensible to them.[92]

That the United States in reality did what it could under the most demanding war conditions to improve the lot of the French people and restore France to a semblance of its old self was not recognized until after the war. By then the French people also realized that France had not been the only country looking to the United States for salvation.

ANGLO-AMERICAN DIFFERENCES

Major policy differences between Great Britain and the United States surfaced throughout the war. Their respective attitudes regarding Vichy seemed to be much further apart than their common interests warranted. Although acting as if it had made a clean break with "anti-British" Vichy, London only too gladly accepted Washington's efforts to keep Franco-German collaboration to a minimum and to maintain contact with the former ally that was on the brink of becoming an enemy. Anglo-American frictions were compounded by their different approaches to the de Gaulle phenomenon. Originally accepted and financed by the British as the leader of a useful auxiliary force, de Gaulle soon made demands completely out of line with France's actual power. The United States refused to treat the nationalistic claims he defended so abrasively and uncompromisingly as merely troublesome pitches. Unlike de Gaulle and Great Britain, who continued to believe in France, the United States had given up on France as a major factor in world politics. The propaganda activities of de Gaulle's organization, the general's suspected political ambitions, and his imperial objectives disturbed American leaders so much that even Churchill, mindful of how much he needed their continued support, declared that in a showdown he would have to side with the United States against France. On several occasions Eden and the Foreign Office also admitted that de Gaulle's obduracy was troublesome. But they were among the

92. U.S. War Department, Military Intelligence Division, Report No. 13741, "Current Political Situation in France," April 20, 1944, in Records of OSS, No. 69442; U.S. War Department, Military Intelligence Division, "Franco-American Relations in Southern France," January 2, 1945, Confidential File, RG 59, Box 3422D, 711.51/1-245, NA.

French leader's staunchest supporters and used such admissions as soothing appeasers.[93]

Weighty considerations motivated Britain's desire to see France restored to its former status and to promote de Gaulle as the most effective instrument to accomplish this goal. The policy was intended as insurance against the United States, the Soviet Union, and the resurgence of Germany. Realizing that FDR's emphasis on cooperation with the Soviet Union and China would for a time reduce Great Britain to being a junior partner of the United States, the British looked upon a strong France as an essential force on the Continent. Remembering Rapallo, Britain speculated about the possibilities of Franco-German, Franco-Russian, and German-Russian alignments in the postwar era, any of which might be simultaneously accompanied by withdrawal of American forces from the Continent. Such a scenario of course assumed the worst possible situation in which Britain could find herself. Realistically assessing the Soviet Union's paramount position in Eastern Europe and its determination to have an equal voice with Great Britain and the United States in the Pacific, the British cabinet saw great merit in being on friendly terms with both the Soviet Union and France. It was apprehensive, however, that Washington's antagonistic treatment of de Gaulle might move France much closer to the Soviet Union than the defense of Western interests should allow. Britain's balancing policies in Europe and around the globe called for counterweights to America's overwhelming economic influence and for safeguards against the Soviet Union's cynical resumption of its ideologically motivated imperialism. Churchill's special relationship with Roosevelt accelerated the defeat of Hitler's Germany; it did not extend to coordinating policies designed to contain the expansion of Soviet communism. Thus, at the end of both world wars the leaders of Great Britain and the United States failed to act in complete harmony.[94]

The widest breach in Anglo-American views existed with regard to colonial questions. FDR made no secret of it that in his judgment the end of the exploitation of colonial peoples would be a vital contribution to the future peace of the world. But just as Churchill did

93. "British Policy and Procedures in Relation to France and the French," June 2, 1943, in Records of OSS, No. 35949.

94. DeWitt C. Poole to Cordell Hull, August 10, 1943, in Confidential File, RG 59, 851.01/2886, NA.

not intend to preside over the dissolution of the British Empire, so General de Gaulle could not envision France's recovery without the resources of its empire. The leaders of Britain and France solidified the identity of their imperial interests by jointly opposing FDR's anticolonialism. In spite of this common interest, though, they also suspected each other of casting eyes on their respective possessions.[95]

Neither France nor Britain welcomed America's influential presence in North Africa after 1943. They resented this unprecedented factor as a latent threat to their spheres of influence in the region. And what were they to think of the idea, suggested by FDR at the Casablanca conference in 1943 and subsequently reiterated at the Cairo, Teheran, and Yalta conferences, of establishing trusteeships that would eventually lead to independence for such French colonies as Morocco and Indochina? How far would the president go in advocating national liberation for peoples whom he considered flagrantly downtrodden natives? Such views had traditionally distinguished America from Europe. France was frightened by such talk. At Yalta, Churchill objected strenuously to Roosevelt's advocacy of a global imperial dismemberment under an international system of trusteeships. Contravening FDR's rather vague anticolonial notions, Churchill belittled China's capacity as a big power, and he persevered in the restoration of Anglo-French influence in Southeast Asia. That Stalin and Chiang Kai-shek reacted enthusiastically to the president's idea of trusteeships scared the British statesman. It was hard for him to understand how the generally sophisticated and subtle American chief executive could fail to see cynical motives in their approval.[96]

FDR's anticolonialism had never been shaped into a coherent policy. He postponed its firm development until the end of the war. Once he had articulated it, the president felt honor-bound not to disappoint the national aspirations of the colonial peoples counting on his leadership. Like Wilson at Versailles, FDR had not thought through the international consequences of the establishment of many relatively small and weak new national states. The British and French governments attributed FDR's anticolonial attitude to his grasp for global hegemony and world markets. As they interpreted it, FDR

95. Britain, Prime Minister's Office, Dominions Office, PREM 3/178/2.

96. Berle Diary, January 4, 1943, Container 214, Berle Papers.

was veiling America's emerging imperialism with humanitarian and democratic principles.

Knowing Roosevelt's thoughts on this subject, Churchill wisely did not press him on it. Instead, he welcomed discussion of the question between the State Department and the Foreign Office. As it turned out, it was a mistake to refer to "America's" anticolonial policy, because the State Department by and large did not share the president's views. Unlike the president, it preferred to see France and its empire fully restored. Pressed by the European allies, blocked by the chief of the State Department's European office, James Clement Dunn, and persuaded by Harry Hopkins and others, FDR weakened in his anticolonial stand. As was the case after the American Civil War, after the Second World War the United States would need additional military and naval bases. The Joint Chiefs of Staff did not want their acquisition blocked by inflexible policies. While the president kept his mind open to such arguments, he never gave up his goal of promoting the independence of the colonial peoples.[97]

Not surprisingly, after FDR's death his policies vis-à-vis France were abandoned. President Truman, a novice in the field of diplomacy, had little choice but to follow the State Department's recommendations. In due course, however, the disasters of Dienbienphu and the Viet Nam War suggested that FDR's idealistic notions might have saved France and the United States from painful experiences.

Already during the war President Roosevelt kept his mind on its economic consequences. Prevention of Germany's autarchic direction of Europe's economy constituted only one of his major objectives. Another was decolonization, which he saw as another way to open up enlarged trade opportunities for American business. As in the First World War, each national government, though more or less militarily allied with others, tried to emerge from the war not merely victorious, but with its own economic foundation better secured. France and Great Britain therefore fought against any notion depriving them of essential colonial resources and markets. As a matter of fact, as much as French and British leaders wanted to harness

97. Walter La Feber, "Roosevelt, Churchill and Indochina: 1942–1945," *AHR*, LXXX (1975), 1277–95; Christopher Thorne, "Indochina and Anglo-American Relations, 1942–1945," *Pacific Historical Review*, XLV (1976), 73–96.

America's enormous industrial and financial might for the revival of their economies, they were also frightened of it.[98]

The likelihood of Anglo-American commercial rivalry influenced Churchill in his otherwise friendly dealings with the United States. In the past, the American share in international trade had been limited. But at the end of World War II, Churchill was fully aware, its greatly expanded industrial capacity would have to search for expanded markets. In a strictly confidential departmental report, dated December 12, 1941, Secretary of State Hull was alerted to the possibility of Anglo-American economic conflicts in the postwar era. Whereas the United States considered the worldwide adoption of its most-favored-nation principle as essential for postwar economic reconstruction and growth, highly influential persons in Britain recommended policies that represented the antithesis of America's conception. They advocated foreign-exchange controls to help give Britain a favorable balance of international payments and to regulate imports as a means of forcing exports. Some preferred bilateral trade agreements; others staunchly defended a system of imperial preferences. Obviously, if after the war Britain engaged in potentially calamitous economic warfare, the economic desiderata of the Atlantic Charter could not be met. It would also play into the hands of those Americans who preferred trade regimentation to protect their interests. If Britain pursued such restrictive policies, it would greatly retard world economic recovery. Following an immensely destructive and costly war, neither France, the United States, nor the rest of the world could tolerate any policies not designed to further speedy reconstruction.

Admittedly, during the war Britain experienced financial hardships because after the collapse of France it lost the European markets that it had used in the past to exchange coal, tin, and textiles for food and other needed supplies. To raise enough American dollars to pay for imports from the United States, it was obliged to reduce its supplies of gold while countries like France, Belgium, and Holland maintained large amounts of gold in American vaults. It griped Britain to fight for these countries "while they were not doing a thing to aid the fight and Britain, who was making the fight on which their ultimate safety depended." Clearly, the competitive na-

98. J. C. Paris to René Massigli, August 25, 1944, in Guerre 1939–45, FCLN Alger, No. 1108, Questions Economiques, AMAE.

tional state system nurtured political and economic rivalries under which nations found it in their self-interest to join in a measure of cooperation only under the most compelling conditions in war or peace.[99]

The Lend-Lease Act of March, 1941, demonstrated such cooperation on a grand scale. From the moment of its enactment the leader of the Free French was keenly interested in obtaining American economic and military assistance. America's relations with Vichy, however, precluded such a development. Instead, the United States asked Britain to transfer a certain portion of its Lend-Lease aid to de Gaulle. Both the British and de Gaulle took strong exception, for political reasons, to American economic aid for Vichy France and for North Africa. For its part, Vichy expressed its resentment of the financial arrangements that were set up for Lend-Lease. Unlike England, Russia, and China, Vichy was expected to pay cash for civilian goods, a condition it could afford to meet. Still, such inequitable treatment caused it to be irritated. Basically, though, French forces in North Africa received a great boost from Lend-Lease aid starting in November, 1942.

A quite unforeseen by-product of America's assistance and military accomplishments produced more than irritation. Because Arab leaders increasingly looked upon Americans as their benefactors, they hoped the United States might help them to get out from under the French colonial system. Although the Americans had not given any thought to taking advantage of such friendly Arab sentiments, the French could not quite suppress their apprehensions. Even after the fighting in North Africa had ended, the French exploited Lend-Lease as much as possible to recapture their domination in that region. As a result of this process the United States lost the sympathy of the Arab nationalists, who were greatly disillusioned.[100]

Discussions between Free France and the United States over Lend-Lease went on for some time. Prior to the recognition of the Provisional Government on October 23, 1944, the State and Treasury departments took opposing positions with respect to existing French funds. Secretary of State Hull argued that they belonged to France and not to the FCNL. Less legalistic, Secretary of the Treasury Morgenthau held that in view of French holdings of over $2.5 billion in

99. Stimson, Diary, January 13, 1941, in Stimson Papers.

100. James J. Dougherty, *The Politics of Wartime Aid: American Economic Assistance to France and French Northwest Africa, 1941–1946* (Westport, Conn., 1978), 3–8.

gold and American dollars, it would be legitimate to use "these assets . . . to pay for the equipping of a French Army on a credit lend-lease basis." In subsequent negotiations Monnet tried hard to conclude very favorable long-term Lend-Lease arrangements. Good-natured Harry Hopkins went along with such an approach as a means of improving the far-from-satisfactory state of Franco-American relations. Morgenthau carried the day by reminding FDR and the secretaries of state and war that Congress had approved Lend-Lease as a war measure, not as postwar reconstruction aid. By the time the United States signed a Lend-Lease Master Agreement with France on February 28, 1945, it had already equipped eight French divisions. But this agreement raised a storm of protest when it became known that by evidently deliberate subterfuges it did provide France with many items contributing to postwar reconstruction. In addition to other reasons, this experience influenced President Truman when he abruptly terminated Lend-Lease altogether after V-J Day.[101]

Up to that date "the total French military and civilian lend-lease account amounted to approximately $2.842 billion." It was worth equipping nearly 400,000 men, including nineteen air squadrons and supporting units, to join the struggle against the Axis.

FDR AND DE GAULLE: PREJUDICES AND APPREHENSIONS

FDR's handling of developing foreign political problems did not provide for much, if any, French influence on them. He manifested a flagrant disregard of French interests, for instance, in connection with the collapse of Fascist Italy. On August 2, 1943, the FCNL considered it its "imperative duty" to request French participation in the armistice negotiations and the implementation of terms imposed upon Italy. It felt morally and materially entitled to such participation. To the chagrin of the FCNL, the Anglo-Americans concluded the Italian armistice without conferring with the French. Noting that neither had the Soviet Union been present on this occasion, de Gaulle lost no time establishing common ground with Stalin to remind the Western Allies of their partnership in the war. The presence of the French in the Italian occupation discussions, FDR explained to Stalin, would engender extreme resentment on the part

101. *Ibid.*, 112–13, 178–98.

of both civil and military elements in Italy whose wholehearted support of the occupation troops was most desirable. As in other instances, the president followed the road of least resistance, even if it meant an offense to French amour-propre.

The French and the Russians were not inspired with confidence by the Anglo-Americans' handling of their protests against their exclusion. At the Moscow Conference of Foreign Ministers in October, 1943, a plan for a Mediterranean commission that would have satisfied all parties concerned led only to the establishment of the Italian Advisory Commission. The advisory nature of this commission was of limited value, of course, and France and the Soviet Union soon discovered that the Anglo-American command had formed an Allied Control Commission for Italy, which for all practical purposes left them out of the effective decision-making process on Mediterranean and Italian affairs.[102]

The Soviet Union was in a much stronger position to assert itself than France, which had constantly to remember its dependent status. Given the very *raison d'être* of the FCNL, it could accept nothing less than equality, and its admission to the Allied bodies discussing the future occupied a place of priority. For the time being, however, ostensibly because FDR did not want to make difficult problems more complex, France was systematically excluded from commissions taking up matters of direct and indirect importance to it. As far as the European Advisory Commission (EAC) was concerned, France demanded immediate full membership in it. Reminiscent of Laval's eagerness to serve as middleman between Hitler's Germany and the United States was Foreign Minister Georges Bidault's allusion to the contribution French presence on the EAC could make "toward eliminating the possibilities of friction between east and west."[103]

How could France regain self-confidence if the United States looked down on it? How could the multitude of problems arising from the approaching end of hostilities and the future security and role of France be decided without French input? What did the Allies have in mind when they originally did not grant France a seat on the

102. FCNL to U.S. Department of State, in FRUS, *The Conferences at Washington and Quebec, 1943: Substantive Papers* (Washington, D.C., 1970), 532–33; Franklin D. Roosevelt to Joseph Stalin, September 4, 1943, in FRUS, *Diplomatic Papers, 1943*, I, 784.

103. Jefferson Caffery to Cordell Hull, November 14, 1944, in Container 42, PSF.

Security Council of the United Nations? Why did they originally exclude France from the control commission of the powers occupying Germany? Only reluctantly did they eventually yield to France's insistent presentations. Having not been invited to take part in the initial formulation of the proposals for the United Nations Organization and hurt by its exclusion from the Big Three's conference at Yalta, the Provisional Government of France, to signal its displeasure at these intolerable snubs, delayed sponsoring the Dumbarton Oaks proposals when it was finally asked to back them. But what really gave the Allies something to worry about was the Provisional Government's repeated warnings that it would not consider itself bound by decisions affecting vital French interests if it had not taken part in making them. "These decisions would therefore be ineffective," as de Gaulle said.[104]

It should be noted that Churchill and Eden strongly supported the French at Yalta. In fact, Churchill made himself the spokesman for French interests. De Gaulle appreciated this service, although he had no illusion about Britain's role as an honest broker. While Stalin was basically more interested in Eastern Europe than in France, he used the French question as a pawn in the larger game of international politics. He saw potential profits in dividing the Western powers and pleasing the French working classes.[105]

To gain a balanced view of FDR's attitudes, one must distinguish between what he said he intended to do and what he actually did. After all, the American president is not an entirely free agent in the determination of foreign policy. In January, 1945, the coordination committee of the Departments of State, War, and the Navy presented a memorandum to Roosevelt concerning American policy toward France. Its mere enumeration of America's actions regarding France corrected many unfavorable impressions the French had received. On November 11, 1944, the American government invited France to accept full membership in the EAC. Subsequently the president approved in principle the FCNL's proposals for French participation in the Allies' postwar governing authority for Germany, French participation in the signing of the German instrument of surrender, the allocation of a French occupation zone in Germany, and the setting up of a quadripartite, instead of tripartite,

104. De Gaulle, *War Memoirs*, III, 110.
105. Woodward, *British Foreign Policy in the Second World War*, V, 276–77.

control commission. The president furthermore approved the outfitting of a substantial number of French combat and supply troops, as well as arms and equipment primarily for use in the immediate postwar era. To avert social and political instability in France, the memorandum recommended "the most sympathetic consideration" for French requests for all kinds of supplies. Finally, it strongly underwrote a permanent seat for France on the Security Council "on a basis of full equality."

In a conversation between de Gaulle and Monnet in May, 1943, the general indicated that the "mounting threat" of Anglo-Saxon domination in Europe might induce France in the postwar world to strengthen its ties with the Soviet Union. Even during the war, to gain concessions and greater independence from the Anglo-Americans and to break down his diplomatic isolation, de Gaulle played his Soviet card shrewdly. He reinforced this tendency through a close working relationship between French Communists and his resistance movement. Satisfied with de Gaulle's leanings, Moscow in September, 1942, recognized the FCNL "as the only body qualified to represent French interests and to organize French participation in the war."[106]

Considering that de Gaulle, French Communists, and Stalin had a long-range political stake in belittling or discrediting America's massive contribution to the liberation of France, it would seem prudent not to take Stalin's apparently anti-French attitudes at Teheran and Yalta at face value. The general's visit to Moscow in December, 1944, and the negotiation of the Franco-Soviet alliance confirmed the usefulness of such contracts.[107] As Ambassador Averell Harriman reported to Washington at the time, de Gaulle's keen analytical mind perceived during his visit to Moscow the danger "that Soviet policy was directed not only toward expanding its sphere of influence in Eastern Europe but also toward incorporating states within the Union." What the future held out, though somewhat exaggerated, amounted to a choice between Anglo-American domination and ac-

106. James C. Dunn, "Analytical Report," February 7, 1943, in France—General, 1937–43, Hull Papers. See also "De Gaulle and the Communists," March 2, 1943, in Records of OSS, No. 29551, and Alfred J. Rieber, *Stalin and the French Communist Party, 1941–1947* (New York, 1962).

107. Unlike Churchill, who would have preferred an Anglo-French-Soviet pact, FDR did not object to a Franco-Soviet pact. Britain, Prime Minister's Office, Operational Papers, Joseph Stalin to Winston Churchill, December 10, 1944, PREM 3/173/1.

ceptance of the reality of Soviet imperialism. In a world of superpowers, there would under no circumstances be a return for France to its past status in the family of nations. Even talk of France's developing into a "Third Force" serving as a link and mediator between the superpowers overrated its capacity.[108]

Roosevelt, who believed that since World War I France had been more a liability than an asset to the United States, was not convinced that it would soon recover from the many wounds it had suffered. He was sympathetic toward France and wanted to help it recover. But because of certain prejudices he developed in the 1930s and because of the shock caused by the sudden collapse in 1940, the president's confidence in French recovery was enveloped in doubt.

On the recommendation of his diplomatic advisers in the State Department, President Harry S. Truman bypassed Roosevelt's doubts with his readiness "to treat France in all respects on the basis of her potential power and influence rather than on the basis of her present strength." One of the underlying differences in the two presidents' approaches toward France involved the Soviet Union. Failing to see how lasting peace could be established and maintained without the Soviet Union, FDR deemed it essential to cooperate with this powerful country. He reckoned that it would take years before France would be strong enough to take care of more than its parochial needs. In contrast, Truman and de Gaulle were guided by their growing fear of the Soviet Union. Recognizing the advisability of a coalition against the spread of communism, they agreed to accelerate the reconstruction of France as a vigorous member in it.[109]

De Gaulle found Truman less subtle and more direct than Roosevelt. He appreciated the respect shown him and the fact that the United States had no designs on French territorial possessions. Naturally he was satisfied that in the post-Roosevelt era America no longer questioned French sovereignty over Indochina, even though it continued to advocate movement toward self-determination for the Indo-Chinese. De Gaulle himself hinted vaguely at colonial reforms. Once the uncertainties surrounding his own leadership had

108. Averell Harriman to Edward Stettinius, December 8, 1944, in Container 42, PSF.

109. Britain, Prime Minister's Office, Operational Papers, Duff Cooper to Foreign Office, April 5, 1945, PREM 3/173/3.

been removed, the general found it easier to acknowledge America's great help.

Although France had long been outside the halls of Allied foreign-policy discussions, de Gaulle and his more suave foreign minister, Georges Bidault, used every opportunity in private conversations and public speeches to make their views known. As in the past, they saw France's security largely in terms of the German menace. Accordingly, they advanced France's traditional remedy for safeguarding its security—breaking up the left bank of the Rhine "into small, semi-independent states operating under French influence." The Ruhr industrial area, they believed, should be under international control, and its mines and industries should "be operated for the benefit of all Western European countries." Prophetically, de Gaulle put the Big Three on notice that France continued to take the position that no lasting peace could be secured without the independence of Poland, Czechoslovakia, Austria, and the Balkan nations. He also assured Italy that, with the exception of minor frontier rectifications, France did not covet any of its territories. And as in the past, de Gaulle expressed the desirability of bilateral pacts with England, Belgium, Luxembourg, and Holland, in addition to his support for an international peace organization "in which the United States will be in the first line." As vital as he considered America's aid to Europe, he never abandoned his apprehension of the Anglo-Saxons' domination of Europe. But for America to carry a major share of the international peacekeeping burden was a different matter.[110]

The main trend of Franco-American relations after 1943 conveyed a more balanced picture of the progress made than the elaboration of unusual incidents and extreme statements. But they were part of the picture. Roosevelt never rid himself of his distrust of General de Gaulle. When in mid-1943 he was concerned about the general's possible threat to the safety of the British and American military operations in North and West Africa, he was mentally prepared to send several regiments and naval vessels to Dakar to prevent him from dominating French West Africa. The president was also prepared to

110. Jefferson Caffery to Edward Stettinius, February 6, 1945, CS/EG Confidential File, in RG 59, 851.01/2-645, NA; Caffery to Stettinius, April 20, 1945, Confidential File, RG 59, 711.51/4-2045, NA. See also "Preconference Documents" (January, 1945), in FRUS, *The Conferences at Malta and Yalta* (Washington, D.C., 1945), 292–306.

stop arming French forces unless he could be completely satisfied that they would unreservedly cooperate in the Allies' military operations and not endanger lines of communications.[111]

The French were eager to fight, not only to qualify as a full-fledged participant in the peace conference, but as Bidault frankly indicated, "they have also to avenge the past." If there was any truth to de Gaulle's charge in November, 1944, that Americans were arming French soldiers "as sort of watchmen," not for combat, he had contributed to certain Allied reservations. Although the French had accepted the condition that their forces, equipped by the United States, must operate under the orders of the supreme Allied commander, Generals Giraud and de Gaulle soon began to equivocate on this absolutely essential condition. Giraud asserted that as the supreme French military commander he could observe this condition only with his prior approval. De Gaulle went further by insisting that the employment of sovereign France's troops must be subject to prior agreement on a government-to-government basis.[112]

Once the general was satisfied that the United Nations would win the war, he placed the resurrection of France ahead of the military phase of the war. In view of the many slights he had suffered as the leader of France, he reportedly confided late in September, 1944, to a circle of compatriots: "France is allied to no one. She is entirely on her own." Time and again he did not seem to care if his reach for recognition interfered with Allied plans. The president, the secretaries of state and war, and the Joint Chiefs of Staff were outraged, for example, by his conduct in the currency controversy. Although advised by the commissioner for foreign affairs of the FCNL that it would be a psychological mistake to use Allied military currency in France, American officials went ahead with it. They took the position that since no French governmental authority existed to issue currency, only an Allied military currency could legally be used. Since Jean Monnet and Pierre Mendès-France of the FCNL had not objected to this solution, it came as a shock that de Gaulle vehemently opposed "the issuance of a so-called French currency in France without any agreement" with him. He was obviously trying to stampede the Allies into according the FCNL full recognition. That refusal of invasion money would automatically depreciate the franc

111. Franklin D. Roosevelt to Winston Churchill, June 10, 1943, Roosevelt to Dwight D. Eisenhower, June 17, 1943, in Elsey Papers.

112. De Gaulle, *War Memoirs*, III, 70.

gave more concern to American officials than to the French leader. Secretary Morgenthau despaired: "With our men fighting on the beaches of France, this fellow comes along and holds . . . a gun to our backs."[113]

In a memorable scene in London, in the course of which Anthony Eden pushed for recognition of the provisional French government, the usually restrained General Marshall could no longer hold back his white fury at de Gaulle. If the American people were told how he hampered the invasion and obstructed the cause their boys were dying for, "there would be a tremendous explosive reaction against the French themselves . . . and make our people anxious to drop France altogether and drop her for good," Marshall said. But he did not want to pour oil on the isolationists' fire. Instead, to the relief of the supreme Allied commander, a political settlement of the currency question was reached on July 7, 1944.[114]

The more certain Hitler's defeat appeared, the more de Gaulle asserted his independence. In a number of instances he went so far as to disregard the Allied chain of command. For example, on January 1, 1945, he ordered General Jean de Lattre de Tassigny not to abandon the sacred ground of Strasbourg despite the fact that General Eisenhower had found it strategically advisable to shift his lines. De Gaulle informed Ike: "Whatever may happen, the French will defend Strasbourg," a city dear to the hearts of all Frenchmen. To avoid an undesirable clash, Eisenhower gave in, but not without alluding to the possibility of cutting the French First Army off American fuel and munitions supplies if it were to operate independently of the Allied armies. Unimpressed by this allusion, de Gaulle retorted with one of his own. If the Americans deprived French forces of the means of combat, they should not be surprised if "the outraged French people forbid the use of its railroads and communications."[115]

When the instruction to evacuate Stuttgart was disobeyed on de Gaulle's orders, at least until the French zone of occupation had been defined, Eisenhower sent the French leader what was for him an unusually blunt note, dated April 28, 1945. He rebuked the general for giving direct orders to the First French Army for political rea-

113. Blum, *Morgenthau Diaries*, III, 172–77.

114. Stimson, Diary, June 15, 1944, in Stimson Papers; Forrest C. Pogue, *George C. Marshall: Organizer of Victory, 1943–1945* (New York, 1973), 398–403.

115. De Gaulle, *War Memoirs*, III, 168–71, 204–207; Joseph Patrick Hobbs, *Dear General: Eisenhower's Wartime Letters to Marshall* (Baltimore, 1971), 184–213.

sons. Fed up with this violation of the original agreements, he declared, "In present circumstances, I can do nothing but inform the Combined Commanders-in-Chief of this affair in detail, stressing the fact that I could no longer, with complete certainty, count on French forces which they may consider re-arming in the future." On May 2, a deeply offended President Truman cautioned de Gaulle not to compel the United States to adopt "a complete reorganization of the military command." Nevertheless, the French leader claimed the right "to see that French forces were employed in the interests of France, the only interests which they are bound to serve."[116]

A month later, this attitude reached ugly proportions over a withdrawal order to General Paul André Doyen, commanding general of the French army in the Alps. On de Gaulle's order he defied an attempt to establish an Allied military government in the province of Cumeo. Having valiantly fought against the Italians in this region, the French general had been instructed to occupy and administer this territory for France without waiting for a final peace treaty that would settle such territorial questions. So as to leave no doubt about his determination, he warned the American commander that Alllied insistence on carrying out the military government plan "would assume a clearly unfriendly character, even a hostile character, and could have grave consequences." Totally misjudging the American character, the French officer threatened to implement de Gaulle's orders "by all necessary means without exception." The almost unbelievable threat that French soldiers bearing American arms would combat Allied soldiers, including Americans, who had liberated France prompted President Truman to dispatch a blistering note to de Gaulle. It concluded tersely "I regret that I have no alternative but to issue instructions that no further issues of military equipment or munitions can be made to French troops."[117] Evidently Truman's stern reaction struck the right note.

Perhaps even more sobering was de Gaulle's realization that France would need massive economic and financial aid to get on its feet again. De Gaulle had gone too far; the time had come to take this need into account. Despite the fact that General Eisenhower was leaning over backward to give France and de Gaulle their proper due, and despite his acknowledgment that French combat troops gave an

116. De Gaulle, *War Memoirs*, III, 220–25.

117. Harry S. Truman to Charles de Gaulle, June 6, 1945, FRUS, *Diplomatic Papers, 1945*, IV, 734–35.

excellent account of themselves, whether affiliated with Vichy or de Gaulle, Frenchmen had tried his patience beyond human endurance. He placed them second only to the weather in causing him the greatest difficulties.

Months before D-day, London and Washington gave some thought to the administration of France during the early phase of the liberation. Proceeding from different premises, they came to different conclusions. The British optimistically believed that the French people would quickly rally to support de Gaulle, enabling him to take charge and maintain order. FDR anticipated disorder and perhaps a bloody revolution. He was therefore inclined to treat France as an occupied country for a while and to entrust the civil administration to the supreme Allied commander. But instead of keeping law and order, such an arrangement would have been rejected by the French as an outrageous provocation. It also ran counter to the British conception not to permit important political decisions to be made by a military commander. Besides, being anxious to see the French control their own affairs as soon as possible, the British, almost as much as de Gaulle, wanted to foreclose even the possibility of a deal with surviving remnants of the Vichy regime. This "ridiculous" suspicion had not died with Hull's unequivocal statement on March 21, 1944, that the United States would not have any relations with Vichy "except for the purpose of abolishing it."[118]

In FDR's directive of March 15, he specifically provided for the nonretention and nonemployment of Vichy collaborators. But while permitting FCNL consultation on setting up civilian administration locally, he insisted on the military commander's privilege not to be exclusively limited to the FCNL in this respect. The Franco-American agreement finally ratified on August 26 gave Eisenhower the power to deal with the FCNL as the de facto authority in France. It established various zones facilitating close cooperation between French and American authorities, with the military situation always being the prime consideration. This proviso applied also to the zone of the interior in which French authorities assumed full administrative responsibilities. Ike tried earnestly not to ruffle French feathers,

118. Memorandum entitled "Relations with France," May 6, 1944, and President's Directive, March 15, 1944, both in Box 13, Hickerson-Matthews File, France, RG 59.

but he did not like it at all that so many political problems had been thrown into his lap.[119]

As the final assault against Japan got under way, liberated France was eager to take part in it. A noticeable change had come about between 1940 and 1945 in French policy vis-à-vis Japan. As had been previously observed, Vichy France was too weak to resist Japanese pressures for concessions. In August, 1940, Japan acquired air bases in northern French Indochina. A year later it received permission to build air and naval bases in southern Indochina. Early in 1942, negotiations were going on to charter to Japan fifty thousand tons of French shipping in Chinese and Indo-Chinese ports. Darlan's assurance that these ships were destined to engage in purely commercial traffic and would definitely not be used for military purposes against the United States had of course to be taken with a grain of salt. Fortunately, Japan's decisive defeat in the battle of Midway came early enough to benefit France as well as the United States.

According to United States Naval Intelligence, one of Japan's long-range objectives was the exclusion of France and the United States from Asia altogether. It was prepared to accept Britain as an Asian power and as "a naval partner along with whom it can top United States naval power." Neither Russia, France, nor China qualified in this respect. But the Japanese endeavored to enlist Russia's cooperation in support of their policy to break up the Sino-American friendship, which presented the greatest potential roadblock to Japan's and Russia's expansion in Asia. They drew encouragement from the fact that while the Soviet Union had given the Allies air bases from where they could attack Rumania, Bulgaria, and Hungary, it turned "a deaf ear to Washington's urgent request for air bases in Vladivostok against Japan."[120]

Since, by 1944, the defeat of the Axis became largely a question of time, France reasserted its sovereign rights in Indochina, notwithstanding Roosevelt's allusions to its eventual independence. To protect its ancient rights, France offered its military support in the war against Japan.[121] But FDR, bent on a course of decolonization, stubbornly resisted this offer. There was, however, little he could

119. President's Directive, March 15, 1945, and H. F. Matthews, memorandum of May 6, 1945, both in Box 13, Hickerson-Matthews File, France, RG 59, NA.

120. Intelligence Report, Office of Naval Operations, June 21, 1944, in Records of OSS, No. 85922.

121. Interviews with General Brossin de Saint Didier, October 20, 1944, July 7,

do when Great Britain overtly and covertly tried to bypass his objection. Inasmuch as Indochina was French, General de Gaulle resented the interference of an outside power trying to interdict the legitimate defense of French territory by French soldiers. He instructed his delegate general in Indochina that "the French forces in Indochina must not on any account be allowed to be put in a position where they cannot fight." Vice Admiral Fenard, chief of the French naval mission in the United States, pleaded more diplomatically for the president to agree at least in principle to the participation of French forces in the Far East "where and how the Combined Chiefs of Staff may see fit." Such an act, he stressed, would give the French people a tremendous morale boost.[122]

The president's reluctant modification of his stand in this matter came very late in the fighting. Within limits, his military advisers did not object to it. Diplomatically, the United States faced the dilemma of seeking to deprive parent countries of some of their colonies in the Pacific region while promoting close cooperation with them in Europe. Secretary of State Hull described this dilemma succinctly: "We could not alienate them in the Orient and expect to work with them in Europe." Even this persuasive argument did not deter President Roosevelt from his ultimate political goals.[123]

A BALANCED APPRAISAL

From Versailles to Hitler's assumption of power, meaningful Franco-American cooperation was canceled out by the larger policy objectives of the two countries. France's search for security and leadership on the Continent not only conflicted with Germany's legitimate right to self-determination but also projected an economic status for Germany detrimental to the world economy. Whether France understood it or not, the United States was not interested in Europe per se; it was interested in Europe as a vigorous economic entity. America's program of peace through trade and disarmament aimed at the internationalization of business. It was designed to

---

1945, French Military Mission to the United States, in Box 70, Marshall Papers. See also Joseph C. Grew's memorandum entitled "French Position," May 18, 1945, in Box 13, Hickerson-Matthews File, France, RG 59, NA.

122. Gary R. Hess, "Franklin Roosevelt and Indochina," *JAH*, LIX (September, 1972), 353–68.

123. Hull, *Memoirs*, II, 1599.

benefit the whole world, not a single power. It did not seek domination. Rather it tried to give direction to a more satisfactory economic world order. In contrast to France's European orientation, the United States had a global outlook, in which Germany's dynamic economic potential played such an integral and positive part that France's essentially negative approach to Germany conflicted fundamentally with America's policy.

Irreconcilable ideological differences between Nazi Germany and the United States assumed a more sinister character when Hitler threatened to upset America's vision of a peaceful world economic order. Unwilling to tolerate this challenge, the United States slowly but surely turned not against Hitler or Germany, but against the so-called new order the Fuehrer set out to impose on the world. Once again the United States was guided by global considerations that would benefit the rest of the world as well as itself. Such benevolent imperialism suited American business interests. But the United States also conceived it as the safest road to genuine peace.

Despite the conflicts and contradictions in Franco-American diplomatic relations during this period, there were enough long-term factors pulling the two nations together to stave off a complete breakdown. Essentially, the peoples of both countries continued to believe in human rights, democratic principles, and a certain degree of Franco-American political solidarity. They were quick to criticize each other, and they demanded more of each other than their respective governments were usually willing to grant. To avoid an undesirable degree of disillusionment, they were often kept in the dark. Americans were not told when General de Gaulle hampered Allied military operations. Many Frenchmen lived in a dreamworld assuming that Marshal Pétain and General de Gaulle were cooperating with each other to advance the liberation of France and that the general and the Americans got along harmoniously.

Remarkably, their differences and quarrels notwithstanding, Pétain and de Gaulle had more in common than met the eye. Both emphasized the sovereignty of France and the urgency of its rebirth, and both stressed the value of strong governmental authority. Both were touchy at the slightest American disregard of French sensitivities, and both considered the United States a vital factor in France's future. As much as they might challenge the United States, neither dared to go beyond the point of tolerable risk.

Ignoring incriminating charges, the United States tried to utilize the special contribution each had to make. It cooperated with Vichy until the end of the North African campaign, and from then on, it cooperated increasingly with the Free, or Fighting, French. Depending on the situation, Washington deemed it important to encourage both active and passive French resistance to the Axis. In this endeavor FDR reckoned with the French people as a third force, probably anti-Pétain by 1944 but not yet certain whether de Gaulle came as a soldier or politician.

The fact standing out in the historical balance sheet is that Vichy's promises and procrastinations in its dealings with Hitler were a ploy. Although in a few instances Darlan's collaboration with Hitler was open to question, the Vichy leaders rendered invaluable service to the anti-Hitler cause by not surrendering their fleet and colonies. Had these assets been in the hands of Germany before the invasion of Russia, they could have perilously influenced the sequence of Hitler's next theaters of operation. From the Allied point of view, by the time the United States entered the war, though fragmented politically, France had remained intact. De Gaulle's energetic campaign to unify it and overcome its great humiliation was greatly aided by the positive nature of his challenge and by his resourcefulness. FDR was compelled to make compromises.

The various powers on the international chessboard behaved in similar fashion. Great Britain and the United States differed on imperial, strategic, political, and economic questions, but they compromised sufficiently to win the war first before settling the affairs of a more peaceful world. The same held true with respect to the Soviet Union. Since self-preservation is the first law of international existence, national survival in wartime takes precedence over coexistence in peacetime. However disillusioning peace terms and their political ramifications may be, they depend largely on the state of affairs at the end of the war. To lay the foundation for lasting peace calls for restraint and wisdom. But the competitive national state system tolerates political compromises for victory more readily than for a peace without victory.

Conclusion

In considering Franco-American diplomatic relations from World War I to the end of World War II, it is interesting to observe the recurrence of the same problems. The governments of France and the United States, their peoples, and their politicians had themselves to blame for having permitted calamitous situations to arise that it was in their power to avert. Both France and Germany dreamed of at least continental supremacy, in violation of modern principles of self-determination. The kaiser and Hitler pretended to be broad-minded by suggesting a dignified role for France in a German-dominated Europe. Clemenceau, Foch, and de Gaulle considered peace with Germany possible if France controlled the Rhine and if Germany's industrial and war-making capacities were made harmless. In both wars France looked to the United States for rescue, whether the republic across the Atlantic considered undertaking such a mission or not. In both wars England proved to be a much more helpful partner than French prejudices were willing to acknowledge. And as much trouble as Russia caused in postwar years, it made invaluable contributions and enormous sacrifices during these wars. Italy's weaknesses, on the other hand, merely confirmed its limited power-political capacity.

Strategic considerations belatedly moved America to enter the two world wars. Its national interests demanded that Great Britain and France not be defeated by the Germans. Both wars advanced its power status and diminished Europe's vitality. The United States, moreover, lost no time moving into the vacuum created by these wars, to conquer the markets in Europe, Africa, and Latin America previously dominated by the newly distracted nations. To cite merely one other important parallel, the United States, whether under Wilson or Roosevelt, considered open world trade the best medicine for the well-being of mankind. In contrast, Europe's outdated political and economic rivalries, culminating in frequent crises leading to war, demonstrated that its leaders had not outgrown the tradition of past centuries. But the twentieth century called for more than illusory national supremacy.

France and the United States learned to live with their persistent frictions, realizing that they needed each other. France valued America's contributions in both world wars and its vital economic assistance following them. Aware of its ancient historic ties and its strategically important geographic link with France, the United States also looked upon it as a dynamic cultural and democratic center. The two countries usually found enough in common to perpetuate their mutual relationship. But since the First World War the United States has repeatedly been called upon to make extraordinary sacrifices to help preserve the territorial integrity and financial viability of France.

Naturally, an upheaval like the Second World War prompted human minds to search for explanations. Perhaps the French debacle may be better understood in broad historical terms than by the mass of contemporary details. The national revolutions clamored for by Pétain and de Gaulle, though tilted differently, were both basically of a moral nature. As Léon Blum has suggested, the private and public virtues of France's old bourgeoisie broke down in the environment of twentieth-century capitalism. "Its onetime rigid code of honor has weakened and collapsed under the influence of its contacts with modern big business," Blum wrote. As it lost its own sense of inward dignity, it also lost its "energy and the creative vigor of the mind." Its vulgar attachment to selfish goals stifled its sense of patriotism.

Assistant Secretary of State Adolf A. Berle, Jr., believed that in the long run a ruthless conqueror like Hitler could not "indefinitely eliminate the spiritual quality of things, without breaking up the human organism." Berle attributed to Europe's, not just Hitler's, fantasy of strength Europe's essential weakness. While admitting that America's huge industrial system was also a factor in producing this weakness, he noted a difference. American capitalist barons "achieved their position by strength, as against the European manipulator-intriguer-politician-grafter type which has been the governing class in Europe." Like the court favorites who ruled Europe just before the French Revolution, their modern prototypes failed their nation.[1]

1. Berle Diary, June 30, 1940, in Container 212, Berle Papers.

In the course of his Princeton Seminars in March, 1954, former Secretary of State Dean Acheson went more elaborately back into history to trace the structural factors that had created a government in France so weak that its inability to deal with problems resulted in a revolutionary tradition. These periodic upheavals contributed to the people's distrust of the state. Historically, the effort of the monarchy since long before Louis XIV to weaken the French nobility separated it from any roots in local communities. In Acheson's words, it "produced a propertied class in France which is totally irresponsible and totally without patriotism of any sort." In contrast to the propertied English upper class, which transferred power to the lower classes to maintain jointly with them a fair and stable government, their French counterpart, he observed, took "their money out to avoid taxation, to do everything they can to make life more pleasant for themselves, whereas the position of the workers becomes more difficult." More so than in other countries, in addition, a steady inflation has plagued France since the First World War. In conjunction with an omnipresent bureaucracy, which encourages corruption and evasion, this inflation hurt France badly. As a consequence, France lost not only the confidence of the masses and of world leaders but also its capacity to act decisively. Acheson found it particularly frustrating that France often made the rest of the world wait until it overcame its latest ministerial crisis. Unless France corrected these historically rooted shortcomings, the perpetuation of its inability to act effectively on a global scale would, in his opinion, continue to stymie the entire West. In other words, the recent past had demonstrated that France must reorganize itself internally, in a structural and civic sense, in order to qualify for the world role to which it aspired. In the process of this transformation it had to acquire another discipline: the faculty to function as an international team member. Despite its frequent allusions to collective security, on this goal, too, its past often stood in its way.[2]

America's performance in this war could not have been duplicated by any other power. The rapid mobilization of its industry and military might overawed friends and foes alike, even more so than in World War I. Its ability to move within a short span of time from one extreme to another, from peacetime to wartime production, from

2. "Princeton Seminars," March, 1954, Reel 7, in Dean Acheson Papers (microfilm), Harry S. Truman Library, Independence, Mo.

near pacifism to total war, and from relative isolationism to world leadership, contributed massively to the defeat of the Axis.

But what mattered most to the exhausted peoples and ruined countries at the end of the war was how the United States would treat them in the future. Would it help them, both friends and former foes, get on their feet again? Would it insist on the liquidation of the old empires? Would it not only promote democracy abroad but also practice it by respecting their rights and aspirations? To their relief, America indeed lived up to its traditional concepts of public morality.

Having learned the hard way that its own prosperity and peace were closely linked to sound economic and financial practices around the globe, the United States assumed enlarged responsibilities after World War II. France and England, who ultimately lost their empires following their "victories" in the two world wars, taught the United States that the earnest search for peaceful solutions during peacetime is less costly than modern war. World War II grew out of the policies following World War I. In the 1920s France and the United States lacked the vision and the wisdom to remove potential threats to peace effectively. The attempt to maintain an unsatisfactory status quo was particularly resented by Germany and Japan. Consequently, they chose to go to war and temporarily experienced the illusion of triumph. The ultimate defeat of the Axis powers by the Soviet Union and the Western democracies not only assured the rebirth of France, but it gave mankind another—perhaps a final—chance for the tolerant coexistence of diverse political and economic systems.

Selected Bibliography

My original intention was to write merely a background chapter for the period from 1918 to 1932. It soon became apparent, however, that I needed to go back to 1914 and add my own research to existing works. The systematic consultation of the State Department's *Foreign Relations of the United States* and the available documents in the archives of the French Foreign Ministry has been supplemented by other primary and scholarly secondary publications. What follows is a list of the most important sources for this study.

I
Manuscript Sources

Yale University Library, New Haven

Auchincloss, Gordon. Papers.
House, Colonel Edward. Papers.
McCormick, Vance C. Papers.
Polk, Frank L. Papers.
Stimson, Henry L. Papers.
Wiseman, Sir William. Papers.

Seeley G. Mudd Manuscript Library, Princeton

Lansing, Robert. Papers.

Library of Congress, Washington, D.C.

Hughes, Charles Evans. Papers.
Hull, Cordell. Papers.
Kellogg, Frank B. Papers.
Lansing, Robert. Papers.
Wilson, Woodrow. Papers and Correspondence (microfilm).

National Archives. Diplomatic and Military Branches. Washington, D.C.

Record Group 59. Department of State. Confidential File, Decimal File, and Hickerson-Matthews File, France, 1933–45.
Record Group 218. Admiral Leahy Files.
Record Group 226. Office of Strategic Services. Reports, 1942–45. Relation France–United States.

Franklin D. Roosevelt Library, Hyde Park, New York

Berle, Adolf A., Jr. Papers.
Hopkins, Harry. Papers.
Morgenthau, Henry. Papers.
President's Official File, 1933–45.
President's Personal File, 1933–45.
President's Secretary File, 1933–45.

Houghton Research Library, Harvard University, Cambridge

Messersmith, George S. Correspondence.

Harry S. Truman Library, Independence, Missouri

Acheson, Dean. Papers (microfilm).
Elsey, George M. Papers.

Dwight D. Eisenhower Library, Abilene, Kansas

Eisenhower, Dwight D. Pre-Presidential Papers.
Jackson, C. D. Papers.
Smith, Walter B. Papers. Documents of Allied Command.

General George C. Marshall Research Library, Lexington, Virginia

Marshall, George C. Papers.

Archives du Ministère des Affaires Etrangères, Paris

Affaires Politiques Générales, 1920–1940.
Guerre 1914–1918, Etats-Unis.
Guerre 1939–1945, Papiers Charles de Gaulle à Londres et Algérie.
Herriot, Edouard. Papiers.
Jusserand, J. J. Papiers.
Paul-Boncour, Joseph. Papiers.
Tardieu, André. Papiers.
Série B., Relations Commerciales. Sous-série Délibérations Internationales.
Série Guerre. Sous-série Paix.
Série Société des Nations.

Série Y, 1918–1940, Affaires Internationales.

Fondation des Sciences Politiques, Paris

Blum, Léon. Papiers.
Daladier, Edouard. Papiers.

Prime Minister's Office, London

Operational Papers. May, 1940–July, 1945. PREM 3/1–514 (microfilm).

II
Published Documents

Auswärtiges Amt. *Akten zur deutschen auswärtigen Politik, 1918–1945*. Series D, 1937–1945. Baden-Baden, 1950–52.

———. *Documents on German Foreign Policy, 1918–1945*. Series D, 1937–1945. 13 vols. Washington, D.C., 1949.

Baker, Ray Stannard, and W. E. Dodd, eds. *Woodrow Wilson: Public Papers*. 6 vols. New York, 1925–27.

Dregas, Jane, ed. *Soviet Documents on Foreign Policy, 1917–1941*. London, 1953.

France. *Journal Officiel de la République Française: Débats Parlementaires*, 1920–40.

———. *Le Journal de la France Libre à Londres. La Marseillaise*, 1943–45.

———. Ministère des Affaires Etrangères, Commission de publication des documents relatifs aux origines de la guerre 1939–1945. *Documents Diplomatiques Français, 1932–1939*. 1e et 2e séries. Paris, 1963–81.

———. Ministère des Affaires Etrangères. *The French Yellow Book: Diplomatic Documents, 1938–1939*. New York, 1940.

Goodrich, Leland M., and Marie Carroll, eds. *Documents on American Foreign Relations, 1939–1946*. 8 vols. Boston, 1940–48.

Great Britain, Foreign Office. *Documents on British Foreign Policy, 1919–1939*. Edited by E. L. Woodward and Rohan Butler. 42 vols. London, 1946–71.

Hubatsch, Walter, ed. *Hitler's Weisungen für die Kriegführung, 1939–1945: Dokumente des Oberkommandos der Wehrmacht*. Frankfurt, 1962.

Myers, W. S., ed. *The State Papers and Other Public Writings of Herbert Hoover*. 2 vols. New York, 1970.

Rosenman, Samuel, ed. *Public Papers and Addresses of Franklin D. Roosevelt*. 13 vols. New York, 1938–1950.

U.S. Congress, Senate. *Hearings Before the Committee on Finance, U.S. Senate, June 9, 10, 11 and 18, 1926: French Debt Settlement*. 69th Cong., 1st Sess.

U.S. Department of State. *The Foreign Relations of the United States. Diplomatic Papers, 1914–1945*. Washington, D.C. Issued annually.

———. *The Conference at Quebec, 1944*. Washington, D.C., 1945.

———. *The Conferences at Cairo and Tehran, 1943*. Washington, D.C., 1961.

———. *The Conferences at Malta and Yalta*. Washington, D.C., 1945.

———. *The Conferences at Washington, 1941–42 and Casablanca, 1943*. Washington, D.C., 1968.

———. *The Lansing Papers, 1914–1920*. 2 vols. Washington, D.C., 1940.

U.S. Department of the Navy, and Germany, Kriegsmarine, Oberkommando. *Führer Conferences on Matters Dealing with the German Navy, 1939–1940, 1942–1945*. 7 vols. Washington, D.C., 1946–47.

U.S. World War Foreign Debt Commission. *Combined Annual Reports of the World War Foreign Debt Commission*. Washington, D.C., 1927.

III
Books, Articles, and Dissertations

A. Period 1914–1920

Baker, Ray Stannard. *Woodrow Wilson and World Settlement*. 3 vols. New York, 1922.

Bardoux, Jacques. *De Paris à Spa: La bataille diplomatique pour la paix française*. Paris, 1921.

Birnbaum, Karl E. *Peace Moves and U-Boat Warfare: A Study of Imperial Germany's Policy Toward the United States, April 18, 1916–January 9, 1917*. Hamden, Conn., 1970.

Burnett, Philip M. *Reparation at the Paris Peace Conference from the Standpoint of the American Delegation*. 2 vols. New York, 1965.

Clemenceau, Georges. *Grandeur and Misery of Victory*. Translated by F. M. Atkinson. New York, 1930.

Clémentel, Etienne. *La France et la politique économique interalliée*. Paris, 1931.

Dawes, Warrington, ed. *The War Memoirs of William Graves Sharp, American Ambassador to France, 1914–1919*. London, 1931.

Doerris, Reihard R. "Imperial Berlin and Washington: New Light on Germany's Foreign Policy and America's Entry into World War I." *Central European History*, XI (1978), 23–49.

Fowler, W. B. *British-American Relations, 1917–1918: The Role of Sir William Wiseman*. Princeton, 1969.

Haupts, Leo. *Deutsche Friedenspolitik 1918–19: Eine Alternative zur Machtpolitik des Ersten Weltkrieges*. Düsseldorf, 1976.

Hendrick, Burton J. *The Life and Letters of Walter H. Page*. 4 vols. New York, 1924.

Herwig, Holger H. "Admirals Versus Generals: The War Aims of the Imperial German Navy, 1914–1918." *Central European History*, V (1972), 208–33.

Hogan, Michael J. "The United States and the Problem of International Economic Control: American Attitudes Toward European Reconstruction, 1918–1920." *Pacific Historical Review*, XLIV (1975), 84–103.

Hohlfeld, Andreas. *Versailles und die russische Frage, 1918–1919*. Hamburg, 1940.

House, E. M. *Intimate Papers*. Edited by Charles Seymour. 4 vols. Boston, 1926–28.

Kaspi, André. *Le temps des américains: Le concours américain à la France en 1917–1918*. Paris, 1976.

Kennan, George F. *Soviet-American Relations, 1917–1920*. 2 vols. Princeton, 1956–58.

Levin, N. Gordon, Jr. *Woodrow Wilson and World Politics: America's Response to War and Revolution*. New York, 1969.

Link, Arthur S. *Wilson*. 4 vols. Princeton, 1947–64.

———. *Woodrow Wilson: Revolution, War, and Peace*. Arlington Heights, Ill. 1979.

Link, Arthur S., Jean-Baptiste Duroselle, Ernst Fränkel, and H. G. Nicholas. *Wilson's Diplomacy: An International Symposium*. Cambridge, Mass., 1973.

Lloyd George, David. *Memoirs of the Peace Conference*. 2 vols. New Haven, 1939.

McDougall, Walter A. *France's Rhineland Diplomacy, 1914–1924: The Bid for a Balance of Power in Europe*. Princeton, 1978.

Mantoux, Paul. *Les délibérations du Conseil des Quatre, 24 mars–28 juin, 1919*. 2 vols.; Paris, 1955.

May, Ernest R. *The World War and American Isolation, 1914–1917*. Cambridge, Mass., 1963.

Mayer, Arno. *Politics and Diplomacy of Peacemaking: Containment and Counterrevolution at Versailles, 1918–1919*. New York, 1967.

Miller, David Hunter. *My Diary at the Conference of Paris; With Documents*. 21 vols. New York, 1924.

Néré, Jacques. *The Foreign Policy of France from 1914 to 1945*. Boston, 1975.

Noble, George Bernard. *Wilsonian Diplomacy, the Versailles Peace, and French Public Opinion*. New York, 1935.

Olphe-Galliard, G. *Histoire économique et financière de la guerre (1914–1918)*. Paris, 1923.

Parrini, Carl P. *Heir to Empire: United States Economic Diplomacy, 1916–1923*. Pittsburgh, 1969.

Parsons, Edward B. *Wilsonian Diplomacy: Allied-American Rivalries in War and Peace*. St. Louis, 1978.

Pingaud, Albert. *Histoire diplomatique de la France pendant la guerre*. 2 vols. Paris, 1938.

Renouvin, Pierre. *La crise européenne et la première guerre mondiale (1904–1918)*. Paris, 1969.

———. *War and Aftermath, 1914–1929*. Translated by Rémy Inglis Hall. New York, 1968.

Ribot, Alexandre. *Journal et correspondances inédites d'Alexandre Ribot, 1914–1922*. Paris, 1936.

Rothwell, V. H. *British War Aims and Peace Diplomacy, 1914–1918*. Oxford, 1971.

Schwabe, Klaus. *Deutsche Revolution and Wilson-Frieden: Die amerikanische und deutsche Friedensstrategie zwischen Ideologie und Machtpolitik 1918/19*. Düsseldorf, 1971.

Seymour, Charles. *Letters from the Paris Peace Conference*. Edited by Harold B. Whiteman, Jr. New Haven, 1965.

Tardieu, André. *The Truth About the Treaty*. Indianapolis, 1921.

Temperly, Harold W. *A History of the Peace Conference of Paris*. 6 vols. London, 1920–24.

Tillman, Seth P. *Anglo-American Relations at the Paris Peace Conference of 1919*. Princeton, 1961.

Trask, David F. *The United States in the Supreme War Council: American War Aims and Inter-Allied Strategy, 1917–1918*. Middletown, Conn., 1961.

Truchy, Henri. *The War Finance of France*. New Haven, 1927.

Walworth, Arthur. *America's Moment, 1918: American Diplomacy at the End of World War I*. New York, 1977.

Wright, Gordon. *Raymond Poincaré and the French Presidency*. Stanford, 1942.

Yates, Louis. *United States and French Security, 1917–1921*. New York, 1957.

Zeman, Z. A. B. *A Diplomatic History of the First World War*. London, 1971.

B. Period 1920–1933

Aldcroft, Derek H. *The European Economy, 1914–1970*. New York, 1978.

Artaud, Denise. "Dialogue de sourds de part et d'autre de l'Atlantique." *Revue Historique*, DXXX (1979), 366–82.

———. *La question des dettes interalliées de la reconstruction de l'Europe (1917–1929)*. 2 vols. Lille, 1978.

———. *La reconstruction de l'Europe, 1919–1929*. Paris, 1973.

Bariéty, Jacques. *Les relations franco-allemandes après la première guerre mondiale*. Paris, 1977.

Bennett, Edward W. *Germany and the Diplomacy of the Financial Crisis, 1931*. Cambridge, Mass., 1962.

Brandes, Joseph. *Herbert Hoover and Economic Policy: Department of Commerce Policy, 1921–28*. Pittsburgh, 1962.

Brüning, Heinrich. *Memoiren, 1918–1934*. Stuttgart, 1970.

———. *Die Vereinigten Staaten und Europa*. Stuttgart, 1954.

Buckley, Thomas H. *The United States and the Washington Conference, 1921–1922*. Knoxville, 1970.

Carlton, David. "Great Britain and the Coolidge Naval Disarmament Conference of 1927." *Political Science Quarterly*, LXXXIII (1968), 573–98.

Dawes, Charles G. *Journal as Ambassador to Great Britain*. New York, 1939.

Duroselle, Jean-Baptiste. *From Wilson to Roosevelt: Foreign Policy of the United States, 1913–1945*. Cambridge, Mass., 1963.

Edge, Walter. *Jerseyman's Journal*. Princeton, 1948.

Ellis, L. Ethan. *Republican Foreign Policy, 1921–1933*. New Brunswick, N.J., 1968.

Feis, Herbert. *The Diplomacy of the Dollar: First Era, 1919–1932*. Baltimore, 1950.

Ferrell, Robert H. *American Diplomacy in the Great Depression: Hoover-Stimson Foreign Policy, 1929–1933*. New Haven, 1957.

———. *Peace in Their Time: The Origins of the Kellogg-Briand Pact*. New Haven, 1952.

Flandin, Pierre Étienne. *Politique française, 1919–1940*. Paris, 1947.

Fohlen, Claude. *La France de l'entre-deux-guerres (1917–1939)*. Paris, 1972.

Gescher, Dieter Bruno. *Die Vereinigten Staaten von Nordamerika und die Reparationen, 1920–1924*. Bonn, 1956.

Girard, Jolyon Pitt. "Bridge on the Rhine: American Diplomacy and the Rhineland, 1919–1923." Ph.D. dissertation, University of Maryland, 1973.

Glad, Betty. *Charles Evans Hughes and the Illusions of Innocence: A Study in American Diplomacy*. Urbana, Ill., 1966.

Hirsch, Felix. "Stresemann, Ballin, und die Vereinigten Staaten." *Vierteljahrshefte für Zeitgeschichte*, III (1955), 20–36.

Hogan, Michael J. *Informal Entente: The Private Structure of Cooperation in Anglo-American Economic Diplomacy, 1918–1928*. Columbia, Mo., 1977.

Hoover, Herbert. *The Memoirs of Herbert Hoover, Volume III: The Great Depression 1929–1941*. New York, 1952.

Hughes, Charles Evans. *The Pathway to Peace: Representative Addresses Delivered During His Term as Secretary of State (1921–1925)*. New York, 1925.

Jacobson, Jon. *Locarno Diplomacy: Germany and the West, 1925–1929*. Princeton, 1972.

———. "The Strategies of French Foreign Policy after World War I." *Journal of Modern History*, LV (1983), 78–95.

Kemp, Tom. *The French Economy, 1913–39: The History of a Decline*. London, 1972.

Leffler, Melvin P. *The Elusive Quest: America's Pursuit of European Stability and French Security, 1919–1933*. Chapel Hill, 1979.

Link, Werner. *Die amerikanische Stabilisierungspolitik in Deutschland, 1921–32*. Düsseldorf, 1970.

Maier, Charles S. *Recasting Bourgeois Europe: Stabilization in France, Germany, and Italy in the Decade After World War I.* Princeton, 1975.

Marks, Sally. *The Illusion of Peace: International Relations in Europe, 1918–1933.* New York, 1976.

———. "The Myths of Reparations." *Central European History,* XI (1978), 231–55.

———. "Reparations Reconsidered; a Reminder." *Central European History,* II (1969), 356–65.

Maxelon, Michael-Olaf. *Stresemann und Frankreich: Deutsche Politik der Ost-West Balance.* Düsseldorf, 1972.

Medlicott, W. N. *British Foreign Policy Since Versailles, 1919–1963.* London, 1968.

Miller, David Hunter. *The Peace Pact of Paris: A Study of the Briand-Kellogg Treaty.* New York, 1928.

Myers, William Starr. *The Foreign Policies of Herbert Hoover, 1929–1933.* New York, 1940.

O'Connor, R. G. *Perilous Equilibrium: The United States and the London Naval Conference of 1930.* Lawrence, Kan., 1962.

Petit, Lucien. *Histoire des finances extérieures de la France: Le règlement des dettes interalliées (1919–1929).* Paris, 1932.

Poincaré, Raymond. *Au service de la France: Neuf années de souvenirs.* 10 vols. Paris, 1926–33.

Rössler, Helmut, ed. *Locarno und die Weltpolitik, 1924–1932.* Göttingen, 1969.

Sauvy, A. *Histoire économique de la France entre les deux guerres.* 2 vols. Paris, 1965–67.

Schrecker, Ellen. *The Hired Money: The French Debt to the United States.* New York, 1978.

Schuker, Stephen A. *The End of French Predominance in Europe: The Financial Crisis of 1924 and the Adoption of the Dawes Plan.* Chapel Hill, 1976.

Simonds, Frank. *American Foreign Policy in the Post-War Years.* Baltimore, 1935.

Strauss, David. *Menace in the West: The Rise of French Anti-Americanism in Modern Times.* Westport, Conn., 1978.

Sutton, Eric, ed. and trans. *Gustav Stresemann: His Diaries, Letters, and Papers.* 3 vols. London, 1935–40.

Tardieu, André. *Devant l'obstacle: L'Amérique et nous.* Paris, 1927.

Trachtenberg, Marc. *Reparations in World Politics: France and European Economic Diplomacy, 1916–1923.* New York, 1980.

Wandel, Eckhard. *Die Bedeutung der Vereinigten Staaten von Amerika für das deutsche Reparationsproblem, 1924–1929.* Tübingen, 1971.

Warner, Geoffrey. *Pierre Laval and the Eclipse of France.* London, 1968.

Weill-Reynal, Etienne. *La politique française des réparations.* Paris, 1945.

Weinberg, Gerhard L. "The Defeat of Germany in 1918 and the European Balance of Power." *Central European History,* II (1969), 248–60.

Wilson, Joan Hoff. *American Business and Foreign Policy, 1920–1933*. Lexington, Ky., 1971.
Wolfers, Arnold. *Britain and France Between Two Wars: Conflicting Strategies of Peace Since Versailles*. New York, 1940.
Zimmermann, Ludwig. *Deutsche Aussenpolitik in der Ära der Weimarer Republik*. Göttingen, 1958.
———. *Frankreichs Ruhrpolitik: Von Versailles bis zum Dawesplan*. Zürich, 1971.

C. Period 1933–1939

Adamthwaite, Anthony. *France and the Coming of the Second World War, 1936–1939*. London, 1977.
Bankwitz, Philip C. F. *Maxime Weygand and Civil-Military Relations in Modern France*. Cambridge, Mass., 1967.
Bennett, Edward W. *German Rearmament and the West, 1932–33*. Princeton, N.J., 1979.
Berle, Beatrice B., and Travis B. Jacobs, eds. *Navigating the Rapids, 1918–1971: From the Papers of Adolf A. Berle*. New York, 1973.
Blum, John Morton. *From the Morgenthau Diaries*. 3 vols. Boston, 1959–67.
Blum, Léon. *L'Oeuvre de Léon Blum*. 9 vols. Paris, 1954–72.
Bonnet, Georges. *De Munich à la guerre: Défense de la paix*. Paris, 1967.
———. *Vingt ans de vie politique, 1918–1938: De Clemenceau à Daladier*. Paris, 1969.
Bowers, Claude G. *My Mission to Spain: Watching the Rehearsal for World War II*. New York, 1954.
Challener, Richard D., ed. *From Isolation to Containment, 1921–1952: Three Decades of American Foreign Policy from Harding to Truman*. London, 1970.
Claudel, Paul. *Cahiers Paul Claudel: Claudel diplomate*. Paris, 1962.
Colton, Joel. *Léon Blum: Humanist in Politics*. New York, 1966.
Craig, Gordon A., and Felix Gilbert, eds. *The Diplomats, 1919–1939*. Princeton, 1953.
Dallek, Robert. *Franklin Roosevelt and American Foreign Policy, 1932–1945*. New York, 1979.
Detweiler, D. S. *Hitler, Franco and Gibraltar: Die Frage des spanischen Kriegseintritts in den Zweiten Weltkrieg*. Wiesbaden, 1962.
Divine, Robert A. *The Illusion of Neutrality*. Chicago, 1962.
Dreifort, John E. "France, the Powers, and the Far Eastern Crisis, 1937–1939." *Historian*, XXXIX (1977), 733–53.
———. *Yvon Delbos at the Quai d'Orsay: French Foreign Policy During the Popular Front, 1936–38*. Lawrence, Kan., 1973.
Dülffer, Jost. *Weimar, Hitler und die Marine Reichspolitik und Flottenbau, 1920–1939*. Düsseldorf, 1973.
Duroselle, Jean-Baptiste. *La Décadence: 1932–1939*. Paris, 1979.

François-Poncet, André. *The Fateful Years; Memoirs of a French Ambassador in Berlin, 1931–1938*. Translated by Jacques LeClerq. New York, 1949.

Funke, Manfred. *Sanktionen und Kanonen: Hitler, Mussolini und der internationale Abessinienkonflikt 1934–1936*. Düsseldorf, 1971.

Furnia, Arthur H. *The Diplomacy of Appeasement: Anglo-French Relations and the Prelude to World War II, 1931–1938*. Washington, D.C., 1960.

Gauthier, Alexandre. "Les Etats-Unis et l'Europe." *Revue d'histoire diplomatique*, LI (1937), 241–65.

Haight, John McVickar, Jr. *American Aid to France, 1938–1940*. New York, 1970.

———. "France and the Aftermath of Roosevelt's 'Quarantine Speech.'" *World Politics*, XIV (1962), 283–306.

———. "France, the United States, and the Munich Crisis." *Journal of Modern History*, XXXII (1960), 340–58.

———. "Les négotiations relatives aux achats d'avions américains par la France pendant la période qui précéda immédiatement la guerre." *Revue d'histoire de la deuxième guerre mondiale*, LVIII (April, 1965), 1–34.

Harris, Bruce, Jr. *The United States and the Italo-Ethiopian Crisis*. Stanford, 1964.

Hauser, Oswald. *England und das Dritte Reich: Eine dokumentierte Geschichte der englisch-deutschen Beziehungen von 1933 bis 1939 auf Grund unveröffentlicher Akten aus dem britischen Staatsarchiv*. Stuttgart, 1972.

———, ed. *Weltpolitik 1933–1939: 13 Vorträge*. Frankfurt, 1973.

Herriot, Édouard. *Jadis: D'une guerre à l'autre, 1914–36*. Paris, 1952.

Hildebrand, Klaus. *The Foreign Policy of the Third Reich*. Translated by Anthony Fothergill. Berkeley, 1970.

Hillgruber, Andreas. *Germany and the Two World Wars*. Translated by William C. Kirby. Cambridge, Mass., 1981.

Hooker, Nancy H., ed. *The Moffat Papers: Selections from the Diplomatic Journals of Jay Pierrepont Moffat, 1919–1943*. Cambridge, Mass., 1956.

Hull, Cordell. *The Memoirs of Cordell Hull*. 2 vols. New York, 1948.

Iriye, Akira. *After Imperialism: The Search for a New Order in the Far East, 1921–1931*. Cambridge, Mass., 1965.

Junker, Detlef. *Der unteilbare Weltmarkt: Das ökonomische Interesse in der Aussenpolitik der USA, 1933–1941*. Stuttgart, 1975.

Levy, Roger, Guy Lacam, and Andrew Roth. *French Interests and Policies in the Far East*. New York, 1941.

Meinck, Gerhard. *Hitler und die deutsche Aufrüstung, 1933–1939*. Wiesbaden, 1959.

Merkes, M. *Die deutsche Politik gegenüber dem spanishchen Bürgerkrieg, 1936–1939*. Bonn, 1961.

Offner, Arnold A. *American Appeasement: United States Foreign Policy and Germany, 1933–1938*. Cambridge, Mass., 1969.

———, ed. *America and the Origins of World War II, 1933–1941*. Boston, 1971.

Parker, R. A. C. "Great Britain, France and the Ethiopian Crisis, 1935–1936." *English Historical Review*, LXXXIX (April 1974), 293–332.
Paul-Boncour, Joseph. *Entre deux guerres: Souvenirs sur la IIIe République, sur les chemins de la défaite*. 3 vols. Paris, 1946.
Ratliff, Ann. "Les relations diplomatiques entre la France et les Etats-Unis (du 29 septembre 1938 au 16 juin 1940)." *Revue d'histoire de la deuxième guerre mondiale*, LXXV (1969), 1–40.
Reynaud, Paul. *In the Thick of the Fight, 1930–1945*. Translated by James D. Lambert. New York, 1955.
Roskill, Stephen. *Naval Policy Between the Wars*. 2 vols. Annapolis, 1976.
Schröder, H.-J. *Deutschland und die Vereinigten Staaten 1933–1939. Wirtschaft und Politik in der Entwicklung des deutsch-amerikanischen Gegensatzes*. Wiesbaden, 1970.
Smith, J. J. "FDR and the Brussels Conference, 1937." *Michigan Academician*, XIV (1981), 109–22.
Sommer, Walter. *Die Weltmacht USA im Urteil der Französischen Publizistik, 1924–1939*. Tübingen, 1967.
Traina, Richard P. *American Diplomacy and the Spanish Civil War*. Bloomington, 1968.
Williams, William A. *American-Russian Relations, 1781–1947*. New York, 1952.
Wilson, Hugh Robert. *Diplomat Between Wars*. New York, 1941.
Young, Robert J. "French Policy and the Munich Crisis of 1938: A Reappraisal." Canadian Historical Association *Historical Papers* (1970), 186–206.

D. Period 1939–1945

Baudouin, Paul. *The Private Diaries (March 1940 to January 1941) of Paul Baudouin*. Translated by Charles Petrie. London, 1948.
Birkenhead, Frederick Winston. *The Life of Lord Halifax*. London, 1965.
Bloch, Marc. *Strange Defeat: A Statement of Evidence Written in 1940*. Translated by Gerard Hopkins. New York, 1968.
Brooks, Russell. "A Gentleman's Agreement." *U.S. Naval Institute Proceedings*, LXXVIII (1952), 701–11.
———. "The Unknown Darlan." *U.S. Naval Institute Proceedings*, LXXXI (1955), 879–92.
Butcher, Harry Cecil. *My Three Years with Eisenhower*. New York, 1946.
Cairns, John C. "Great Britain and the Fall of France: A Study in Allied Disunity." *Journal of Modern History*, XXVII (1955), 365–409.
Campbell, Thomas M., and George C. Herring, eds. *The Diaries of Edward R. Stettinius, Jr., 1943–1946*. New York, 1975.
Chandler, Alfred D., Jr., *et al.*, eds. *The Papers of Dwight D. Eisenhower: The War Years*. 5 vols. Baltimore, 1970–78.
Chautemps, Camille. *Cahiers Secrets de l'Armistice, 1939–1940*. Paris, 1963.
Churchill, Winston S. *The Second World War*. 6 vols. Boston, 1948–53.

Clark, Mark. *Calculated Risk*. New York, 1950.

Clarke, Richard. *Anglo-American Economic Collaboration in War and Peace, 1942–1949*. Oxford, 1982.

Colbert, Evelyn. "The Road Not Taken: Decolonization and Independence in Indonesia and Indochina." *Foreign Affairs*, LI (1973), 608–28.

Crozier, Brian. *De Gaulle*. New York, 1973.

De Gaulle, Charles. *War Memoirs*. 3 vols. New York, 1955–60.

Dilks, David, ed. *The Diaries of Sir Alexander Cadogan, O.M., 1938–1945*. New York, 1972.

Dougherty, James. J. *The Politics of Wartime Aid: American Economic Assistance to France and French Northwest Africa, 1941–1946*. Westport, Conn., 1978.

Eckes, Alfred E., Jr. *A Search for Solvency: Bretton Woods and the International Monetary System, 1941–1971*. Austin, 1975.

Eden, Anthony. *The Memoirs of Anthony Eden: The Reckoning*. Boston, 1965.

Eisenhower, Dwight D. *Crusade in Europe*. New York, 1948.

Feis, Herbert. *Between War and Peace: The Potsdam Conference*. Princeton, 1960.

Friedländer, Saul. *Prelude to Downfall: Hitler and the United States (1939–1941)*. Translated from the French by Aline B. and Alexander Werth. New York, 1967.

Funk, Arthur Layton. *Charles de Gaulle: The Crucial Years, 1943–1944*. Norman, Okla., 1959.

———. "Eisenhower, Giraud and the Command of TORCH." *Military Affairs*, XXXV (1971), 103–108.

———. *The Politics of TORCH: The Allied Landings and the Algiers Putsch, 1942*. Lawrence, Kan., 1974.

Funke, Manfred. *Hitler, Deutschland und die Mächte: Materialen zur Aussenpolitik des Dritten Reiches*. Düsseldorf, 1976.

Gibson, Hugh, ed. *The Ciano Diaries, 1939–1943*. New York, 1946.

Giraud, Henri Honoré. *Un seul but, la victoire, Alger 1942–1944*. Paris, 1949.

Gordon, Bertram M. *Collaborationism in France During the Second World War*. Ithaca, N.Y., 1980.

Griffiths, Richard. *Marshal Pétain*. London, 1970.

Hachey, Thomas E. *Confidential Dispatches: Analyses of America by the British Ambassador, 1939–1945*. Evanston, Ill., 1974.

Halder, Franz. *Kriegstagebuch. Tägliche Aufzeichnungen des Chefs des Generalstabes des Heeres, 1939–1942*. Edited by Hans-Adolf Jacobsen. 3 vols. Stuttgart, 1962–64.

Hillgruber, Andreas. "Der Faktor Amerika in Hitler's Strategie, 1938–1941." In Wolfgang Michalka, *Nationalsozialistische Aussenpolitik*. Darmstadt, 1978.

———. *Hitlers Strategie. Politik und Kriegsführung 1940–1941*. Frankfurt, 1965.

Hytier, Adrienne Doris. *Two Years of French Foreign Policy: Vichy, 1940–1942*. Paris, 1958.

Jäckel, Eberhard. *Frankreich in Hitlers Europa*. Stuttgart, 1966.

Jacobsen, Hans-Adolf. *Der Weg zur Teilung der Welt: Politik und Strategie 1939–1945*. Bonn, 1977.

Joliet, Paul Victor II. "French-American Relations and the Political Role of the French Army, 1943–1945." Ph.D. dissertation, State University of New York at Binghamton, 1978.

Kolko, Gabriel. *The Politics of War: The World and United States Foreign Policy, 1943–1945*. New York, 1968.

LaFeber, Walter. "Roosevelt, Churchill and Indochina: 1942–1945." *American Historical Review*, LXXX (1975), 1277–95.

Langer, William L., and S. Everett Gleason. *The Challenge to Isolation, 1937–1940*. New York, 1952.

———. *The Undeclared War, 1940–1941*. New York, 1953.

Laval, Pierre. *The Diary of Pierre Laval*. New York, 1948.

Ledwidge, Bernard. *De Gaulle*. New York, 1982.

Loewenheim, Francis L., Harold D. Langley and Manfred Jonas, eds. *Roosevelt and Churchill: Their Secret Wartime Correspondence*. New York, 1975.

Loveland, William Alan. "Deliverance from Dictatorship: American Diplomacy Towards France During the 1940's." Ph.D. dissertation, Rutgers University, 1979.

Marie de la Gorce, Paul. "De Gaulle et les Américains." *La Nef*, XXVI (February–April, 1966), 59–77.

Massigli, René. *Une comédie des erreurs, 1943–1956: Souvenirs et réflexions sur une étape de la construction européenne*. Paris, 1978.

Mauriac, Claude. *Diaries, 1944–1954: The Other de Gaulle*. Translated by M. Budberg and G. Latta. New York, 1973.

Metzmacher, Helmut. "Deutsch-englische Ausgleichbemühungen im Sommer 1939." *Vierteljahrshefte für Zeitgeschichte*, XIV (1966), 369–412.

Moltmann, Günter. *Amerikas Deutschlandpolitik im Zweiten Weltkrieg: Kriegs- und Friedensziele 1941–1945*. Heidelberg, 1958.

Murphy, Robert. *Diplomat Among Warriors*. New York, 1964.

Paxton, Robert O. *Vichy France: Old Guard and New Order, 1940–1944*. New York, 1972.

Pogue, Forrest C. *George C. Marshall: Ordeal and Hope, 1939-1942*. New York, 1967.

———. *George C. Marshall: Organizer of Victory, 1943–1945*. New York, 1973.

Queille, Pierre. "Les diplomates anglaise et américaine vis-à-vis de la France vaincue (1940–1942): Un schéma d'ensemble." *Revue d'histoire diplomatique*, XCIV (1980), 230–50.

———. *Histoire diplomatique de Vichy: Pétain Diplomate*. Paris, 1977.

Ratliff, Ann. "Le rôle des Etats-Unis dans les conférences de Malte et de Yalta." *Histoire de la deuxième guerre mondiale*, LXXV (1969).

Renouvin, Pierre. *World War II and Its Origins.* Translated by Rémy Inglis Hall. New York, 1969.

Reynaud, Paul. *Mémoires.* 2 vols. Paris, 1960–63.

Rich, Norman. *Hitler's War Aims.* 2 vols. New York, 1973, 1974.

Thomas, R. T. *Britain and Vichy: The Dilemma of Anglo-French Relations, 1940–42.* New York, 1979.

Union of Soviet Socialist Republics. *Stalin's Correspondence with Churchill, Attlee, Roosevelt and Truman, 1941–1945.* New York, 1958.

Vigneras, Marcel. *Rearming the French.* Washington, D.C., 1959.

Viorst, Milton. *Hostile Allies: FDR and de Gaulle.* New York, 1965.

Waites, Neville, ed. *Troubled Neighbours: Franco-British Relations in the Twentieth Century.* London, 1971.

Weygand, Maxime. *Mémoires.* 3 vols. Paris, 1950–57.

White, Dorothy S. *Seeds of Discord: De Gaulle, Free France and the Allies.* Syracuse, 1964.

Wilmot, Chester. *The Struggle for Europe.* New York, 1952.

Woodward, Llewellyn. *British Foreign Policy in the Second World War.* 5 vols. London, 1970–76.

Wright, Gordon. "Ambassador Bullitt and the Fall of France." *World Politics,* X (1957), 63–90.

———. *The Ordeal of Total War, 1939–1945.* New York, 1968.

Zahniser, Marvin. *Uncertain Friendship: American-French Diplomatic Relations Through the Cold War.* New York, 1975.

Index